JEWISH LITERATURE FOR CHILDREN:

A Teaching Guide

Cheryl Silberberg Grossman **Suzy Engman**

Alternatives in Religious Education, Inc.
Denver, Colorado

Published by:
Alternatives in Religious Education, Inc.
Denver, Colorado

Library of Congress Catalog Number 85-70543
ISBN 0-86705-018-7

©Alternatives in Religious Education, Inc. 1985

Printed in the United States of America
10 9 8 7 6 5 4 3 2 1

All rights reserved. No part of this book may be reproduced in any form or by any means without permission in writing from the publisher.

DEDICATION

To my parents, Ruth and Jerry Engman, who first shared with me the joys of Jewish learning and life.

                                      S.E.

To the memory of my grandparents, Irene and Herman Wehrmann; also to my parents, Helen and Murray Silberberg, my husband Fred, and my beloved children Erica Danielle, and Ian David, all of whom inspire me to practice my Judaism with joy and pride.

                                        C.S.G.

... And to the teachers of
Erica Danielle Grossman, Ian David Grossman,
Emily Michelle Engman and Danielle Lauren Engman.

ACKNOWLEDGMENTS

Our Special Thanks To

Dorothy Kennedy, our typist, who encouraged us, supported us, and often went beyond the call of duty in typing this manuscript.

Meriessa Anton, Cheryl Levey, Lorraine Miller, Cynthia Hertz, Beverly Newman, Maxine Goldman Weil, Bonnie Berlman Weinberg, Suzy Wohl, and Fran Wolf, librarians, educators, and Jewish Teacher's Center directors who provided us with the very best in Jewish literature for children.

Russell Doll, for reading portions of this manuscript and making helpful suggestions.

Audrey Friedman Marcus and Rabbi Raymond A. Zwerin for their invaluable editorial assistance.

The authors of the books included in this text, who share their inspiring thoughts, experiences, and visions with us, and with our children.

CONTENTS

Introduction		vii
I.	Bible Stories	1
II.	Death & Dying	21
III.	Ethics	35
IV.	Holidays	53
V.	Holocaust	73
VI.	Israel	93
VII.	Jewish Folklore	114
VIII.	Jewish History	130
IX.	Jewish Identity	160
X.	Prayer	183
Cross-Referencing System		201
General Adult References		207

INTRODUCTION

This is a book about books — Jewish books — books to read to children and books children can read. This is a source book for teachers, parents, librarians — anyone who seeks high quality children's literature on a variety of Jewish themes. This is also a book of creative activities for children and families — meant to bring Jewish literature to life in the classroom, in informal settings, in the library, and in the home.

How the Book is Arranged

The book consists of ten chapters, arranged by topic in alphabetical order. The topics are: Bible Stories, Death and Dying, Ethics, Holidays, Holocaust, Israel, Jewish Folklore, Jewish History, Jewish Identity, and Prayer. Each chapter features ten books on the theme, also listed in alphabetical order by author. For each of these 100 books, there is a brief annotation and a listing of its major ideas.

Following the description of each featured book, there are three clearly defined, original teaching activities which include the use of drama, art, music, field trips, creative writing, etc. (For example, children are invited to take a trip to Israel right in the classroom; they can create and then appreciate Jonah's great fish as it hangs from the ceiling above them; they can "experience" the adjustment of a Russian Jewish immigrant to life in the free world.) All of these 300 activities are meant to promote in children the enthusiasm, knowledge, and insight that are integral to Jewish life. (It is important to note than an activity written for any one specific book might also be readily adapted to use with other books and themes.)

All the books featured, along with their activities, are appropriate for a variety of grade levels ranging from preschool through junior high. As an aid to teachers, grade levels are specified for every book and again for every activity.

At the conclusion of each chapter, there is an extensive annotated bibliography of additional books on the theme for children, as well as a listing of resources on the theme for adult reading. At the end of all of the ten chapters is a further listing of General Adult References. The books in this section contain factual and methodological information of help to teachers, parents, and librarians in planning additional activities for children in all settings.

A Cross-Referencing System is included as the concluding chapter, since many of the 100 books featured in the 10 chapters encompass multiple themes and foci. In this system, each of the featured books is listed first under the specific chapter heading where it appears, then cross-referenced to other chapters/themes to which it also relates.

How to Use This Book

There are numerous applications for this book. For example, it is possible to design a course on a particular theme that has as its central focus the books and activities in a given chapter. Or, the books and activities in a specific chapter can be integrated into an already existing curriculum. The addition of such a Jewish literature component can expand and enrich the curriculum. Another valuable application is the potential use of many of the activities for special observances and celebrations, such as Israel Independence Day, Yom HaShoah, or a particular holiday. Librarians will make excellent use of the book reviews herein when referring young readers to books related to both their secular and religious studies. Of course, the activities and the comprehensive bibliographies are of obvious special benefit to librarians. Last, but not least, the substitute teacher who is not provided with a lesson plan will find the 300 teaching activities useful in planning a meaningful session for students.

Conclusion

The ultimate success of all creative ideas rightfully belongs to the people who will implement them. Hence, the importance of teachers in Jewish tradition cannot be overemphasized. Our Talmudic sages must surely have realized this when they categorized teaching as tantamount to actually having given birth to the child. It is our hope that the ideas in this book, together with your own special resources and love for Jewish life, will creatively combine to make your library, classroom, camp, or family room an interesting, challenging, and exciting learning environment for readers of all ages.

Suzy Engman
Cheryl Silberberg Grossman
June 1985
Tammuz 5745

Bible Stories I

The dynamic element of the Bible lies in its significance for the Jewish faith. To the faithful it offers the word of God which persists for all the ages; each age must search in it for what is most relevant and peculiar to itself. Each generation heard in the Bible's word its own wishes, hopes, and thoughts; each individual their heart's desire. The Bible lay so near to the heart that it could not be viewed from the historical standpoint. Never in Judaism did it become an ancient book to be read during later ages; it remained the book of life, of each new day. Divine revelation is intended for all people and not only for those who lived at the time it was delivered; it speaks to all of us about ourselves.

The Essence of Judaism by Leo Baeck. Copyright © 1948 by Schocken Books, Inc.; copyright © renewed 1976 by Schocken Books, Inc.

OVERVIEW

According to a *Midrash*, when Israel was about to receive the Torah, God asked them for guarantors to insure the preservation of this most precious of gifts. The Israelites responded, "Behold, our children are our guarantors." And the Lord replied, "They are certainly good guarantors. For their sake I give the Torah to you."

If we chose to teach our children nothing more than the words of the Torah, then we would actually have focused their attention on the most basic and complete source of Jewish knowledge. Through the words and between the lines of the Torah, the entire drama of the human experience unfolds before our eyes. In the accounts of biblical heroes we find the strength and the wisdom to deal with virtually every situation we might encounter in life. We discover also the concept of monotheism, the *mitzvot* which lend ethical character to our lives, the source of our prayers and holiday celebrations, and the guarantee of a Jewish homeland.

Having been named *Am HaSefer*, People of the Book, it is only appropriate that we should begin our children's Jewish education with the study of Torah — the Book of Books — for the study of Torah can provide our children with the kind of hopeful and positive start in life that is so vital in this complex world.

The Bible stories selected for this chapter were chosen for the themes and story lines we felt were most interesting and pertinent to children. In *Jonah and the Great Fish*, Jonah's treacherous and exciting journey to Ninevah would certainly hold appeal for young children. The message conveyed in the story, of having compassion for all people, is one children should consider at a very early age.

Sibling rivalry and the importance of striving for family harmony are themes which have reappeared in literature throughout the centuries. Joseph in *Joseph the Dreamer* deals with these issues.

A highly emotional story through which children will discover something of the inner feelings and conflicts which go hand in hand with being a parent is *The Binding of Isaac*. The importance of faith in God is reinforced in this version of the *Akedah*.

Children are usually fascinated by nature and by the nature of our world. *The Seven Days of Creation* will add to their wonder and provide perspective on the natural beauty which surrounds them. The central role of humanity in creation is also emphasized in this story.

Corruption is unfortunately a part of our society today and instances of evil and corruption are also evident in the Bible. The destruction of the city of Sodom in *The Wicked City* is a reminder to all of us that ethical choices must be made in planning our lives as individuals and as a part of society. This retelling is exciting and will place children right into Abraham's adventure. *Noah's Ark* will impress upon youngsters the importance of taking an active part in keeping the world a good place in which to live.

A positive female Jewish role model may be found in *The Story of Ruth*. Ruth made a conscious choice to follow the Jewish way of life, and did so with conviction. In this story, children will also be reminded of the important role women played in biblical times.

The Tower of Babel is a Bible story which attempts to explain the often asked question, "What are the origins of the various languages spoken in the world?" The explanation is thought provoking and the story captivating.

Two additional books which have been included in this chapter, but do not focus on individual stories from the Bible, are *Living Animals of the Bible* and *Ladder of Angels: Scenes from the Bible*. Each adds an interesting dimension to the study of the Bible. The first introduces children to the biblical animal kingdom and the second gives an overview of biblical history illustrated with children's art work.

BIBLE STORIES: BOOKS AND ACTIVITIES

Bulla, Clyde Robert. *Jonah and the Great Fish.* **Illus. by Helga Aichinger. New York: Thomas Y. Crowell Co., 1970. 35 pages. Grade level: K-4.**

The story of Jonah, the reluctant prophet, is masterfully retold by Clyde Robert Bulla. Bulla's narrative follows Jonah from the time he refuses to act as God's messenger to his final acceptance of the task to help the Ninevites put aside their wicked ways. The colors and brush strokes used in the illustrations help to establish the flow of the story and convey the emotions of Jonah as he journeys to Ninevah.

Major Ideas

It is important to have compassion for all people.

We must be willing to take responsibility and provide leadership during difficult times.

All of our experiences provide an opportunity for learning and growth.

God's message is often conveyed through extraordinary means.

Activities

1. Grades K-4: To keep the spirit of Jonah alive in your classroom through the season of Yom Kippur, have students create a stuffed "Great Fish" of their own which will be hung from the ceiling. A step-by-step procedure follows:

    Materials:
    heavy brown wrapping paper   yarn
    markers   scissors
    blunt needles

    Procedure:
    a. Give each student a piece of wrapping paper which is approximately 18″ x 36″ when folded in half.
    b. Instruct the students to draw a great fish on one side of the paper covering as much of the paper as possible, but not touching the fold.
    c. For younger students, the teacher should cut out the shape of the fish through both layers of the paper. Older children can do this themselves.
    d. After the shapes are cut, have the student decorate the fish so that when the two halves are sewn together, the decorated portions will be on the outside.
    e. Using a running stitch, begin sewing the fish together with yarn, leaving a one-inch margin around the edges. Start from the back fin, and continue halfway around the fish.
    f. Stuff the fish with scraps of paper or fabric.
    g. Finish sewing the rest of the way around the fish.
    h. Punch a hole on the uppermost portion of the margin. Tie a string through the hole so it may be hung from the ceiling.

2. Grades K-4: After sharing the story *Jonah and the Great Fish* with students, play "Magic Bag." Tell the students that in front of the room is an invisible magic bag containing *everything* that was in the story. Ask a volunteer to come up and open the bag to take out one of the objects. The student will slowly pantomime use of the object. The student who guesses what is being pantomimed must tell when the object appears in the story, how it is used, and who uses it. That student then gets to take the next object out of the bag. Some of the objects mentioned in the story are:

house	grain	donkey
field	lots	fish
garden	cup	dust
plow	water	gates of the city
camels	plant	ship
worm	silver	stick

3. Grades K-4: Compassion for others is one of the ideas of this story. It is one of the main themes of Yom Kippur. Asking students to think about how the class can help people as an appropriate way to teach compassion through service. Have the students suggest various projects and then have them vote on which they would like to pursue. If the class needs help with ideas, you might suggest the following:

    Collect canned goods for the needy.
    Adopt a grandparent.
    Collect and sell aluminum cans and give the proceeds to a charity.
    Make get well cards for children recuperating in a hospital.

Bible Stories

Bulla, Clyde Robert. *Joseph, the Dreamer.* Illus. by Gordon Laite. New York: Thomas Y. Crowell Co., 1971. 61 pages. Grade level: K-4.

One of the most beloved Bible tales is retold in this colorful book by Clyde Robert Bulla. The basic story line of *Joseph the Dreamer* is given depth through finely drawn characters who exhibit the wide range of emotions which punctuate Joseph's family relations. The artist maintains the flavor of life in the ancient Middle East through his well researched illustrations.

Major Ideas

Family ties have a profound influence on our lives.

Boasting breeds jealousy, as does favoritism.

Change for the better is always within our reach.

Activities

1. Grades K-4: An exciting way to interest young students in the story is for the teacher to come dressed as Joseph in a coat of many colors. The teacher can then begin to introduce ideas from the book by telling about the events in Joseph's life from Joseph's point of view.

2. All ages: At the beginning of the story, Jacob favors Joseph with the special gift of a coat of many colors. Guide the students in realizing that by the end of the story, something special happens to all of Jacob's children. Each has worked at bringing harmony to the family and, thus, all are deserving to be robed in a coat of glorious colors. Plan a classroom feast to celebrate the reunion of Jacob's family. Let each student select from the story the sibling he/she would like to portray. One or more of the students might come as Dinah, Jacob's only daughter. Ask for parents' assistance in converting an old sheet into a robe-like garment which fits their child. To make the sheet into a robe, cut a hole in the center of the sheet. A rope or belt may be used to tie the garment at the mid-section. The students may decorate their "robes" in class. Provide glue, glitter, fabric scraps, and indelible markers. The following week, invite parents to join their robed children in a feast of family togetherness.

3. Grades 3 and 4: After discussing the dreams in the Joseph narrative, have the students write down an imaginary or actual dream that they have had. The students do not need to write their names on the paper. When the descriptions are completed, collect the papers, fold them, and place them in a box. Each student (imagining that he/she is Joseph) will then select one dream and interpret it in writing and with illustration.

Cohen, Barbara. *The Binding of Isaac.* Illus. by Charles Mikolaycak. New York: Lothrop, Lee & Shepard Books, 1978. 29 pages. Grade level: 3-6.

A prolific Jewish author and award winning illustrator worked together to create this stirring version of the *Akedah* (the binding of Isaac). The paintings by Mikolaycak paired with Cohen's writing, convey not only the story, but also the emotional drama of Abraham's sacrifice. Most thought provoking is the last painting which illustrates Cohen's final lines: "And none of you will ever be asked to sacrifice your children. God will not ask anyone to do that again." In the painting, however, we see children burning in the flames of the Holocaust.

Major Ideas

Faith in God is a key component of Jewish life.

Difficult times may test our faith in God.

Our experiences influence us throughout our lives. Maintaining one's Jewish identity can be a challenging task.

Activities

1. Grades 3-6: Have each student choose a partner. One student will assume the role of Isaac and the other, Abraham. Isaac's challenge is to convince Abraham not to follow through with the sacrifice. Abraham's challenge is to convince Isaac that God's wishes must be obeyed. Reverse roles. Follow up discussion questions might include:

    How do you feel about the test God chose for Abraham?

    If you were Abraham, would you sacrifice one of your children to show your love for God? Why or why not?

    As Isaac, what were some of the reasons you gave Abraham to try and convince him not to sacrifice you?

    What are some of the ways *you* show your faith in God?

    Why do you suppose the Rabbis chose this portion of the Torah to be read each year on Rosh Hashanah?

2. Grades 3-6: In this particular retelling of the *Akedah*, Isaac mentions three generations of biblical characters. To help your students gain a clearer picture of these biblical generations, prepare a geneogram (a family tree). An example follows in Diagram 1, which depicts Abraham, Isaac, and Jacob along with their wives, maidservants, and children. Then have students select one of the biblical personalities and

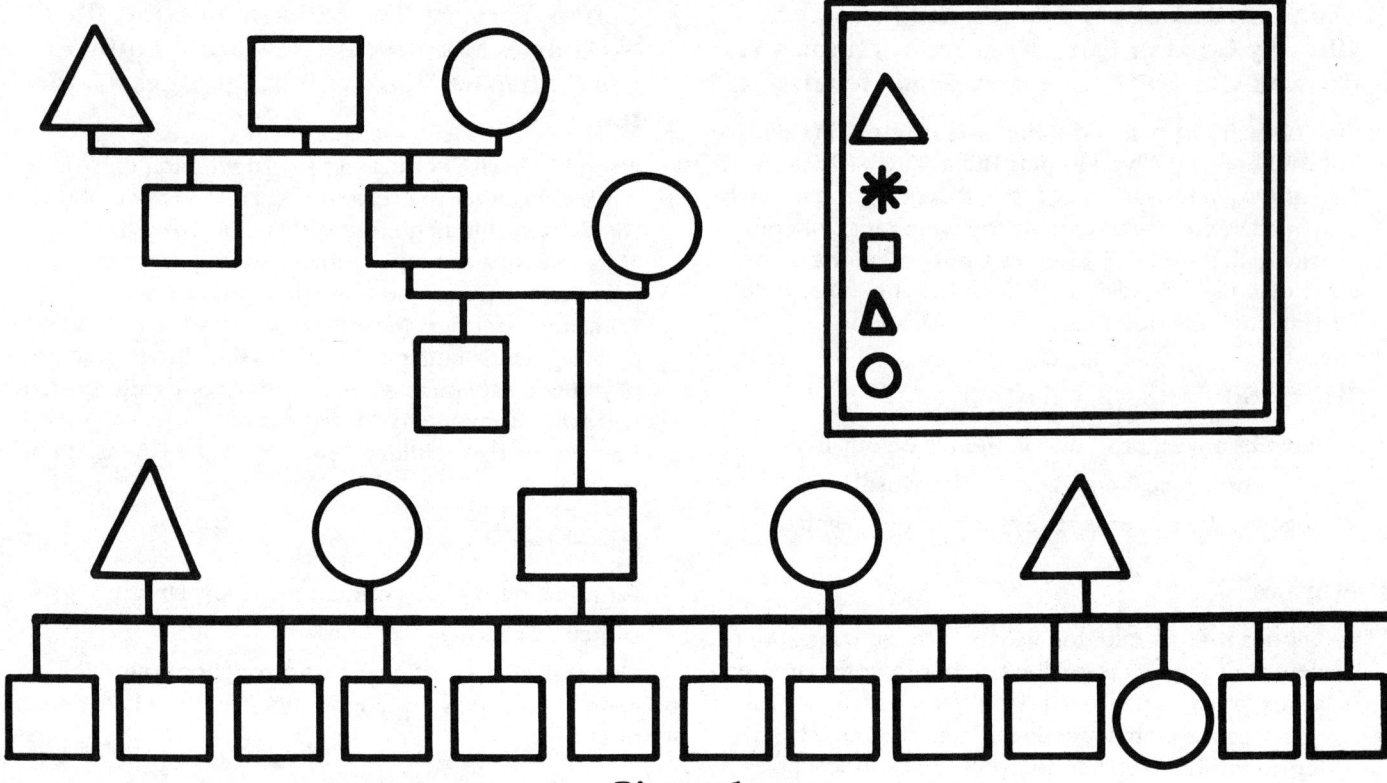

Diagram 1

research that person's role in biblical history. Tell students to cut out words, phrases, and pictures from newspapers and magazines which describe and convey the essence of the individual they have chosen. The cut-outs may be pasted on poster board in an aesthetically pleasing manner. The work can then be shared with members of the class. The students can guess which biblical personality is being portrayed. Display collages around the original geneogram.

3. Grades 3-6: Ask the students to pretend that they are Abraham. Have them keep a diary starting from the time God tells Abraham to sacrifice Isaac. Encourage the students to explore the thoughts of Abraham at this crucial time.

Ferguson, Walter W. *Living Animals of the Bible*. Illus. by the author. New York: Charles Scribner's Sons, no publication date. 95 pages. Grade level: 3 and up.

A colorful and scientific look at the biblical animal kingdom. The author has grouped the animals into major categories such as: mammals, reptiles, amphibians, birds, and insects, and then listed their Hebrew, English, and scientific names. Each animal is then matched to an appropriate biblical passage. The author gives a concise and interesting background. Realistic watercolor illustrations bring each animal to life. This is an artistically pleasing reference book which is a delight to use.

Major Ideas

Some popular Hebrew names are derived from the names of animals.

Animals played an important role in biblical life.

The origins of many of today's existing animals can be traced back to biblical times.

The laws of *kashrut* are based on the animals which existed during biblical times.

Activities

1. Grades 5 and 6: Divide the class into groups of 3 or 4 students. Using this and other books, each group will choose one animal to research. As a means of sharing information, the groups will choose an animal-related tune (i.e., "Rise and Shine," "Old MacDonald," "Animal Crackers in My Soup," *"El Ha Mayan Ba G'dee Katan," "Yesh Lanu Tayish"*). Have them write original lyrics incorporating the characteristics and the Hebrew name of their animal.

2. Grades 3 and 4: Write on separate slips of paper the names of individual biblical animals, as well as the sound that the animal makes. Duplicate this information on another set of paper slips. Make sure you have a slip for each student in the class. Have the students clear a space for themselves. Explain to them that they will become the animal that is written on the piece of paper they receive. The students will assume the body shape of their animal and will softly make the animal sound as they move around the

room, looking and listening for another of their kind. Once they are paired, they will sit quietly waiting for the others to finish. This is an excellent listening activity and will reinforce information about the types of animals found in the Bible. You might also take this opportunity to teach a Hebrew song or two about animals. Here are the lyrics for two favorites:

Yesh Lanu Tayish

Yesh lanu tayish,
l'tayish yesh zakan.
V'lo arba raglayim,
v'gam zanav katan.

We have a goat.
He has a beard and four legs
And also a little tail.

There is also a simple line dance to go along with *"Yesh Lanu Tayish."* The students choose partners and stand in two lines facing each other. As the song is sung, the couple at the head of the group dances in any fashion they choose down the middle of the lines and back. When they return, each goes in the opposite direction along the outside of their line with the others following and singing, "ya la la . . ." The lead couple forms a bridge with their arms and the other couples dance underneath and then again separate into two lines. The dance is complete after each couple has had a turn to lead.

Kum Bachur Atzeyl

Kum bachur atzeyl v'tzey la'avodah (2x)
Kum Kum v'tzey la'avodah. (2x)
Kukuriku kukuriku, Ha tarnigol karah. (2x)

Get up, get up lazy boy
and go to work.
Get up, get up, and go out to work.
Kukuriku, the rooster has crowed.

3. All ages: Have a special day set aside when students can bring in their pets. Check with the principal beforehand. Discuss the importance of keeping the animals under control. Give an award to every pet (best looking, best personality, best bark, best coat, etc.). If there are children who have no pets, ask them to help you judge which award should be given to each animal.

Fisher, Leonard Everett. *The Seven Days of Creation.* **Illus. by the author. New York: Holiday House Inc., 1981. 27 pages. Grade level: K-6.**

The account of Creation is told through a simple, well-written text complemented by beautiful, vibrantly colored acrylic illustrations. Each day of creation is brought to life by the pictures which end with the seventh day when "God . . . saw that it was good, and God rested." The book is a perfect introduction to the Creation account for young students. Older students will appreciate the author's vision of Creation through art.

Major Ideas

The biblical description of the Creation is characterized by a remarkable sense of orderliness.

Creation is an ongoing process in which each of us plays a very important role.

Activities

1. Grades K-6: Have groups of students dramatize the Creation account through creative movement. Each group will enact one of the days of Creation.

2. Grades K-6: Have the class develop ideas for a new world, including both philosophical ideals and the world's physical appearance. This activity could culminate in the creation of a burlap and felt wall hanging depicting their world.

3. Grades K-6: Take your class to a local site of particular beauty. After allowing them some private moments, teach the students the *b'rachah* one says upon seeing a beautiful sight in nature:

ברוך אתה יי אלהינו מלך העולם עושה מעשה בראשית.

Baruch Atah Adonai Eloheynu Melech Ha'Olam Oseh Ma'aseh V'reysheet.
Blessed is the Eternal our God, Ruler of the Universe, who creates and recreates the world anew.

A class picnic might follow.

L'Engle, Madeleine. *Ladder of Angels: Scenes from the Bible.* **Illus. by children of the world. New York: The Seabury Press, 1979. 128 pages. Grade level: 3 and up.**

In this exquisite book, L'Engle has rewritten (in poetry and prose) selected passages from each book of the Tanach (Holy Scriptures). To illustrate her work, L'Engle chose paintings from the exhibition "Children of the World Illustrate the Old Testament." The children's art work adds a unique perspective to this study of the Bible. Although the book is appropriate for grade 3 and up, teachers may need to retell some parts of text to the younger students.

Major Ideas

The Bible is unique in that it holds universal appeal for people of all ages and can be understood on a multitude of levels.

The 39 books of the Tanach offer a dynamic panorama

of ancient Jewish history, from the Creation of the world to the destruction of the Second Temple.

Activities

1. Grades 3 and up: After sharing the book with your students, have each choose two or three passages which they would like to illustrate. When all illustrations are finished and labeled, guide the class in placing the art work in chronological order along a hallway in your school or on a large bulletin board.

2. Grades 3 and up: The title of the book, *Ladder of Angels*, is derived from Genesis 28:10-17. In this passage, Jacob has a dream in which angels are seen ascending into heaven and descending to earth. Jacob awakens to realize that God is with him. Have the children sit quietly for a moment to contemplate ways in which they feel God's presence. Have volunteers share their thoughts with the class.

3. Grades 5 and 6: The last book in the Tanach is Chronicles II, ending in approximately 597 B.C.E. with the Babylonian exile. Have students imagine that they have been given the task of "adding" a new book to the Tanach focusing on Jewish history in the 20th century. Each student will select one aspect of 20th century Jewish life to research. Once the research is completed, the students will convey the events and what can be learned from them through the writing of poetry, prose, or fables. The teacher might choose to put the book together in the same format as L'Engle's, with an illustration accompanying each passage. Important topics to research include:

   The various waves of Jewish immigration to the United States and Canada.
   The Holocaust.
   The establishment of the State of Israel.
   The Middle East wars.
   Persecution of Jews in Russia and other countries.
   Sketches of important Jewish figures in the 20th century.

Petersham, Maud and Mishka. *The Story of Ruth*. Illus. by the authors. New York: Macmillan Publishing Co., Inc., 1958. 30 pages. Grade level: 3-6.

This story of Ruth's dedication to the people of Israel, sensitively retold by the Petershams, is a source of inspiration for the preservation of the Jewish heritage. Rather than returning to her own people, Ruth, a Moabite, chooses to remain with and adopt the faith of her Israelite mother-in-law after the death of Ruth's husband. It is from this valiant woman, Ruth, that the line of King David may be traced. Soft, realistic illustrations complement the text of this moving story.

Major Ideas

We must choose to follow the Jewish way of life and not just follow it because of habit or birth.

Dedication to one's priorities is important, although sometimes difficult.

Women played a prominent role in biblical life and tradition.

Activities

1. Grades 5 and 6: Ruth helped to preserve our Jewish heritage by remaining dedicated to her adopted faith. The following consensus building activity will help students understand that Jewish survival depends upon commitment to and understanding of basic tenets, traditions, and individuals.

   a. Have the entire group offer ideas concerning elements of Jewish life which they feel are important to our survival. List these on the board. Examples might be:

      synagogue
      Rabbi
      Torah
      tzedakah
      mitzvot
      Hebrew
      Israel
      Ten Commandments
      religious school
      holidays
      Shabbat

   b. Separate the class into groups of four or five. Have each group discuss and decide which five of the elements listed on the board are *most* crucial to Jewish survival.

   c. A spokesperson from each group will then report the decision to the class. Keep tally marks on the blackboard. Encourage group members to state what thoughts influenced their choices. List on the board in a separate category those elements not decided on by any of the groups.

   d. Then, take a class vote on the remaining elements, with each student voting five times.

      Explain to the students that although they have chosen only five elements as being the most crucial to Jewish survival, in reality all of the elements mentioned in the discussion work together to strengthen the fabric of Jewish life.

2. Grades 3-6: To reinforce the themes of the Book of Ruth (dedication and making conscious choices of how we live our lives), have the students create a Jewish "coat of arms" about themselves. In advance,

cut stars of David to be given to each student. Give the following instructions:

a. Ruth exhibited dedication to her mother-in-law Naomi and to the Jewish people when she said, "Wherever you go, I will go. Your people will be my people." In the top point, draw a picture of someone who is dedicated to you.

b. In the bottom point, draw a picture of someone to whom you are dedicated.

c. In the top right hand point, draw a picture of something Jewish you and your family do at home.

d. In the lower right hand point, draw a picture of the thing you enjoy most about being Jewish.

e. In the upper left hand point, draw a picture of a character in a Jewish book you have read or a real-life person who has shown dedication to the Jewish people.

f. In the lower left hand point, write three things that we are doing in this classroom which show that we are dedicated to the Jewish way of life.

g. In the middle of the *Magen David,* draw a picture of yourself. Also, write your Hebrew name beneath your self-portrait.

3. Grades 3-6: The Book of Ruth is read on the holiday of Shavuot, which generally falls after the Jewish school year is over. Have your students, in their own words, rewrite and illustrate the story of Ruth so that each has a personal copy to be read on Shavuot.

Singer, Isaac Bashevis. *The Wicked City.* Illus. by Leonard Everett Fisher. New York: Farrar, Straus & Giroux, Inc., 1072. 37 pages. Grade level: 3-6.

Issac Bashevis Singer powerfully captures the evil ways of the ancient people of Sodom in *The Wicked City*. In this Bible story, Abraham bargains with God to save the city of Sodom from destruction. He argues that the just should not be destroyed along with the wicked, and God agrees. If ten righteous people can be found among the Sodomites, then the city will be saved. Abraham's pleas to the Sodomites for repentance go unheeded. But his nephew Lot and his family flee the city before it is destroyed. There is, in the end, poetic justice for Lot when his wife turns into a pillar of salt as she looks back to view the fiery destruction of Sodom. Fisher's expressive block-point illustrations boldly convey the sinful character of the Sodomites in contrast to the goodness of Abraham.

Major Ideas

Moral corruption can destroy a society.

It is important to strive for justice, even against the highest authority.

The gift of a second chance should be used wisely.

Activities

1. Grades 3-6: Before reading *The Wicked City,* dispense with all classroom rules for ten minutes. Inform students that they can do or say anything they want, barring foul language or physically touching another student. After ten minutes, bring the students into a discussion circle and explore such questions as the following:

    You have experienced ten minutes without rules. How might a day without rules affect your usual daily routines?
    How do you think the people in nearby classrooms were affected by our 10 minute lack of rules?
    Why might some people like living without rules?
    On what are rules based?
    Why do we have rules?
    What are some rules in this class which you consider to be constructive?
    Which rules, if any, would you like to change?

    Then, give an introduction to the story, such as: "In Isaac Bashevis Singer's description of the ancient city of Sodom, we learn just how destructive society can be without regard for some of the rules you have just mentioned. Let's listen to the story."

2. Grades 3-6: Point out to the students how the illustrator, Leonard Everett Fisher, through the use of exaggerated and distorted facial features, conveyed the evil nature of the people of Sodom. Give the children a sheet of 12" x 18" drawing paper to be folded in half. On one side, they are to depict themselves as they might look if they had lived in Sodom. On the other side, have them draw what they would look like if they followed the ethics of Abraham. Display these on a bulletin board entitled "Bad Guys and Good Guys."

3. Grades 3-6: Separate the class into four groups. Have two of the groups write a five line marching chant of the Sodomites, focusing on corrupt ways. The remaining groups will compose a five line chant of righteousness for Abraham. Examples follow:

    Lot's Chant

    We are the Sodomites
    We love to steal and fight
    Our life is spent
    Doing nothing right. (2x)

Chant of Righteousness

We are holy gals and guys
Who look so good in God's eyes
We worship each and every day
Which helps us out along the way. (2x)

These chants will be shared with other class members and will be sung as the students leave class that day.

Spier, Peter. *Noah's Ark*. Illus. by the author. Garden City, New York: Doubleday & Co., Inc., 1977. 41 pages. Grade level: K-3.

This book, winner of the coveted Caldecott Medal, tells the story of Noah and the great flood through colorful and detailed illustrations. Unlike other picture books on the same topic, the illustrations vividly depict the reactions and activities of Noah and the animals while they are aboard the ark. Children will delight in Peter Spier's whimsical style.

Major Ideas

All actions bear rewards and/or consequences.

The rainbow symbolizes God's promise never to destroy the world again and also the implication that people must do their share to help God keep this promise.

Activities

1. Grades K-3: Have the class construct papier maché animals to be placed against a mural background of the ark. A recipe for pulp follows:

   Materials:
   newspaper
   water
   wheat flour
   cotton cloth
   sandpaper
   tempera paint
   shellac

   Procedure:
   a. Tear newsprint into small pieces.
   b. Allow the torn paper to soak overnight in water.
   c. Drain excess water. Pulp will remain.
   d. Wring pulp in a cotton cloth so that there is less likelihood of excess moisture deteriorating the paste.
   e. Add about a cup of wheat flour to approximately five cups of pulp. It is now ready.
   f. Mold animals.
   g. Let dry.
   h. The dry substance can be sandpapered. Holes can be bored in it. It can be carved, painted, and shellacked.

2. Grades K-3: Play the record *Noah's Ark*. Music and words by Anne and Paul Barlin (RCA Records). This record provides music and narration for a Noah's ark dance interpretation.

3. Grades K-6: Teach your class "Rise and Shine" or invite the Cantor or song leader to help you. A source for the music is *The Good Times Songbook: One Hundred and Sixty Songs for Informal Singing.*, edited by James Lersy.

Rise and Shine

Chorus:
Rise and Shine and give God your glory glory. (2x)
Rise and shine and give God your glory glory,
Children of the Lord.
The Lord said to Noah there's gonna be a floody floody. (2x)
Get those children out of the muddy muddy,
Children of the Lord.

Chorus

Noah, he built Him, he built Him an arky arky. (2x)
Made it out of hickory barky barky,
Children of the Lord.

Chorus

The animals, they came in, they came in by twosies twosies. (2x)
Elephants and kangaroosies roosies,
Children of the Lord.

Chorus

It rained and poured for forty daysies daysies. (2x)
Drove those animals nearly crazy crazy,
Children of the Lord.

Chorus

The sun came out and dried up the landy landy. (2x)
Everything was fine and dandy dandy,
Children of the Lord.

Chorus

The animals, they came out, they came out by threesies threesies. (2x)
Cats and rats and chimpanzeezies zeezies,
Children of the Lord.

Chorus

Bible Stories

Weisner, William. *The Tower of Babel.* New York: Viking Press, Inc., 1968. 30 pages. Grade level: 2-4.

A colorful rendition, both in narrative and illustration, of a favorite Bible tale. When King Nimrod and his subjects arrogantly attempted to build a great tower reaching higher than God, God caused each to speak a different language. This hampered their ability to communicate and complete the project. The detailed illustrations capture the rush of activity and the ultimate demise of the Tower.

Major Ideas

The tale of the biblical Tower of Babel offers a possible explanation for the development of different languages. God is omnipotent.

Attempting to reach higher than God is arrogant and often destructive.

Clear communication is vital to relationships.

Activities

1. Grades 2-4: Separate the class into groups of 4 or 5. Seat each group around a table. To illustrate the importance of communication among people, engage children in the following activity. Designate one child in each group as the leader. The teacher should provide an illustration of an imaginary Tower of Babel made from a variety of geometric shapes to the leaders. Give each child in the group a handful of the shapes needed to build a replication of the tower held by the leaders. The job of the leader is to communicate instructions for building the tower to the team members. The catch is that each leader will communicate instructions through gibberish. To simplify this just a bit, code names for each shape may be given. Any questions members of the group may have of the leader must also be conveyed in gibberish. The complexity of the design should depend on the age of the children. One possible blueprint of a Tower for older children is demonstrated in Diagram 2.

Diagram 2

A follow-up discussion could include the following questions:

What was it like trying to complete the task with each person speaking a different language?

What were some of the ways you helped to make your questions or instructions clearer to your teammates?

Why do you suppose God decided to confuse the languages of King Nimrod and his subjects?

What would the world be like if all people spoke the same language?

2. Grades 2-4: The Tower of Babel is considered negative because its purpose is to reach higher than God. After a brief discussion exploring the negative aspects of the Tower, have students talk about ways they can be holy or good right here on earth. Then build a Tower of Tov (goodness), following these directions:

Materials:
empty large ice cream drums secured from ice cream stores
12" x 18" colored construction paper
oil pastels, crayons or markers
masking tape

Procedures:
Give each student construction paper and a drawing implement. Instruct them to illustrate an example(s) of their deeds on earth. Leave a one inch margin on one end of the paper.

Adhere completed drawings to the ice cream drums, securing with masking tape so that the margin is covered.

Build a tower to be displayed in the hall for all to see.

3. Grades 2-4: The story of the *Tower of Babel* will spark students' interest in learning about languages spoken throughout the world. Take this opportunity to introduce words and phrases spoken in countries other than our own. It would be interesting to select countries where there are large or culturally different Jewish populations.

BIBLE STORIES: BOOKS FOR CHILDREN

Armstrong, H. William. *Hadassah-Esther, the Orphan Queen*. Illus. by Barbara Byfield. Garden City, New York: Doubleday & Co., Inc., 1972. Grade level: 5 and up.

A captivating retelling of Esther's courageous effort to save the Jewish people from Haman's extermination plot. The book reveals how Esther's intelligent planning led to the present celebration of the Feast of Purim.

Asch, Sholem. *In the Beginning: Stories From the Bible*. Trans. by Caroline Cunningham. New York: Schocken Books, Inc., 1966. Grade level: 4 and up.

Asch combines folklore style and elements of *Midrash* in retelling favorite stories from the Book of Genesis. The volume contains thirty-four stories from Adam to the burial of Jacob, all excellent to read on one's own or out loud.

Asimov, Isaac. *Animals of the Bible*. Illus. by Howard Berelson. New York: Doubleday & Co., Inc., 1978. Grade level: 4-6.

Asimov not only describes the animals named in the Bible, but also gives an explanation of the symbolic significance of each animal named. The illustrations by Berelson are beautiful and imaginative.

Asimov, Isaac. *The Story of Ruth*. New York: Doubleday & Co., Inc., 1972. Grade level: 5 and up.

Asimov uses Psalms from the Bible and quotations directly from the Book of Ruth to complement his own narrative retelling of Ruth's story. Written in an interesting style, Asimov has made the book a memorable one for the young reader.

Banks, Lynne Reid. *Sarah and After: Five Women of the Old Testament*. New York: Doubleday and Co., Inc., 1975. Grade level: 5 and up.

The lives of Sarah, Rebekah, Leah, Rachel, and Dinah, are dramatically revealed by the author. The author's interpretation of the original stories helps the reader understand the forces which shaped the destiny of these five important biblical women.

Bearman, Jane. *Jonathan: Bible Heroes Library*. Illus. by the author. Middle Village, New York: Jonathan David Publishers, Inc., 1965. Grade level: 2-4.

The relationship between Jonathan and David is retold focusing on the importance and beauty of true friendship. The book begins with a poem entitled "What Is A Friend" explaining that Jonathan and David were the type of friends described in the poem. Thereafter, the story of the two biblical heroes and friends unfolds.

Bollinger, Max. *Noah and the Rainbow: An Ancient Story*. Translated by Clyde Robert Bulla. Illus. by Helga Aichinger. New York: Thomas Y. Crowell Co., 1972. Grade level: K-3.

Noah's story is retold in the form of a narrative poem. The muted oriental-style illustrations complement the text.

Bollinger, Max. *Daniel*. Translated by Marion Koenig. Illus. by Edith Schindler. New York: Delacorte Press, 1968. Grade level: 4 and up.

The biblical hero Daniel comes to life in this fast paced retelling of an exciting story from the Hebrew Bible. Realistic pen and ink drawings portraying the biblical personalities accompany the text.

Bollinger, Max. *David*. Translated by Marion Koenig. Illus. by Edith Schindler. New York: Delacorte Press, 1967. Grade level: 5 and up.

This book recounts David's early life as a shepherd boy, his days of glory following an encounter with the giant Goliath, his final battle with the Philistines, and, finally, his reign as King of the House of Judah. Winner of the National German Children's Book Award, the lively narrative and dialogue help bring David to life.

Brin, Ruth F. *The Story of Esther*. Illus. by H. Hechtkopf. Minneapolis: Lerner Publications Co., 1976. Grade level: K-3.

Told in fairy tale form, the story of how Queen Esther saved her people is revealed. The realistic illustrations accurately convey the styles and decor of Esther's time.

Brodsky, Beverly. *Jonah: An Old Testament Story*. Illus. by the author. New York: J.B. Lippincott Co., 1977. Grade level: K-3.

In first person narrative, Brodsky reveals to the reader the lesson Jonah learns from God. Brodsky's stunning watercolor paintings add to the appeal of the book.

Burnford, Shelia. *Mr. Noah and the Second Flood.* Illus. by Michael Foreman. New York: Praeger Publishing, 1973. Grade level: 4 and up.

The year is 1973 and another flood is imminent. Descendants of the original Noah decide to build the second ark. The outcome of this tale is not quite as hopeful as the original. The book forces the reader to reflect on the individual's responsibility for this earth.

Chaikin, Miriam. *Joshua in the Promised Land.* Illus. by David Frampton. New York: Clarion Books, 1982. Grade level: 5 and up.

The story of Joshua's role in the fight for the Promised Land is vividly told by Chaikin. Frampton's woodcuts add visual appeal to the story.

Cioni, Ray and Sally. *The Droodles Storybook of Proverbs.* Illus. by the authors. Elgin, Illinois: David C. Cook Publishing Co., no publication date. Grade level: K-4.

Humorous illustrations help to bring the wisdom of the Book of Proverbs within the grasp of young children.

Cohen, Barbara. *I Am Joseph.* Illus. by Charles Mikolaycak. New York: Lothrop, Lee & Shepard Books, 1980. Grade level: 6 and up.

The biblical story of Joseph is retold from Joseph's point of view. The text and beautiful illustrations by Charles Mikolaycak combine to make this book magnificent to read and look at.

Delessert, Etienne, and Schmid, Eleanore. *The Endless Party.* New York: Harlin Quist Books, 1967. Grade level: K-3.

This is a whimsical tale revealing the shenanigans of the animals while aboard Noah's ark. Surrealistic illustrations perfectly match the mood of the story.

DeRegniers, Beatrice Schenk. *David and Goliath.* Illus. by Richard M. Powers. New York: Viking Press, Inc., 1965. Grade level: 1-4.

An exciting retelling of the events which preceeded and directly followed David's killing of the giant Goliath. The illustrations help to carry the suspense of the story.

Evslin, Bernard. *Signs & Wonders: Tales from the Old Testament.* Illus. by Charles Mikolaycak. Bristol, FL: Four Winds Press, 1981. Grade level: 6 and up.

Dialogue has been created to add interest to the child's reading of tales from the Hebrew Bible. Biblical characters are given life as their emotions are revealed. The illustrator has done a superb job of depicting characters and settings.

Farber, Norma. *A Ship in a Storm On the Way to Tarshish.* Illus. by Victoria Chess. New York: Greenwillow Books, 1977. Grade level: K-2.

This ancient legend of Jonah, told in the form of a narrative poem, takes children to the sea on the way to Tarshish. Humorous illustrations convey the sometimes treacherous nature of a long sea voyage. A fun and exciting book.

Gaines, M.C. (ed). *Picture Stories From the Bible–The Old Testament in Full Color Comic Strip Form.* Illus. by the author. New York: Scarf Press, 1979. Grade level: 2 and up.

Children will thoroughly enjoy these delightful comic strip renditions of favorite biblical stories. A refreshing and lively addition to the traditional biblical curriculum.

Garfield, Leon, and Bragg, Michael. *The Writing on the Wall.* New York: Lothrop, Lee & Shepard Books, 1983. Grade level: K-2.

Young Samuel and his cat Mordecai are the main characters in this glorious retelling of the legend of King Belshazzar from the Book of Daniel. Bragg's full page illustrations add to the grandeur of the book.

Garfield, Leon, and Bragg, Michael. *King Nimrod's Tower.* New York: Lothrop, Lee & Shepard Books, 1982. Grade level: 2-5.

A little boy and his dog watch as King Nimrod's workmen try to build a tower as high as heaven. This creative twist adds appeal to this story from the Book of Genesis. Powerful illustrations convey the frustrations of King Nimrod and his men as their attempts fail.

Goffstein, M.B. *My Noah's Ark*. Illus. by the author. New York: Harper & Row Publishers, Inc., 1978. Grade level: PK and up.

> More than retelling the story itself, this book captures the joy which biblical tales bring to young and old alike as they are passed within families from one generation to the next. Goffstein's distinctive text and line drawings are comparable to the old women's toy ark in that they do indeed "warm (us) like sunshine."

Graham, Lorenz. *David He No Fear*. Illus. by Ann Grifalconi. New York: Thomas Y. Crowell Co., 1971. Grade level: 1-4.

_____. *God Wash the World and Start Again*. Ilus. by Clare Romano Ross. New York: Thomas Y. Crowell Co., 1971. Grade level: 1-4.

> In these two books, the use of poetic English by African tribesmen recounts the adventures of two beloved biblical heroes, David and Noah. Finely detailed illustrations show us the life and times of these men.

Hogan, Bernice. *Deborah*. Illus. by Joan Berg. Nashville: Abingdon Press, 1964. Grade level: 5 and up.

> Although this book is classified as fictional biography, the author has relied heavily on biblical events to share with the reader the life of one of the Jewish people's early leaders. An engaging and informative book.

Hirsh, Marilyn. *Tower of Babel*. Illus. by the author. New York: Holiday House, Inc., 1981. Grade level: K-3.

> The biblical explanation for the origins of language is retold by Hirsh in this simple, yet engaging story. Biblical times are convincingly portayed through Hirsh's black and white line drawings and interesting style of writing.

Hutton, Warwick. *Jonah and the Great Fish*. Illus. by the author. New York: Atheneum Publishers, 1983. Grade level: K-3.

> Hutton's radiant watercolor illustrations powerfully communicate Jonah's plight and God's anger. The book is an excellent introduction to this popular Bible tale.

Hutton, Warwick. *Noah and the Great Flood*. Illus. by the author. New York: Atheneum Publishers, 1977. Grade level: K-3.

> Hutton's gentle watercolor illustrations convey Noah's awesome task and God's promise never to destroy the earth again. A beautiful book to share with children.

Kasuya, Masahiro. *The Beginning of the World*. Illus. by the author. New York: Thomas Y. Crowell Co., 1948. Grade level: K-1.

> The creation account is told with very simple text and vibrant illustrations. The reader is reminded of the ongoing beauty of creation as the author tells us that "new people are being born everyday, and God gives each person a special face — yours too."

Kossoff, David. *Bible Stories*. Illus. by Gino D'Achille. Cleveland: William Collins and Sons & Co., 1968. Grade level: 5 and up.

> The Hebrew Bible comes to life through Kossoff's great storytelling techniques. Every character and every event can be vividly pictured. The illustrations help the reader to understand biblical history and its personalities.

Lerner, Carol. *A Biblical Garden*. Translation from the Hebrew Bible by Ralph Lerner. Illus. by the author. New York: William Morrow & Co., Inc. 1982. Grade level: 3-6.

> Pictures and descriptions of twenty plants mentioned in the Bible are included in this book. Both Hebrew and scientific names are given as well as the biblical quotation in which the plant appears.

McKellar, Shona. *The Beginning of the Rainbow*. Illus. by Masahiro Kasuya. Nashville: Abingdon Press, 1982. Grade level: PK-2.

> The significance of the rainbow is explained in McKellar's interpretation of Noah's story. Realistic and vivid illustrations of the animals and the rainbow against a muted background add to the beauty of the book.

Mee, Charles L., Jr. *Moses, Moses*. Illus. by Ken Munowitz. New York: Harper & Row Publishers, Inc., 1977. Grade level: PK-3.

> This is a fine retelling of the story of Moses. Stylized illustrations add to the appeal of the book.

Mee, Charles L., Jr. *Noah*. Illus. by Ken Munowitz. New York: Harper & Row Publishers, Inc., 1978. Grade level: PK-1.

Perhaps one of the most simple retellings of the Noah story, this book is filled with charm. Stylized pen and ink drawings are delightful and convey the hope for a better world.

Miyoshi, Sekiya. *Jonah and the Big Fish*. Nashville: Abingdon Press, 1982. Grade level: K-3.

Jonah's travels to Nineveh are vigorously retold in this book for young children. Bold illustrations highlight Jonah's trip and the variety of emotions he feels.

Miyoshi, Sekiya. *The Oldest Story in the World*. Illus. by the author, adapted by Barbara L. Jensk. Valley Forge, PA: Judson Press, 1969. Grade level: PK-3.

Against a dark background, vibrant colors illustrate the creation story. The storytelling voice of the oral tradition adds a special dimension to this book.

Miyoshi, Sekiya. *Singing David*. Illus. by the author. New York: Franklin Watts, Inc., 1970. Grade level: PK-2.

This is a simply written story of how David was able to express his love for a little lamb through song. Primitive crayon etchings warmly convey the emotions of the story.

Palmer, Robin. *Wings of the Morning: Verses from the Bible*. Illus. by Tony Palazzo. New York: Henry Z. Walck, Inc., 1968. Grade level: 3 and up.

This selection of verses from the Bible with soft illustrations reads like a book of poetry. The book serves as a perfect motivation for children to research the original source.

Pomerantz, Charlotte. *Noah's and Namah's Ark*. Illus. by Kelly K.M. Carson. New York: Holt, Rinehart & Winston, Inc., 1981. Grade level: 2-4.

In humorous verse, Pomerantz imaginatively interprets the story of Noah. Noah's wife Namah is rightly included in the action of the story. Detailed black and white illustrations add greatly to the whimsical nature of the book.

Reed, Allison. *Adam and Eve*. Illus. by Helen Siegl. New York: Lothrop, Lee & Shepard Books, 1968. Grade level: 3 and up.

The text of this well known Bible story is extended by the beauty and vitality of the intricate woodcuts. Descriptive language helps the reader to experience creation, and Adam and Eve's knowledge of both good and evil.

Rice, Tim, and Webber, Andrew Lloyd. *Joseph and the Amazing Technicolor Dreamcoat*. Illus. by Quentin Blake. New York: Holt, Rinehart & Winston, Inc., 1982. Grade level: 3-6.

The words to the hit musical *Joseph and the Amazing Technicolor Dreamcoat* have been illustrated in this updated version of the biblical tale of Joseph. A useful book to serve as background for the planning of a class musical presentation.

Saporta, Raphael. *A Basket in the Reeds*. Illus. by H. Hechtkopf. Minneapolis: Lerner Publications Co., 1965. Grade level: 1-3.

This story reveals the agony and courage in Yoheved's decision to place her son, Moses, in the river and the goodness of Pharaoh's daughter in her decision to protect the young child. The illustrations accurately depict biblical times and the inner thoughts of the characters.

Singer, Isaac Bashevis. *Why Noah Chose the Dove*. Illus. by Eric Carle. New York: Farrar, Straus & Giroux, Inc., 1974. Grade level: K-3.

As the animals try to outdo one another to win Noah's favor, the dove sits silently. The bird modestly helps Noah make his decision. Brightly colored illustrations which personify each animal work harmoniously with the narrative.

Tellenback, Margret Haubensak. *The Story of Noah's Ark*. Illus. by Erna Embardt. New York: Crown Publishers, Inc., 1977. Grade level: 2-3.

Although the next is engaging and well written, the illustrations are the most striking aspect of this book. Each vibrant painting helps the reader to fully experience Noah's adventure and communication with God.

Taubes, Helen. *The Bible Speaks.* (Three Volumes) Illus. by Dan Bar-Giora. London: Soncino Press, 1965, 1971. Grade level: 2-4.

> The author has retold stories from the Hebrew Bible in this three volume series intended for young children. Each story is short and perfect for individual reading or storytelling sessions provided by the teacher.

Tresselt, Alvin. *Stories from the Bible.* Illus. by Lynd Ward. New York: Coward, McCann & Geoghegan, Inc., 1971. Grade level: 2-5.

> Two giants in the field of children's literature pool their talents in this collection of Bible stories. Full page lithographs and powerful text combine to make this book a treasure for the young reader.

Van Eyssen, Shirley. *In the Beginning: A New Interpretation of the Old Testament.* Illus. by Nicole Claveloux, Charles Claveloux, Charles Louis Lasalle Loup, and Jean-Claude Perrouin. New York: Harlin Quist Books, 1970. Grade level: 4 and up.

> Starting with the Creation and ending with the story of Jonah, this is an excellent introduction to Bible study for the intermediate and upper grade elementary student. Magnificent illustrations in a variety of styles accompany the well written text.

Waddell, Helen, and Moss, Elaine. Abridged by Doreen Roberts. *The Story of Saul the King.* Illus. by Doreen Roberts. New York: David White, 1966. Grade level: 3-5.

> With language reminiscent of biblical style and form, Waddell has retold the story of King Saul. The excitement of Saul's life and his often self-destructive nature are brought to life through Waddell's art of storytelling and Robert's finely drawn illustrations.

Wahl, Jan. *Runaway Jonah and Other Tales.* Illus. by Uri Shulevitz. New York: Macmillan Publishing Co., Inc., 1968. Grade level: K-3.

> This book is comprised of five chapters, each retelling the story of a famous biblical hero. The stories included are about Daniel, Noah, Jonah, David, and Joseph. Shulevitz's gold toned illustrations, sometimes whimsical, other times serious, add just the right touch to these lovely Bible tales.

Weil, Lisl. *The Very First Story Ever Told.* Illus. by the author. New York: Atheneum Publishers, 1976. Grade level: PK-1.

> Black drawings against a tan background illustrate God's creation of the world. Both the text and illustrations brilliantly convey God's joy at what God had created. A fine book for the very young.

Wengrov, Rabbi Charles. *Tales of King Saul: Retold for Jewish Youth.* Illus. by Zalman Kleinman, New York: Shulsinger Brothers, Inc., 1969. Grade level: 1-3.

> Material from *Midrash* and *Aggadah* is interwoven with this retelling of the story of Saul. The tale is fast paced and interesting, enhanced by line drawings washed with color that illustrate the most important events of Saul's life.

Wengrov, Charles. *Tales of the Prophet Samuel.* Illus. by Aharon Shevo. New York: Shulsinger Brothers, Inc., 1969. Grade level: K-4.

> Samuel's life from the time he is an infant until his old age is captured in this portrayal of one of the great early prophets. Simple line drawings illustrate the text.

White, Anne Terry. *David the Giantkiller.* Illus. by Phero Thomas. New York: Thomas Y. Crowell Co., 1970. Grade level: 4 and up.

> The story of David becomes an exciting tale of adventure through White's smoothly written prose. Expressive woodcuts illuminate David's heroic deeds.

BIBLE STORIES: RESOURCES FOR ADULTS

The Torah

The Torah: The Five Books of Moses. Philadelphia: The Jewish Publication Society of America, 1982.

Ben Asher, Aaron. *The Aleppo Codex.* Edited by Moshe Goshen-Gottstein. Jerusalem: Hebrew University, 1976.

Epstein, Morris. *A Book of Torah Readings.* Illus. by Ezekiel Schloss. New York: KTAV Publishing House, Inc., 1960.

Greenberg, Moshe. *Understanding Genesis.* New York: Behrman House, Inc., 1969.

Sarna, Nahum. *Understanding Genesis.* New York: Schocken Books, Inc., 1966.

The Prophets

The Prophets: Nevi'im. Philadelphia: The Jewish Publication Society of America, 1978.

Brickner, Balfour, and Vorspan, Albert. *Searching the Prophets for Values.* New York: Union of American Hebrew Congregations, 1981.

Coote, Robert. *Amos Among the Prophets: Composition and Theology.* Philadelphia: Fortess Press, 1981.

Freehof, Solomon. *Ezekiel: A Commentary.* New York: Union of American Hebrew Congregations, 1973.

Gross, Chaim (illus). *Isaiah: A New Tradition.* Philadelphia: The Jewish Publication Society of America, 1973.

Heschel, Abraham Joshua. *The Prophets.* Philadelphia: The Jewish Publication Society of America, 1962.

Pearlman, Moshe. *In the Footsteps of the Prophets.* New York: Leon Amiel, Publishers, 1975.

Rosenberg, David. *Light-Works: The Prophet Isaiah in a Poet's Bible.* New York: Harper & Row Publishers, Inc., 1978.

Stavroulakis, Nikos (illus.). *Jeremiah: A New Translation.* Philadelphia: The Jewish Publication Society of America, 1973.

Woundstra, Martin. *The Book of Joshua.* Grand Rapids, MI: Eerdman's Publishing Co., 1981.

The Writings

The Writings: Kethubim. Philadelphia: The Jewish Publication Society of America, 1982.

Anderson, Robert A. *Signs and Wonders: A Commentary on the Book of Daniel.* Grand Rapids, MI: Eerdman's Publishing Co., 1984.

Bronstein, Herbert, and Friedlander, Albert. *Five Megillot.* Illus. by Leonard Baskin. New York: Central Conference of American Rabbis, 1984.

Fensham, F. Charles. *The Books of Ezra and Nehemiah.* Grand Rapids, MI: Eerdman's Publishing Co., 1983.

Ginsberg, H.L. *The Five Megilloth and the Book of Jonah.* Illus. by Ismar David. Philadelphia: The Jewish Publication Society of America, 1969.

Glatzer, Nahum (ed). *The Dimensions of Job: A Study and Selected Readings.* New York: Schocken Books, Inc., 1969.

Goldin, Grace. *Come Under the Wing: A Midrash on Ruth.* Philadelphia: The Jewish Publication Society of America, 1980.

Gordis, Robert. *Koheleth, The Man and His World.* New York: Schocken Books, Inc., 1968.

Greenberg, Moshe; Greenfield, Jonas; and Sarna, Nahum. *The Book of Job.* Philadelphia: The Jewish Publication Society of America, 1980.

Hann, Robert. *The Manuscript History of the Psalms of Solomon.* Chico, CA: Scholars Press, 1982.

Intrator, Aaron, and Spotts, Leon. *The Voice of Wisdom: A Guide to the Literature of the Bible For Youth and Adults.* Cleveland: Bureau of Jewish Education. 1965.

Rosenberg, David. *Blues of the Sky: Interpreted from the Original Hebrew Book of Psalms.* New York: Harper & Row Publishers, Inc., 1976.

Rosenberg, David. *Job Speaks: The Book of Job in a Poet's Bible.* New York: Harper & Row Publishers, Inc., 1977.

Shahn, Ben. *Ecclesiastes Or, The Preacher.* Handwritten and Illuminated by the author. Paris: Trianon Press, 1971.

Aprocryphal Writings

Charlesworth, J.H. *The Odes of Solomon.* London: Oxford University Press, 1973.

Craven, Toni. *Artistry and Faith in the Book of Judith.* Chico, CA: Scholars Press, 1983.

Delange, Nicholas. *Apocrypha: Jewish Literature of the Hellenistic Age.* New York: Viking Press, Inc., 1978.

Enslin, M.S. and Zeitlin, S. *The Book of Judith.* New York: KTAV Publishing House, Inc., 1973.

Goldstein, Jonathan. *Maccabees One and Two: A New Translation with Introduction and Commentary.* New York: Doubleday & Co., Inc., 1983. (Two Volumes)

Goodspeed, Edgar J. *The Apocrypha: An American Translation.* New York: Vintage Books, 1959.

Hadas, Moses. *The Third and Fourth Books of Maccabees.* New York: KTAV Publishing House, Inc., 1953.

Lawrence, Richard (trans). *The Book of Enoch the Prophet.* San Diego: Wizards Bookshelf, 1976.

Metzger, Bruce M. (ed). *The Apocrypha of the Old Testament.* London: Oxford University Press, 1975.

Pearlman, Moshe. *The Maccabees.* New York: Macmillan Publishing Co., Inc., 1973.

Vermes, G. (trans). *The Dead Sea Scrolls in English.* New York: Penguin Books, Inc., 1968.

Wacholder, Ben Zion. *The Dawn of Qumran: The Sectarian Torah and the Teacher of Righteousness.* New York: Hebrew Union College Press, 1983.

Wilson, Edmund. *The Scrolls from the Dead Sea.* London: Oxford University Press, 1955.

Zimmerman, F. *The Book of Tobit.* New York: KTAV Publishing House, Inc., 1958.

Biblical Archaeology and History

Dayan, Moshe. *Living With the Bible.* New York: William Morrow & Co., Inc., 1978.

Everyday Life in Bible Times. Washington, DC: National Geographic Society, 1967.

May, Herbert. (ed). *Oxford Bible Atlas.* London: Oxford University Press, 1974.

Orlinsky, Harry. *Understanding the Bible Through History and Archaeology.* New York: KTAV Publishing House, Inc., 1972.

Pearlman, Moshe. *Digging Up the Bible.* New York: William Morrow & Co., Inc., 1980.

Biblical Commentaries

Alter, Robert. *The Art of Biblical Narrative.* New York: Basic Books, Inc., 1981.

Anderson, Bernhard. *Understanding the Old Testament.* Englewood Cliffs, NJ: Prentice-Hall, Inc., 1975.

Ben-Isaiah, Rabbi Abraham, and Sharfman, Rabbi Benjamin (eds). *The Pentateuch and Rashi's Commentary: A Linear Translation.* New York: S.S. & R. Publishing Co., Inc., 1949.

Bickerman, Elias. *Four Strange Books of the Bible: Jonah, Daniel, Koheleth, Esther.* New York: Schocken Books, Inc., 1984.

Cohen, M. J. *Pathways Through the Bible.* Philadelphia: The Jewish Publication Society of America, 1946.

Culi, Rabbi Yaakov. *The Torah Anthology Series: Me'Am Lo'ez.* New York: Maznaim Publishing Corporation, 1977.

Faier, Dr. Zvi (trans). *Malbim: Commentary On Bereishis.* Jersey City, NJ: M.P. Press, Inc., 1984.

Hertz, J.H. ed. *The Pentateuch and Haftorahs.* London: Soncino Press, 1966.

Maimonides, Moses. *A Maimonides Reader: Excerpts from the Mishnah Torah.* Edited by Isadore Twersky. New York: Behrman House, Inc., 1972.

Maimonides, Moses. *Mishneh Torah*. New Haven, CT: Yale University Press. (Series)

The Anchor Bible Series. New York: Doubleday & Co., Inc.

The Artscroll Tanach Series. New York: Mesorah Publications, Ltd.

The Interpreter's Bible. New York/Nashville: Abingdon-Cokesberry Press, 1953. (Twelve Volumes)

The Rambam Commentary on the Torah. Trans. by Rabbi Dr. Charles Chavel. New York: Shilo Publishing House, Inc., 1971-1976.

Plaut, Gunther, and Bamberger, Bernard. *The Torah: A Modern Commentary.* New York: Union of American Hebrew Congregations, 1981.

Samuel, Edith (ed). *In the Beginning, LOVE: Dialogues on the Bible Between Mark Van Doren and Maurice Samuel.* New York: John Day Company, 1973.

Biblical Folklore and Legends

Frazer, James G. *Folklore in the Old Testament.* New York: Hart Publishing, Co., Inc., 1975.

Gaster, Theodor H. *Myth, Legend and Custom in the Old Testament.* New York: Harper & Row Publishers, Inc., 1969.

Ginzberg, Louis. *Legends of the Bible.* Intro. by Shalom Spiegel. Philadelphia: The Jewish Publication Society of America, 1966. (Compiled from the original seven volume work of 1910)

O'Brien, Joan, and Major, Wilfred. *In the Beginning: Creation Myths From Ancient Mesopotamia, Israel and Greece.* Chico, CA: Scholars Press, 1982.

Zevin, Shlomo. *A Treasury of Chassidic Tales on the Torah.* New York: Mesorah Publications, Ltd., 1980.

Nature and the Bible

Hareuveni, Nogah. *Nature in Our Biblical Heritage.* Kiryat Ono, Israel: Neot Kedumim Ltd., 1980.

James, Wilma. *Gardening With Biblical Plants: Handbook for the Home Gardener.* Chicago: Nelson-Hall, Inc., 1983.

Rubin, Gail. *Psalmist With a Camera.* New York: Abbeville Press, 1979.

Origins of Biblical Customs

Abraham P. *The Biblical and Historical Background of Jewish Customs and Ceremonies.* New York: KTAV Publishing House, Inc., 1980.

_____. *The Biblical and Historical Background of the Jewish Holy Days.* New York: KTAV Publishing House, Inc., 1978.

Chill, Abraham. *The Minhagim: Customs and Ceremonies of Judaism, Their Origins and Rationale.* New York: Sepher-Hermon Press, 1979.

Miller, Madelaine S., and Miller, J. Lane. *Harper's Encyclopedia of Bible Life.* Edited by Boyce M. Bennett and David H. Scott. New York: Harper & Row Publishers, Inc., 1983.

Psychological Perspectives on Biblical Personalities

Arieti, Silvano. *Abraham and the Contemporary Mind.* New York: Basic Books, Inc., 1981.

Freud, Sigmund. *Moses and Monotheism.* New York: Vintage Books, 1955.

Fromm, Erich. *You Shall Be As Gods: A Radical Interpretation of the Old Testament and Its Traditions.* New York: Holt, Rinehart & Winston, Inc., 1966.

Mellinkoff, Ruth. *The Mark of Cain.* Berkley, CA: University of California Press, 1981.

Reik, Theodor. *The Creation of Woman: A Psychoanalytic Inquiry into the Myth of Eve.* New York: George Braziller, Inc., 1960.

Spiegel, Shalom. *The Last Trial: On the Legends and Lore of the Command to Abraham to Offer Isaac as a Sacrifice.* New York: Behrman House, Inc., 1979.

Wellisch, E. *Isaac and Oedipus*. London: Routeledge & Kegan Paul, 1954.

Zeligs, Dorothy. *Psychoanalysis and the Bible: A Study In Depth of Seven Leaders*. New York: Bloch Publishing Co., 1974.

Selected Biblical Portraits

Carlisle, Thomas John. *Eve and After: Old Testament Women in Portrait*. Grand Rapids, MI: Eerdman's Publishing Co., 1984.

Cox, Janice N. *Foremothers: Women of the Bible*. New York: Seabury Press, Inc., 1981.

Heller, Joseph. *God Knows*. New York: Alfred A. Knopf, Inc., 1984.

Samuel, Maurice. *Certain People of the Book*. New York: Union of American Hebrew Congregations, 1955.

Silver, Daniel Jeremy. *Images of Moses*. New York: Basic Books, Inc., 1982.

Steinsaltz, Adin. *Biblical Images: Men and Women of the Book*. New York: Basic Books, Inc., 1984.

Stern, Chaim. *Isaac: The Link in the Chain*. New York: Speller Publications, 1977.

Teubal, Savina J. *Sarah the Priestess: The First Matriarch of Genesis*. Athens, OH: Ohio University Press, 1984.

Stern, Jossi. *People of the Book*. Cleveland OH: Collins Publications, 1979.

Wiesel, Elie. *Five Biblical Portraits*. Notre Dame, IN: University of Notre Dame Press, 1981.

_____. *Images From the Bible: the Paintings of Shalom of Safed, the Words of Elie Wiesel*. New York: Overlook Press, 1980.

_____. *Messengers of God: Biblical Portraits and Legends*. New York: Pocket Books, 1977.

Wildavsky, Aaron. *The Nursing Father: Moses as a Political Leader*. Montogomery: University of Alabama Press, 1984.

Talmud, Mishnah, and Midrash

Danby, Herbert (trans). *The Mishnah*. London: Oxford University Press, 1933.

Epstein, I., (ed). *The Babylonian Talmud*. London: Soncino Press, 1952. (Eighteen Volumes)

Freedman, Rabbi H., and Simon, Maurice (eds). *Midrash Rabbah*. London: Soncino Press, 1961. (Ten Volumes)

Glatzer, Nahum (ed). *Hammer on the Rock: A Midrash Reader*. New York: Schocken Books, Inc., 1962.

Herford, R. Travers. *Pirke Avoth, The Ethics of the Talmud: Sayings of The Fathers*. New York: Schocken Books, Inc., 1971.

Kolatch, Alfred. *Who's Who in the Talmud*. New York: Jonathan David Publishers, Inc., 1981.

Lipman, Eugene (ed). *The Mishnah: Oral Teachings of Judaism*. New York: W.W. Norton & Co. Inc., 1970.

Malter, Henry (ed). *The Treatise Ta'anit of the Baylonian Talmud*. Philadelphia: The Jewish Publication Society of America, 1967.

Neusner, Jacob. *Invitation to the Talmud: A Teaching Book*. New York: Harper & Row Publishers, Inc., 1973.

Neusner, Jacob. *Judaism: The Evidence of the Mishnah*. Chicago: University of Chicago Press, 1981.

_____. *Learn Mishnah*. New York: Behrman House, Inc., 1978.

_____. *Learn Talmud*. New York: Behrman House, Inc., 1979.

_____. *The Talmud of Babylonia: An American Translation*. Chico, CA: Scholars Press, 1984.

Rabbinowitz, J. (trans). *Midrash Rabbah* (Genesis, Exodus, Leviticus, Numbers, Deuteronomy). New York: Sanhedrin Press, 1977.

Rapaport, Samuel. *A Treasury of the Midrash*. New York: KTAV Publishing House, Inc., 1968.

Steinsaltz, Adin. *The Essential Talmud*. New York: Basic Books, Inc., 1976.

Strack, Hermann. *Introduction to the Talmud and Midrash*. New York: Meridian Books, 1959.

The Artscroll Mishnah Series. New York: Mesorah Publications, Ltd.

Zakom, Miriam Stark (trans). *Tz'enah Ur'enah: The Classic Anthology of Torah Lore and Midrashic Comment*. New York: Mesorah Publications, Ltd., 1983.

Teaching Bible

Adler, David A. *The Bible Fun Book*. New York: Bonim Books, 1979.

Becker, Joyce. *Bible Crafts*. New York: Holiday House Inc., 1982.

Beiner, Stan. *Sedra Scenes: Skits for Every Torah Portion*. Denver: Alternatives in Religious Education, Inc., 1982.

Goodis, Karen Lipschutz. *The Learning Center Book of Bible People Grades 2-4*. Denver: Alternatives in Religious Education, Inc., 1981.

Grishaver, Joel Lurie. *Bible People Book One*. Denver: Alternatives in Religious Education, Inc., 1980.

_____. *Bible People Book Two*. Denver: Alternatives in Religious Education, Inc., 1981.

_____. *Bible Places Ditto Pak*. Denver: Alternatives in Religious Education, Inc., 1983.

Klepper, Jeff, and Salkin, Jeff. *Bible People Songs*. (Cassette and song books). Denver: Alternatives in Religious Education, Inc., 1981.

Loeb, Sorel Goldberg, and Kadden, Barbara Binder. *Teaching Torah: A Treasury of Insights and Activities*. Denver: Alternatives in Religious Education, Inc., 1984.

Moses and the Exodus: Nashville, TN: Abingdon Press. (Simulation Game)

Newman, Shirley. *A Child's Introduction to Torah*. New York: Behrman House, Inc., 1972.

_____. *A Child's Introduction to the Early Prophets*. New York: Behrman House, Inc., 1975.

Prophets and the Exile. Nashville, TN: Abingdon Press. (Simulation Game)

Provinceland: A Biblical Simulation of the Judges and Kings Era. Nashville, TN: Abingdon Press.

Simon, Solomon. *The Rabbis' Bible*. New York: Behrman House, Inc., 1966, 1969, 1974. (Three Volumes)

Death & Dying II

Judaism teaches us to understand death as a part of the divine pattern of the universe. Actually we could not have our sensitivity without fragility. Mortality is the price we pay for the privilege of love, thought, creative work — the toll on the bridge of being from which clods of earth and snow peaked mountain summits are exempt. Just because we are human, we are prisoners of the years, yet that very prison is the room of discipline in which we, driven by the urgency of time, create.

Joshua Loth Liebman, quoted in Likrat Shabbat: Worship, Study, and Song for Sabbath and Festival Services and for the Home, *edited by Sidney Greenberg, p. 176. © 1973, by The Prayer Book Press of Media Judaica, Inc.*

OVERVIEW

More than a chapter about death and dying, this is a chapter about life and living. This is so because, in reality, it is we the living who must cope both with our own mortality and the death of loved ones. Judaism accepts death as an inevitable part of the life cycle. Our religion attaches to this final rite of passage a unique set of customs which, after affirming the finality of death, gradually enable the mourner to reaffirm the continuation of life.

The subject is an extremely painful one, and especially so when death occurs tragically or out of season. Yet, we do our children a great service by teaching them about the grieving process and the Jewish way of death and dying. To avoid the subject of death is tantamount to avoiding life itself, an action whose consequences can be devastating.

Yet, today's children are often sheltered from the realities associated with death and dying. Elizabeth Kübler-Ross, who has written extensively on the topic of death education, condemns the society which deals with death by denial or avoidance. She contends that children need to understand that death is a natural process of life. Ignoring the topic or avoiding children's questions can cause children to fear death.

Although all children need to have their questions about death answered, this is especially important when a child has been faced with the death of a loved one. It is not uncommon for such a child to feel somehow responsible for the death or that he/she could have made the person happier when that person was alive. The books and activities in this chapter will familiarize children with Jewish mourning customs, help them to see death as a normal part of life, and encourage them to consider the importance of leading a good and fulfilling life. A variety of situations in which death has occurred is included in the books.

Note that books on aging are also included in this chapter. This is not to say that aging is synonymous with death, but rather that there is much we can learn about life and, ultimately, about facing death from the shared perspective of those who have lived a very long time. In the Talmud we read a beautiful story on this theme about a king who stops to observe an old man who is planting a tree. When asked why he is planting the tree, the fruit of which he will obviously not live long enough to enjoy, the old man replies, "As my fathers planted for me, so too will I plant for my children."

The wisdom of the old man speaks eloquently to the value of cherishing life for as long as we live. It takes the "*Shehecheyanu*," which is normally recited on special occasions, and literally gives it a place in our everyday lives. It teaches through action that, as wonderful as it is to say the blessing, it is far more important to strive toward actually being the blessing.

Perhaps one of life's greatest ironies is that although death leaves us sad and empty, our knowledge that it will inevitably come can help us to live each day more fully. Both the joy and the sorrow of life are thus very much a part of this chapter.

The loss of a parent or sibling is particularly devastating for a young child. In *How It Feels When a Parent Dies*, interviews with eighteen children who have experienced the death of a parent are reported. Robbie, in *There Are Two Kinds of Terrible*, must cope with his mother's death from cancer and also bridge the communication gap he has with his father so that each can act to comfort the other. In *A Summer to Die*, a young girl eventually adjusts to the fact that her sister is dying of leukemia.

The sudden death of a special friend is also difficult to accept. However, children do adjust, especially with adult guidance. *Thank you Jackie Robinson* describes a young boy's friendship with an older man. When the man dies, the boy's mother — as well as his own introspection — act as a comfort for him. In *Bridge to Terabithia*, Jess Aarons is devasted when he learns his best friend Leslie has drowned. With the help of a teacher at school, Jess discovers that his life will go on and that he will always remember Leslie.

The death of an elderly loved one is an experience which most children will encounter. Included here are three books which deal sensitively with this topic. *Bubby, Me, and Memories* is specifically Jewish in content and reveals a young girl's warm recollections of times spent with her grandmother. A young boy's recollections are recounted in *Pop's Secret*. In *Annie and the Old One*, an American Indian girl tries to hold back time so that her grandmother does not die. The girl eventually learns that death is inevitable. So that children will realize that one can continue to live a fulfilled life in old age, the book entitled *Growing Older* is also included. This book contains a compilation of interviews with vibrant, elderly people.

The loss of a pet is frequently the first experience a child has with death and often the best place to begin death education. A young boy discovers that death is not easy to bear in *The Tenth Good Thing About Barney*. However, participating in Barney's funeral and remembering the good times aid the youngster in the mourning process, and ultimately lead to acceptance.

DEATH & DYING: BOOKS AND ACTIVITIES

Ancona, George. *Growing Older*. Photo. by the author. New York: E.P. Dutton, 1978. 48 pages. Grade level: 4-6.

Ancona has compiled a collection of anecdotal remembrances and photographs of elderly people from a variety of backgrounds. As each of these individuals reminisces about life, we come to realize that one can enter old age with a strong sense of pride and integrity. Thus, in this moving book, the stereotypes so often attributed to the aged are debunked

Major Ideas

Even in old age we can continue to be vibrant and vital human beings.

The elderly have much wisdom to offer the younger generations if only we take the time to listen.

Activities

1. Grades 4-6: Show the film for children entitled *Teeny Tiny and the Witch Woman* (Weston Woods), in which an elderly woman is narrator. At the end of the film, the woman tells the children that this story is one of her favorites; it was told to her and now she is passing it on to them. She then beckons the children with her gently wrinkled hands to remember her story and pass it on one day. Have each student prepare this story or another folktale to be told when the class visits a Jewish or non-Jewish geriatric facility in your community. Each student should be paired with one of the residents for the telling. The residents should also be prepared in advance so that they can share a favorite folktale or personal experience story with the student.

2. Grades 4-6: Set up a center in your classroom entitled "A Touch of Grey – A Touch of Gold." Create a display of pictures of older people. Place a tape recorder in the center. On a laminated direction card, write the following:

   Look around at all the faces and think about what these people might have experienced during their lives. Pick one and imagine you are that person. Talk into the tape recorder and recall some of the memorable moments in your life. Later in the week, we will play the recording back for the entire class to hear.

   As part of this center, you can have older members of the community prepare tapes about their lives for your students' listening pleasure. Be sure to encourage these people to be as creative as they desire on the tapes, perhaps including songs and favorite stories.

3. Grades 4-6: Recite Psalm 92, explaining to students that the Psalm expresses the idea that faith in God can lead to a longer and better life. Next, have students design a picture of elderly people living productively. These may be used on a bulletin board to illustrate the quote from Psalm 92: "They shall still bring forth fruit in old age; they shall be full of sap and richness."

Cohen, Barbara. *Thank You, Jackie Robinson*. Illus. by Richard Cuffari. New York: Lothrop, Lee and Shepard Co., 1974. 125 pages. Grade level: 5 and up.

What could make Davy, a sixty-year-old man, and Sam, an elementary student, best friends? Both are enthusiastic fans of the Dodgers baseball team. The bond is especially close because Sam's own father is no longer living. When Davy has a heart attack, Sam risks being evicted from the Dodgers game to go into the dugout and ask a special favor of Jackie Robinson. Robinson agrees to the favor, which is to have the entire team sign one of the game balls as a get well wish for Davy. Sam sneaks into Davy's hospital room and gives him the ball, realizing that this is the last time he will see his friend. A week after Davy's funeral, Sam is able to turn on a Dodgers game and listen, knowing that each time the team plays, his love for Davy will be remembered.

Death & Dying

Major Ideas

A surrogate parent can play an important role in the life of a child who has lost a parent.

Friendships should not be based on age alone.

Comfort can be found in continuing to enjoy the activities once shared with a deceased loved one.

Activities

1. Grades 5 and up: When Davy dies, Sam attends the wake. He notes that Jewish burial customs are different. To help your students understand the Jewish way of burial, take them to a funeral home which handles Jewish burials. Have the funeral director and also a Rabbi present to explain how a body is prepared for burial, and what takes place during the ceremony and during the period of mourning after the burial. Ample time should be left for students to ask questions.

2. Grades 2 and up: Davy and Sam are friends and share common interests despite their age difference. To illustrate to the students how people older than they may have interests similar to theirs, pair each student with a teacher or other member of the school support staff for a 15 minute rap session. Have the children return to the classroom and share their findings with their classmates. While it is possible that some of the students may have little in common with the person with whom they talked, others may discover similar interests and be motivated to spend some time getting to know the particular staff member because of similar interests. A nice fringe benefit of this exercise is that it promotes a strong sense of community within the school. The rap session may need to be scheduled outside of regular class hours.

3. All ages: Since students spend so much time in hard work and study, why not let them live it up and enjoy the activity that added so much pleasure to Sam's and Davy's lives? Take them to a baseball game. If this is not feasible, plan a class picnic and let them play ball.

Krementz, Jill. *How It Feels When A Parent Dies.* **New York: Alfred A. Knopf., Inc., 1981. 110 pages. Grade level: 5 and up.**

All children feel pain when a parent dies. Krementz has put together a stirring collection of interviews with eighteen children of varying ages and backgrounds. All have experienced the pain associated with the death of a parent. Children who have experienced similar losses will derive comfort from the honest expression of emotions found in these pages, a comfort based on the knowledge that their emotional reactions are shared by others. The author has dealt with a difficult topic in an extraordinary manner, making this book a most significant contribution to children's literature.

Major Idea

We deal with death in both shared and individual ways, but the most important thing is to express one's feelings openly.

Activities

1. Grades 5 and up: The stories in this book are so moving that a good beginning activity is simply to allow the students to voice their responses to the selections you choose to read out loud.

2. Grades 5 and up: Another way of allowing students to express their feelings about the stories is to have them write a letter to the person whose story particularly touched them. Mail letters with stamped envelopes to the author. Request that she forward the letters to the designated people. The author's address is:
   Jill Krementz
   c/o Alfred A. Knopf
   201 E. 50th Street
   New York, New York 10022

3. Grades 5 and up: The twelfth century Spanish-Hebrew poet Bahya Ibn Paquda wrote "Our days are scrolls: write on them what you want to be remembered for." The children in this book remember their parents fondly. Tell your students to imagine that they are now parents with children. Have them create a scroll on which they write or draw what they want their children to remember about them. Encourage the students to take the scrolls home to share with their parents.

Lois, Lowry. *A Summer To Die.* **Illus. by Jenni Oliver. Boston: Houghton Mifflin Co., 1977. 154 pages. Grade level: 6 and up.**

Molly and Meg are sisters. Meg, two years younger than Molly, is jealous of her sister's beauty and popularity. When Molly becomes ill, those feelings are intensified as Molly seemingly takes advantage of her illness to gain special attention. What Meg does not know is that her sister has leukemia. When Molly is hospitalized for the last time, Meg comes to realize that her sister is dying. Molly's death is juxtaposed to Meg's experience of witnessing and photographing the birth of the child of a close friend. Because Molly herself could not witness the event, Meg brings a photograph to the hospital for her sister to see. Molly is weak and on life support systems, yet she still manages a smile to celebrate this new life. After Molly's funeral, Meg attends a photographic exhibition where she views a portrait of herself taken by a friend at Molly's funeral. She is comforted to see many of her sister's qualities mirrored in herself. Lowry has written a touching story of sibling rivalry and sibling love.

Major Ideas

It is acceptable to have and express both positive and negative feelings about those we love.

Life continues to move on, even in the face of death.

Life is not always fair, especially when death comes tragically and out of season.

When dealing with people who are ill, it is important to look beyond the effects of the illness and continue to relate to the individual as a person with special qualities.

Activities

1. Grades 6 and up: The devastating effects of leukemia are graphically described in the narrative of this book. It helps the reader to realize that children are suffering with cancer. As a way of helping children with cancer, involve your students in a fund-raising project for cancer research, a local children's oncology unit, or a Ronald McDonald house. One project idea would be to hold an auction of items donated by the students and their family and friends. All of the items should be in good condition.

2. Grades 6 and up: In the book, the sadness of death and the joy of birth are juxtaposed. While Molly is dying, Meg observes the birth of their friend's child. Allow your students to experience sharing the delight of a new child. Using your synagogue bulletin and the Jewish community news, select a family that has recently given birth or adopted a child. Have your students plan a special way of expressing *Mazel Tov* to the family. Some suggestions are:

    Donate a book to the library in the baby's honor.
    Prepare a Shabbat meal for the family.
    Make *Mazel Tov* cards.
    Hold a party for the baby's sibling(s).
    Provide babysitting so the parents can have some time to themselves.

3. Grades 6 and up: Meg looked upon her sister with envy, when, in fact, each had special qualities and talents. Ask the students to provide a photograph of themselves and a photograph of a sibling or close friend. The photographs should not be larger than 4" x 5" and should be mounted on two separate pieces of 18" x 12" construction paper. Around each photograph have them write the words and phrases which describe the positive qualities and talents of the person reflected in the snapshot. This is a perfect opportunity to teach a little known blessing which speaks of the importance of individuality: "Blessed is the Eternal who discerns secrets, for the mind of each is different from the other as is the face of each different from the other." The students work may then be displayed on a bulletin board entitled: "Blessed Are Our Differences." The inspiration for this title came from an article of the same title by Rabbi Harold Schulweis in the September 1983 issue of *Moment* magazine.

Mann, Peggy. *There Are Two Kinds of Terrible*. New York: Doubleday and Co., Inc., 1977. Grade level: 5 and up. 132 p.

Peggy Mann's story provides a contrast between two kinds of pain experienced by a young boy. The first is the physical, yet curable pain of breaking an arm at the beginning of summer vacation. The second is the emotional trauma of losing a mother to cancer. The narrative realistically captures the intensity of Robbie's emotions during his mother's ordeal with cancer and after her death. His denial, anger, pain, and grief are not eased by his loving, yet distant father. It is not until the end of the story, when Robbie discovers a hidden photo album of his parent's life together, that he is able to feel not only his own grief, but his father's as well. At this point, Robbie reaches out to comfort his father and they are able to reach understandings and to continue their life together.

Major Ideas:

Part of coping with grief is reaching out and caring for others.

The fact that life goes on even without those we love is a harsh, yet sometimes comforting reality.

All pain is relative.

We sometimes need to look beyond a defensive facade in order to find the goodness and/or true feelings of one another.

Activities

1. Grades 5 and up: As demonstrated in the book, it often takes a crisis to jar us into showing our concern and appreciation for another person. Robbie does not reach out to his father until he realizes that his father, too, has suffered a terrible loss. The caring letter he writes to his father established a bond between the two for the first time. Have your students write a letter to each of their parents which shows appreciation for the good qualities in the parent. In doing so, it is hoped that the students will realize the importance of taking the opportunity to care at all times.

2. Grades 5 and up: Most people did not know how to comfort Robbie when his mother died. To help prepare students to act as comforters, invite people to your classroom who have experienced various kinds of losses through death. This could include loss of a parent, grandparent, sibling, friends, or pet. It is best not to invite people whose grief is very recent. Have the guests share their feelings about their loss and

what they found to be most comforting. Leave ample time for students to ask questions.

3. Grades 5 and up: In the description of the funeral, Robbie talks about the minister's sermon on God's wisdom. Each religion has its own special ways of comforting those who are bereaved. First give an explanation of the *Kaddish* to students. The following narrative contains major points which can be included in your explanation:

> In Judaism, it is traditional to recite a prayer called the *Kaddish* for a full year after a loved one dies, and then once a year on the anniversary (*yahrzeit*) of the loved one's death. The *Kaddish* is actually a prayer which praises the virtues of God. It serves as a comfort to the bereaved because it is recited in the supportive atmosphere of one's congregation. By saying the *Kaddish,* loved ones also pay tribute to the dead. Interestingly enough, this Aramaic prayer talks not about the sadness of death, but rather about the greatness of God, demonstrating that even in our grief we must continue to praise God.

After the explanation, introduce students to the following story from the Dubner Maggid which appears in the prayer book *Likrat Shabbat,* compiled and translated by Rabbi Sidney Greenberg, edited by Rabbi Jonathan D. Levine (The Prayer Book Press, 1973).

> Once there was a king who owned a large diamond which was beautiful and pure. He was very proud of the diamond, as there was no other like it. When the diamond was accidentally scratched, the king offered a great reward to any diamond cutter who could return the diamond to its original splendor. But, no one could repair the jewel. The king was heartbroken. After awhile, a craftsman came to the king telling him that he could make the diamond even more beautiful than it was before. The king allowed the craftsman to try. The man was able to do what he promised. Around the imperfection, he engraved a lovely rosebud and used the scratch to make the stem. We can be like the craftsman. When we are bruised by life, we can take even the scratches and build a life of beauty and charm.

After reading this to the students, hold a class discussion focusing on how Robbie can use the wounds of his mother's death to build a life of beauty.

Miles, Miska. *Annie and the Old One.* **Illus. by Peter Parnall. Boston: Little, Brown & Co., 1971. 44 pages. Grade level: 2-5.**

Although not specifically Jewish in content, this book's approach to life and death parallels that of Judaism. The passing on of tradition from generation to generation and the idea of death as a natural part of life are common threads in both Jewish and American Indian culture. In Annie's conversations with her grandmother, she learns that although she would like it to be so, time cannot be held back. "The sun sets and rises, a cactus does not bloom forever and all of us must one day return to the earth." With this realization, Annie is able to pick up a weaving stick given to her by her grandmother. She continues work with the knowledge that as the rug is completed, her grandmother's life is coming to an end. Line drawings washed with brown and gold earth tones capture the feeling of Annie's desert home.

Major Ideas

There is a variety of emotions which mark the dying process and death.

We should value the sharing which takes place between generations.

Opening up lines of communication inside and outside of the family is especially crucial in dealing with death.

How we live has a great impact on how we die.

The fact that time cannot be held back is an important reality of the natural cycle of life.

It is important to appreciate and live each moment and day productively.

Activities

1. Grades 2-5: Annie learned to weave in the manner taught to her by the "Old One." Teach your students the art of paper weaving. A step-by-step procedure follows:

   Materials:
   12" x 18" colored construction paper
   crayons or markers

   Procedure:
   a. Display a variety of 12" x 18" colored sheets of construction paper from which students may select their "looms."
   b. Have pre-cut strips of construction paper in a variety of colors available. Strips may be cut in different widths and lengths. The style of the edge may vary (scalloped, straight, zig-zagged, etc.).
   c. Fold the loom paper in half, either way.
   d. Leaving a border of ½" to 1" all the way around, cut lines across from the fold at ½" intervals. (For a kinetic effect, such as that used by the Israeli artist Yaacov Agam, have the students draw a picture on the 12" x 18" paper before doing this step.)
   e. Using one paper strip at a time, weave in and out of the cuts made on the loom.

f. If necessary, snip off the weaving strips so they are even along the edge.

2. Grades 2-5: The "Old One" taught Annie to weave. Ask the students to share with the class things that they have learned from their grandparents or an older member of their family. Arrange with each student to prepare a simple demonstration of what their "Older One" taught them.

3. Grades 4 and 5: Teach the song based on Ecclesiastics 3:1-8: "Turn! Turn! Turn!" Music may be found in *Great Songs of the Sixties,* ed. Milton Okun, Times Books, 1975. A recording of the song may also be found on "Pete Seeger's Greatest Hits" (Columbia Records/CBS Inc., CS9416).

Paterson, Katherine. *Bridge to Terabithia.* Illus. by Donna Diamond. New York: Thomas Y. Crowell Co., 1978. 128 pages. Grade level: 5 and up.

Jess Aarons and Leslie Burke are friends. Together, they create Terabithia, a secret kingdom in the woods. There they share their dreams and are saved from the world. The other special person in Jess's life is Miss Edmunds, his music teacher. When Miss Edmunds calls Jess to accompany her to the Smithsonian Institution, he excitedly accepts the invitation. It does not occur to Jess until they are well on their way that he might have asked his teacher if Leslie could join them. When Jess returns home after a perfect day, he is informed by his sister that Leslie has drowned in an attempt to cross the gully to Terabithia. Jess is helped to accept Leslie's death by another teacher who guides him to understand that Leslie will never be forgotten. Paterson, who wrote this book after her son experienced the death of his friend, has created comfort for all who experience such a loss.

Major Ideas

The memories of a special friendship endure, even after death.

"It is up to (the survivor) to pay back to the world in beauty and caring what (the deceased) . . . (loans) in vision and strength" *(Bridge to Terabithia,* p. 126).

Activities

1. Grades 5 and up: One of the things that made Leslie so alive and creative was her stimulating family life. In Leslie's home, lively communication and the arts replaced the hours that many people spend in front of the television. In fact, in Leslie's home there was no T.V. Make a class pact that for one week the students and teacher will not watch television. After the week has passed, have a class discussion in which each member shares some of the activities they found to replace watching television. If possible, recruit parent involvement, asking *all* family members to abstain from watching television that week. At the end of the trial period, ask how the experimental week might influence their choice of leisure activities in the future. Also ask what they missed and what they gained during the week.

2. Grades 5 and up: Leslie was cremated. Therefore, she did not have an epitaph written for her. To prepare students to write an epitaph for Leslie, take them to a Jewish cemetery to observe different types of headstones. After the trip, have each student design a headstone and epitaph in tribute to Leslie.

3. Grades 5 and up: Jess's relationship with Leslie helped him to change and grow into maturity. Lead a discussion in which the students focus on how they used to be and how they are now. Next, have each student write a poem of any length using the following format:

    I used to _____
    but now _____

This and other poetry writing suggestions appear in *Wishes, Lies and Dreams: Teaching Children to Write Poetry* by Kenneth Koch (Vintage Books, 1970).

Pomerantz, Barbara. *Bubby, Me, and Memories.* Photo. by Leon Lurie. New York: Union of American Hebrew Congregations, 1983. 31 pages. Grade level: K-3.

This written and photographic recollection of a young girl's memories of her grandmother help the reader to experience more fully the child's grief upon her grandmother's death. Common questions raised by children about death are sensitively addressed in the child's conversation with her parents. A unique aspect of this book is that the family observes traditional Jewish mourning customs. At the end of the book, the child is comforted as she sees many of the qualities of her grandmother living on in herself.

Major Ideas

Acknowledging grief is necessary before one can accept death and go on with life.

Children's questions about death should be answered honestly.

Jewish mourning customs are designed to allow people to experience fully the grief process.

Activities

1. Grades K-3: The little girl in the book loved to listen to the lullaby that Bubby used to sing. This is reminiscent of the old Yiddish songs which many of our grandparents and great-grandparents brought with them from Europe. To pass the beauty and warmth of these songs on to your students, ask the Cantor or music specialist to teach the following songs: *"Az Der Rebbe Est," "Oifen Pripetchok,"* and *"Chiri Bim."* The words and music to these (and other) Yiddish

songs may be found in: *Voices of a People* by Ruth Rubin (Philadelphia: The Jewish Publication Society of America, 1979); *A Treasury of Jewish Folklore*, edited by Nathan Ausubel (New York: Crown Publishers, Inc., 1979); and *The Yiddish Song Book* by Jerry Silverman (Briarcliff Manor, NY: Stein & Day Publishers, 1983).

2. Grades K-3: As does the Bubby in this story, grandparents have a special way of providing all sorts of presents and delights for their grandchildren. One day the little girl surprised her Bubby with a puppet that she had made. Have students make a gift to be given to their grandparent(s) or to another special person in their lives. If necessary, the teacher can find elderly people in the community who would welcome a surrogate grandchild. A wide selection of craft ideas may be found in *Arts and Crafts The Year Round* (Volumes I and II) by Ruth Sharon, United Synagogue Commission on Jewish Education, 1965.

3. Grades K-3: One photograph in the book shows the little girl looking into Bubby's mirror. She is comforted by the fact that she is able to see some of her Bubby's traits in herself. Tell students to bring in small photographs of themselves, their parents, and their grandparents. So that all the students can observe the resemblance among family members, mount the photographs on a bulletin board entitled: "Meet Our Mishpocha."

Townsend, Maryann, and Stern, Ronnie. *Pop's Secret.* **New York: Addison-Wesley Publishing Co., Inc., 1980. 26 pages. Grade level: 1-3.**

Through narrative and photographs, a young boy shares memories of his grandfather. The opening pictures show Pop living with his grandsons. These are followed by snapshots from Pop's collection which depict his grieving for his grandfather. The warmth of the intergenerational relationships which Pop inspired within his family act as a comfort to the boy.

Major Ideas

The life we lead can be a source of inspiration to those we leave behind.

Loved ones live on through our memories.

Activities

1. Grades 1-3: As a way of allowing your students to share the experience of this book with their parents, have them take a note home which reads as follows:

    Dear Parents,
    Today we read the book *Pop's Secret* in class. The book contains photographs and narrative about the life of one grandfather. Please take time this week to pull out some photographs depicting the generations of your family and enjoy them together with your child. Special memorabilia may also be shared. If your child wishes, he or she may bring one or two favorite photos or items to class for show and tell.

2. Grades 2 and 3: Pops was born in 1896. Have students find out the year in which one of their grandparents was born. They should also find out how things were different in those times from the way they are today. If the grandparent is living, the information may be gleaned from a direct conversation. If not, parents can supply the facts. Some research may need to be done. In the next class session, have students creatively present how life was different during the time their grandparents were born. Suggestions for creative presentations are:

    drama
    poetry reading
    drawings
    presentation of actual photographs
    musical numbers

3. Grades 1-3: Pop lived to celebrate 83 happy birthdays. To bring the special atmosphere of an eighty-third birthday celebration to your classroom, invite several people from the community who are 83 to a birthday party in their honor. Set aside class time before the party to make cup cakes and decorations. In addition to enjoying the refreshments and singing happy birthday and other songs, allow time for the students and their guests to talk informally.

Viorst, Judith. *The Tenth Good Thing About Barney.* **Illus. by Erik Blegvad. New York: Atheneum Publishers, 1971. 25 pages. Grade level: K-2.**

When Barney the cat dies, the young boy with whom he lived is so sad, that he can't even eat his chocolate pudding. The boy's mother encourages him to participate in the funeral. She suggests that he recite a list of ten good things about Barney. The boy, however, can only think of nine good things. He continues to grieve, but ultimately finds comfort in a discussion he has with his father who is planting seeds in the garden. He learns that things change in the ground, and that Barney will help to make the soil rich so that the flowers, trees, and grass can grow. As he is being put to bed by his mother, the boy informs her that he has discovered the tenth good thing about Barney.

Major Ideas

Ashes to ashes, dust to dust, is a concept rooted in reality.

Participating in the planning and carrying out of a funeral is an important part of the grieving process.

Activities

1. Grades K-2: Explain to students that a eulogy is delivered at a funeral to remind us about the good qualities of the person who has just died. Remind them that in *The Tenth Good Thing About Barney,* the boy's mother asked him to think of a list of good things about his cat to be recited at Barney's burial. Also, tell them that it is especially important to remember the good qualities of people and other special living things while they are still alive. To help stress this concept of appreciation, have each student select a person (or another living thing such as a pet) and create a list of good qualities about him or her. These may then be shared out loud with the rest of the class. For those students who cannot yet write, the teacher can act as a scribe. Or, younger students may simply be asked to complete the following sentence out loud: "My _____ is good because _____."

2. Grades K-2: Reiterate the concept explained by the father to the son that when a living thing dies and is buried in the ground, it changes into substances that help make the soil a better place for things to grow. The soil is then able to give life to seedlings. To illustrate part of this process, bring some potting soil into the classroom and have each student fill a small pot and plant some rapidly growing seeds.

3. Grades K-2: Using the theme of the ten good things about Barney, separate your class into ten small groups. Assign the students in each group the task of drawing a large picture illustrating one of Barney's good qualities. The ten qualities are:

    1. Brave
    2. Smart
    3. Funny
    4. Clean
    5. Cuddly
    6. Handsome
    7. Only once ate a bird
    8. Purred sweetly
    9. Slept on boy's belly
    10. Helps to grow flowers

As a visual attraction to a listening center in the library, display your students' pictures on colorful poster board. Prepare a reading of the story on a cassette tape. Other students in the school may then come to the center to listen to the story and view your students' illustrations.

DEATH & DYING: BOOKS FOR CHILDREN

Alexander, Sue. *Nadia the Willful.* Illus. by Lloyd Bloom. New York: Pantheon Books, 1983. Grade level: 2-4.

A young Bedouin girl keeps the memory of her brother alive by thinking and speaking of him often in spite of her father's objections. Ultimately, she helps her father through the grief process by encouraging him to do the same. The emotions of each character are captured by Bloom's black and white illustrations.

Aliki. *The Two of Them.* Illus. by the author. New York: Greenwillow Books, 1979. Grade level: PK and up.

This book focuses on the loving relationship between a little girl and her grandfather from the time of her birth to his death. Pencil and crayon drawings illustrate the love between "the two of them."

Anderson, Lydia. *Death.* Photographs by the author. New York: Franklin Watts, Inc., 1980. Grade level: 4-6.

Almost every aspect of death is briefly covered in this simple, yet direct book.

Bernstein, Joanne E. *Loss and How To Cope With It.* New York: Seabury Press, Inc., 1977. Grade level: 6 and up.

This book is intended for children who have been confronted with the death of a family member. The list of service organizations provided is a valuable resource for those seeking outside assistance in coping with death.

Bernstein, Joanne E., and Gullo, Stephen V. *When People Die.* Photo. by Rosmarie Hausherr. New York: E.P. Dutton & Co., Inc., 1977. Grade level: K-3.

This book answers many of the questions children have about burial customs, religious beliefs, afterlife, causes and time of death, and how individuals react to losing someone they love. The text ends with the thought "There is a time to be born, a time to live, and a time to die." The photographs are well chosen and reflect the concepts and feelings discussed in the book.

Blue, Rose. *The Thirteenth Year: A Bar Mitzvah Story.* Illus. by Ted Lewin. New York: Franklin Watts, 1977. Grade level: 3-6.

A young boy changes the original plans for his Bar Mitzvah when he discovers his grandfather is dying of cancer. When his grandfather dies, Barry is grateful that he has become a Bar Mitzvah so that he may be a part of the *minyan*. A beautiful story emphasizing the significance of Bar Mitzvah and importance of commitment to family.

Blume, Judy. *Tiger Eyes.* Scarsdale, New York: Bradbury Press, 1981. Grade level: 6 and up.

After Davey Wexler's father is killed in a robbery, the family moves from Atlantic City to live with an aunt in another state. Through his friendships with a boy whose father has terminal cancer and with a teen-age alcoholic, Davey learns to deal with is own grief. Blume has written a very sensitive novel for more mature young readers.

Bunting, Eve. *The Empty Window.* Illus. by Judy Clifford. New York: Frederick Warne & Co., Inc., 1980. Grade level: 3-5.

C.G. has not been to visit Joe for quite some time. Joe is dying of leukemia and C.G. feels uncomfortable in his presence. However, when he discovers that Joe enjoys watching the parrots which fly outside his window, C.G. is determined to capture one as a present for Joe. When the parrot is presented to Joe, he asks C.G. to let the parrot go, for it is the freedom that the parrot has that Joe admires, a freedom Joe does not have. When Joe dies, C.G. watches the parrots and cries realizing that Joe is not there to see them. A sad yet beautiful story.

Bunting, Eve. *The Happy Funeral.* Illus. by Vo-Dinh Mai. New York: Harper & Row Publishers, Inc., 1982. Grade level: K-3.

This story is told by Laura, whose grandfather has just died and is lying in an open casket. Laura cannot uderstand how her Mother has prophesied that this will be a "happy funeral." Finally she comes to the realization that if a person has had a long and happy life, then death is not necessarily tragic. Ceremonial customs of Chinese-Americans are included.

Cleaver, Vera and Bill. *Grover.* Illus. by Frederick Marvin. New York: J.B. Lippincott Co., 1970. Grade level: 5 and up.

In this moving book, a young boy must cope with his mother's death by suicide. This is made all the more difficult because Grover and his father each handle their grief differently and provide little support for one another. Eventually, they each accept the death and cope with their sorrow.

DePaola, Tomie. *Nana Upstairs and Nana Downstairs.* Illus. by the author. New York: G.P. Putnam's Sons, 1973. Grade level: K-3.

> Every Sunday Tommy visits Nana upstairs (his grandmother who is confined to bed) and Nana downstairs (who is usually busy doing the housework). When both die, Tommy has a very special way of dealing with his grief. An excellent book showing the love between grandparent and grandchild, and the child's ultimate acceptance of his relatives' death.

Geller, Norman. *Talk to God . . . I'll Get the Message* (Jewish Version). Lewiston, ME: Norman Geller, Publisher, 1983. Grade level: 1-4.

> Geller has written a series of books to help children cope with death, each one reflecting the beliefs of a different religion. This particular version sensitively addresses the issues of death and dying from a Jewish perspective, helping the young child to understand death as a natural part of life. Faith in God is presented as still possible and even comforting when death is experienced.

Girion, Barbara. *A Tangle of Roots.* New York: Charles Scribner's Sons, 1979. Grade level: 6 and up.

> Girion's novel is a moving exploration of a teen-age girl's experiences after she learns suddenly of her mother's death.

Greenberg, Jan. *A Season In-Between.* New York: Four Winds Press, 1979. Grade level: 5 and up.

> The memories that a young girl has of her father help her to cope with his death and go on with her life. The story is beautifully developed.

Greene, Constance C. *Beat the Turtle Drum.* Illus. by Donna Diamond. New York: Viking Press, Inc., 1976. Grade level: 4-6.

> Joss and Kate are sisters. When Joss dies as a result of a climbing accident, Kate must go on. She realizes that time eases the pain but remarks that "It's the now that hurts." The author writes with great sensitivity and warmth. Joss's special qualities are described so powerfully that it is especially disturbing when she dies.

Hermes, Patricia. *Who Will Take Care of Me?* San Diego: Harcourt Brace Jovanovich, Inc., 1983. Grade level: 4-6.

> When Mark and his younger brother Pete are orphaned, they go to live with their grandmother. When she dies, Mark is grief stricken and fearful. He is worried about who will take care of him and about his brother Pete, who is mentally retarded. Mark's story is poignant, believable, and inspiring.

Hermes, Patricia. *You Shouldn't Have to Say Goodbye.* San Diego: Harcourt Brace Jovanovich, Inc., 1982. Grade Level: 5 and up.

> When Sarah is told that her mother is dying of cancer, she experiences many common grief reactions. The warm relationship between mother and child adds to the beauty of the story and to the painful reality of the mother's death.

Hughes, Monica. *Hunter in the Dark.* New York: Atheneum Publishers, 1983. Grade level: 6 and up.

> Through flashbacks, a young boy, Mike, who is dying of leukemia, depicts the effects of the disease on his parents and himself. At the end of the book, Mike, who has always longed to be a hunter, finds that he cannot kill a beautiful animal. He also begins to accept his own death. A sensitively told story about the courage of a young man who is dying.

Hurd, Edith Thacher. *The Black Dog Who Went Into the Woods.* Illus. by Emily Arnold McCully. Harper & Row Publishers., Inc., 1980. Grade level: PK-2.

> An old dog goes into the woods to die and each member of the family has a dream about the dog which is shared with other family members. The shared memories help the family to adjust to the pet's death. Soft line and wash illustrations convey the mood of the story.

Kaplan, Bess. *The Empty Chair.* New York: Harper & Row Publishers, Inc., 1978. Grade level: 6-8.

> This is a story about a young Jewish girl's adjustment to the death of her mother and her acceptance of the woman her father decides to marry. Touching and humourous family scenes add to the beauty of the book.

Kidd, Ronald. *That's What Friends Are For*. New York: Elsevier/Nelson Books, 1978. Grade level: 6 and up.

Gary, a young teen-ager, learns to cope with the guilt he feels because he neglected his friend Scott who was dying of leukemia. Gary vows in his written report of their friendship that Scott will never be forgotten. A well constructed and perceptive book.

Lee, Virginia. *The Magic Moth*. New York: Seabury Press, Inc., 1972. Grade level: 4-6.

A family copes with the death of a young child from heart disease by remaining with her throughout her ordeal and symbolically views the flight of a moth at the time of her death as her spirit rising to heaven. Warm family relationships are depicted in this moving story.

LeShan, Eda. *Learning to Say Good-by, When a Parent Dies*. Illus. by Paul Giovanopoulos. New York: Macmillan Publishing Co., 1976. Grade level: 5-7.

The author addresses the reader directly in this book which describes the emotions that children have when a parent dies. Anecdotes help to show how children react, then adjust to the parent's death. A fine and much needed piece of informational literature for children.

Mazer, Norma Fox. *A Figure of Speech*. New York: Delacorte Press, 1973. Grade level: 6 and up.

Jenny has a very special relationship with her grandfather. When she discovers that her parents have decided to move him to an old age home, she runs with him to the farmhouse where he lived when he was young. Once there, Grandpa dies. Jenny is appalled at her parents' kind words for Grandpa after his death. A very well written book to help build compassion for the problems of the elderly.

Orgel, Doris. *The Mulberry Music*. New York: Harper & Row Publishers, Inc., 1971. Grade level: 5 and up.

When Libby discovers that her grandmother is dying, she runs to the hospital to see her one last time. What she sees is not her grandmother, but a gray figure who is attached to tubes. It is when she finally reaches her grandmother's home and begins to reminisce about their relationship that she finds the real grandma. Libby then decides to participate actively in the planning of her grandmother's funeral. This is a lovely story about the value of intergenerational love and understanding.

Peavy, Linda. *Alison's Grandfather*. Illus. by Ronald Himler. New York: Charles Scribner's Sons, 1981. Grade level: 3-4.

The death of Alison's grandfather is seen from the point of view of Erica, Alison's friend. Erica remembers all the good things about Alison's grandfather, especially how much he enjoyed his life. Erica's mother, who was at the hospital when the old man died, reports that he died peacefully with a smile on his face. Himler's realistic illustrations show grandpa's life, as well as Erica's reaction to his illness.

Schecter, Ben. *Someplace Else*. Illus. by the author. New York: Harper & Row Publishers, Inc., 1971. Grade level: 3 and up.

This story about how twelve-year-old Arnie Schiffman copes with moving, his mother's operation, and his father's death is punctuated with compassion, humor, and courage.

Sherman, Eileen Bluestone. *The Odd Potato: A Chanukah Story*. Illus. by Katherine Janus Kahn. Rockville, MD: Kar-Ben Copies, Inc., 1984. Grade level: K-3.

A young girl, through love and determination, helps her grieving father celebrate Chanukah as he did when his wife was alive. This is a heart-warming story of close family relationships.

Simon, Norma. *We Remember Philip*. Illus. by Ruth Sanderson. Niles, IL: Albert Whitman & Co., 1979. Grade level: 2-4.

A class of children helps their teacher adjust to the death of his son in this beautiful book. The importance of sharing grief is clearly stated and realistic illustrations appropriately convey the warmth of the story.

Slote, Alfred. *Hang Tough, Paul Mather*. New York: J.B. Lippincott Co., 1973. Grade level: 4-7.

Paul's main interest is baseball. However, he is dying of leukemia and has been given orders not to play the game. Not to be held down easily, he finds a way to help his teamates win an important game. A sad story about a young boy who shows courage through the hardest times.

Smith, Doris Buchanan. *A Taste of Blackberries*. Illus. by Charles Robinson. New York: Thomas Y. Crowell Co., 1973. Grade level: 4-6.

> When Jamie, who is somewhat overdramatic, falls on the ground after he is stung by a bee, his best friend goes home doubting Jamie's sincerity. When he learns that Jamie has died, the friend feels guilty and begins to grieve. The young boy eventually adjusts to Jamie's death and helps Jamie's mother to cope. A sensitive and perceptively written story.

Stolz, Mary Slattery. *The Edge of Next Year*. New York: Harper & Row Publishers, Inc., 1974. Grade level: 5 and up.

> When Ben is fourteen and Victor is ten, their mother is killed in a car accident. Their father then becomes an alcoholic as he tries to escape the reality of the situation. Eventually, Dad realizes that he needs help and the book ends hopefully. This is a realistic story of the adjustment which follows the death of a close family member — honest and well written.

Tobias, Tobi. *Petey*. Illus. by Symeon Shimin. New York: G.P. Putnam's Sons, 1978. Grade level: 2-4.

> Emily is dismayed when she discovers one afternoon that her gerbil does not respond to her. Emily's father comforts her, explaining that Emily has done her best to give the gerbil a happy life and that the gerbil is old. Soft, realistic illustrations convey the mood of the text.

Tolan, Stephanie S. *Grandpa and Me*. New York: Charles Scribner's Sons, 1978. Grade level: 5-7.

> In her diary, eleven-year-old Kelly relates her unhappiness as she watches her grandfather becoming senile. Grandpa eventually makes a decision during one of his lucid moments to commit suicide. A well written book with convincing dialogue and characters.

Tresselt, Alvin. *The Dead Tree*. Illus. by Charles Robinson. New York: Parents Magazine Press, 1972. Grade level: 1-4.

> The death of a tree is portrayed as part of the natural ecological process. Readers may draw an analogy between the tree and the aging process of a human being. The illustrations vividly depict the life process of the tree.

Warburg, Sandol. *Growing Time*. Illus. by Leonard Weisbourd. New York: Houghton Mifflin Co., 1969. Grade level: K-3.

> When Jamie's mother tells him that his dog King is dead, Jamie turns to his family to provide him with an explanation of his dog's death. A variety of answers are given, each aiding somewhat in the mourning process. When Jamie's parents bring home a new dog, he rejects it at first, but eventually decides that he will help the dog to grow. Soft illustrations enhance the mood of the story.

White, E.B. *Charlotte's Web*. New York: Harper & Row Publishers, Inc., 1952. Grade level: 4-6.

> When Charlotte the spider saves Wilbur the pig's life, a special relationship between the two begins. After Charlotte dies, Wilbur is heartbroken, but finds solace in the memories he has of his friend, as well as in the friendship he builds with her children. A heartwarming story.

Zolotow, Charlotte. *A Father Like That*. Illus. by Ben Schecter. New York: Haarper & Row Publishers, Inc., 1971. Grade level: PK-2.

> A young boy who has no father imagines life as it would be if his father was there. His mother comforts the boy, stressing that one day the little boy can provide a life like the one he imagines for his own child.

Zolotow, Charlotte. *My Grandfather Lew.*. Illus. by William Pene DuBois. New York: Harper & Row Publishers, Inc., Grade level: PK-2.

When Lew calls his mother in the middle of the night, she is surprised to discover that Lew remembers many joyful moments he spent in his grandfather's care. Together mother and son reminisce. Nicely drawn illustrations convey the love between the generations.

DEATH & DYING: RESOURCES FOR ADULTS

Children's Personal Reflections on Death and Dying

Bluebond-Langer, Myra. *The Private Worlds of Dying Children.* Princeton, NJ: Princeton University Press, 1980.

Zelig, R. *Children's Experiences With Death.* Springfield, IL: Charles C. Thomas, Publisher, 1974.

Helping Children Cope With Death

Fassler, Joan. *Helping Children Cope.* New York: Macmillan Publishing Co., Inc., 1978.

Green, Betty, and Irish, Donald P. *Death Education: Preparation for Living.* Cambridge, MA: Schenkman, 1971.

Grollman, Earl (ed). *Explaining Death to Children.* Boston: Beacon Press, Inc., 1967.

Joseph, Samuel K. *A Time To Die: A Course on Death in 7 Units for Third and Fourth Grade Students.* New York: Union of American Hebrew Congregations, 1977.

Grollman, Earl. *Talking About Death: A Dialogue Between Parent and Child.* Boston: Beacon Press, Inc., 1976.

Kübler-Ross, Elisabeth. *On Children and Dying.* New York: Macmillan Publishing Co., Inc., 1983.

Mills, G.C.; Reisler, R.; Robinson A.E; and Vermilye, G. *Discussing Death: A Guide to Death Education.* Palm Springs, CA: ETC Publications, 1976.

Wolf, Anna. *Helping Your Child to Understand Death.* New York: Child Study Press, 1973.

Yamamoto, Kaoru. *Death in the Life of Children.* West Lafayette, IN: Kappa Delta Pi, 1978.

Jewish Perspectives on Death and Dying

Goodman, Arnold M. *A Plain Pine Box: A Return to Simple Jewish Funerals and Eternal Traditions.* New York: KTAV Publishing House, Inc., 1981.

Klein, Isaac. *A Time To Be Born, A Time To Die.* New York: United Synagogue of America, Department of Youth Activities, 1976.

Lamm, Maurice. *The Jewish Way in Death and Mourning.* New York: Jonathan David Publishers, Inc., 1969.

Marcus, Audrey Friedman; Bissell, Sherry; and Lipschutz, Karen S. *Death, Burial and Mourning in the Jewish Tradition.* Denver: Alternatives in Religious Education, Inc., 1976.

Riemer, Jack (ed). *Jewish Reflections on Death.* New York: Schocken Books, Inc., 1981.

Philosophical Perspectives on Life and Death

Bulka, Reuven P. *Torah Therapy: Reflections on the Weekly Sedra and Special Occasions.* New York: KTAV Publishing House, Inc., 1983.

Forman, Max L. *Rx for Living, Take As Needed.* New York: Bloch Publishing Co., 1983.

Greenberg, Sidney (ed). *A Treasury of the Art of Living.* Bridgeport, CT: Hartmore House, 1963.

Harlow, Jules (ed). *The Bond of Life.* New York: Rabbinical Assembly, 1975.

Kavanaugh, Robert. *Facing Death.* New York: Penguin Books, Inc., 1972.

Kübler-Ross, Elisabeth. *Death: The Final Stage of Growth.* Englewood Cliffs, NJ: Prentice-Hall, Inc., 1975.

Kübler-Ross, Elisabeth, and Warshaw, M. *To Live Until We Say Goodbye.* Englewood Cliffs, NJ: Prentice-Hall, Inc., 1978.

Kushner, Harold S. *When Bad Things Happen to Good People.* New York: Schocken Books, Inc., 1981.

Lifton, Robert Jay, and Olson, Eric. *Living and Dying.* New York: Bantam Books, Inc., 1974.

Pliskin, Zelig. *Gateway to Happiness.* Monsey, NY: Jewish Learning Exchange, 1983.

Silverman, William, and Cinnamon, Kenneth. *When Mourning Comes: A Book of Comfort For the Grieving.* Chicago: Nelson-Hall, 1982.

Practical Guides and Theoretical Perspectives

Feifel, Herman. *New Meanings of Death*. New York: McGraw-Hill, Book Co., 1977.

Grollman, Earl. *Concerning Death*. Boston: Beacon Press, 1974.

Habenstein, Robert, and Lamers, William M. *Funeral Customs the World Over*. Milwaukee, WI: Bulletin Printers, Inc., 1973.

Hendon, David. *Death as a Fact of Life*. New York: Warner Paperback Library, 1973.

Kübler-Ross, Elisabeth. *Questions and Answers on Death and Dying*. New York: Collier Publishing, 1974.

Stanford, Gene, and Perry, Deborah. *Death Out of the Closet*. New York: Bantam Books, Inc. 1976.

Ethics III

A mitzvah is like a musical score, and its performance is not a mechanical performance but an artistic act. The music in a score is open only to him who has music in his soul. It is not enough to do the mitzvah, one must live what he does. The goal is to find access to the sacred deed.
The Wisdom of Heschel *by Abraham Joshua Heschel. Copyright Farrar, Straus & Giroux, Inc. 1975, p. 272.*

OVERVIEW

There is a very special Yiddish word to denote the highest level of being. The word is "*mensch*," which means literally, "human being." To refer to someone as a *mensch* is to bestow upon that person the greatest possible compliment, because the term signifies neither wealth, success, nor social status, but, rather, a high degree of personal character, integrity, and honorable conduct.

With this in mind, the task of being human, in the Jewish sense, becomes particularly challenging. And to complicate matters, the overwhelming amount of freedom which has been both a blessing and curse to humanity since time immemorial must be contended with. As an aid in dealing with these challenges, Jewish tradition has an abundance of ethical literature. Such literature falls into two major categories. First, there is *halachah* (law) which informs and governs the practical observances and is rooted in the 613 *mitzvot* (commandments) contained in the Torah. The second type of ethical literature takes on a wide variety of literary forms and is geared toward moral and spiritual perfection. Among the popular components of this category are the Wisdom Literature of the Bible (such as the Book of Proverbs), the Tractate *Avot* (Sayings of the Fathers) from the Mishnah, and various folk literature.

The importance of ethical behavior can be integrated with virtually every topic in the Jewish curriculum. It is exemplified in the acts of favorite biblical heroes and heroines, in concepts such as *teshuvah* (repenting for our wrongdoings) during the High Holy Days, and in customs such as *shelach manot* (taking gifts of food to the needy on Chanukah and Purim). It is seen also in the customs associated with each phase of the life cycle, in the uniquely Jewish concept of *tzedakah,* and in the lessons of history which demonstrate both the very best and the very worst of our human capabilities.

As for the best starting point, there is none more motivating than Hillel's response to the stranger who wanted to hear the entire Torah as he stood on one foot. From the maxim "Do not do unto others that which is hateful to yourself," we learn to value the wisdom that only learning and experience can bring, as Hillel stated, "The rest you must go and study."

The books included here are intended to help children develop an ethical set of values. In "teaching" values to children, it is important that ideas are not didactically presented, but rather that role models of exemplary behavior are provided for the children to consider. The characters in children's literature may act as those role models.

Many ethical concepts are presented in the books in this chapter. Bringing about change through constructive means is the theme in three of the books. An editorial written by Summer Smith in *Summer Begins* helps a predominantly Christian community become sensitive to the needs of its Jewish members. The participation of Jews in the Civil Rights movement is illuminated in *Northern Fried Chicken.* In Snyder's *The Great Condominium Rebellion,* a set of condominium rules is changed through cooperation and intergenerrational dialogue.

The consequences of not giving in to temptation and engaging in dishonest behavior are themes found in *Finders Weepers* and in *Ike and Mama and the Once-In-A-Lifetime Movie.* In both of these stories, the main characters repent through action. Positive feelings are their reward.

Rabbi Simon and His Friends: Values and *A Mitzvah is Something Special* deal specifically with a Jewish code of ethics. Rabbi Simon introduces the young reader to ethical issues through stories from the Bible and the Talmud. In *A Mitzvah is Something Special*, the inner process one engages in when doing a *mitzvah* is seen as being as important as doing the act itself.

Understanding, accepting, and relating to people who are different from us is essential background for treating our neighbors and friends with compassion. Grandpa Izzy in *The Bagel Baker of Mulliner Lane* creates holiday gifts for his neighbors who are from a variety of ethnic and religious backgrounds. With the mandating of mainstreaming today, it is especially important that children are tolerant and accepting of those who are handicapped. *The Blue Rose* will aid children in understanding that although people like Jenny, the main character, may be somewhat different, they experience the same emotions as everyone else.

Finally, the pleasure that is derived from giving without thought of receiving is depicted in *The Giving Tree*, a beautiful story conveying the intrinsic rewards of *tzedakah*.

The two most crucial questions children must be encouraged to think about when forming an ethical code by which to live are: What kind of person am I? What kind of person do I wish to be? Just to tell a child to live as a good person is not enough. Children must recognize their abilities and their limitations and realize that the decisions they make today will have a direct influence on the life they and others lead tomorrow.

ETHICS: BOOKS AND ACTIVITIES

Asher, Sandy. *Summer Begins*. New York: Elsevier/Nelson Books, 1980. 288 pages. Grade level: 5 and up.

Eighth grade is a time of new beginnings for Summer Smith. Once a quiet, reserved girl, she now has her first romance and becomes an outspoken supporter for freedom of religion. It all begins when Summer must write an article for the *Eighth Grade Reporter*. She is unable to think of a topic until the day she overhears a conversation between the mothers of two of her Jewish classmates. The mothers express concern about their daughters' discomfort in singing the songs for the traditional University School Christmas program. Summer then decides to write an editorial which advocates a more ecumenical holiday program. Summer's editorial causes a great stir in the community. Through the resolution of the problem, Summer and all of the members of the University School community come to realize the importance of freedom of religion and freedom of the press. Sandy Asher's novel is both entertaining and pertinent.

Major Ideas

As citizens of a democratic society, we are fortunate to be guaranteed freedom of religion and freedom of the press.

Upholding one's values can result in both positive and negative consequences.

It is important to establish constructive means for promoting ethical behavior.

Activities

1. Grades 5 and up: One of the major themes of this book is freedom of the press. To help students better understand this concept, plan a field trip to the local Jewish or secular newspaper. Arrange for the editor or another key member of the newspaper staff to discuss freedom of the press with your students. The talk should focus on particular times in the individual's experience when a decision had to be made on whether to print controversial issues. A tour of the facility should also be included as a part of the field trip.

2. Grades 5 and up: One solution to winter holiday customs which place more emphasis on one group's beliefs over others is to plan programs and design decorations and greetings which are ecumenical. Have students design ecumenical season's greetings cards which may be sent to a class in another school, children in the hospital, or nursing home residents.

Materials:

construction paper in various colors
crayons
felt tipped markers
scrap material
tempera paint
glitter
glue

3. Grades 5 and up: Have your students imagine that Summer's editorial is picked up by the Associated Press and published nationally. Then, have each student pick a piece of paper (from a shoebox) on which the teacher has written a personality and role description. After briefly explaining to your students the proper format for writing a telegram, have them write a short telegram to Summer imagining that they are writing as the character selected from the shoebox. The telegram should express their feelings about the editorial. Sample descriptions follow:

> You are a fundamentalist Baptist minister from Oklahoma.
>
> You are a Lubavitcher Jew from Brooklyn, New York.
>
> You are a steelworker from Detroit whose children attend parochial school.
>
> You are a Christian housewife with six children, married to a Jewish man.

Blau, Judith Hope. *The Bagel Baker of Mulliner Lane*. Illus. by the author. New York: McGraw-Hill Book Company, 1976. 38 pages. Grade level: K-2.

Judith Hope Blau has taken memories of her childhood and spun them into a delightful tale of neighborly love and magical bagels. Grandpa Izzy is a bagel baker who thoroughly enjoys his work. Grandma Sonny tolerates her husband's bagel obsession in the best of humor. One year, when Chanukah and Christmas fall at the same time, a snowstorm traps Grandpa Izzy in the bakery. Undaunted by his predicament, he proceeds to make all kinds of bagel animals. When the neighbors and friends finally dig their way through the snow to rescue Grandpa Izzy, they find him happily dancing among the bagel creations he has made as holiday gifts for them. Zany illustrations add to the humor of the story.

Major Ideas

Good neighbors can live together in peace, even though they have religious and ethnic differences.

It is helpful to try to make the best of a difficult situation.

Activities

1. Grades K-2: It is written in the book of Leviticus 19:18: "You shall love your neighbor as yourself." When Grandpa Izzy is trapped in the bakery and his neighbors are trying to dig him out, he passes the time making gifts for his neighbors. This is a fine example of the kind of neighborly reciprocity emphasized by the Torah. Extend this concept by planning an ethnic food exchange between your students and a neighboring school or church with an ethnic orientation.

Have students make bagels. Use the following recipe from *Tom Tov: Good Taste*, Agudas Achim Sisterhood (Iowa City, Iowa: Uni-print, Inc., p. 182). Used with permission.

Bagels

Ingredients:

3 C. sifted flour
1½ tsp. salt
2 tbl. sugar
½ oz. or 2½ tsp. dried yeast (2 pkgs.)
1⅛ C. water
3 tbl. oil

Glaze:
egg yolk
water
poppy seed
caraway seed
salt crystals
onion flakes

Procedure:

Mix flour with salt and sugar. Dissolve yeast in water. Stir well. Add oil to the yeast. Knead to a firm, smooth dough. Cover with a cloth. Let rise one hour in a warm place. Knead again until dough is elastic. Divide into 12 portions. Shape each into a cylinder 5 inches long and ¾ inch thick. Shape into rings, pinching ends together. Cover and let rise ten minutes. Add 3 tablespoons sugar to 4 quarts boiling water. Drop in bagels one by one. Make sure the water is boiling as each is immersed. Let simmer 10 minutes. Remove, drain and place on lightly oiled baking sheet. Brush with beaten egg yolk and a little water while still warm. Sprinkle with seasoning of choice as listed above. Bake 30 to 35 minutes at 400 degrees. Recipe makes 16, 1⅓ ounce bagels.

Serve the bagels with a choice of butter, cream cheese, or jelly. To add an Israeli flavor, bring in chocolate nut spread which may be made at home or purchased at a gourmet specialty shop. Ask the visiting students to bring in one ethnic delicacy of their choice. Also, plan some special activities, such as storytelling or songs, to be enjoyed before or after the refreshments are served.

2. Grades K-2: Grandpa Izzy fashioned all kinds of imaginary bagel creations. Using leftover bagels from your ethnic food celebration, have students design bagel creations of their own. A list of materials and the procedure follow.

Materials:

heavy duty glue
shellacked bagels
pieces of 8-1/2 x 11 heavy weight white cardboard
felt tipped markers
scrap materials (string, felt, beads, buttons, etc.)

Procedures:

a. Glue the bagel in a desired position onto the piece of cardboard using Tacky Glue or 527 Clear Craft Cement. The position of the bagel will depend on whether it will used as the head, the body, or another part of the creature being designed.

b. Using the markers and scrap materials, embellish the bagel in such a way that it becomes a bagel creature.

c. Grandpa Izzy named all of his creations using a part of the word bagel such as duckagel, lionagel, and pelicanagel. Have students name their creations in a similar fashion and print the name on the cardboard. Before the creations are sent home, display them on a bulletin board entitled "The Bagelagels of _____" (fill in with name of your class, school or synagogue).

3. Grade 2: Grandpa Izzy wrote a song about his beloved bagels. To prepare students to write a food oriented song, have a discussion about traditional Jewish foods. Take a vote to decide on the one food about which students would like to write a song. Choose a familiar melody and then collectively com-

pose lyrics about your chosen "nosh." The following example uses the tune "If I Had a Hammer."

> If I had a chicken,
> I'd make me some chicken soup.
> I'd make it good and hot
> with lots of spice.
> I'd eat it with *matzah* balls,
> I'd eat it with kreplach,
> I'd eat it with noodles and rice and everything nice morning, noon, and night.

Chaiken, Miriam. *Finders Weepers*. Illus. by Richard Egielski. New York: Harper & Row Publishers, Inc., 1980. 120 pages. Grade level 3-6.

When Molly finds a gold ring on the way home from visiting with a friend, she decides to keep it. She lies to her mother, saying that the ring fell out of a moving car. Molly enjoys wearing the ring, but when her little brother is admitted to the hospital for asthma, Molly worries that God is dealing out a punishment for her sin. On Rosh Hashanah, Molly discovers that the ring belongs to Hanna Gittel, a German refugee whose father was killed by Hitler. The ring Molly is wearing was a gift to Hanna from her father. Molly then decides that she must return the ring, but she cannot remove it from her finger. It isn't until Yom Kippur that Molly is able to give the ring back to its proper owner. Chaiken's story realistically depicts a young girl's struggle to fight against what is wrong and to do what is right.

Major Ideas

A person should make a concerted effort to return something which has been found to its rightful owner.

Even though there may not be an external punishment for our wrongdoing, we must live with our inner guilt.

Doing what is right can bring a happy, peaceful feeling to ourselves, as well as to others.

Activities

1. Grades 3-6: Miriam Chaiken entitled her book *Finders Weepers* which is a take-off of the saying "finders keepers, losers weepers." Have students think up a rhyming couplet of their own which teaches a lesson. Examples follow:

   > Cheat on a test,
   > You'll never be best.
   >
   > Hurt a friend,
   > The friendship may end.
   >
   > Stealing money
   > Is not very funny.

   Give each student triangle-shaped banners of construction paper on which the couplet may be printed. A small illustration or border design should accompany the saying. Display these around the room.

2. Grades 3-6: Hanna Gittel suffered as a result of Molly's selfishness. Tell students to imagine that they are in Hanna's place and have lost one of their prized possessions. Then have each student write a lost and found ad. The ad should attempt to convince the "finder" to return the possession to its rightful owner. Remind students to not only describe the object, but also to explain its personal significance and value.

3. Grades 3-6: Like most children, Molly is not always a considerate friend. This is especially true when she excludes Hanna. Take this opportunity to hold a discussion in your classroom about the meaning of friendship. Questions might include:

   > Think about your best friend. What do you value about that person's friendship?
   >
   > What do you suppose people value about your friendship?
   >
   > How do you make friends?
   >
   > When you've done something that hurts a friend, how do you make up?
   >
   > There is a song by Bette Midler entitled "You've Got To Have Friends." Why do you have to have friends?

   To conclude the session, have students stand and form a circle with linked arms. Sing *"Shalom Chaverim."* The words and music may be found in *Great Songs of Israel*, edited by Velvel Pasternak.

Eisenberg, Phyllis Rose. *A Mitzvah is Something Special*. Illus. by Susan Jeschke. New York: Harper & Row Publishers, Inc., 1978. 31 pages. Grade level: 2-5.

Eisenberg explores the concept of doing a *mitzvah* from the heart, keeping the reader aware of the inner growth which must be experienced before a *mitzvah* is completed. Lisa, a young girl, is torn between two very different grandmothers, but comes to love that which is unique in each. Grandma Esther loves to cook and bake. Grandma Dorri hates cooking and loves playing the flute and telling funny stories. Lisa learns from each of her grandmothers different ways of enjoying life and giving to others. In the end, she triumphantly puts all the pieces together into a *mitzvah* of her own, inviting both grandmothers together to sleep at her house. Pencil drawings enhance the joyous growth which takes place in this sharing between generations.

Major Ideas

Working through conflicting loves and developing the ability to synthesize takes time and understanding.

Ethics

It is important to do *mitzvot* with the proper *kavanah* (intent).

Values such as doing *mitzvot* are learned and passed on from generation to generation.

Activities

1. Grades 2-5: Lead a discussion on qualities that the students believe important in becoming a *tzadik* (one who does what he/she can do in order to make the world a just and good place). To accomplish this, you might ask the following questions:

   What makes Lisa a good person?

   What are some other things that make a person good?

Diagram 3

   Who are some of the good people you have known and what did they do to qualify as a *tzadik*? (Introduce the term at this point.)

   What qualities do you have now that make you a *tzadik*?

   What qualities would you like to acquire which will help you to make this world a just and good place in which to live?

2. Grades 2-5: Have students select and illustrate one example of *tzedakah* (righteousness) which they have fulfilled. Use these illustrations to create a "Trailways to Tzedakah" bulletin board. See Diagram 3 for a model of the board:

3. Grades 2-5: Teach students one or more of the following songs: "Al Shlosha Devarim," "Amar Rabbi," "Amar Rabbi Akiva."

Klein, Gerda. *The Blue Rose*. Photographs by Norma Holt. New York: Lawrence Hill & Co., Inc., 1974. 62 pages. Grade level: 2-6.

This is the moving story of a little girl named Jenny who is different, not because she doesn't experience the same emotions as others, but because she was born retarded. Gerda Klein's sensitive and powerfully descriptive style reaches out to people of all ages, capturing what it is like to be Jenny. Norma Holt's photographs show Jenny in every facet of her life. This book explores the emotional effects of retardation, rather than its physical causes. It is a biography which is a must for all, because of its ability to teach compassion.

Major Ideas

Compassion for those who are different or less fortunate is important.

It is good to take the time necessary to appreciate the uniqueness of every individual.

All people need love.

Education should be geared to the specific needs of the individual.

Activities

1. Grades 2-6: In the book it is suggested that Jenny may be "marching to the beat of a different drummer." To develop the idea that we are all unique, bring in different types of music and allow students to express themselves through movement. To achieve continuity, the teacher can tape the music onto one cassette.

2. Grades 2-6: As a means of allowing the students to find out a little about what it is like to be handicapped, one or more of the following activities may be used:

   Each student is paired with another for a blind walk. One is blindfolded. The other student is responsible for being the leader. Roles should then be reversed.

   Find somebody who knows sign language and have him or her come to your classroom to give a short talk in sign language without the class's prior knowledge. Ask the person doing the signing to translate what he/she said and perhaps teach the class some basic signs. Then, divide the class into pairs and have the students observe lip movements to see if they can get their partner's meaning.

Assign one highly sophisticated scientific article to each student. Tell them to read the article and be prepared to report to the class on its content. This should demonstrate how a developmentally delayed child might feel when confronted with even simple material.

3. Grades 2-6: Prepare a room in the school as a specialized art museum, focusing on paintings of famous people throughout history who have overcome handicaps. The students will be the artists. Each student will also be responsible for providing a short biographical sketch on their subject. Provide a list of people from whom to choose and have books set aside in the library for research. Some people you might want to include on your list are:

   Jacob - limp
   Isaac - blind
   Moses - speech impediment
   Nelson Rockefeller - dyslexia
   Helen Keller - deaf, blind, and mute
   Patricia O'Neal (actress) - stroke victim
   Franklin Delano Roosevelt - polio victim
   Itzak Perlman (violinist) - polio victim
   Albert Einstein - speech delay

Rittner, Stephen. *Rabbi Simon and His Friends: Values.* Photographs by the author. Milwaukee: Arbit Books, Inc., 1978. 144 pages. Grade level: PK-3.

This book, combining dialogue and colorful photographs of puppets interacting, exposes children to a variety of ethical issues. Two children, Sue and Jeff, and Rabbi Simon are the three main puppet characters. Throughout the book, Sue and Jeff grapple with questions pertaining to ethical behavior. Rabbi Simon helps the children resolve their questions through pointed stories from the Bible and the Talmud. The text, often punctuated with humor, is both entertaining and meaningful.

Major Idea

The Jewish way of life includes a code of ethics by which we are to live.

Activities

1. Grade K: The puppet characters make the point that all of the human race is part of a team which must work together to make the world a better place in which to live. Have the class search magazines and newspapers for pictures of people working together as a team. The pictures can depict a group of people or just one person helping another. Choose your magazines so that different ethnic groups are represented. Cut each picture out of the magazine. Also, take photographs of your students involved in various activities which call for group cooperation. Finally, arrange the photographs and pictures as a bulletin board collage entitled: "Tzedakah: A Caring Way of Life."

2. Grades PK-3: A story about Rabbi Gamliel is told in the book. When the Rabbi sent his servant to the market to bring back the best thing there, he brought back a tongue, and when the Rabbi sent his servant to the market to bring back the worst thing there, he once again brought back a tongue. From this story a lesson is learned: "... there is nothing better than a good tongue (someone who talks nicely) and nothing worse than a bad tongue (someone who is always hurting others with his or her words)." To help reinforce this lesson, have the students draw a picture of themselves with their mouths opened very wide. Give each student a sheet of paper listing five other students in the class. Tell the students to write something nice about each student on their list in the space of the open mouth. Each student's name should be used. For example: "Rachel is a good friend." For younger students, the teacher may need to act as a scribe.

3. Grades PK-3: Rabbi Hillel said, "If I am not for myself, who will be for me? If I am only for myself, what kind of person am I?" In this book this statement is used to illustrate the concept of *tzedakah*. Hold a discussion with students, asking them what things they need to do to be nice to themselves and what they can do to be nice to others. Then teach the song "*Im Eyn Ani Li*" by Debbie Friedman. You might want to ask for the Cantor or music specialist's help. Music may be found on the record "If Not Now, When?" (Sing Unto God). Words and music are in the songbook available from the same source.

Schotter, Roni. *Northern Fried Chicken.* New York: Philomel Books, 1983. 143 pages. Grade level: 5 and up.

The year 1962 marked a turning point in both the Civil Rights Movement and in the friendship between two teen-age girls living in Providence, Rhode Island. Unlike her best friend Bernie, Betsy Bergman had never been known as fashionable or assertive. She walked in Bernie's shadow until the two of them became involved in the Providence Jewish Educational and Cultural Task Force. Known as PROJECT, the group participated in various equal rights activities in the community including Food for Freedom and a fair housing demonstration. As usual, Bernie provided Betsy with the initial push into action. However, by the time of the demonstration, Betsy proved herself to be the greater freedom fighter as Bernie's interests drifted in other directions. Roni Schotter's novel movingly captures the fervor of the Civil

Rights movement and the struggle of two friends who have reached a parting of the ways.

Major Ideas

There are times when personal beliefs and goals must take priority over friendship.

As friends grow and change, new interests may cause them to become either closer or more distant.

"All that is necessary for evil to triumph in the world is for good people to do nothing" (Edmund Burke).

Activities

1. Grades 5 and up: Betsy and Bernie are active in the PROJECT's Food for Freedom drive. As a means of teaching your students the importance of caring for the needy in your community, sponsor a school canned food drive. Once dates have been cleared with the principal, students from your class can visit the other classes in the school to publicize the *tzedakah* project. Send a flyer home with each student. Posters created by your class will encourage participation in the project. On the scheduled collection dates, bring the canned food to your classroom and place it in boxes or grocery sacks. The food may then be taken to an agency in the community for distribution to the needy. If you are unaware of which agencies in your community are involved in this type of service, find out by contacting your city government or a family service agency.

2. Grades 5 and up: There are a number of excellent films available on the topics of prejudice and equal rights. The following may be rented from Contemporary Films, Inc.:

   Willie Catches On - A candid film which explores how prejudice begins and spreads.

   Brotherhood of Man - Animated color cartoons and music add to the appeal of this film on promoting brotherhood.

   Fable for Friendship - An animated and humorous film about the efforts of UNESCO to destroy the walls of prejudice which separate nations.

   The House on Cedar Hill - A lively film biography of Fredrick Douglas, a Black writer and statesman, who helped his people move from slavery into freedom.

   A Chance for Change - Black children in a Mississippi Head Start center are shown learning to voice thoughts and opinions constructively.

   Vision Quest - The story of a fourteen-year-old American Indian boy living in Montana.

   I Wonder Why - A young Black girl explores why some people don't like her in this moving film.

   A City Decides - The true story of the integration of the St. Louis school system.

   Also contact the audiovisual department of the local public library to see what films they have available on the topics of prejudice, equal rights, or famous Black or Jewish "freedom fighters." Be sure to check that the films are appropriate for your students' grade level.

3. Grades 5 and up: When Betsy attends the March on Washington, she is pleased to find that Rabbi Joachim Prinz is there along with Martin Luther King, Jr. to support civil rights for Blacks. Betsy makes the following comment about religion and taking a stand on critical social issues:

   "Even though I didn't know the rabbi who was speaking, I felt connected to him, almost as if he were a relative of mine. In a way he was. We shared the same religion, and it was this kind of religion — the reaching-out kind that made me proud to be Jewish. Using your own particular experience to reach beyond yourself and help other people was what I felt religion should be all about" (p. 139).

   Active concern for freedom and civil rights is an important aspect of Judaism. Whether the people whose rights are at stake are Jewish or non-Jewish, it is important for Jews to take a strong stand because we have known firsthand throughout history the horrors of persecution. After sharing Betsy's comments, remind your students that even today there are Jews living in countries such as Russia where their civil rights are being violated. One of the ways your students can help Soviet Jewry is by writing letters to their Congresspersons and Senators asking them for support legislation to pressure the Soviet government to allow Jews to emigrate. Check with the reference department of your public library for the addresses of these public officials. Divide the work among the students so that each Senator and Representative from your state receives several letters. You may also send letters to the President of the United States, The White House, 1600 Pennsylvania Ave. N.W., Washington, DC 20500 and the Secretary General of the United Nations, The United Nations, New York, NY 10017. If desired, the project may be extended by having your students suggest that the school adopt a Russian Jewish family which has been denied exit visas. Information for this can be obtained from one of the following organizations: Union of Councils for Soviet Jews, National Conference on Soviet Jewry, Student Struggle for Soviet Jewry.

Snyder, Carol. *The Great Condominium Rebellion*. Illus. by Anthony Kramer. New

York: Delacorte Press, 1981. 149 pages. Grade level: 5 and up.

When Stacy and Marc are invited to spend Chanukah and their winter break with their grandparents in Florida, they eagerly look forward to their idea of a good time. However, upon arriving at Lemon Cove Condominiums, they find a restrictive set of condominium rules which threaten to spoil their fun. Through committee meetings, compromise, and intergenerational cooperation, Stacy, Marc, and the other young visitors manage to make their vacation an enjoyable one. Carol Snyder's understanding of the needs of both the young and the old is expressed with humor and sensitivity.

Major Ideas

Some rules, whether we like them or not, are really in our best interest.

When rules are deemed unjust or too restrictive, it is important to try and change them through constructive means.

Cooperation between generations can lead to satisfaction for all.

Activities

1. Grades 5 and up: Stacy and Marc were given postcards by their parents so they could write home about their vacation in Florida. The postcards they write reflect an emerging sense of ethics. The following activity allows students to express Jewish ethics through a picture postcard design. The teacher should first make available the following sources which contain examples of Jewish ethical concepts:

   The Holy Scriptures: According to the Masoretic Text. (Philadelphia: The Jewish Publication Society of America, 1917.) (Look particularly in the books of Exodus, Leviticus, Numbers, Deuteronomy, and Proverbs.)

   Ethics of the Fathers, translated and annotated by Hyman Goldin.

   Treasury of Jewish Quotations by Leo Rosten (New York: Bantam Books, 1972.)

   Each student should select one saying which is personally meaningful (i.e., "Love your neighbor as yourself," "Whoever loves peace should pursue peace and preserve it"). Then, on a 4" x 6" blank index card, have the students create a picture postcard design, which is either abstract or realistic, illustrating the chosen saying. The saying itself should be printed somewhere within the design. Have the students imagine that they are on vacation in a location where their chosen maxim is actually the way of life. On the reverse side of the postcard, tell the students to write a note to a family member or friend describing how the particular ethic has affected their vacation and how they plan to carry on that ethic once they return home.

2. Grades 5 and up: While visiting their grandparents, the children were able to change life for the betterment of all through constructive suggestions and committee efforts. As a means of teaching your students that they can effect change through constructive means, place a suggestion box in your classroom for the entire year. Tell the students that when they are dissatisfied with something which has occurred in the class or have an idea for something they would like to see happen, they can drop a note into the box. Impress upon them that if they are dissatisfied and wish to write about it, they should do so in a sensitive manner and also include a suggestion for improving the situation. These notes will be read by the teacher and, when appropriate, discussed with the entire class. A student committee can be elected to engage in further discussion and implementation of a solution.

3. Grades 5 and up: When Stacy and Marc arrive at Lemon Cove Condominiums, they expect their vacation to be all play and no work. However, after spending time at committee meetings in order to improve the quality of life for everyone in the condominium, they realize how much satisfaction can be derived from consciously working to help others. To guide your students to do works of *tzedakah*, encourage them to participate in the Chai Program designed by Rabbi Raymond A. Zwerin of Temple Sinai, Denver, Colorado. To follow this program, the students will commit themselves to complete eighteen hours of *tzedakah* during the given year. To begin, brainstorm ways of doing *tzedakah* in your synagogue, school, or community. Have students keep a journal documenting their good works and any reactions to what they have done. Compile selected entries in a newspaper entitled the *Tzedakah Times* and send home for the students and their parents to enjoy.

Snyder, Carol. *Ike and Mama and the Once-In-A-Lifetime Movie*. Illus. by Charles Robinson. New York: Coward, McCann & Geoghegan, Inc., 1981. 96 pages. Grade level: 3-5.

This story, set in New York City in the 1920s, illustrates that people can achieve their goals through hard work and honest means. At the beginning of the story, a young boy named Ike and his friends are reprimanded for trying to sneak a penniless friend into a movie theater. Ike's mother reminds the boys that it is their obligation to pay back the owner of the theater. To earn money, the boys plan to become paid extras in a D.W. Griffith movie which is being filmed in a suburb of the city. After a long and arduous bicycle trip to the filming site, they are offered only a nickel apiece for shovelling snow. However, after the camera man is instructed to film the boys' spontaneous snowball fight, the director pays each $1.50 for his role in the film. The boys must then resist the temptation to spend the money so they can follow through on their promise to repay the theater owner and realize their secret plan to take their families to the movie in which they "star." Snyder has created believable characters with whom children can identify.

Major Ideas

One must resist the temptation to fulfill one's goals in what might be an easy, but dishonest, way.

To say we are sorry is good, but to show through our behavior that we have repented is better.

We can learn and grow from our past mistakes.

Activities

1. Grades 3-5: Ike and his friends learn a valuable lesson in ethics when they participate in a film and earn enough money to pay back the movie theater owner for sneaking into a movie. The following activity is designed to allow your students to enjoy being a part of a film, while at the same time exploring ethical issues. Separate your class into groups of three to five students. Give each group a card on which an ethical dilemma is posed. Examples follow:

   You are at the shopping mall with a friend and see something you really want to buy. You do not have enough money to purchase the item. As you are walking, you look down and see a wallet which someone has lost. You pick it up. You and your friend look inside and find fifty dollars. You do not realize that another shopper has noticed your action. What do you, your friend, and the onlooker do?

   It is Saturday afternoon and you are an Orthodox Jew who observes Shabbat in the traditional way. You see that there has been a serious accident in front of your house. You run downstairs to see how you can help. You are the only witness to the accident in which an elderly man has been critically injured. His wife begs you to drive your car to get their daughter who lives eight blocks away so that she may see her father before he dies. What do you do?

   You and your classmates are sitting in class taking a test when you notice that one of your friends is cheating. When the tests are returned the following day, the teacher raves about how well your cheating friend has done. What do you and your classmates do?

   Give each group a private place in which to plan and rehearse a skit based on their ethical dilemma. The skits should end with a solution to the dilemma. Each skit should be videotaped with only the actors in that specific skit present. Plan a day on which the videotapes will be shown to the whole class. Just before the point in each tape where a solution is reached, press the pause button and encourage class members to share their own solutions to the problem. Then, play the remainder of the tape. These tapes may then be kept as a resource in the school library.

2. Grades 3-5: The boys in the story learned from their past mistake that there are ways to earn money that will enable a person to do what he/she wants to do and also benefit others. Have students either think of a time when they personally have turned a past mistake into something pleasant or have them imagine such an event. Ask them to write a narrative poem which tells of the experience. Have volunteers share their poems with the entire class.

3. Grades 4-5: The boys in the story have a goal to earn money to set their record straight. To do so, they must come up with a plan, overcome obstacles, and develop inner characteristics which will enable them to fulfill their goal. To help your students learn this same problem solving and self-evaluation process, engage them in the following activity. It is a modification of an activity suggested in *100 Ways to Enhance Self Concept in the Classroom: A Handbook for Teachers and Parents* by Jack Canfield and Harold C. Wells. Give each child a piece of 12" x 18" white construction paper and a box of crayons or felt tipped markers. Tell the students to fold their paper into four equal sections. Ask them to close their eyes and create a mental image of one important goal they would like to accomplish in the present or future. Once they have opened their eyes, ask them to draw a picture of their goal in the upper right-hand box. In the upper left-hand box, have them draw a self-portrait. In the lower right-hand box, have them draw a picture of the obstacles they might face in reaching their goal. Finally, in the last box, have them write down the inner qualities they must develop in order to overcome the obstacles to attaining their goal. Display the drawings on a bulletin board entitled "Alei B'hatzlachah: Reaching For Our Dreams."

Silverstein, Shel. *The Giving Tree*. Illus. by the author. New York: Harper & Row Publishers, Inc., 1964. 55 pages. Grade level: PK and up.

The joy of giving is beautifully expressed in this book depicting the relationship between a tree and the little boy it loves. At the beginning of the story, the child is content to swing playfully on the tree's branches. But the child becomes a man and his desires change. He asks the tree to provide him with money, a house, and a boat. The tree, by giving of itself, is able to fulfill the wishes of the boy. At the end of the book, both are old. The tree has given everything to the boy and believes that it has nothing left to give. But, it is mistaken. Companionship and comfort can still be provided. The simple black on white line drawings help to carry the emotional impact of the story.

Major Ideas

Giving is its own reward.

In a good relationship, there is a balance between giving and receiving.

One's needs and goals change throughout the life cycle.

Activities

1. Grade 2 and up: Give each child a sheet of 12" x 18" white construction paper, crayons, and a set of watercolors. Then, ask the students to imagine themselves as a giving tree and to think about the ways in which they give to others. Using the crayons, have the students draw a self-portrait of their entire body standing straight with their arms reaching up. From the arms, more branches should be added. Along the branches, each child should draw images of ways in which they give. After the drawings are completed, use the water colors to paint a light wash over the picture. See Diagram 4 for an example.

2. Grades 4 and up: As a basis for a discussion on the importance of giving, tell students to fill out the following questionnaire:

Questions of Ethics

a. When was the last time you felt good about doing something for someone else?

b. What have you done for someone else that you really didn't want to do? Why did you do it?

c. What are some of the ways in which you can give now that you may not be able to give when you are eighty?

d. When you are eighty, how might you be able to give differently?

e. How do you give to your parents? Siblings? Grandparents?

f. How do your parents, siblings, grandparents give to you?

g. Which of the characters in the book *The Giving Tree* would you rather be? Why?

If you choose to type the questionnaire please remember to leave space for the students to reply.

3. All grades: The tree takes pleasure in giving the boy apples. Plan a field trip to a local apple or other fruit orchard so that students may experience the "giving nature of trees." Have the students pick the fruit and bring it back to the classroom. In the classroom, make two or three different recipes with the fruit (e.g., apple sauce, fruit pie, etc.). Check your favorite cookbooks for recipes. So that others may experience the giving nature of your students, invite another class to enjoy the fruit dishes. The blessing over apples is:

ברוך אתה יי אלהינו מלך העולם בורא פרי העץ .

Baruch Atah Adonai Eloheynu Melech Ha'olam Boray P'ri Ha'eytz.

Blessed is the Eternal our God, Ruler of the universe, who creates the fruit of the tree.

Diagram 4

ETHICS: BOOKS FOR CHILDREN

Adoff, Arnold. *All the Colors of the Race*. Illus. by John Steptoe. New York: Lothrop, Lee & Shepard Books, 1982. Grade level: 2-6.

   The poetry in this book makes a plea for religious and racial tolerance. Steptoe's impressionistic illustrations extend and refine the text.

Ames, Mildred. *What Are Friends For*. New York: Charles Scribner's Sons, 1978. Grade level: 4 and up.

   Amy and Michelle are close friends. When Amy discovers that her friend has been shoplifting, she must reflect on the true meaning of friendship. After this book is read, a class discussion focusing on ethical values concerning friendship and stealing would be appropriate.

Belsky, Judith Benoliel. *All About Rivkah*. Illus. by Harvey Klineman. New York: Feldheim Publishers, 1980. Grade level: PK-2.

   A charming book about seven-year-old Rivkah who fantasizes about the *mitzvot* she will perform at different ages. She finds the "right sized" *mitzvah* for her current age in her own neighborhood. The illustrations of Rivkah engaged in doing *mitzvot* are lively and colorful.

Blume, Judy. *Blubber*. New York: Bradbury Press, 1974. Grade level: 4-6.

   This is a story about peer group cruelty. Linda is the scapegoat in her class. The cruel acts against Linda by her classmates are not unrealistic. This book is thought provoking and can act as a springboard for discussing an individual's responsibility to his peers.

Bogot, Howard, and Syme Daniel. *I'm Growing*. Illus. by Janet Compere. New York: Union of American Hebrew Congregations, 1982. Grade level: PK-2.

   In an unusual and special way, Bogot and Syme help very young children to realize that as they grow, so, too, will their responsibilities both Jewishly and otherwise.

Bunting, Eve. *Terrible Things*. Illus. by Stephen Gammell. New York: Harper & Row Publishers, Inc., 1980. Grade level: PK-2.

   The story of a little bunny who learns that hate is a "terrible thing" and that to be concerned about others is important. Gammell's illustrations are charming.

Cauley, Lorinda Bryan. *The Ugly Duckling*. Illus. by the author. San Diego: Harcourt Brace Jovanovich, Inc. 1979. Grade level: PK-1.

   Large, colorful illustrations enhance the retelling of this story about the beauty and potential in all living things. A discussion about kindness and respect for others would be an appropriate follow-up to the reading of this book.

Chaikin, Miriam. *Getting Even*. Illus. by Richard Egielski. New York: Harper & Row Publishers, Inc., 1982. Grade level: 4-6.

   This is the third in a series of books about the growing-up years of Molly, a young girl living in Brooklyn in the 1930s. In this book, Molly reveals a secret told to her by a friend and must deal with the consequences of her decision. A thought provoking story.

Chaikin, Miriam. *How Yossi Beat the Evil Urge*. Illus. by Petra Mathers. New York: Harper & Row Publishers, Inc., 1983. Grade level: 2-4.

   Yossi is able to beat the evil urge by engaging in prayer and responding to "the urge" with song and dance. A green imp is used to portray the evil urge and primitive style illustrations add to the serious yet entertaining tone of the story.

Clifton, Lucille. *My Friend Jacob*. Illus. by Thomas di Grazia. New York: E.P. Dutton, 1980. Grade level: 1-3.

   The warm relationship depicted in this book between a young boy and his older mentally retarded friend illustrates the importance of accepting those in society who are handicapped. The mood of the story is extended by the beautifully drawn realistic illustrations.

Cohen, Barbara. *The Innkeeper's Daughter*. New York: Lothrop, Lee & Shepard Books, 1979. Grade level: 5 and up.

Rachel is overweight, has no boyfriend, and perceives her mother as being perfect. Her only escape from life at the Inn, which she dislikes, is through reading. It is only through a disaster that Rachel and her mother begin to accept one another. Cohen has written a superb novel which defines the intricacies of mother-daughter relationships and the problems of being an unpopular child.

Cohen, Barbara. *Unicorns in the Rain*. New York: Atheneum Publishers, 1980. Grade level: 6 and up.

A modern day Noah story about a world which no longer adheres to a basic code of ethics following the Judeo-Christian value system. As a result, a present day Noah and his family are forced to build an ark. The descriptive setting and good pace provides a story which is thought provoking and logical.

Colish, Chana. *The Great Mitzvah Fair*. Illus. by Michoel Muchnik. New York: Merkos L'Inyonei Chinuch, 1982. Grade level: K-3.

As children view the lively illustrations of the Mitzvah Fair, they are "taken" on amusement park rides with Jewish themes. Children participate in eating *hamantaschen*, a tour of the Torah, riding in a *dreidle*, bouncing on *challah* dough, and sliding down a *mezzuzah*. The book provides an entertaining introduction to a discussion of *mitzvot*.

dePaola, Tomie. *Now One Foot Now the Other*. New York: G.P. Putnam's Sons, 1981. Grade level: K-2.

When Bobby was a baby, his grandfather taught him to walk, played with him, and made him feel special. When Bobby's grandfather has a stroke, Bobby reciprocates by spending time with his grandfather, helping him accomplish what were once easy tasks. A beautiful book about the importance of caring for the elderly.

Derman, Martha. *The Friendstone*. New York: Dial Press, 1982. Grade level: 3-6.

Sally Moffat must work very hard to adopt values different from those of her bigoted family. However, as her friendship with Evie Grauber blossoms, the task of doing away with previously held stereotypes becomes much simpler and even pleasurable.

Gackenbach, Dick. *Do You Love Me?* Illus. by the author. New York: Seabury Press, Inc., 1975. Grade level: PK-4.

The importance of gentle and appropriate treatment of animals is stressed in this warm book about a young boy who learns that the love given to a pet will be reciprocated. The author's illustrations convey the message of the story.

Gervitz, Eliezer. *The Mystery of the Missing Pushke*. Illus. by Chanan Mazel. New York: Feldheim Publishers, 1982. Grade level: 4 and up.

Swift and sensitive detective work on the part of Binyamin helps to solve the theft of the *pushke* (*tzedakah* box), while at the same time protecting the reputation of a new boy in school.

Girion, Barbara. *A Handful of Stars*. New York: Charles Scribner's Sons, 1981. Grade level: 6 and up.

Jewish values abound in this novel about how a high school freshman's family helps her to cope with epilepsy. The relationship between Julie and her grandmother is particularly touching and the facts about epilepsy add to the realistic quality of the story.

Goffstein, M.B. *Natural History*. Illus. by the author. New York: Farrar, Straus & Giroux, Inc., 1979. Grade level: All grades.

The responsibility that we all have to preserve the dignity and peace of the universe is the message of this simple book. Goffstein's line drawings illustrating a quiet, tender world are effectively enhanced by watercolors.

Gotleib, Yaffa. *The Gift of Challahs*. Illus. by Aidel Backman. New York: Aura Publishing Co., 1982. Grade level: 1-4.

This is a beautifully written tale which contrasts two very different ways of showing reverence and gratitude to God. Gotleib helps the young reader to understand that the special gift prepared for God by the pious, uneducated couple is just as appreciated as accomplishments of a scholarly nature. The most important qualities of giving and doing are thus the intent and effort which go into the action.

Haley, Gail E. *Noah's Ark*. Illus. by the author. New York: Atheneum Publishers, 1971. Grade level: K-2.

A modern day story of a man named Noah who fights to save animals from extinction. The message of our responsibility for our environment is clearly conveyed.

Ethics

Harlow, Jules. (ed). *Lessons From Our Living Past*. Illus. by Erika Weihs. New York: Behrman House, Inc., 1972. Grade level: 3-5.

"The moral possibilities of our own lives" are presented through a diverse collection of stories selected from Jewish tradition. Nicely illustrated.

Hest, Amy. *Maybe Next Year*. New York: Clarion Books, 1982. Grade level: 4 and up.

A young girl who was orphaned must learn to share her Nana's love when the woman chooses to remarry. Hest has approached this sensitive topic with a pleasing combination of philosophy and wit.

Jones, Penelope. *The Stealing Thing*. New York: Bradbury Press, 1983. Grade level: 3-5.

Hope, an only child whose parents work and whose babysitter cannot take care of her in the summer, begins to steal. She feels guilty and ashamed. The ending is happy and the author shows much insight into Hope's behavior and its causes.

Kleinbard, Gitel. *"Oh Zalmy! Or the Tale of the Porcelain Pony, Book 1*. Illus. by Shmuel Kunda. Brooklyn, NY: Mah Tov Publishers, 1976. Grade level: PK-2.

By being honest and forgiving, a young Orthodox boy is able to resolve a family problem. The illustrations are lively, often humorous and will appeal to the young child.

Kleinbard, Gitel. *"Oh! Zalmy" or The Tale of the Tooth; Book 2*. Illus. by Shmuel Kunda. New York: Mah Tov Publishers, 1977.

Zalmy doesn't want to lose the tooth that is hanging by a thread after an accident, so he decides to keep his mouth closed until he gets home. However, in order to save a kitten, he must talk. A delightful story about the importance of doing *mitzvot*. A glossary of Hebrew and Yiddish words used in the story is included.

Konecky, Edith. *Allegra Maud Goldman*. New York: Dell Publishing Co., Inc., 1978. Grade level: 2 and up.

Allegra Maud Goldman is an absolutely lovable character even with her streak of devilishness. This story recounts Allegra's years between the ages of three and thirteen when she tests out everyone in her world to determine just how much mischief she can get away with.

Lehrman, Robert. *Juggling*. New York: Harper & Row Publishers, Inc., 1982. Grade level: 6 and up.

Although Howie is a star when it comes to doing tricks with a soccer ball, learning to juggle love, sex, and relationships with family and peers presents an even greater challenge for him. This story will appeal not only to the sports buff, but to any youngster entering into adolescence.

Levitin, Sonia. *The Year of Sweet Senior Insanity*. New York: Atheneum Publishers, 1982. Grade level: 6 and up.

Levitin has done a powerful yet sensitive job of helping children to realize the consequences of placing infatuation and fun above good judgment. Through the character of Leni, the issues of strained parent-child relationships, sex, and responsibility are insightfully explored.

Maruki, Toshi. *Hiroshima No Pika*. Illus. by the author. New York: Lothrop, Lee & Shepard Books, 1982. Grade level: 4-6.

The effect of the atom bomb dropped on Hiroshima is the subject of this tragic story. Vivid expressionistic paintings depict the horror of war. The text clearly states the message that "It can't happen again . . . if no one drops the bomb."

Muchnik, Michael. *Hershel's Houseboat*. Illus. by the author. New York: Merkos L'Inyonei Chinuch, 1977. Grade level: PK-1.

While on a houseboat trip, children learn about God's commandments. Pleasant illustrations complement the text.

Muchnik, Michael. *Tuvia's Train That Had No End*. Illus. by the author. New York: Merkos L'Inyonei Chinuch, 1978. Grade level: K-3.

When the Rabbi becomes sick, the Orthodox children in his congregation engage in performing *mitzvot* which will help to speed his recovery. The illustrations nicely convey the essence and moral of the story.

Rosenthal, Jaffa. *Mitzvos We Can Do*. Illus. by Rabbi Shmuel Kunda. New York: Mesorah Publications, Ltd., 1982. Grade level: PK-2.

    Rosenthal and Kunda have colorfully utilized the letters of the Hebrew alphabet to teach very young children about those commandments which they are personally capable of fulfilling.

Ruckman, Ivy. *In a Class by Herself*. Harcourt Brace Jovanovich, Inc., 1983. Grade level: 6-9.

    Dyna is on probation for participating in a burglary. When transferred to a new school, she realizes that in order to register, she must pay a fee. She decides to participate in one more burglary to get the money. Dyna makes friends at her new school who support her at the hearing for her burglary. At the end, it is clear that Dyna realized the mistake she has made and vows to change her behavior. A strong, believable story.

Schiffman, Ruth. *Turning the Corner*. New York: Dial Press, 1981. Grade level: 6 and up.

    Jewish values are apparent in the family lives and decisions made by Rebecca, an eighteen-year-old who must decide whether to pursue her education or help her family during the Depression.

Segel, Yocheved. *Our Sages Show the Way*. Illus. by Naama Northman, Trans. by Esther Falk. New York: Feldheim Publishers, 1979. Grade level: 4 and up.

    This collection of Talmudic tales contains a wealth of Jewish ethical values. Segel has chosen parables and expositions from a number of Talmudic scholars and retold them in a most appealing manner.

Simon, Norma. *All Kinds of Families*. Illus. by Joe Lasker. Niles, IL: Albert Whitman & Company, 1976. Grade level: 2-4.

    Simon has written an exquisite book about the important roles families play in our lives. The many different forms of family life are sensitively depicted through moving text and a variety of black and white and colored "family portraits."

Snyder, Carol. *Ike and Mama and the Block Wedding*. Illus. by Charles Robinson. New York: Coward, McCann & Geoghegan, Inc., 1979.

    Through example, Mama teaches Ike a lesson in compassion when she makes a wedding party for a couple who cannot afford to make their own. Snyder excels in writing stories which are entertaining and contain an "ethical" message as well.

Snyder, Carol. *Ike and Mama and Trouble at School*. Illus. by Charles Robinson. New York: Putnam Publishing Group, 1983. Grade level: 3-6.

    In this volume of the *Ike and Mama Series*, Ike must contend with the consequences of the letter from the school principal to his parents, Ziggy the school bully who is out to get him, and Sylvia who wants to sit next to him on the school outing. As usual, Ike's Mama and the boys from his neighborhood help him to solve these dilemmas in an ethical fashion.

Wade, Anna. *A Promise Is For Keeping*. Photographs by Jon Peterson. Chicago: Children's Press, 1979. Grade level: 1-3.

    A discussion of honesty and reliability would be an appropriate follow-up to this book about two friends who promise to take turns wearing a lost bracelet they find at the beach. The full page color photographs illustrate the action of the story.

Weilerstein, Sadie Rose. *K'tonton on an Island in the Sea*. Illus. by Michael Berenstein. Philadelphia: The Jewish Publication Society of America, 1976. Grade level: 2-5.

    A Jewish Tom Thumb-like character, K'tonton, finds himself stranded on an island. There he must discover a way to practice his religious beliefs. Simple drawings reflect K'tonton's life on the island.

Wittman, Sally. *A Special Trade*. Illus. by Karen Gundersheimer. New York: Harper & Row Publishers, Inc., 1978. Grade level: PK-1.

    Little Nellie and elderly Bartholomew have a special relationship. He takes care of her, strolling through the neighborhood everyday. When Bartholomew grows older, he is the one that needs to be wheeled around. Nellie does the job; it is a very special trade. Humorous pen drawings illustrate the warmth between the two individuals from different generations.

Zakutinsky, Ruth. *The Case of the Missing Baseball Cards.* New York: Aura Publishing Co., 1982. Grade level: 3-6.

The situation in this story becomes a rather awkward one when a young boy corners two classmates he suspects have stolen another boy's baseball cards.

Zuber-Sharfstein, Chana. *The Secret of Success and Other Stories.* Illus. by Zalman Kleinman. New York: Merkos L'Inyonei Chinuch, 1976. Grade level: 2-6.

The personal benefits of doing *mitzvot* for others are highlighted in this well written collection of six stories.

Zola, Meguido. *Only the Best.* Illus. by Valerie Littlewood. New York: Julia MacRae Books, 1981. Grade level: K-3.

The question of what is the "best" gift to give to a new baby is raised in this beautifully illustrated book. The father discovers in his search that material gifts are not nearly as good as the love a father can give to a child.

ETHICS: RESOURCES FOR ADULTS

Anthologies of Jewish Wisdom for Everyday Living

Greenberg, Sidney. *Say Yes to Life: A Book of Thoughts for Better Living.* New York: Crown Publishers, Inc. 1982.

Klagsbrun, Francine. *Voices of Wisdom: Jewish Ideals and Ethics for Everyday Living.* Illus by Mark Podwal. New York: Pantheon Books, 1980.

Riemer, Jack, and Stampfer, Nathaniel (eds). *Ethical Wills: A Modern Treasury.* New York: Schocken Books, Inc., 1983.

Ethical Writings of Selected Jewish Philosophers

Aryeh, Isaiah, and Dvorkes, Joshua (eds). *The Baal Shem Tov on Pirkey Avot.* Jerusalem: Feldheim Publishers, 1974.

Bokser, Ben Zion. *The Legacy of Maimonides.* New York: Hebrew Publishing Co., 1962.

Borowitz, Euguene. *Choices in Modern Jewish Thought: A Partisan Guide.* New York: Behrman House, Inc., 1983.

Buber, Martin. *I and Thou.* Translation and notes by Walter Kaufmann. New York: Charles Scribner's Sons, 1970.

Friedman, Maurice. *Martin Buber's Life and Work: The Middle Years 1923-1945.* New York: E.P. Dutton, 1983.

Goodhill, Ruth Marcus (ed). *The Wisdom of Heschel.* New York: Farrar, Straus & Giroux, Inc., 1975.

Heschel, Abraham Joshua. *The Insecurity of Freedom.* New York: Schocken Books, Inc., 1975.

Lewy, Hans; Altman, Alexander; and Heinemann, Isaak (eds). *Three Jewish Philosophers.* New York: Atheneum Publishers, 1969.

Liebman, Joshua Loth. *Hope For Man.* New York: Simon & Schuster, Inc., 1966.

_____. *Peace of Mind.* New York: Simon & Schuster, Inc., 1965.

Maimonides, Moses. *The Guide of the Perplexed.* Chicago: University of Chicago Press, 1963.

Minkin, Jacob. *The World of Moses Maimonides.* New York: Thomas Yoseloff, 1957.

Rosenthal, Gilbert. *Maimonides: His Wisdom For Our Time.* New York: Sabra Books, 1969.

Rosner, Fred. *Medicine in the Mishneh Torah of Maimonides.* New York: KTAV Publishing House, Inc., 1984.

Guides to Values Development and Social Action

American Jewish Committee. *Publications Catalogue of the Institute of Human Relations: Resources for Human Relations Agencies, Schools, Religious and Civic Organizations and Individuals.* New York: American Jewish Committee.

Brown, Steven M. *Higher and Higher.* New York: United Synagogue Department of Youth Activities, 1979.

Casteel, J. Doyle. *Learning to Think and Choose.* Santa Monica, CA: Goodyear Publishing Co., Inc., 1978.

Fowler, James W. *Stages of Faith.* New York: Harper & Row Publishers, Inc., 1981.

Fraenkel, Jack R. *Helping Students Think and Value.* Englewood Cliffs, NJ: Prentice-Hall, Inc., 1973.

Galbraith, Ronald E., and Jones, Thomas M. *Moral Reasoning: A Teaching Handbook for Adapting Kohlberg to the Classroom.* St. Paul, MN: Greenhaven Press, 1976.

Grishaver, Joel Lurie; Feinstein, Morley; and Wasserman, Howard. *The Jewish Values Game.* Denver: Alternatives in Religious Education, Inc., 1979.

Grishaver, Joel Lurie, and Huppin, Beth. *Tzedakah, Gemilut Chasadim and Ahavah.* Denver: Alternatives in Religious Education, Inc., 1983.

Hawley, Robert C. *Values Exploration Through Role Playing.* New York: Hart Publishing Co., 1974.

Howe, Leland W., and Howe, Mary Martha. *Personalizing Education: Values Clarification and Beyond.* New York: Hart Publishing Co., 1975.

Jewish Value Prompters. Denver: Alternatives in Religious Education, Inc., 1973. (Game)

Neusner, Jacob. *Mitzvah*. Chappaqua, NY: Rossel Books, 1982.

Olitzky, Kerry M. *My Jewish Community Ditto Pak*. Denver: Alternatives in Religious Education, Inc., 1981.

Schwartz, Earl. *Moral Development: A Practical Guide for Jewish Teachers*. Denver: Alternatives in Religious Education, Inc., 1983.

Simon, Sidney; Howe, Leland; and Kirschenbaum, Howard. *Values Clarification: A Handbook of Practical Strategies for Teachers and Students*. New York: Hart Publishing Co., Inc., 1978.

Summers, Barbara Fortang. *Community and Responsibility in the Jewish Tradition: A Study and Action Program*. New York: United Synagogue of America, 1978.

There Is a Season: A Values Clarification Approach to Jewish Holidays. Denver: Alternatives in Religious Education, Inc., 1978.

Vorspan, Albert. *Jewish Values and Social Crisis: A Casebook for Social Action*. New York: Union of American Hebrew Congregations, 1977.

Zwerin, Raymond A. *For One Another: Jewish Organizations That Help Us All*. New York: Union of American Hebrew Congregations, 1975.

Hasidic Thought

Buber, Martin (ed). *Ten Rungs: Hasidic Sayings*. New York: Schocken Books, Inc., 1962.

Langer, Jiri. *Nine Gates to the Chasidic Mysteries*. New York: David McKay Co., 1961.

Newman, Louis (ed). *The Hasidic Anthology*. New York: Schocken Books, Inc., 1963.

Schachter, Zalman M., and Hoffman, Edward. *Sparks of Light: Counseling in the Hasidic Tradition*. Boulder, CO: Shambhala Publications, 1983.

Historical Development of Jewish Ethics and Law

Berkovits, Eliezer. *Not in Heaven: The Nature and Function of Halakha*. New York: KTAV Publishing House, Inc., 1983.

Ginzberg, Louis. *On Jewish Law and Lore*. New York: Atheneum Publishers, 1970.

Herzog, Chief Rabbi Isaac. *Judaism: Law & Ethics*. London: Soncino Press, 1974.

Silver, Daniel J. (ed). *Judaism and Ethics*. New York: KTAV Publishing House, Inc., 1970.

Jewish Ethics Concerning Love, Marriage, and Sex

Benson, Paulette, and Bissell, Sherry. *Divorce in Jewish Life and Tradition*. Denver: Alternatives in Religious Education, Inc., 1977.

Borowitz, Eugene. *Choosing A Sex Ethic: A Jewish Inquiry*. New York: Schocken Books, Inc., 1969.

Gittelsohn, Roland. *The Extra Dimension: A Jewish View of Marriage*. New York: Union of American Hebrew Congregations, 1983.

Gordis, Robert. *Love & Sex: A Modern Jewish Perspective*. New York: Farrar, Straus & Giroux, Inc., 1978.

Green, Alan. *Sex, God and the Sabbath: The Mystery of Jewish Marriage*. Cleveland: Temple Emanu El, 1979.

Grollman, Earl. *Talking About Divorce*. Boston: Beacon Press, Inc., 1975.

Haut, Irwin H. *Divorce in Jewish Law and Life*. New York: Sepher-Hermon Press, 1983.

Jung, Leo. *Love and Life*. New York: Philosophical Library, Inc., 1979.

Lamm, Maurice. *The Jewish Way in Love and Marriage*. New York: Harper & Row Publishers, Inc., 1980.

Mirel, Barbara, and Mirel, Jeff. *Relationships: A Jewish View*. Denver: Alternatives in Religious Education, Inc., 1981.

Seltzer, Sanford. *Jews and Non-Jews Falling in Love*. New York: Union of American Hebrew Congregations, 1976.

Siegel, Robert and Debbie. *Intermarriage: A Guide for Jewish Parents*. Charleston, SC: Rashi Press, 1979.

Zwerin, Raymond A., and Marcus, Audrey Friedman. *Marriage in Jewish Life and Tradition*. Denver: Alternatives in Religious Education, Inc., 1978.

Jewish Perspectives on Contemporary Ethical Issues

Biale, Rachel. *Women and Jewish Law: An Exploration of Women's Issues in Halakhic Sources*. New York: Schocken Books, Inc., 1984.

Bloch, Abraham P. *A Book of Jewish Ethical Concepts: Biblical and Postbiblical*. New York: KTAV Publishing House, Inc., 1984.

Cohn, Haim. *Human Rights in Jewish Law*. New York: KTAV Publishing House, Inc., 1984.

Goldman, Alex J. *Judaism Confronts Contemporary Issues*. New York: Shengold Publishers, Inc. 1978.

Jacobs, Louis. *A Tree of Life: Diversity, Creativity, and Flexibility in Jewish Law*. New York: Oxford University Press, 1983.

Kellner, Menachem Marc (ed). *Contemporary Jewish Ethics*. New York: Shengold Publishers, Inc., 1978.

Levi, Leo. *Torah and Science: Their Interplay in the World Scheme*. New York: Feldheim Publishers, 1983.

Nelson, J. Robert. *Human Life: A Biblical Perspective of Bioethics*. Philadelphia: Fortress Press, 1984.

Rotenstreich, Natan. *Man and His Dignity*. Jerusalem: Magnes Press, 1983.

Schochet, Elijah Judah. *Animal Life in Jewish Tradition: Attitudes and Relationships*. New York: KTAV Publishing House, Inc., 1984.

Sidorsky, David (ed). *Essays on Human Rights: Contemporary Issues and Jewish Perspectives*. Philadelphia: The Jewish Publication Society of America, 1978.

Simon, James L.; Zwerin, Raymond A.; and Marcus, Audrey Friedman. *Bioethics: A Jewish View*. Denver: Alternatives in Religious Education, Inc., 1984.

Vorspan, Albert. *Great Jewish Debates and Dilemmas: Jewish Perspectives in Conflict in the Eighties*. New York: Union of American Hebrew Congregations, 1980.

Zipperstein, Edward. *Business Ethics in Jewish Law*. New York: KTAV Publishing House, Inc., 1983.

MITZVOT AND THE JEWISH WAY OF LIFE

Chill, Abraham. *The Minhagim: The Customs and Ceremonies of Judaism, Their Origins and Rationale*. New York: Sepher-Hermon Press, 1979.

_____. *The Mitzvot: The Commandments and Their Rationale*. New York: Bloch Publishing Co., 1974.

Dresner, Samuel. *The Jewish Dietary Laws: Their Meaning For Our Time*. New York: Rabbinical Assembly, 1982.

Lebeau, James M. *The Jewish Dietary Laws: Sanctify Life*. Edited by Stephan Garfinkel. New York: United Synagogue of America, Department of Youth Activities, 1983.

Maimonides, Moses. *The Commandments*. Trans. by Charles Chavel. London: Soncino Press, 1967. (Two Volumes)

Munk, Michael L. *The Wisdom in the Hebrew Alphabet: The Sacred Letters as a Guide to Jewish Deed and Thought*. New York: Mesorah Publications, Ltd., 1983.

Siegel, Danny. *Gym Shoes and Irises: Personalized Tzedakah*. Spring Valley, NY: The Town House Press, 1982.

RABBINIC JUDAISM

Goldin, Hyman (ed). *Pirke Avot: Ethics of the Fathers*. New York: Hebrew Publishing Co., 1962.

Montefiore, C.G., and Loewe, H. *A Rabbinic Anthology*. New York: Schocken Books, Inc., 1974.

Neusner, Jacob. *Understanding Rabbinic Judaism*. New York: KTAV Publishing House, Inc., 1974.

Holidays IV

An artist cannot be continually wielding his brush. He must stop at times in his painting to freshen his vision of the object, the meaning of which he wishes to express on his canvas. Living is also an art. We dare not become absorbed in its technical processes and lose our consciousness of its general plan . . . The Sabbath represents those moments when we pause in our brushwork to renew our vision of this object. Having done so we take ourselves to our painting with clarified vision and renewed energy.

Mordecai Kaplan, quoted in Likrat Shabbat: Worship, Study, and Song for Sabbath and Festival Services and for the Home, edited by Sidney Greenberg, p. 10. ©1973 The Prayer Book Press of Media Judaica, Inc.

OVERVIEW

Celebration is inherent to the Jewish way of life. The biblical injunction *"samachta b'chagecha"* (rejoice in your festival) resounds throughout the cycle of the Jewish year as seven major holidays, fourteen minor holidays, and the weekly Shabbat are celebrated. The major holidays are: Rosh Hashanah, Yom Kippur, Sukkot, Shemini Atzeret, Simchat Torah, Pesach, and Shavuot. The minor holidays are: Fast of Gedalia, Hoshanah Rabbah, Chanukah, Fast of the Tenth of Tevet, Tu B'Shevat, Fast of Esther, Purim, Fast of the First Born, Yom HaShoah (Holocaust Commemoration), Yom HaAtzma'ut (Israel Independence Day), Lag B'Omer, Fast of the Seventeenth of Tammuz, Tisha B'Av, and the Fifteenth of Av.

Each holiday is distinguished by its own biblical and historical origins, customs, prayers, and emotional tone. Educators must therefore design holiday learning experiences for students that include each of these dimensions. The task of planning and learning during the holidays is particularly enjoyable, as we can appeal to each of the five senses. We can listen to the sound of the *shofar* on the High Holy Days, smell the sweet spices of Havdalah, feel the rich earth while planting trees on Tu B'Shevat, taste the bitter herbs at the *Seder*, and view the new moon after Rosh Chodesh, the beginning of each month.

But above and beyond these concrete holiday experiences, we must also contemplate the true meaning of celebration. Lest we become too wrapped up in the physical indulgences of the holidays, the philosopher Philo suggested that "the true significance of the festival is to find pleasure and enjoyment through meditation about the world and the harmony within it." Rabbi Akiba carried this definition of celebration as "quiet exaltation" beyond the festivals and into everyday life as he offered to his disciples the simple phrase, "A song every day, a song every day" (*The Wisdom of Heschel*, Farrar, Straus & Giroux, Inc., 1970, p. 159).

To encourage students to sing their songs of celebration, we have selected a variety of books which emphasize holiday joy and meditation. *The House on the Roof: A Sukkot Story* will help students to understand the importance of fighting to uphold Jewish traditions, and motivate them to partake in Sukkah construction and Sukkot celebration. The spendor of Shabbat and necessity for *tzedakah* are interwoven with the history of the Jewish people in the beautiful story *The Secret of the Sabbath Fish*.

Although Shavuot usually falls after school is over, it should not be neglected during the academic year. *Who Knows Ten?* may be used to tie the giving of the Law to the holiday of Shavuot. This book will undoubtedly add meaning to the student's celebration of the holiday and their understanding of each of the Ten Commandments.

Both *Yussel's Prayer*, a book for Yom Kippur, and *A Sound to Remember*, a book for Rosh Hashanah, emphasize the importance and value of participating actively and sincerely in holiday rituals. This belief is also shared by a little boy and his grandfather in *The Wineglass*, an excellent story to be shared at Passover.

Chanukah and Purim are favorite holidays for children. If the students have never tasted a potato *latke*, they will taste the "best ever" in *Potato Pancakes All Around: A Hanukkah Tale*, and if they are not aware of the story behind Purim, the book *Esther* will surely provide that background.

Tu B'Shevat is widely celebrated in Jewish schools. To add to the celebration and to remind students of the beauty and importance of trees, read *A Tree is Nice*.

Finally, for a review of all the Jewish holidays, we suggest *Jewish Days and Holidays*, an informative book which also provides activity pages.

HOLIDAYS: BOOKS AND ACTIVITIES

Adler, David A. *The House on the Roof: A Sukkot Story.* **Illustrations by Marilyn Hirsh. New York: Bonim Books, 1976. 28 pages. Grade level: K-4.**

The House on the Roof tells the story of an elderly man who builds a *sukkah* on the roof of his apartment building as a surprise for his grandchildren. One is moved by the extraordinary effort and love he puts into the *sukkah*, the joy it brings to his grandchildren, and the sadness and anger stirred up by the landlord who takes the old man to court to have the *sukkah* removed. Upon hearing the tenant's explanation for the *sukkah*, the judge rules that the man may leave the booth standing for no more than the duration of the holiday. Marilyn Hirsh's lovely illustrations set a lively background for the story.

Major Ideas

Religious freedom is a basic human right.

It is important to strive toward justice for all.

To rejoice in the celebration of life and the festival is a major theme of Sukkot.

Activities

1. Grades K-4: In keeping with the spirit of Sukkot, have the students decorate the classroom as a *sukkah*. Chains of construction paper may be strung across the ceiling. The students may create paper fruit and other decorations to be suspended from the chains.

2. Grades K-4: At the end of the book, the old man explains the meaning of Sukkot to the judge. Since Sukkot is the celebration of the harvest, nature-oriented projects are appropriate at this time. The week before you plan to share the book with the class, send a letter to the students' parents asking them to choose three or more of the vegetables suggested on a list you provide. The list should include only vegetables with textures or interesting shapes that will show up when used as a printing implement (examples: onions, cabbage, green peppers, carrots, artichokes, etc.). Discuss the book again, as well as the holiday's meaning. Tell the students that in addition to celebrating Sukkot by hanging fruits and vegetables from the *sukkah*, they are going to use the vegetables to create lasting works of art. The students will then do vegetable printing using the procedure described below:

Materials:
vegetables
dry powder or tempera
plain drawing paper

Procedure:

   a. The teacher cuts the vegetable in half.

   b. Each student will press the vegetable into a printing pad made with twenty thicknesses of newspaper cut 9" x 12". The pad is saturated with water, and sprinkled with dry powder or moist tempera paints.

   c. The vegetable is then pressed against a paper on which the print is to appear. This process is repeated with each print.

   d. To re-use the vegetable, wash it with water.

   e. Display the prints on a bulletin board entitled: *Boray P'ri Ha'adamah* (from the blessing thanking God for creating fruits of the earth).

3. Grades 3 and 4: According to the historical explanation of Sukkot given in the book, the Israelites lived in portable huts during their wanderings in the desert. The *sukkah* built each fall reminds us of the Israelites' huts. To help the students experience what it was like to live outdoors, plan a Sukkot Shabbaton. Have the students spend Friday night and Saturday at the synagogue. If necessary, boys and girls can sleep in classrooms which have been decorated as *sukkot*. Eat meals in the outdoor *sukkah*. Invite parents to help with supervision and activities. The Oneg Shabbat should also be held in the outdoor *sukkah* so that the students can enjoy the night sky.

Aronim, Ben. *The Secret of the Sabbath Fish.* **Illus. by Shay Rieger. Philadelphia: The Jewish Publication Society of America, 1978. 43 pages. Grade level: 2-4.**

According to the author, gefilte fish as a Sabbath delicacy had its beginnings in the Russian village of Barisev some two hundred years ago. At that time, a very special fish was purchased by Tante Mashe from the Prophet Elijah, who appears in the guise of a fisherman. As Tante Mashe prepares the fish as a gift of *tzedakah* for the villagers, she tells the story of the Jewish people. She uses each ingredient to symbolize both the harsh realities and the joys of our experience. Through black and white line drawings and imaginative narrative, Shay Rieger and Ben Aronim have spun a masterful tale of creation.

Major Ideas

Warmth and beauty can be found even within the harshest environments.

Sometimes individuals of the most humble means are the most giving.

The combining of love, skill, and creativity can result in a very special creation.

Holidays

Activities

1. Grades 3 and 4: Have the students write an original recipe for gefilte fish. Then reproduce these for the parents and/or send them to the local Jewish newspaper for publication.

2. Grades 3 and 4: Involve the entire class in making gefilte fish that will be eaten at a Kabbalat Shabbat to be held before the end of the day on Friday. The teacher should obtain the ingredients in advance to make the process easier and less time consuming. Prepare the fish the day before, or even the week before, and freeze it.

3. Grades 2-4: Have the students imagine that they have just come to earth from another planet. Arriving early Friday morning, they meet a young Jewish child who asks them to participate in a Shabbat celebration. When told that one of the delicacies they will savor is gefilte fish, an image very different from ours comes to mind. Have each student create a crayon resist drawing depicting the stranger's concept of the fish in its natural surroundings. A step-by-step procedure for crayon resist follows.

Materials:

crayons
tempera paint
light colored construction paper
water
newspaper

Procedure:

a. With heavy pressure, apply crayon to light colored construction paper. Use several layers of newspaper padding underneath.

b. Leave some areas not crayoned — both between objects and within.

c. Add detail to negative space.

d. Paint over drawing with water diluted tempera.

Cashman, Greer Fay. *Jewish Days and Holidays.* **Illus. by Alona Frankel. Englewood, NJ: SBS Publishing, Inc., 1979. 64 pages. Grade level: 2-5.**

This book provides an excellent overview of the Jewish holidays. Dynamic illustrations and interesting text combine to communicate the essence of each holiday. At the end of the book, there is an activity page which enables the child to review the symbols for each holiday.

Major Ideas

The festivals of the Jewish year follow a specific cycle.

Each holiday has unique symbols and customs.

Each holiday has a biblical root.

Activities

1. All ages: Holiday material can be enjoyably reviewed by playing the game "Jewpardy" (a take-off of the television game show "Jeopardy"). Decide on five to seven category titles. For example: Holiday Heroes; Holiday Munchies; Symbols and Ceremonies; Holiday Villains; Name That Holiday, etc. Categories should be created based on information covered both in the book and during other classroom activities. After the selection of categories, prepare the game as follows:

   a. Write each category title on a 4" x 6" index card using broad felt tipped pens.

   b. For each category, formulate a list of five to seven appropriate questions on scrap paper.

   c. Write the answer to these questions on one side of individual 4" x 6" index cards. These cards will be the clue cards.

   d. On the other side of the clue cards, use a broad felt tipped pen to mark the money or point value of each clue, depending on its difficulty. Use a 10, 20, 30, 40, 50 system or use letters of the Hebrew alphabet to indicate point value.

   e. Tape cards to the chalkboard as in Diagram 5.

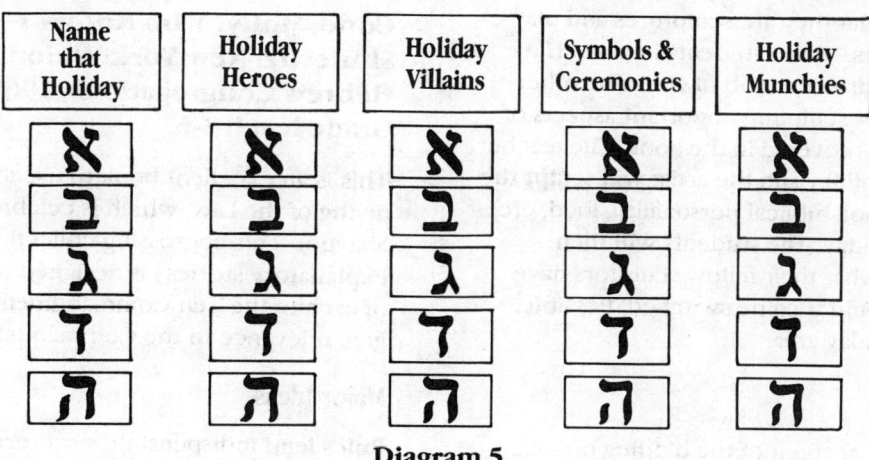

Diagram 5

f. Depending on the size of the class, separate the students into two or more teams and name the teams by Jewish symbols, such as *Magen David* and *Chai*. Tell them that they will be selecting from the board the clue cards on which an answer is written. Their job is to supply the question.

g. Begin by having a member of team #1 select a category. Although a student may choose any category, he/she must begin by choosing the easiest clue (starting with a point value of 10). That student then attempts to supply the question for the answer written on the clue card. If the student does not answer correctly, the member of the next team who has raised his/her hand first may take the turn and accrue the points. If the correct question is not given after all the teams have had a chance, the point value of the clue can be cut in half. Then, another individual from the team which originally chose the clue will begin a second round of attempting to answer correctly. When the correct question is supplied, team #2 then selects a category (either a new category or the clue card worth 20 points under the first category chosen) and the above stated rules continue to be followed. The teacher should keep a tally of the points.

2. Grades 3-5: Among the outstanding qualities of this book are the beautiful collage illustrations. Have each student choose one of the holidays and create a collage depicting that holiday. A simple collage may be created by cutting and pasting colored construction paper, fluorescent and day-glo papers, scraps of material, tin foil, wallpaper samples, ads from magazines, and other colorful and textured odds and ends onto a background surface (construction paper, poster board, cardboard, etc.). Place these on a bulletin board entitled *Shanah Tovah* (A Good Year), making sure to create a collage for each holiday during the Jewish year.

3. Grades 3-5: In a poem that appears in the High Holy Day Machzor (prayer book), people are described as being like clay in the hands of a potter. Ask the students to imagine that they are sculptures and play "Holiday Sculptures." Place students in pairs. Have one assume the shape of a blob of clay. The other will be the sculptor sculpting important aspects of the Jewish holidays covered in the book. The teacher will call out the holiday and the artist will sculpt the "blob" into a symbol, biblical personality, food, etc., related to that holiday. The students will then attempt to guess what their fellow sculptors have created. Roles should then be switched. Possible ideas for each holiday area:

Rosh Hashanah:
shofar
the ram (in the account of the binding of Isaac)

Sukkot:
lulav
etrog
sukkah

Chanukah:
menorah
dreidle
jelly donut or *latke*

Passover:
matzah
cup of wine
egg

Shavuot:
Ten Commandments
Mount Sinai
fruit

Shabbat:
Havdalah candle
challah
spice box

Yom Kippur:
the great fish (Jonah)
chicken (*kapparah*)
The Book of Life

Simchat Torah:
Torah
a flag
the sun (symbol of creation)

Purim:
gragger
hamentaschen
Megillah

Yom HaAtzma'ut:
Israeli flag
parade float
David Ben-Gurion

Tisha B'Av:
flames (destruction of the Temple)
Ner Tamid (Eternal Light)
a person mourning

Cone, Molly. *Who Knows Ten?* Illus. by Uri Shulevitz; New York: Union of American Hebrew Congregations, 1965. 107 pages. Grade level: 3-6.

This is an excellent book to use in teaching about the giving of the Law, which is celebrated on the holiday of Shavuot. This engrossing collection of *Midrashim* (short explanatory stories) is designed to explain the meaning of each of the Ten Commandments. Each story helps to give relevance to the Commandment in the child's life.

Major Ideas

Rules lend indispensible structure to life.

Holidays

God chose to give the Israelites the Commandments and they, in turn, chose to accept that gift.

There are ten commandments basic to all humanity.

Activities

Note: When doing these activities, remind the students that the giving of the Law is tied to the holiday of Shavuot. They may need this reminder, since Shavuot does not ordinarily fall during the school year.

1. Grades 3-6: Hold a discussion about how the original Ten Commandments influence our lives. Then ask each student to create ten new commandments which would benefit humanity. Write these on tablets shaped like those handed down at Sinai. Display the completed tablets on a bulletin board entitled "We Know Ten."

2. Grades 3-6: Have the students choose one of their new commandments and write a story, as the author did, to help explain how and why that commandment could benefit humanity. For example, if a student wrote "Thou shalt not pollute the environment," he or she might write a story which tells of the ill effects of pollution. Volunteers may share their stories aloud in class.

3. Grades 3-6: It is written in the book of Deuteronomy that "you shall write them (the Commandments) upon the doorposts of your house and upon your gates." The students can have the opportunity to fulfill this commandment by creating their own "*mezzuzot.*" Materials and procedure follow.

Materials:

self-hardening clay
acrylic paint
scrolls (may be handwritten on nice quality writing paper; kosher scrolls may be purchased from a synagogue)

Procedure:

a. Design on paper a shape for the *mezzuzah* holder.

b. Using a thin layer of self-hardening clay, shape the *mezzuzah* holder as designed, leaving the inside hollow and one end open. The back side of the *mezzuzah* holder should be flat and a nail hole should be placed at the top and the bottom.

c. Slip the scroll inside and close the opening.

d. Before allowing the clay to dry, designs may be etched into the *mezzuzah* holder.

e. Paint with acrylics.

f. Before students take their *mezzuzot* home, teach them the blessing which is said when affixing a *mezzuzah* to one's door.

ברוך אתה יי אלהינו מלך העולם אשר קדשנו במצותיו וצונו לקבוע מזוזה.

Baruch Atah Adonai Eloheynu Melech Ha'olam, Asher Kid'shanu B'mitzvotav, V'tzivanu Likboa Mezzuzah.

Blessed are You O Eternal our God, Ruler of the universe, who sanctifies us by Your commandments and commands us to affix this *mezzuzah*.

Cohen, Barbara. *Yussel's Prayer: A Yom Kippur Story.* **Illus. by Michael J. Deraney. New York: Lothrop, Lee & Shepard Books, 1981. 28 pages. Grade level: 2-4.**

This book tells the story of a poor young shepherd boy, Yussel, who successfully opens the gates of heaven on Yom Kippur so that the prayers of the people in his village are received. Prior to Yussel's heartfelt prayer, the gates remained closed, because the prayers of the villagers had not been offered with sincerity. This book, warmly illustrated in shades of brown and white, is excellent for teaching children the purpose and spirit of prayer.

Major Idea

A true prayer comes from the heart and need not follow traditional form.

Activities

1. Grades 3 and 4: Yussel's prayer was conveyed to God through music. Have the students draw a picture of Yussel expressing a musical prayer through his reed pipe. At the bottom of the page, ask the students to write a caption translating the music into words.

2. Grades 2-4: Yussel prayed with a reed pipe. Have the students create simple rhythm instruments to be used in an orchestral prayer. Directions for making various types follow.

   Drum – Use any large, metal can. The top can be an old piece of inner tube held in place with baling wire.

   Drum – Use shellacked muslin stretched and laced over both ends of a coffee can. Soak muslin in cold water and put on wet. Apply the first coat of the shellack after muslin dries. It must be shellacked 3 times and allowed to dry thoroughly between coats.

   Tom-tom – A tympani drum head over both ends of a coffee can. Drum head must be soaked 10 minutes until soft. Twine is used for laces, and heads are gradually stretched, tightening as they dry. The lacing is then shellacked.

   Tambourine – Use an old drum head or muslin between 2 embroidery hoops. Six bottle caps hammered flat are attached around the rim with string or wire.

Cymbals – Use 2 can tops (coffee cans may be used). Edges are hammered flat, and empty spools nailed on for handles.

Plate shaker – Lace two paper plates together with dry corn inside.

Cup shaker – Use paper cup holding dried corn.

Clothespin kids – Use clothespin for body. For the hat, one flat bottle cap and one regular bottle cap can be held on with a screw. The hat rattles.

Can shaker – Partially fill tooth powder can with dried corn or pebbles.

Maracas – Use 2 worn-out light bulbs covered with thin strips of paper toweling pasted on with flour and water paste. Apply 4 or 5 layers and allow to dry. Decorate with a design in colors. Then break the bulb by hitting it on a cement floor. The broken glass inside makes the sound.

Jingle sticks – Use 2 dowel rods 12" long (from a lumber yard) and 2 flattened bottle caps fastened to one end of each stick with a screw.

Rhythm sticks – Use 2 dowel rods 12" long (from a lumber yard) painted red.

Sand blocks – Use two blocks of wood 3¾" long, 3" wide, and ⅞" thick (lumber yard again). Sandpaper is put on with thumb tacks.

Wood blocks – These have the same measurements as the sand blocks above. Sandpaper the rough edges.

Picket fence – Use a board with 10 clothespins, upside down, attached with screws. A dowel rod is used to "play" up and down the fence. This may also be used by primary teachers for number work by painting clothespins different colors.

Bells – Sew three bells on a band of ribbon.

Triangles – Use a 6" long nail with a string tied to the head to serve as a handle. For the striker, use a 3" long nail. Another sort of triangle is made from a piece of bent metal.

Rhythm instruments can be made from many other things, such as oatmeal boxes or gourds filled with pebbles, paper plates to which buttons have been sewn, and so on.

3. All ages: Ask the Rabbi to come into your classroom to explain the purpose of a sermon to the students. After the Rabbi leaves, ask the students to imagine that they are Rabbis planning a sermon for Yom Kippur. Have them write down their thoughts. If possible, have the Rabbi incorporate some of the children's sermons into the Yom Kippur service.

Hirsh, Marilyn. *Potato Pancakes All Around: A Hanukkah Tale.* **Illus. by the author. New York: Bonim Books, 1978. 34 pages. Grade level: K-3.**

While Grandma Yetta and Grandma Sophie argue over which potato *latke* recipe to use on the first night of Chanukah, Samuel the peddler steps in and dazzles the family with a recipe made from bread crust. To this base, Samuel adds ingredients as suggested by each member of the family. The potato pancakes were "the best ever." Action packed illustrations washed in gold and brown add to the excitement and humor in the story. They also depict the festive customs of Chanukah. Included at the end of the book are Grandma Yetta's and Grandma Sophie's recipes for potato pancakes.

Major Ideas

Chanukah is a joyous, family-oriented celebration.

Cooperation and integration of varying ideas are the keys to any successful group effort.

Activities

1. Grades K-3: Two weeks before reading the story, say to the students, "In a couple of weeks a surprise visitor (the teacher dressed as the peddler) will be coming to our class to share a Chanukah story about a very special Jewish recipe. I will be giving you a letter which asks your parents to send in a favorite Jewish recipe enjoyed by *your* family. Then, we will put the recipes together in a cookbook with a drawing from each of you to give your parents for a surprise Chanukah present." The letter should read as follows:

   Dear Parent(s),

   In conjunction with our study of Jewish holidays, we often talk about Jewish food. To facilitate our class discussion next week, please send in two favorite Jewish recipes you are willing to share. (I am asking for two to minimize duplication of delicacies.)

   Thank you for your help.

   B'shalom,

   (Your name)

   Once you have received the recipes, type at least one recipe from each family on dittos. Have the students draw an appropriate illustration for their family's recipe on separate dittos. The drawing might depict a holiday during which the food is eaten or a picture of the food being prepared or eaten. Once the cookbook is compiled, each student can color the illustrations with crayon. The cover should be a blank page so that each student can name his/her own cookbook, or one title can be decided upon by the class.

2. Grades K-3: Rather than simply reading this story to your class, commit it to memory so that you can mix the potato pancake ingredients (listed at the end of the book) as you tell the story to the class. The potatoes, onions, and bread crumbs should be grated and measured beforehand, along with all the other ingredients. An electric skillet can be brought into the classroom to fry the pancakes, or the entire activity may be done in the kitchen.

3. Grades K-3: At the end of the book, the characters take part in Chanukah festivities, including playing games. After the class has eaten the *latkes* and learned about the holiday, play a game of Chanukah Bingo. Make up cards with pictures of the various Chanukah symbols and historical characters. Draw the symbols and historical characters on dittos or trace them from books onto the dittos. After duplicating the symbols and historical characters, cut them out and create cards of varying combinations. Give out chocolate Chanukah *gelt* as markers. Prepare a selection of riddles for yourself. Use these in calling the game. (The difficulty of the riddles should be geared to the students' grade level). For example:

> This Chanukah delicacy is referred to in Yiddish as *latkes*, or in Hebrew as *levivot* ...
>
> The oil in this burned for eight days ...
>
> He led the battle against the Assyrian army. His name means hammer ...

Levitin, Sonia. *A Sound to Remember.* **Illus. by Gabriel Lisowski. New York: Harcourt Brace Jovanovich, Inc., 1979. 28 pages. Grade level: 2-4.**

When a young boy is chosen by the Rabbi of his small European village to sound the *shofar* in celebration of the New Year, the boy, his parents, and the villagers question the wisdom of the Rabbi's judgment. After the boy's failure on Rosh Hashanah, the reader is kept in suspense as to whether the end of Yom Kippur will be marked with silence as well. Through the warmth of sensitive narrative and detailed pencil drawings, the pain, the frustration of struggle, and the ultimate joy of success are experienced.

Major Ideas

The call of the *shofar* has both traditional and personal meanings.

In order for traditions to survive, older generations must allow the young to learn and practice rituals.

The wisdom of a certain choice may not be immediately evident.

Accomplishing a task successfully takes patience, practice, and strong faith.

Activities

1. Grades 2-4: Engage the students in a discussion focusing on the following questions:

    Why do you think the Rabbi chose the young boy rather than an adult for the privilege of sounding the *shofar*?

    What are some of the rituals that take place in your family that you hope will be carried on to the next generation?

    The young boy in the story eventually met with success. What have been some of your successes over the past year?

    What are some of your goals for the coming year?

2. Grades 2-4: Have the Cantor or the Rabbi bring a *shofar* to your class to demonstrate how it is sounded. Allow each student to try it. Be sure to explain the meaning of the different *shofar* sounds.

3. Grades 3 and 4: To explain why the *shofar* is sounded, introduce the students to the Torah portion of Abraham and the binding of Isaac (the *Akedah*). Reinforce key points by providing them with an age appropriate crossword puzzle based on what has been taught. Diagram 6 is an example of a puzzle appropriate for third or fourth graders.

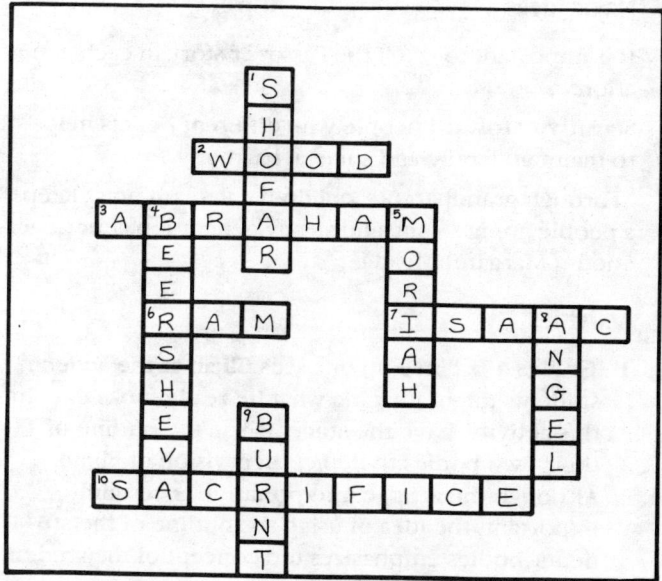

Diagram 6

Across

2. It was Isaac's job to carry this.

3. He was put to the test by God.

6. This was sacrificed in place of Isaac.

7. Abraham's most prized possession.

10. Another way of saying to give something up.

Down

1. Hebrew name for a ram's horn.

4. Place to which Abraham and Isaac returned after leaving Moriah.

5. The land where the sacrifice was to take place.

8. Sent by God to stop Abraham from killing Isaac.

9. _____ offering.

Rosten, Norman. *The Wineglass*. Illus. by Kaethe Zemach. New York: Walker & Co., 1978. 30 pages. Grade level: 4-6.

The biblical injunction "*v'chigadeta l'bincha bayom hahu*" (to teach one's children the story of Passover) is poignantly conveyed in this tale. In *The Wineglass*, a young boy and his grandfather share the belief that the Prophet Elijah comes as a guest to every *Seder* to sip a bit of wine from the special cup. The little boy's enthusiasm is contrasted to the disinterest and disbelief of the other family members. Only the mother understands the miracle of Elijah in her young son's eyes. This is a tale of great wisdom and one that wields a powerful message. For, as the author quotes on the cover page, "if the sun and the moon should doubt, they would surely go out."

Major Ideas

It is important to retell the Passover story in each generation.

Sensitivity toward people with different beliefs helps to maintain family and societal harmony.

"Through grandparents, children can learn what keeps a people going strong and steady generation after generation" (Margaret Mead).

Activities

1. Grades 4-6: Since no one sees Elijah at the *Seder*, students might imagine what he really looks like. In this activity, have the students use the outline of their own bodies to depict their vision of Elijah. Although the artistic interpretation is certainly important, the idea of using the outline of the students' bodies emphasizes the concept of the students adopting Elijah's compassionate inner qualities. A step-by-step procedure for this art project follows.

Materials:

roll of brown wrapping paper
scissors
markers
yarn
scraps of paper
newspaper

Procedure:

a. Pair the students so that they may outline one another while lying down on paper.

b. Have the outline drawn in duplicate to allow for two parts which can be sewn together and stuffed.

c. Once the outlines are cut out, have the children decorate their paper person to look like their idea of Elijah. Both front and back should be decorated.

d. Staple around the edges of the two pieces beginning at the top of the head and staple down halfway on each side.

e. Stuff the upper body and head with crumpled newspaper.

f. Continue stapling down the legs to bottom of feet, leaving openings to stuff the lower half of the body.

g. Complete stapling.

h. Have the students take their "Elijahs" home to sit in a place of honor at their *Seder*.

2. Grades 4-6: A prophet is a messenger between God and the people. Ask the students to imagine that they are Elijah and must deliver a message at their family's *Seder*. Have them prepare the messages in writing so they may be shared as a special addition at the actual *Seder*.

3. Grades 4-6: One of the striking features of this story is the warm relationship shared by the young boy and his grandfather. To allow the students to share some of this same warmth with a grandparent (or another family elder), and to add a different twist to the *Seder* as well, arrange for them to recite the Four Questions at their family *Seder* together with the grandparent. Make sure the older person will be attending the student's *Seder* and, if possible, have these elderly individuals come to class to practice the Four Questions. This intergenerational recitation of the Four Questions could also be done at the class or school's model *Seder*.

Udry, Janice May. *A Tree is Nice*. Illus. by Marc Simont; New York: Harper & Row Publishers, Inc., 1956. 29 pages. Grade level: K-2.

Janice Udry's book *A Tree is Nice* extols the many delights of trees. Marc Simont's illustrations enhance the short, but poetic text. A Caldecott winner, this book will make a nice addition to any classroom celebration of Tu B'Shevat.

Holidays

Major Ideas

Trees are both useful and beautiful.

Like all living things, trees require care.

Activities

1. Grades K-2: Ask the students to clear a space for themselves in the middle of the room and tell them that they will be " growing" from a tiny seed in the ground into a full grown tree. Say to them:

   > Curl up as small as you can and become a tiny seed resting beneath the ground on a hillside in Jerusalem. As the spring rain falls, you slowly feel yourself breaking out of your shell and sprouting up through the soil.
   >
   > As time passes, you continue to grow taller and taller and taller until you are a full grown tree. Your branches are spreading out and your leaves are slowly breaking through. Your branches sway in the breeze as the wind blows. Now rain begins to fall and the wind blows harder and harder, pressing your leaves and branches downward. The rain stops, as does the wind, and you soak in the sunshine. You stand tall and proud above the earth. A tree is nice.

   Read the passage slowly, pausing to give the students an opportunity to dramatize the tree's growth.

2. Grades K-2: In the book, it is mentioned that "... leaves whisper in the breeze..." Since the format of the book is tall and narrow, pre-cut pieces of light colored construction paper which are 15" long by 7" wide. Tell the students to draw a tree as it looks in spring, summer, or fall, leaving room underneath to write what the leaves are whispering. For students who cannot yet write, the teacher can act as a scribe.

3. Grades K-2: In Israel on Tu B'Shevat, students are given the afternoon off from school to go on picnics and tree planting outings. It is customary for Jews living in the Diaspora (outside of Israel) to send money to Jewish National Fund at this time of year. The money is used to purchase trees to be planted in Israel. Ask each of the students to bring 25 cents so that a tree may be planted in honor of the class. Tell them that a special certificate will be sent stating that a tree in their honor was planted in Israel. If you know of someone who is traveling to Israel, perhaps they would be willing to carry the collected money and personally fulfill the class's *mitzvah* of planting a tree. Ask the person to take a picture of the site.

Weil, Lisl. *Esther.* **Illus. by the author. New York: Atheneum Publishers, 1980. 43 pages. Grade level: 2-4.**

Lisl Weil retells the story of the Purim heroine Esther. After becoming the wife of the Persian King Ahasuerus, Esther learns of a plot by Haman, the wicked advisor to the King, to kill the Jewish people. Esther, through her own plotting and with the help of her cousin Mordecai, is able to save herself and her people. The illustrations accurately convey the time and place of the story.

Major Ideas

Taking a stand for justice can involve risks.

As Jews, we are responsible for the well-being of our people.

Even in the face of danger, we must not bow down to tyrants, but rather remain faithful to God.

Activities

1. All ages: Teach the following Purim songs which may then be used in Activity 2: "*Elimelech of Gilhofen,*" "*Utzu Eytza*" and "*Chag Purim.*" The words and music to these and other Purim songs may be found in *The New Jewish Song Book*, edited by Harry Coopersmith.

2. Grades 2-4: In Weil's book it is stated: "The time that might have been a time of death became a time of laughter." Jews are thus commanded to celebrate with great fervor the holiday of Purim. To add to the carnival atmosphere, tell the students to come dressed as wacky Purim characters. Then, singing the songs taught in the first activity, have them parade from class to class. The students might also make a special appearance at the *Megillah* reading at the synagogue or school. Older children might be challenged to design costumes of Purim characters as these might look in future decades or centuries.

3. All ages: Masks were worn by primitive people to ward off evil spirits. Haman was the evil instigator of Purim. Have the younger children create paper plate masks to ward him off. Older children can create their masks from papier maché. Materials and procedure follow.

Paper Plate Masks

Materials:

paper plates
string
scissors
paste
tempera paint
scraps of paper and material

Procedure:

a. The teacher should cut holes for the eyes and slits for the nose, leaving the bridge intact.

b. Using the materials provided, have the children decorate their masks as desired.

Papier Maché Masks

Materials:

newspaper
masking tape
wax paper
wheat paste
water
tempera paint
shellac
scraps of material

Procedure:

a. Use newsprint to establish the correct size. Fold the paper into a strip about 3" or 4" wide, then fit the strip under the chin and over the head. When secured with masking tape, the oval of paper indicates the outside dimensions of the mask.

b. Stuff the oval with wads of slightly dampened newspaper. A mound should be formed within the oval.

c. Pinch the dampened newsprint to make a lump for the nose. Push down on newsprint to form eye sockets.

d. Place pieces of wax paper over the mound. This way the next layers will not adhere to the mold just completed.

e. Cover the entire mask with strips of newsprint and paper toweling that have been dipped in wheat paste. Each layer of paper should be laid down in the opposite direction from the preceding layer. Alternate newsprint and paper toweling so that the pupils will know when each layer is completed. Six layers are needed.

f. When the paper has dried, the inner wads of newsprint can be removed.

g. Holes may then be cut for the eyes and nostrils.

h. Hair, ears, and noses may be built up further from paper and various scraps of materials can be added.

i. Paint and shellac when dry.

HOLIDAYS: BOOKS FOR CHILDREN

Adler, David. *A Picture Book of Jewish Holidays*. Illus. by Linda Heller. New York: Holiday House, Inc., 1981. Grade level: K-3.

    Adler and Heller were awarded the American Library Association's Notable Book Citation for this colorful, large format book. Simple text explaining the basics of each holiday and exquisite paintings are sure to capture the interest of young readers.

Adler, David. *A Picture Book of Hanukkah*. Illus. by Linda Heller. New York: Holiday House, Inc., 1982. Grade level: PK-2.

    Decorative, earth-toned illustrations and simple narrative are the hallmarks of this retelling of the Chanukah story.

Adler, David. *A Picture Book of Passover*. Illus. by Linda Heller. New York: Holiday House, Inc., 1982. Grade level: PK-2.

    From the story of Joseph through the Exodus from Egypt, the events of Passover are dramatically retold. Holiday customs are also described in a manner easily understood by the young reader. The text is complemented by Egyptian-style illustrations in pastel tones.

Aleichem, Sholom. *Hanukah Money*. Illus. by Uri Shulevitz. New York: Greenwillow Books, 1978. Grade level: K-3.

    There is a touch of old world flavor in this tale of the happiness which the festival of Chanukah brings into the lives of a *shtetl* family. Shulevitz's illustrations capture the character of each family member, but most especially the children who revel in the gift of Chanukah *gelt*.

Aleichem, Sholom. *Holiday Tales of Sholom Aleichem*. Trans. by Aliza Shevrin. Illus. by Thomas di Grazia. New York: Charles Scribner's Sons, 1979. Grade level: 4-6.

    Aliza Shevrin has translated seven holiday tales by Sholom Aleichem, one of the world's most beloved Jewish writers and humorists. The stories take place in Kasrilevka and are told from the perspective of the young boys who experience a variety of events during the holidays. Di Grazia's illustrations help to recreate the warmth and spirit of Sholom Aleichem's world.

Bearman, Jane. *The Eight Nights: A Chanukah Counting Book*. Illus. by the author. New York: Union of American Hebrew Congregations, 1979. Grade level: PK-1.

    Melodic rhymes and vivid illustrations of the numbers one through eight sing out the joys of Chanukah, from one night to the next. Blessings for the candle lighting and a glossary of Chanukah terms are also included.

Brin, Ruth. *The Shabbat Catalogue*. New York: KTAV Publishing House, Inc., 1978. Grade level: 2 and up.

    Brin has put together a collection of Shabbat stories and activities aimed to please the interests of a variety of "shoppers."

Brodsky, Beverly. *Jonah: An Old Testament Story*. Illus. by the author. New York: J.B. Lippincott Co., 1977. Grade level: K-3.

    Told in first person narrative, Brodsky reveals to the reader the lesson Jonah learns from God. Brodsky's stunning watercolor paintings add to the appeal of the book.

Burstein, Chaya. *A First Jewish Holiday Cookbook*. Illus. by the author. New York: Hebrew Publishing Co., 1979. Grade level: 3 and up.

    An easy to use holiday cookbook for aspiring kitchen wizards. The book includes many international recipes, procedures for cooking and information concerning the laws of *kashrut*. Numerous cartoons add an extra touch of pleasure to the cooking experience.

Burstein, Chaya. *The Jewish Kids Catalogue*. Illus. by the author. Philadelphia: The Jewish Publication Society of America, 1983. Grade level: 3 and up.

    Designed along the same lines as the three well-known Jewish catalogs, this volume is a vital resource of knowledge and activities for children, teachers, and parents. Stories, games, songs, crafts, and a mini-encyclopedia are among the media employed to cover such topics as holidays, history, and Israel.

Chaikin, Miriam. *Light Another Candle: The Story and Meaning of Hanukkah*. Illus. by Demi. Boston: Houghton-Mifflin Co., 1981. Grade Level: 3-6.

The spiritual and military victories of the Maccabees are described in this anecdotal account of the Chanukah story.

Chaikin, Miriam. *Make Noise, Make Merry: The Story and Meaning of Purim*. Illus. by Demi. New York: Clarion Books, 1983. Grade level: 3-6.

Chaikin's retelling of the Purim story is both factual and fanciful, blending little known "facts" with more obvious highlights. Demi's purple and white line drawings add to the appeal of this interesting book.

Chaikin, Miriam. *Shake a Palm Branch: The Story and Meaning of Sukkot*. Illus. by Marvin Friedman. New York: Clarion Books, 1984. Grade level: 3-5.

Chaikin continues her holiday series with this informative volume about Sukkot. The historical development of the festival is discussed and the customs, songs, prayers, and foods that continue to be a part of contemporary celebrations are presented. Friedman's illustrations highlight major themes and rituals.

Chaikin, Miriam. *The Seventh Day: The Story of the Jewish Sabbath*. Illus. by David Frampton. New York: Schocken Books, 1983. Grade level: 4-6.

Beginning with the Creation account and culminating with the Israelites' celebration of the Sabbath after entering the Promised Land, the history of Shabbat is retold through fascinating narrative and bold woodcuts.

Charles, Freda. *The Mystery of the Missing Challah*. Illus. by Lil Goldstein. New York: Jonathan David Publishers, Inc., 1981. Grade level: PK-K.

Very young children will delight in this engaging mystery story for Shabbat.

Cohen, Barbara. *The Carp in the Bathtub*. Illus. by Joan Halpern. New York: Dell Publishing Co., Inc., 1972. Grade level: K-3.

When two young children befriend a carp that is supposed to become the main ingredient for the family's Passover gefilte fish, their father must come up with a quick compromise. Halpern's illustrations enhance both the humorous and serious moments in the story.

Cohen, Barbara. *Here Come the Purim Players*. Illus. by Beverly Brodsky. New York: Lothrop, Lee & Shepard Books, 1984. Grade level: 1-4.

Cohen and Brodsky have drawn a poignant connection between two historical events in this tale which captures the true beauty and meaning of Purim. Although faced with imminent destruction, the Jews of the Prague Ghetto are portrayed joyously celebrating the survival of their ancestors in Persia.

Cohen, Barbara. *Queen For a Day*. New York: Lothrop, Lee & Shepard Books, 1981. Grade level: 4 and up.

This Jewish Cinderella story is about a thirteen-year-old girl who has her chance to shine when asked to play Queen Esther in a Purim play. Cohen has sensitively captured the emotional pain of the young main character who must live with her grandmother and two aunts, each of whom are incapable of providing positive emotional support.

Cuyler, Margery. *Jewish Holidays*. New York: Holt, Rinehart & Winston, Inc., 1978. Grade level: 2-5.

Besides exploring the background of each Jewish holiday and its customs, this book contains a calendar of the Hebrew months and craft ideas for each holiday.

Devorah-leah. *Lost Erev Shabbos in the Zoo*. Illus. by Siegmund Forst. New York: Judaica Press, 1983. Grade level: PK-1.

When two little children get lost in the zoo, the animals help them to get home before Shabbat begins. The rhyming text and colorful illustrations of animals getting ready for Shabbat are sure to please any young child.

Drucker, Malka. *Hanukkah: Eight Nights, Eight Lights*. 1980.
Passover: A Season of Freedom. 1981.
Rosh Hashanah and Yom Kippur: Sweet Beginnings. 1981.
Shabbat: A Peaceful Island. 1983.
Sukkot: A Time to Rejoice. 1982.

Holidays

Illus. by Brom Hoban. New York: Holiday House, Inc. Grade level: 3-6.

In each of these books, Drucker explores the history, customs, and significance of the respective holiday. Each volume also includes holiday recipes, songs, games, puzzles, and crafts.

Fass, David. *The Shofar that Lost its Voice*. Illus. by Marlene Lobell Ruthen. New York: Union of American Hebrew Congregations, 1982. Grade level: PK-2.

An entertaining mystery tale about a young boy who suddenly finds himself inside a *shofar* where he learns about the meaning of Rosh Hashanah. Ruthen's illustrations add a colorful, adventurous tone to the story.

Ganz, Yaffa. *Follow the Moon: A Journey Through the Jewish Year*. Illus. by Harvey Klineman. New York: Feldheim Publishers, 1984. Grade level: 1-4.

Ganz and Klineman have created an excellent introduction to the holidays as they occur within the cycle of the Jewish year. Historical facts and customs related to each holiday and season are provided. Brightly colored illustrations make this a very attractive book.

Ganz, Yaffa. *Savta Simcha and the Incredible Shabbos Bag*. Illus. by Bina Gewirtz. New York: Feldheim Publishers, 1980. Grade level: 3-4.

This story of a Jewish Mary Poppins is sure to bring pleasure to young readers in the same spirited way Savta Simcha brought Jewish experiences to the children of Wintergreen City. Ink and water color illustrations highlight key moments in the story.

Ganz, Yaffa. *Savta Simcha and the Cinnamon Tree*. Illus. by Bina Gewirtz. New York: Feldheim Publishers, 1984. Grade level: 2-4.

The fanciful adventures of Savta Simcha continue in this sequel to *Savta Simcha and the Incredible Shabbos Bag*. Ganz's lively approach to storytelling and Gewirtz's color washed ink drawings educate as well as entertain. This volume contains stories appropriate for Purim, Passover, Lag B'Omer, Shavuot, and Tisha B'Av, each of which can be enjoyed when read aloud or on one's own.

Gersh, Harry. *When a Jew Celebrates*. Illus. by Erika Weihs. New York: Behrman House, Inc., 1971. Grade level: 5-6.

Often used as a text in Jewish classrooms, this book provides a very readable and interesting discussion of the history and meaning of each Jewish holiday and its customs. Chapters on the Jewish calendar and life cycle events are also included.

Goffstein, M.B. *Laughing Latkes*. Illus. by the author. New York: Farrar, Straus & Giroux, Inc., 1980. Grade level: PK-3.

Animated *latkes* are the major characters of this entertaining Chanukah story. As always, Goffstein's highly polished text and simple line drawings are exquisite.

Greene, Jaqueline. *The Hanukah Tooth*. Illus. by Pauline Quellet. Wellesley, MA: Pascal Publications, 1981. Grade level: PK-2.

Greene and Quellet have creatively combined two very important events in the lives of young Jewish children: losing a tooth and, of course, Chanukah.

Greenfeld, Howard. *Chanukah*. 1976.
Passover. 1978.
Purim. 1983.
Rosh Hashanah and Yom Kippur. 1979.
Illus. by Elaine Grove and Linda Heller. New York: Holt, Rinehart & Winston, Inc. Grade level: 3-6.

Each of these factual holiday narratives is concisely retold with a focus on the holiday's historical significance and explanation of related customs. Grove and Heller's decorative illustrations emphasize the major concepts of each holiday.

Halpern, Chaiky. *The Dangerous Dreidle Ride*. Illus. by the author. New York: Feldheim Publishers, 1981. Grade level: PK-1.

Little children will enjoy this fanciful tale about one of King Dimpu's servants who captures a giant runaway *dreidle* and allows the Chanukah *gelt* within to be distributed to the children of the kingdom. Whimsical illustrations add to the appeal of this Chanukah adventure.

Hirsh, Marilyn. *I Love Hanukkah*. Illus. by the author. New York: Holiday House, Inc., 1984. Grade level: PK-2.

A three-year-old boy's love for Chanukah resounds throughout this story about how one family celebrates the holiday. The story is unique in that the reader learns about Chanukah through the story read to the little boy by his grandfather. Hirsh's illustrations capture the warmth and beauty of this family celebration.

Hirsh, Marilyn. *The Hanukkah Story*. Illus. by the author. New York: Hebrew Publishing Co., 1977. Grade level: K-3.

Archaeological findings are the prime vehicle for this retelling of the Chanukah story. Realistic illustrations portray the costumes and architecture of the era in which the events occur.

Hirsh, Marilyn. *One Little Goat: A Passover Song*. Illus. by the author. New York: Holiday House, Inc., 1979. Grade level: 1 and up.

Hirsh has transformed the words of the song "*Chad Gadya*" into an action packed play which is followed by the musical score to the song and brief explanations of Passover and the song's meaning. The author's richly detailed drawings in black, red, and white add to the excitement of the tale.

Kozodoy, Ruth. *The Book of Jewish Holidays*. Illus. by Suzanne Suba. New York: Behrman House, Inc., 1981. Grade level: 4-5.

Kozodoy provides an informative look at the Jewish holidays for children who are ready to begin more in-depth study.

Lebovics, Aydel. *The Sukkah and the Big Wind*. Illus. by Rochelle Cohen. New York: Merkos L'Inyonei Chinuch, 1982. Grade level: K-2.

When a whirlwind blows through an Orthodox neighborhood, pieces of everyone's *sukkah* land in Mr. Levi's yard. He is the only person on the block who has never built a *sukkah*. Through rhyming narrative and colorful illustrations, the story of how Mr. Levi is helped by his neighbors to celebrate Sukkot happily unfolds.

Levoy, Myron. *The Hanukah of Great-Uncle Otto*. Illus. by Donna Ruff. Philadelphia: The Jewish Publication Society of America, 1984. Grade level: 3-6.

Joshua's Great Uncle Otto seems a little melancholy as Chanukah approaches. He explains to Joshua that he remembers the *menorah* his family had lit for generations back in Germany. However, when he fled from the Nazis, Uncle Otto was unable to bring the treasured *menorah*. With hard work, Joshua and Uncle Otto are able to construct a replica of the *menorah* in time for the family's Chanukah celebration. Levoy and Ruff have combined their talents to create a very special Chanukah story that captures the richness of intergenerational relationships.

Lieberman, Donald. *Heroes of Hanukkah*. New York: KTAV Publishing House, Inc., 1980. Grade level: 6 and up.

A dynamic historical novel about the brothers Maccabee and how each contributed to the fight for freedom against the tyranny of Antiochus.

Lubavitch Women's Organization. *A Candle of My Own: Thoughts on Shabbos Candles by Girls Who Light Them*. Illus. by Michoel Muchnik. New York: Lubavitch Women's Organization, 1979. Grade level: 3 and up.

A collection of moving poetry and prose by girls, ages six to fourteen, who light Shabbos candles. The book is beautifully illustrated with color photographs and artwork.

Marcus, Audrey Friedman, and Zwerin, Raymond A. *High Holy Day Do-It-Yourself Dictionary*. Illus. by Marlene Lobell Ruthen. New York: Union of American Hebrew Congregations, 1983. Grade level: K-3.

Brightly colored drawings and bold text illumine the significance of the major aspects of the Passover *Seder* to primary grade children. The line from the Four Questions, "But this night is different," is used repeatedly throughout the text to highlight the significant features of the Passover celebration. The authors' skillful use of all the actions involved in the *Seder* invites active participation from children. A page of Hebrew blessings with transliterations and translations is also provided.

Marcus, Audrey Friedman, and Zwerin, Raymond A. *High Holy Day Do-It-Yourself Dictionary*. Illus. by Marlene L. Ruthen. New York: Union of American Hebrew Congregations, 1983. Grade level: K-3.

The warm narrative and brilliant colored pencil drawings bring the meaning of the High Holy Days alive for very young students in a most enjoyable way. The authors have provided students with the opportunity to fill in key vocabulary throughout the text. This helps to reinforce major High Holy Day concepts, as well as to engage the students actively in study of the topic.

Holidays

Medoff, Francine. *The Mouse in the Matzah Factory*. Illus. by David Goldstein. Rockville, MD: Kar-Ben Copies, Inc., 1983. Grade level: PK-1.

Readers are led on a journey by a little mouse from the picking of wheat on a farm through the process of baking *matzah* in a factory. The earthy tones of this book, giving the appearance of *matzah*, are sure to capture young readers' interest.

Miller, Deborah. *Only Nine Chairs: A Tall Tale for Passover*. Illus. by Karen Ostrove. Rockville, MD: Kar-Ben Copies, Inc., 1982. Grade level: PK-3.

This humorous, rhyming tall tale explains how nineteen people solved the problem of who was going to sit where at a *Seder* table set only for nine.

Miller, Deborah. *Poppy Seeds, Too*. Illus. by Karen Ostrove. Rockville, MD: Kar-Ben Copies, Inc., 1982. Grade level: PK-3.

There is definitely a humorous twist to this story about baking *challah*! Delightful illustrations, a *challah* recipe, and the blessing over bread complete the fun filled baking lesson.

Mindel, Nissan. *Complete Story of Tishrei*. Brooklyn, NY: Merkos L'Inyonei Chinuch, 1982. Grade level: 5 and up.

Mindel has compiled an invaluable treasury of Torah readings, allegories, legends, philosophical and historical writings about the holidays which occur in Tishre, the seventh month of the Jewish year.

Purdy, Susan Gold. *Jewish Holiday Cookbook*. New York: Franklin Watts, 1979. Grade level: 4 and up.

Purdy devotes a chapter of recipes for each of thirteen holidays, as well as a special chapter on cooking skills. Recipes are concise and easy to follow.

Rosen, Anne, Jonathan, and Norma. *Family Passover*. Photographs by Laurence Salzmann. Philadelphia: The Jewish Publication Society of America, 1980. Grade level: 2 and up.

A beautiful photographic essay which, together with narrative, describes how one family celebrates Passover.

Ross, Betty Ann. *Dates as Sweet as Honey*. Illus. by Tali Krivolet. New York: Board of Jewish Education, Inc., 1982. Grade level: PK-3.

Although written for Tu B'Shevat, this unique book is also appropriate for sharing on Sukkot and Tisha B'Av. The reader is told how the ancient Israelites made pilgrimages to the Temple in Jerusalem each year, bringing as gifts portions of the seven native species, including dates. After the Temple was destroyed, the taste of the sweet dates continued to remind Jews of Israel and of the time when we still had our Temple. The green and brown cartoon style illustrations help the text build to the climax when children are shown planting trees on Tu B'Shevat and savoring the taste of sweet dates.

Rugill, Peter. *The Return of the Golem: A Chanukah Story*. New York: Holt, Rinehart & Winston, Inc., 1979. Grade level: 1-4.

Rugill has blended elements of folklore and science fiction in this special Chanukah retelling of the legend of the Golem.

Saypol, Judith, and Wikler, Madeline. *Let's Have a Party: 100 Mix-And Match Party Ideas For the Jewish Holidays*. Rockville, MD: Kar-Ben Copies, Inc., 1981. Grade level: K and up.

This volume contains a multitude of creative Jewish party ideas for Shabbat and other holidays. Suggestions are included for invitations, decorations, games, and menus. The book format, together with the illustrations, allows for easy and enjoyable implementation.

Saypol, Judith, and Wikler, Madeline. *My Very Own Jewish Book Series*. Illus. by Madeline Winkler. Rockville, MD: Kar-Ben Copies, Inc., 1977-1982. Grade leavel: K-2.

Each book in this series contains stories, songs, blessings, and discussion starters for families with primary grade children. Book topics include Rosh Hashanah, Yom Kippur, Sukkot, Simchat Torah, Chanukah, the Purim Megillah, the Passover Haggadah, Shavuot, and Shabbat.

Schwartz, Amy. *Mrs. Moskowitz and the Sabbath Candlesticks*. Philadelphia: The Jewish Publication Society of America, 1983. Grade level: 5 and up.

> When Mrs. Moskowitz moves with her cat into a new apartment, she is sad and lonely until her son brings her what turns out to be a "magical box." Inside the box, Mrs. Moskowitz finds her old Shabbat candlesticks which lend a feeling of warmth to her new home.

Singer, Isaac Bashevis. *The Power of Light: Eight Stories for Hanukkah*. Illus. by Irene Lieblich. New York: Farrar, Straus & Giroux, Inc., 1980. Grade level: 1 and up.

> A collection of eight miraculous and heartwarming Chanukah stories set in Poland. Singer's eloquent style harmoniously combines the spirit and meaning of Chanukah with the ambience of the setting.

Singer, Isaac Bashevis. *A Tale of Three Wishes*. Illus. by Irene Lieblich. New York: Farrar, Straus & Giroux, Inc., 1975. Grade level: PK-3.

> According to legend, late on the night of Hoshanah Rabbah, the heavens open up for a brief moment to accept and grant the wishes of those fortunate enough to witness the event. When Shlomoh, Esther, and Moshe look toward the sky, they find themselves making some rather curious wishes. The magic of the tale is further enhanced by Lieblich's illustrations.

Sofer, Barbara. *The Holiday Adventures of Achbar*. Illus. by Nina Gaelen. Rockville, MD: Kar-Ben Copies, Inc., 1983. Grade level: 1-3.

> Achbar, the mouse-detective, comes to the rescue of the Schuster family when they are plagued with various mysteries during Jewish holidays.

Spector, Shoshanah. *The Seder That Almost Wasn't*. Illus. by Raphael Wettenstein. New York: Shengold Publications, Inc., 1967. Grade level: PK-1.

> Children will enjoy this captivating story of what happens to a young boy at Passover when he wants to recite the Four Questions.

Steinkoler, Ronnie. *A Jewish Cookbook for Children*. Illus. by Sonja Glassman. New York: Julian Messner, 1980. Grade level: 3-6.

> Eastern European and Middle Eastern foods are included in this book of easy to prepare recipes. The foods are arranged according to holiday.

Stern, Shirley. *Exploring Jewish Holidays and Customs*. New York: KTAV Publishing House, Inc., 1981. Grade level: 4 and up.

> Stern has designed a very useful source book combining key symbols, customs, and historical background on each holiday. The book also includes information on life cycle events from birth through marriage, a chapter on Jewish education, as well as activity suggestions, blessings, and a glossary.

Suhl, Yuri. *The Purim Goat*. Illus. by Kaethe Zemach. Bristol, FL: Four Winds Press, 1980. Grade level: 2-4.

> A young boy teaches his goat to dance to the noise of the Purim *graggers*. In doing so, he hopes to prove the goat's previously debatable worth and save it from slaughter.

Taylor, Sydney. *Danny Loves a Holiday*. Illus. by Gail Owens. New York: E.P. Dutton, 1980. Grade level: 1-3.

> Unusual things happen as Danny celebrates the Jewish holidays which he loves so passionately. Soft pencil drawings add to the warmth and humor of Danny's holiday adventures.

Weilerstein, Sadie Rose. *The Best of K'Tonton*. Illus. by Marilyn Hirsh. Philadelphia: The Jewish Publication Society of America, 1980. Grade level: PK-3.

> This special volume clebrates the 50th anniversary of the adventures of the Jewish Tom Thumb, K'Tonton Ben Baruch Reuben. The holiday tales included are among K'Tonton's most popular adventures and are beautifully brought to life again in Hirsh's vibrant illustrations.

Weilerstein, Sadie Rose. *K'Tonton in the Circus: A Hanukkah Adventure*. Illus. by Marilyn Hirsh. Philadelphia: The Jewish Publication Society of America, 1981. Grade level: 2-4.

> When K'Tonton is held captive by a circus troupe, he takes the opportunity to teach them about Chanukah.

Weilerstein, Sadie Rose. *Ten and A Kid*. Illus. by Janina Domanska. Philadelphia: The Jewish Publication Society of America, 1973. Grade level: 6 and up.

> After Gadya the goat mysteriously appears at the Passover *Seder* of Reizel and her family, Reizel embarks with Gadya on a journey through the years that is filled with holiday celebrations. The book is a most deserving winner of the National Jewish Book Award.

Weilerstein, Sadie Rose. *What The Moon Brought*. Philadelphia: The Jewish Publication Society of America, 1942. Grade level: 1-3.

> A collection of stories about each significant day in the Jewish calendar by one of the most beloved American Jewish children's writers.

Wurtzel, Yehuda and Sara. *Lights: A Fable About Hanukkah*. Illus. by Noam Nadav. Chappaqua, NY: Rossel Books, 1984. Grade level: K and up.

> This fanciful Chanukah allegory was based on the television cartoon special, *Lights*. The Hebrew letters of the Torah serve as the lights of learning and courage which help to drown out the oppressive darkness thrown upon the Jews by the Syrians. In the end, it is the single jar of these miraculous "letter lights" that is used to rekindle the Temple *menorah*. Nadav's vibrant cartoon illustrations lend a special magic to the text.

Zola, Meguido. *Only the Best*. Illus. by Valerie Littlewood. New York: Franklin Watts, 1981. Grade level: K-3.

> A young father's love for his newborn daughter sends him on a search to find the very best possible Sukkot gift for her. After looking everywhere, from the toy shop to the apothecary, he realizes that the very best gift he can give the child is his love. So the father leaves the harvest of material gifts behind and returns home to kiss his infant daughter. Like the father's kiss, the detailed, color illustrations and warm text are sure to bring smiles to the reader.

Zusman, Evelyn. *The Passover Parrot*. Illus. by Janus Kahn. Rockville, MD: Kar-Ben Copies, Inc., 1983. Grade level: K-2.

> Leba gets more than she bargains for when her parrot, who is the only one willing to listen as she practices the Four Questions, decides that he, too, will participate in the family *Seder*. Dynamic line drawings add to the humor of the story.

Zwerin, Raymond A., and Marcus, Audrey Friedman. *A Purim Album*. Illus. by Marlene Lobell Ruthen. New York: Union of American Hebrew Congregations, 1981. Grade level: K-2.

> The story of Purim is retold in picture album style. A colored pencil drawing of one scene from a Purim play starring Robin, a young girl, is mounted on each page. The book concludes with some provocative thoughts from Robin about what she has learned from the Purim story. A wonderful introduction to Purim for young and old alike.

Zwerin, Raymond A., and Marcus, Audrey Friedman. *Shabbat Can Be*. Illus. by Yuri Salzman. New York: Union of American Hebrew Congregations, 1979. Grade level: PK-2.

> Zwerin and Marcus have written a book which carries the reader into the joyous dimensions of Shabbat. The text on each page begins with the enticing words "Shabbat can be." In each case this is followed by a description of a special activity and feeling which may be experienced on Shabbat. The book provides an excellent introduction to Shabbat blessings and rituals, and invites young readers to explore what Shabbat means to them. Delightful illustrations of children enjoying Shabbat together with family and friends add to the text's beautiful depiction of this treasured day in Jewish life. A separate Parent-Teacher Guide illuminates concepts and values associated with Shabbat.

HOLIDAYS: RESOURCES FOR ADULTS

Artistic and Culinary Celebrations

Goodman, Hannah. *Jewish Cooking Around the World*. Philadelphia: The Jewish Publication Society of America, 1974.

International Council of Jewish Women. *Cooking Time Around the World*. New York: International Council of Jewish Women, 1982.

Nathan, Joan. *The Jewish Holiday Kitchen*. New York: Schocken Books, Inc., 1979.

Rockland, Mae Shafter. *The Jewish Party Book: A Contemporary Guide to Customs, Crafts and Foods*. New York: Schocken Books, Inc., 1979.

Rosenberg, David. *Chosen Days: Celebrating Jewish Festivals in Poetry and Art*. Illus. by Leonard Baskin. Doubleday & Co., Inc., 1980.

Shostek, Patti. *A Lexicon of Jewish Cooking: A Collection Folklore, Foodlore, History, Customs and Recipes*. Chicago: Contemporary Books, Inc., 1981.

Family Celebrations

Cardozo, Arlene Rossen. *Jewish Family Celebrations: The Sabbath, Festivals, and Ceremonies*. New York: St. Martin's Press, Inc., 1982.

Lieberman, Susan. *Let's Celebrate: Creating New Family Traditions*. Illus. by Mary Engelbreit. New York: Pedigree Books, 1984.

Syme, Daniel. *The Jewish Home Holiday Series*. New York: Union of American Hebrew Congregations, no publication date. (Six Booklets)

Holiday Teaching Aids

Adler, David A. *Hanukkah Fun Book: Puzzles, Riddles, Magic and More*. New York: Bonim Books, 1976.

_____. *Hanukkah Game Book: Games, Riddles, Puzzles and More*. New York: Bonim Books, 1978.

_____. *Passover Fun Book: Puzzles, Riddles, Magic and More*. New York: Bonim Books, 1978.

Becker, Joyce. *Jewish Holiday Crafts*. New York: Bonim Books, 1977.

Berman, Bonnie, and Glatstein, Laura. *Holiday Game Pak*. Denver: Alternatives in Religious Education, Inc., 1977.

Borovetz, Frances. *Second Holiday Ditto Pak 4-6*. Denver: Alternatives in Religious Education, Inc., 1981.

Chait, Ruth. *Second Holiday Ditto Pak K-3*. Denver: Alternatives in Religious Education, Inc., 1983.

Elefant, Leah, and Gary, Esther. *Holiday Crafts Come Alive*. New York: Feldheim Publishers, 1981.

Eichenbaum, Sharon; Goldin, Alice; and Korman, Michael. *Jewish Awareness Worksheets I and II: The Jewish Holidays*. New York: Behrman House, Inc., 1977.

Everyman's University. *Hanukah Kit*. Distributed by Alternatives in Religious Education, Inc., 1982.

Fun-In-Learning About Passover. New York: Jonathan David Publishers, Inc., no publication date.

Glassman, Barbara. *Holiday Ditto Pak K-3*. Denver: Alternatives in Religious Education, Inc., 1982.

_____. *Holiday Ditto Pak 4-6*. Denver: Alternatives in Religious Education, Inc., 1983.

_____. *Shabbat Ditto Pak K-2*. Denver: Alternatives in Religious Education, Inc., 1978.

Goodman, Robert. *A Teachers Guide to Jewish Holidays*. Denver: Alternatives in Religious Education, Inc., 1983.

Hebrew Holiday Lotto (Pesach and Shabbat). Denver: Alternatives in Religious Education, Inc., 1976.

Holman, Marilyn. *Using Our Senses: Hands-on Activities for the Jewish Classroom*. Denver: Alternatives in Religious Education Inc., 1980.

Kopin, Rita. *The Lively Jewish Classroom*. Denver: Alternatives in Religious Education, Inc., 1980.

Levy, Deborah, and Marcus, Audrey Friedman. *The Learning Center Book of Jewish Holidays and Symbols Grades 1-3.* Denver: Alternatives in Religious Education, Inc., 19766.

Reuben, Steve, and Kinneret. *Especially Wonderful Days: Sing-Along Jewish Holiday Songs for the Primary Grades.* Denver: Alternatives in Religious Education, Inc., 1976. (Cassette and Song Book)

There is a Season: A Values Clarification Approach to Jewish Holidays. Denver: Alternatives in Religious Education, Inc., 1978.

Zisenwine, David, and Abramovitz, Karen. *The Sabbath: Time & Existence.* Tel Aviv: Everyman's University Publishing House, 1982. Distributed by Alternatives in Religious Education, Inc.

Zwerin, Raymond A. *The Jewish Calendar.* Denver: Alternatives in Religious Education Inc., 1975.

Holiday Anthologies

Goodman, Philip (ed). *Chanukah.* Philadelphia: The Jewish Publication Society of America, 1976.

——————— (ed). *Passover.* Philadelphia: The Jewish Publication Society of America, 1973.

——————— (ed). *Purim.* Philadelphia: The Jewish Publication Society of America, 1964.

——————— (ed). *Rosh Hashanah.* Philadelphia: The Jewish Publication Society of America, 1970.

——————— (ed). *Shavuot.* Philadelphia: The Jewish Publication Society of America, 1974.

——————— (ed). *Sukkot and Simhat Torah.* Philadelphia: The Jewish Publication Society of America, 1973.

——————— (ed). *Yom Kippur.* Philadelphia: The Jewish Publication Society of America, 1971.

Holiday Tales

Rush, Barbara. *Seventy and One Tales for the Jewish Year.* New York: American Zionist Youth Foundation, 1980.

Shevrin, Aliza (trans). *Holiday Tales of Sholom Aleichem.* New York: Charles Scribner's Sons, 1979.

Singer, I.B. *Zlateh the Goat and Other Stories.* New York: Harper & Row Publishers, Inc., 1966.

Zevin, Shlomo. *A Treasury of Chassidic Tales on the Festivals.* New York: Mesorah Publications, Ltd., 1981.

Rosh Hashanah and Yom Kippur

Agnon, S.Y. *Days of Awe: A Treasury of Tradition, Legends and Learned Commentaries Concerning Rosh Hashanah, Yom Kippur and the Days Between.* New York: Schocken Books, Inc., 1965.

Cooper, Martin and Zephyr. *Rosh Hashanah: The Jewish New Year.* New York: Zephyr Graphics, 1978.

Greenberg, Sydney (ed). *Teaching and Preaching High Holy Day Themes: A Resource Book.* Bridgeport, CT: Hartmore House, 1973. (Two Volumes)

Raskin, Saul. *Avinu Malkeinu: Our Father Our King.* Drawings by the author. Flint, MI: Genesis Publishing Corporation, 1966.

Rotberg, Tzvi. *Rosh Hashanah: The Akeda.* Trans. by Sholom Ziskind. New York: Maznaim Publishing Corporation, 1983.

Chanukah

Pearlson, Jordon (ed). *These Lights: Haneirot Halalu.* Illus. by Leonard Baskin. New York: Central Conference of American Rabbis, 1984.

Rockland, Mae Shafter. *The Hanukah Book.* New York: Schocken Books, Inc., 1975.

Rosenberg, David. *Blazing Fountain: A Book for Hanukkah.* New York: Schocken Books, Inc., 1978.

Passover

Bronstein, Herbert (ed). *A Passover Haggadah.* Illus. by Leonard Baskin. New York: Central Conference of American Rabbis, 1975.

Fredman, Ruth. *The Passover Seder: Afikoman in Exile*. Philadelphia: University of Pennsylvania Press, 1981.

Rabinowicz, Rachel A. (ed). *Passover Haggadah: The Feast of Freedom*. Illus. by Dan Reisinger. New York: The Rabbinical Assembly, 1982.

Raphael, Haim. *A Feast of History*. New York: Simon & Schuster, Inc., 1972.

Raskin, Saul. *Haggadah For Passover*. Drawings by the author. New York: Academy Photo Offset, Inc., 1941.

Roth, Cecil. *The Sarajevo Haggadah*. Yugoslavia: Izadavacki Zavod, 1970.

Scherman, Rabbi Nosson. *The Haggadah Treasury*. New York: Mesorah Publications, Ltd., 1978.

Shahn, Ben. *Ben Shahn's Haggadah For Passover*. Trans. by Cecil Roth. Paris: Trianon Press, 1965.

Yerushalmi, Yosef Hayim. *Haggadah and History: A Panorama in Facsimile of Five Centuries of the Printed Haggadah*. Philadelphia: The Jewish Publication Society of America, 1975.

Shabbat

Dresner, Samuel. *The Sabbath*. New York: Burning Bush Press, 1970.

Heschel, Abraham Joshua. *The Sabbath: Its Meaning for Modern Man*. New York: Farrar, Straus & Giroux, Inc., 1951.

Millgram, Abraham. *Sabbath: The Day of Delight*. Philadelphia: The Jewish Publication Society of America, 1944.

Shabbat Manual. New York: Central Conference of American Rabbis, 1972.

Strassfeld, Michael. *A Shabbat Haggadah for Celebration and Study*. New York: Institute of Human Relations Programs of American Jewish Committee, 1981.

Zisenwine, David, and Abramovitz, Karen. *The Sabbath: Time & Existence*. Tel Aviv: Everyman's University Publishing House, 1982. Distributed by Alternatives in Religious Education, Inc.

Scholarly Explorations of the Jewish Festivals

Berg, Philip S. *The Kabbalah Connection: Jewish Festivals as a Path to Pure Awareness*. Jerusalem: Research Center of Kabbalah, 1983.

Bloch, Abraham. *The Biblical and Historical Background of Jewish Customs and Ceremonies*. New York: KTAV Publishing House, Inc., 1980.

Gaster, Theodor. *Festivals of the Jewish Year*. New York: William Morrow & Co., Inc., 1961.

Kitov, Eliyahu. *The Book of Our Heritage: The Jewish Year and its Days of Significance*. New York: Feldheim Publishers, 1978.

Knobel, Peter (ed). *Shaarei Mo-eid: Gates of the Seasons – A Guide to the Jewish Holidays*. Illus. by Ismar David. New York: Central Conference of American Rabbis, 1983.

Rosenfel, Abraham (trans). *Tisha B'av Compendium*. New York: Judaic Press, 1983.

Rotberg, Tzvi. *Sefiras HaOmer*. New York: Maznaim Publishing Corporation, 1983.

Strassfeld, Michael. *The Jewish Holidays: A Guide and Commentary*. Illus. by Betsy Teutsch. New York: Harper & Row Publishers, Inc., 1985.

Trepp, Leo. *The Complete Book of Jewish Observance: A Practical Manual for The Modern Jew*. New York: Behrman House, Inc./Summit Books, 1980.

Waskow, Arthur. *Seasons of Our Joy: A Celebration of Modern Jewish Renewal*. New York: Bantam Books, Inc., 1982.

Wolpin, Nissim (ed). *Seasons of the Soul: Religious, Historical and Philanthropical Perspectives on the Jewish Year and its Milestones*. New York: Mesorah Publications, Ltd., 1981.

Zevin, Rabbi Shlomo. *The Artscroll Festivals in Halachah Series*.
Yom Tov, Rosh Hashanah Yom Kippur, Succos. 1981.
Chanukah, Purim, Fast Days, Tishah Beav, Minor Festivals. 1981.
Pesach, Omer, Shavuos. 1982.
New York: Mesorah Publications, Ltd.

Holocaust

V

*He doesn't know the world at all
who stays in his nest and doesn't go out.
He doesn't know what birds know best
Nor what I want to sing about,
That the world is full of loveliness.
When dewdrops sparkle in the grass
And earth's aflood with morning light,
A blackbird sings upon a bush
To greet the dawning after night.
Then I know how fine it is to live.
Hey, try to open up your heart
To beauty; go to the woods someday
And weave a wreath of memory there.
Then if the tears obscure your way
You'll know how wonderful it is to be alive.*

*Anonymous, Terezin, 1941
From the book* I Never Saw Another Butterfly *— with permission of Dr. Hana Volavkova, editor.*

OVERVIEW

The words of the anonymous child of Terezin which appear in the moving and meaningful poem above seem almost too beautiful to bear, particularly when cast against the harsh realities of the Holocaust. How do we even begin to take children whose Jewish education has thus far consisted only of the sweetness of apples and honey, blessings, and Bible heroes, and teach them that Auschwitz, too, is what it means to be Jewish? How do we explain to children generations removed from the experience that there was a time in Jewish history when a man named Hitler ordered his willing followers to brutally murder six million of our people, as well as millions of others, while the rest of the world sat idly by? How should we respond as these children view the concentration camp victims stripped of their human dignity and ask, why?

Perhaps the Holocaust experience and the answers to these questions will never be fully understood. But what must be understood most emphatically is that in order to help prevent such a tragedy from ever again defacing the history of humanity, the Holocaust must always be an integral part of both Jewish and secular education.

The books which have been selected for inclusion in this chapter compel children to consider the power in all of us to choose between good and evil, right and wrong. They also show the extreme courage of ordinary people during this tragic period of history.

The bravery of young children during the war can be seen in *The Boys Who Saved the Children*, a factual account of a thirteen-year-old Jewish boy who is able, through an intelligent plan, to prevent temporarily the children of the Lodz Ghetto from being transported to a concentration camp. In *The Devil in Vienna*, a Christian girl maintains correspondence with her best friend, who is Jewish, in spite of her parent's protests. In the end, she helps her friend to survive.

Friendship is also the theme of *Alan and Naomi*. The story is a moving account of the relationship between an American boy who is "untouched" by the persecution of Jews in Europe and a French girl who has experienced Nazi tyranny.

A view of the power of Nazi propaganda is evident in *Friedrich*, the story of one German family's experience during World War II. The book focuses on the effects the war had not only on the narrator, but on his Jewish friend, Friedrich, as well.

Two stories of survival are *A Pocket Full of Seeds* and *Upon the Head of the Goat*. The persistence and hope of both of the young female protagonists assist them in their struggle to remain alive during the Nazi regime in Europe.

January 1942, marked the birth of the Unified Partisan organization. Thereafter, resistance groups began to grow throughout Eastern Europe. In *Uncle Misha's Partisans*, the strength of the resistance movement is seen as a young boy wires Nazi headquarters with explosives.

As an introduction to this difficult topic for children, *I Never Saw Another Butterfly* and *Promise of a New Spring: The Holocaust and Renewal* were selected. The first book is for older children and reflects both the suffering and hope of children who were detained and most often died in concentration camps. *Promise of a New Spring* was written for younger children and emphasizes the importance of carrying on the legacy of the Holocaust. *The Tattooed Torah* depicts one way in which this legacy continues to live, as a congregation purchases for its children a little Torah that was saved from destruction during the Holocaust.

HOLOCAUST: BOOKS AND ACTIVITIES

Baldwin, Margaret. *The Boys Who Saved the Children.* **Photographs unknown. New York: Julian Messner, 1981. 62 pages. Grade level: 5-8.**

This is the true story of a group of teen-age boys, led by Ben Edelbaum, whose courageous efforts delay the deportment of the children of the Lodz ghetto to concentration camps. Each night after a long day of repairing the coats of German soliders, the boys labored over a special fur coat to be given to the Commandant's wife. It was hoped that in presenting the coat on her birthday, a kind word would be offered on the children's behalf. After she received the coat, the rumors of the impending action stop and the children are saved for a while. The powerful story, combined with photographs of ghetto children and concentration camp victims, clearly illustrates the evil of the Nazi regime. At the same time, one is touched by the love and support that people can provide for one another as demonstrated by the relationships within Ben's family.

Major Ideas

A key to survival is allowing one's spirit to remain undaunted, even in the face of impending tragedy.

Family ties can be a comfort during difficult times.

It takes fortitude to be a leader.

Activities

1. Grades 5-8: The reader is informed at the end of the book that out of the 160,000 residents of the Lodz Ghetto, only 1,000 survived. The number of lives lost during the Holocaust is staggering. In preparation for your community's Holocaust commemoration (Yom HaShoah), have each student create a wood burned plaque in memory of those who died in a specific extermination camp, concentration camp, ghetto, paratisan movement, or pogrom. It is also fitting to create a plaque in memory of the non-Jewish population who fought the Nazi's tyranny against the Jews. Necessaary materials and procedure follow.

    Materials:

    wood burner
    wood
    protective coating (lacquer or other wood finish)
    newsprint

    Procedure:

    a. Sketch a design for the plaque on newsprint.

    b. Transfer the design to the wood.

    c. The teacher can arrange for these plaques to be displayed at the community commemorative service or in the synagogue.

2. Grades 5-8: Ben Edelbaum possessed three qualities which helped him and others to stay alive: a high degree of self-esteem, strong leadership abilities, and a firm belief in his right to live. Discuss with the students which of these qualities of self-esteem they themselves possess. Next have each student draw a self-portrait on 12" x 18" white drawing paper using pastels, leaving space around the portrait to write. Across the top all of the students should write "L'CHAYIM!" (To Life!), in large print. The rest of the space around the self-portrait will then be used to write adjectives describing important aspects of the student's self-esteem (i.e., strength, humor, creativity, courage). Each student should write his/her name in the middle of the self-portrait.

3. Grades 5-8: In the book, the reader is informed that although any type of Jewish religious service was prohibited in the ghetto, the ghetto inhabitants still managed to preserve their Jewish traditions by holding secret services and celebrations. To help the students understand what it would be like to have to practice Judaism secretly, have them choose Shabbat or another holiday as their theme and secretly plan and execute a service celebration. The class must decide on the following regarding the service or celebration:

    Where, in or around the building, to hold the service.
    Which rituals or prayers are to be included.
    Assignment of responsibilities.

    In order for this activity to be effective, caution the students against telling anyone about their plans. Further, it is important for them to choose a location where they will not be discovered. On the actual day of the event, an honored guest should be escorted blindfolded to the secret celebration. Possible guests could be the principal or director of the particular setting in which you work, the Rabbi, or the students' parents.

Ginsburg, Marvel. *The Tattooed Torah* **Illus. by Jo Gershman. New York: Union of American Hebrew Congregations, 1983. 28 pages. Grade level: K-3.**

This is the story of a little Torah which survived the Holocaust and eventually found a new home in an American synagogue. Before the rise of Hitler, the reader is told that the Torah lived a peaceful life in Brno, Czechoslovakia. The Holocaust, however, brings desecration and sorrow to " . . . the most precious possession

Holocaust

of the Jewish people . . . " The young reader of this book will gain a sense of the tragedy of the Holocaust, as well as the sacredness of the Torah. The illustrations nicely capture the varied emotions the Torah experiences.

Major Ideas

The Torah provides a special link to those who came before us and those who will follow us.

The extreme cruelty of the Nazis is evident not only in their attempt to destroy Jewish lives, but also in their effort to destroy all that is important to the Jewish way of life.

Activities

1. Grades 2 and 3: For many years, all of the Torahs confiscated in Czechoslavakia during the Holocaust were kept in a warehouse in Prague. Have the students imagine what the Torahs might have "talked about" during their captivity. Select pairs of students to carry on imaginary conversations as Torahs. Following the role plays, tell the students that it is also possible that the Torahs may have spoken the important words which are actually written inside of them. Take this opportunity to introduce students to some of the narrative from each of the books of the Torah in simplified form. This can be accomplished through storytelling sessions carried on over a period of time. Some suggested passages are:

   Genesis:
   The Creation Story
   Noah's Ark
   The Tower of Babel

   Exodus:
   Bondage in Egypt
   The Ten Plagues
   Crossing the Red Sea

   Leviticus:
   23:1-16 Celebration of the Major Holidays, Shabbat, Sukkot, Passover, and Shavuot.

   Numbers:
   16: The Uprising of Korach

   Deuteronomy:
   The *Shema*
   The Ten Commandments
   The Death of Moses

   As a means of creatively extending these lessons, you may wish to involve the students in dramatic reenactments of the stories.

2. Grades K-3: Inform the Rabbi that the class has read *The Tattooed Torah* and that students are currently involved in learning some of the stories from the Torah. Ask if he/she would be willing to arrange for the students to be called to the Torah for a special blessing during Simchat Torah or Shabbat.

3. Grades K-3: A special *parochet* was made for the little Torah. With permission of the Rabbi, principal, or Board of Trustees, have the students create a *parochet* (curtain for the Holy Ark), to be used during special times. Use the tie-dye technique. Materials and procedure follow.

   Materials:

   appropriate size light weight cotton or muslin fabric
   packages of dye in a variety of colors
   strong thread

   Procedure:

   a. Either knot the fabric or push the fabric into tentlike shapes and tightly bind together.

   b. Mix the dye according to the directions on the package.

   c. Dip the fabric into the dye (the tied areas will not take the dye).

   d. Once the fabric is dry, untie the knots of thread. A pattern will be evident.

   e. Use Vogart pens to embellish the *parochet* with Jewish symbols. (Vogart pens are tubes of paint with a ballpoint pen tip which are made specifically for fabric.)

I Never Saw Another Butterfly . . . **Children's drawings and poems from Terezin Concentration Camp 1942-1944. New York: McGraw-Hill Book Company, 1971. 81 pages. Grade level: 5 and up.**

This moving collection of poetry and drawings carries the reader into the world of the Holocaust as seen and experienced by children who were prisoners at Terezin, a concentration camp. These poems and drawings are testimonial to both the best and the worst of our human capabilities.

Major Ideas

Hardship can result in a greater appreciation of the things in life which are often taken for granted.

Painful experiences can sometimes inspire creations of lasting beauty.

Humanity must never again remain silent in the face of inhumanity.

Activities

1. Grades 5 and up: Yom HaShoah is a time when the events of the Holocaust are remembered. Ironically, this comes in the spring when one is surrounded by reminders of the rebirth or rejuvenation of life. A major theme in many of the poems is the beauty and solace that can be found in nature. Therefore, reading these poems outside is particularly appropriate.

2. Grades 5 and up: As supplementary reading, recommend that your students read *The Diary of Anne Frank*. Have them keep a diary as if they, too, were in hiding. Before they begin, hold a class discussion, focusing on the following:

> The feeling of having to leave one's home and go into hiding in a strange place.
>
> What it might be like to be robbed of basic freedoms.
>
> What types of things might be good to take along to the hiding place and how choices might be narrowed down.
>
> How time might be spent in hiding.

3. Grades 5 and up: The Holocaust destroyed the lives and dreams of millions of people. Yet, the children of Terezin continued to dream and to express their emotions through their art, despite the death around them. A symbolic representation of the bleakness of the Holocaust, as well as the visions it inspired, may be achieved through a crayon etching project. The bright and varied colors applied first to the paper can represent the students' dreams. Next, their dreams will be blackened out by a solid layer of black crayon covering the entire surface. Using a pointed object such as a toothpick to scrape off the black, the students will symbolically realize that dreams can shine through even during the harshest of times. A step-by-step procedure for crayon etching follows:

Materials:

crayons
white drawing paper, manila or oak tag, 9" x 12"
newspapers
sharp pointed tool such as a nail file or bobby pin

Procedure:

a. Place a newspaper on your working area.

b. Apply a light or bright color wax crayon to the paper with medium pressure.

c. Apply a dark or grayed color heavily over the light or bright color.

d. Scratch off the dark or grayed color in some areas, letting the light or bright color show and making a drawing or composition.

e. Keep all shavings on the newspaper, as they are hard to clean from any surface.

Klein, Gerda Weissmann, *Promise of a New Spring. The Holocaust and Renewal*. Illus. by Vincent Tartaro. Chappaqua, New York: Rossel Books, 1981. 43 pages. Grade level: 2-4.

In this book, Gerda Klein gently introduces to young children the devastating effects of the Holocaust on the Jewish people and on all humanity. *Promise of a New Spring* opens with photographs, sepia-toned drawings, and factual narrative depicting the Nazi plan for destruction of the Jews. The author then creates an analogy between the Holocaust and a purposefully set forest fire in which only a remnant of life remains. The book ends with a promise of a new spring, but only if the survivors and those of us who inherit the legacy of the Holocaust will ensure that the event is neither forgotten nor repeated.

Major Ideas

"Those who cannot remember the past are condemned to repeat it" (Santayana).

Drawing strength from one's Jewish heritage can help one cope in the face of adversity.

Activities

1. Grades 3 and 4: The book emphasizes the importance of passing down and keeping alive the memories of the survivors by sharing them with all who will listen. Invite a Holocaust survivor to the classroom to share his/her experiences and to field any questions that the students may have. Prepare a list of questions in advance with the class.

2. Grade 4: The analogy of the forest fire to the Holocaust as created by Gerda Klein is reminiscent of the burning bush described in the Torah. One interpretation of Exodus 3:2 "*V'hasneh Einenu U'kal*" (And there was a bush all aflame, yet the bush was not consumed) is that the burning bush can serve as a metaphor for the survival of the Jewish people. Gerda Klein reminds the reader that although survivors of the Holocaust were "burned," it is important for them to build a new life, to "find water below the charred forest floor." After discussing the relevance of this Torah portion to the Holocaust experience, ask the students to draw a scene of a Holocaust survivor in an activity that renews and affirms life. For example: marriage, family activities, work, travel, Jewish celebrations, or even mourning of loved ones killed during the Holocaust. After the drawings are completed, arrange them on a bulletin board around a construction paper replica of the burning bush. Title the bulletin board "And the bush was not consumed. Our lives go on."

3. Grades 2-4: The author notes that it was the Nazi's intention "... to destroy every memory of the Jewish people ..." This is an ideal time to ask the students to reflect upon memories which they cherish and would like to share. Have the students first write a letter to their parents informing them of their Holocaust studies. Then have them relate how *Promise of a New Spring* has caused them to reflect upon special memories from their own lives. Each child

should then complete the letter by sharing his/her memory with the parent(s). If necessary, or if the student prefers, a letter may be written to a special person other than a parent.

Levoy, Myron. *Alan and Naomi*. New York: Harper & Row Publishers, Inc., 1977. 192 pages. Grade level: 6-8.

Alan is a young boy growing up in Brooklyn in the early 1940s. Naomi, who is Alan's age, is a Jewish refugee from France who has been traumatized by the war. Alan begrudgingly spends time with Naomi and unravels the roots of her withdrawn and often bizarre behavior. Naomi gradually makes an adjustment to her new life. However, when she witnesses a prejudiced attack against Alan, she is reminded of her past and once again regresses. Alan blames Naomi's illness not only on the Nazis, but on all the prejudiced individuals in this world. Levoy's story is unique in that it illustrates the permanent psychological devastation caused by Nazi tactics.

Major Ideas

Close friendship eases pain.

People must take great care in how they treat others, for thoughtless actions may inflict lifelong pain.

Activities

1. Grades 6-8: Alan uses a puppet to reach and communicate with Naomi. His creative use of the puppet enables Naomi to express her feelings more comfortably. Utilizing the theme of creatively reaching out to others, have students prepare a puppet show for young children who are institutionalized. Possibilities for institutional settings include a hospital, convalescent home, or a school for the emotionally or physically disabled. Separate the students in the class into four groups. Have each group create a puppet show based on a short fairy-tale or folktale. To allow time for all groups to present, limit shows to approximately ten minutes in length.

2. Grades 6-8: Note: Before doing this activity, it is necessary that the students have prior knowledge of the living conditions in the concentration camps. Alan, living in the United States during World War II, is physically untouched by the war. In the opening chapters of the story, one of Alan's greatest concerns is that nothing interfere with his baseball games. To contrast life as it was during world War II for Jewish youth in the United States and Europe, have the students keep two different journals for three days. In one, they should imagine that they are Jewish children living in America and, in the other, that they are in a Nazi concentration camp in Europe. After the journals are completed, portions may be shared aloud in class.

3. Grades 6-8: In Naomi's case, the psychological impact of her experiences in France during World War II left her unable to cope with rebuilding her life in a new country where prejudice also existed. Explain to the students that there were other survivors who did not have an easy time adjusting to their new lives. Have the students share their ideas on how the German government might have better helped survivors to rebuild their lives after the war and to cope with the psychological wounds inflicted by the Nazis. After this discussion, ask the children the following questions:

   When have you purposely hurt another human being?

   In retrospect, what might you have done to help the person you hurt recover from the pain you caused them?

   When have you been purposefully hurt by another human being?

   What could that person have done to help you recover from the pain?

Orgel, Doris. *The Devil in Vienna*. New York: Dial Press, 1978. 256 pages. Grade level: 6-8.

Inge Dornenvald and Lieselotte Vessely have a special friendship which is threatened by the Nazi's rise to power in Austria. Lieselotte is Christian and her father is a Nazi. Inge is Jewish. When Lieselotte moves to Germany, she and Inge try to keep in touch. Lieselotte's father, however, forbids their correspondence. Lieselott's uncle, a priest, helps the girls maintain their friendship and, in doing so, risks his own safety. This story, based on the author's personal experiences, is a poignant illustration of how children can rise above the politics and prejudice created by adults.

Major Ideas

Remaining true to one's personal convictions can be risky, but rewarding.

The strongest friendships survive even in the face of the most destructive forces.

Activities

1. Grades 6-8: Inge and Lieselotte provide a model for positive interaction among Jews and gentiles. They transcend the prejudice of the society in which they live. Although they come from different backgrounds, they are able to play together, work together, and enjoy each other's company. Take this opportunity to involve the class in a joint brotherhood project with students from a neighboring church. Pair each of the students with a student from the church. Have the pairs work together on a poster, focusing on a theme that promotes brotherhood among ethnic, racial, and religious groups. Materials and procedure follow.

Materials:

poster board
felt tipped markers
construction paper
paste
a variety of scrap material (i.e., string, tin foil, glitter, and anything else that might be used for a collage)

Procedure:

a. Have each pair brainstorm ideas for their poster.

b. After selecting one idea, a sketch can be made on scrap paper.

c. The design can then be drawn onto the poster board and completed using whatever materials the pair desires.

d. The posters may be displayed in the church and synagogue. Or, arrangements may be made with local businesses, organizations, or an art museum to display the students' work.

2. Grades 6-8: Ask the students what they think the title *The Devil in Vienna* means. When they arrive at the realization that there were many evil forces prior to and during the Nazi's reign of power, ask them to think about any "devils" that are present in society today. Then read sample Letters to the Editor from local secular and Jewish newspapers and nationally circulated periodicals. The selected letters should voice citizen concerns about crucial issues. These will provide a model for students in writing their own letters. Tell the students to select an issue which is of particular interest to them and write a letter expressing their ideas on the topic. These will be mailed to the periodical or newspaper of the student's choice.

3. Grades 6-8: When Inge is forced to leave Vienna because of the persecution of the Jews, a song comes to her mind: "Vienna, Vienna, you alone shall be the city of my dreams." Inge, however, is not sad to leave the city in which she was born and raised. She is aware of the danger in remaining behind. Throughout history, the Jewish people have found it necessary to leave their homes as a result of persecution. Ask the students to imagine how they might feel and what they might miss about their community or country if they were forced to leave because of discrimination against the Jewish people. Then have them write a farewell poem about their community or country. A nice example of a farewell to a community is the song "Anatevka" from *Fiddler on the Roof*.

Richter, Hans Peter. *Friedrich*. Translated from the German by Edite Kroll. New York: Holt, Rinehart & Winston, Inc., 1961. 149 pages. Grade level: 6-8.

The sheer brutality of the Nazi regime becomes painfully apparent to a young gentile boy as he witnesses a friend, Friedrich, being denied his basic rights simply because he is Jewish. Through Friedrich's experiences, the book accurately chronicles the prejudice and resulting violence against German Jewry between 1925 and 1942. The fate of the Jews living in Europe during this time is symbolized by the ultimate death of Friedrich as he is denied entry to a bomb shelter. The horror of this period is demonstrated by the actions of uncaring German citizens. Yet, the reader is also exposed to people who are not sympathetic to Hitler's cause, but who comply with his orders because of a fear for their own lives. Richter's moving style is obviously a product of having been there himself.

Major Ideas

Each of us has the capacity to choose between good and evil.

Choosing evil over good and — sometimes — even good over evil, has its consequences.

It is often difficult to go against the authority of the crowd.

Activities

1. Grades 6-8: Before introducing the book, tell the students to make a list of the activities they most enjoy and another list of activities which they do on a daily basis. The teacher, in the role of a Nazi officer, will then recite the restrictions placed on Jews beginning in 1933 when Adolph Hitler became Chancellor of the German Reich and continuing to the end of the war. As the decrees are read, the students must cross off all activities on their lists which would defy the decree in any way. Have volunteers compare their original list of activities with the activities that remain after the decrees are read. Finally, introduce the book saying: "*Friedrich* is a story of a young Jewish boy who was actually forced to live by the laws, decrees, and regulations of the Nazi regime."

2. Grades 6-8: Certain scenes from this book lend themselves well to dramatic reenactment. Separate the class into four groups and assign roles for dramatizing each of the following chapters. Questions are provided for brief discussion after each scene.

"The Jungvolk" (Scene I)
1933

In this scene, Friedrich attends a meeting of Hitler Youth and is forced to chant "The Jews are our affliction."

Discussion:

Friedrich is excited about the prospect of being a member of the Jungvolk, even though the group is anti-Semitic. Why would a Jewish person want to affiliate with such a group?

Can you relate this to any situation in your life? What might Friedrich have been thinking about when he was forced to recite "The Jews are our affliction"? How would you react in a similar situation?

"The Pogrom" (Scene II)
1938

At this time, Friedrich's gentile friend (the narrator) witnesses and participates in a violent pogrom against Jewish citizens.

Discussion:

Influenced by the pressure of the group, Friedrich's friend takes part in the violence against the Jews. How does peer pressure influence or provide an excuse for a person to do something that they may not have chosen to do alone?

After the pogrom, Friedrich's friend looks into a piece of broken mirror and then runs home. What might he have been thinking as he viewed his own reflection in the mirror?

"In the Shelter" (Scene III)
1942

This chapter describes the events which occur as Friedrich is denied entry to the bomb shelter.

Discussion:

If you have been a German citizen in the bomb shelter, would you have argued for or against allowing Friedrich to enter, or would you have remained silent? Give reasons for your decisions.

"The End" (Scene IV)
1942

It is discovered that Friedrich has died as a result of the bombing.

Discussion:

This is a very intense scene which may best be followed by some time to think, rather than immediate discussion. After time for reflection, ask the following: How do you imagine Friedrich's death affected those who found him throughout their lives?

3. Grades 6-8: Remind the students that as Friedrich's friend joins the pogrom, he is told, "Today you'll see something, boy... that you can tell your grandchildren about." Tell them to imagine that they are Friedrich's friend many years after the war. Have them write a letter to their grandchildren recalling the day of the pogrom. The letter should describe what actually happened, how they feel about having participated in the act, and any wisdom gained from the experiences that they believe should be passed on.

Sachs, Marilyn. *A Pocket Full of Seeds.* Illus. by Ben Stahl. New York: Doubleday & Co., Inc., 1973. 137 pages. Grade level: 5-7.

The story begins with Nicole, a young girl, reflecting on how it feels to be in a girls' school not knowing where her parents and younger sister are. Nicole is Jewish and living in Nazi occupied France. Upon returning from an overnight visit with friends, she discovers her family has been taken away by the Nazis. She seeks refuge with a Christian family who keep her until they feel their own lives are in danger. Although they offer to send her to live with their elderly uncle, she refuses, opting instead to remain close to home so that she may be there when her family returns. Nicole bicycles to her school and is taken in by her teacher, who is a suspected Nazi sympathizer. Sachs has written a touching story which teaches the value of hope in stressful times.

Major Ideas

A person's Jewish heritage is something that cannot be denied.

Hope can carry us through hard times.

"Life goes on," be it in joy or in sorrow.

Activities

1. Grades 5-7: In the book, Nicole is offended by the laughter of a man whose wife and children have been taken away by the Nazis. Her mother explains to Nicole that the man's laughter is indicative of the hope held by the man that he will be reunited with his family. When Nicole is separated from her family, she, too, relies on hope for a good future to carry her through. Have each student draw a scene depicting one of Nicole's dreams for the future. After the drawings are completed, display them in a self-adhesive photograph album. Adhere letters to the cover spelling "NICOLE'S HOPE." The album may be displayed in the school library as part of a Holocaust literature display.

2. Grades 5-7: Nicole's family begins to feel closer to their Judaism because of the Nazi threat that their right to observe Jewish tradition freely will be taken away from them. Ask each student to share one aspect of Jewish life they would cling to most tightly if there were a threat that it would be taken away. Have the students decorate a box which, upon completion, will hold a symbol of their most cherished aspect of Judaism. Materials and procedure follow.

Materials:

a box commonly found in the kitchen (i.e., cereal,

sugar, cookie, toothpick, etc.)
construction paper
felt tipped markers

Procedure:

a. Cut construction paper to size so that it may be pasted over the selected box. The original box should be completely covered.

b. Using markers and/or pieces of scrap construction paper, decorate the covered box.

c. Using a piece of construction paper, have the children draw or construct a symbol of their most cherished aspect of Judaism.

d. Place the symbol inside the box.

e. When the art project is finished, seat students in a circle. Place the boxes in the center of the circle. One at a time, the students will select a box and open it. The student whose box is opened will then explain the symbol and its special significance.

3. Grades 5-7: Nicole's gentile teacher gives her a safe haven in the boarding school. Apprise the students of the fact that there were other gentile citizens who were willing to risk their own lives to save Jews. Many of these helpful citizens were discovered and executed or sent to concentration camps without proper legal trials. Tell the students to assume that the attempt of Nicole's teacher to save her Jewish student was eventually discovered. Arrange a mock trial to determine whether Nicole's teacher has indeed committed a crime. The following roles will need to be assigned:

> Nicole
> Nicole's teacher
> the judge
> jury
> Nazi lawyer
> Defense lawyer
> Witnesses for the defense
> Witnesses for the prosecution

Siegal, Aranka. *Upon the Head of the Goat: A Childhood in Hungary 1939-1944.* **New York: Farrar, Straus & Giroux, Inc., 1981. 192 pages. Grade level: 6-9.**

This Newbery Honor Book is a moving recollection of the author's childhood prior to and during the Nazi occupation of Hungary. When Piri (Aranka Siegal) returns to Hungary after a visit to her grandmother's farm in the Ukraine, she finds that things are not quite the same as when she left. There are outbreaks of anti-Semitism. Her mother has become a part of the Jewish underground, and her aunt commits suicide in order to protect the family when her Zionist acts are discovered. In spite of all these changes, the family clings tightly to their Jewish traditions and remains dedicated to one another. In the Afterword, the reader is informed that out of this large and courageous family, only Piri and one sister survived.

Major Ideas

It is important to retain one's dignity and integrity even under the most adverse of circumstances.

The vibrant spirit of Judaism, if deeply ingrained, cannot be crushed.

That there may not be justice is an unfortunate reality of the world in which we live.

The only reward for goodness is goodness itself.

Family commitment is a key component to maintaining psychological well-being through difficult times.

Activities

1. Grades 6-9: In the final chapter of the book, Aranka Siegel reveals the source for her story's title. The reader is informed that in biblical times, the sins of the Israelites were symbolically placed upon the head of the goat. The Temple Priest would then send the goat into the wilderness, thus ridding the people of their sins. As a springboard for discussion, reread out loud the dialogue of Piri, her friend Judi, and Mr. Shuster about what it means to be a scapegoat (page 205 from "It is the times . . ." through page 206, "If this is the way God chooses to use His people, I'd rather not be chosen"). Discussion questions could include the following:

   How were the Jews and other minority groups used as scapegoats by Hitler's government?

   Give some examples of how certain groups are used as scapegoats in today's world.

   Can you think of a time when you have become another person's scapegoat or when you have used another person as a scapegoat?

   Judi mentions that she would prefer not to be one of God's chosen people. What does it mean to be "chosen"? What are the positive and negative consequences of being chosen?

2. Grades 6-9: Conditions in the ghetto were deplorable. Piri's mother encouraged her family to make use of scarce resources in order to make their living space as comfortable as possible. Rope off the room into four sections and separate the class into four family groups. Assign a section of the room to each group. Provide each group with a collection of material that Piri's family had available to them in the

ghetto, such as bricks, boards, bedspreads, nails, rocks, pots, boxes, pencil, and paper. Other materials may also be used. Tell the students to imagine that this roped off section of the room is their space in the ghetto. As a family, they must decide how to create a home using the materials provided. (The students need to be cautioned against pounding nails into classroom walls, ceilings, and floors, or hanging things from electrical fixtures.) After completing the task, students should be asked to compare this ghetto environment to their own homes. What is similar? What is different? They should also share the decision making process in which they engaged as they determined how to design and utilize their space. As this discussion is taking place, you might want to serve a ghetto meal of chunks of bread and potatoes.

3. Grades 6-9: As deportation to the ghetto becomes imminent, Piri chooses to say goodbye to a close friend. She asks the girl to take care of her cherished phonograph and records. Have the students consider what cherished item they would give to a friend for safekeeping if they were deported to a ghetto. Then separate the class into pairs to role play saying goodbye. Each student in the pair should have the opportunity to play the person leaving. The teacher can periodically freeze the action to focus on the dialogue taking place between a single pair.

Suhl, Yuri. *Uncle Misha's Partisans*. Bristol, Florida: Four Winds Press, 1973. 211 pages. Grade level: 6-9.

This book is a suspenseful retelling of the role played by a real group of partisans during the Holocaust. Young Motele, returning from a violin lesson, finds that his sister, mother, and father have all been murdered by the Nazis. Vowing to avenge their deaths, he joins a partisan group in the Ukraine. Eventually he is given the opportunity to carry out his vow. Posing as a Ukranian peasant, Motele secures a position playing violin at the Nazi officer's headquarters. He wires the building with explosives and observes the devastation. The story concludes with a partisan friend assuring Motele that the burning building is a just a "... *yahrzeit* candle for our dead."

Major Ideas

Survival is often dependent on collective action.

Innocent people are frequently scapegoated because of society's ills.

There is much strength and comfort to be found in the extended family of the Jewish people.

Activities

1. Grades 6-9: Motele opted to avenge the death of his family through a violent act against the Nazi perpetrators. To help the students understand Motele's decision to defy, rather than to become a passive victim of the Nazis, discuss the following questions:

    What are the possible actions you might take if you were in Motele's position?

    What would be the consequences of each of these actions?

    Why do you suppose Motele chose to become a partisan?

    Motele risked his life to wire the headquarters with explosives. For what kinds of things would you personally be willing to risk your life?

    What might Motele have been thinking about as he watched the Nazi headquarters burn?

2. Grades 6-9: Songs acted as an inspiration for partisan defiance against Nazi brutality. Teach the "Jewish Partisan Song" in Yiddish or in Hebrew. Yiddish words and music may be found in *Never To Forget: The Jews of the Holocaust* by Milton Meltzer. The Hebrew version of the song, "*Shir Hapartizanim*," may be found in *Great Songs of Israel*, edited and arranged by Velvel Pastnernak.

3. Grades 6-9: Introduce the idea that during difficult times it often becomes necessary to utilize one's personal ingenuity and resources in order to cope or survive. Motele uses his ability to play the violin to stay alive and to aid the partisan effort. Tell the students to imagine that they are in Motele's situation. Have them write a story focusing on how they use their own talent or ingenuity to stay alive and aid the partisan cause.

HOLOCAUST: BOOKS FOR CHILDREN

Aaron, Chester. *Gideon.* New York: J.B. Lippincott Co., 1982. Grade level: 6 and up.

Told in first person, the author relates the dangers he experienced as a smuggler in the Warsaw Ghetto. His escape from Treblinka concentration camp is also recalled.

Abells, Chana Byers. *The Children We Remember.* Photographs from the Archives of Yad Vashem. Rockville, MD: Kar-Ben Copies, Inc., 1983. Grade level: 2-6.

The author of this heart-rending book about the children of the Holocaust immediately establishes a sense of identification between Jewish children of today and those who actually experienced the horrors of the Holocaust. A superb book which, in photographs and very few words, captures the Holocaust experience.

Baer, Edith. *A Frost in the Night: A Childhood on the Eve of the Third Reich.* New York: Pantheon Books, 1980. Grade level: 6 and up.

In this chilling novel, the Nazis' terrifying rise to power in 1932 is retold from the perspective of a young girl. Baer sensitively delves into the life of Eva, whose childhood is shattered when Hitler becomes the leader of Germany.

Bishop, Clair. *Twenty and Ten.* New York: Viking Press, Inc., 1952. Grade level: 5 and up.

An exciting story about the students and nuns in a French parochial school who manage to hide ten Jewish refugee children from the Nazis.

Block, Marie Halum. *Displaced Person.* New York: Lothrop, Lee & Shepard Books, 1978. Grade level: 5 and up.

Through the experiences of Stephan, a non-Jewish refugee in a DP camp in Nazi Germany during the final days of World War II, Block provides young readers with a very different perspective of the Holocaust.

Demetz, Hana. *The House on Prague Street.* New York: St. Martin's Press, 1980. Grade level: 6 and up.

The themes of love, survival, peace, and terror are juxtaposed in the life of the adolescent Helen Richter. Helen's world is painfully altered when her family is sent to a concentration camp and the war separates her from her young German boyfriend. Demetz skillfully untangles the intricacies of each of the issues facing Helen.

Eisner, Jack. *The Survivor.* New York: Bantam Books, Inc., 1982. Grade level: 6 and up.

Eisner's account of how he survived the Warsaw Ghetto and concentration camps at the age of thirteen is filled with the same courageous spirit which allowed him to remain persistent in his struggle for life.

Eliav, Arie. *The Voyage of Ulua.* New York: Funk and Wagnalls Co., 1969. Grade level: 6 and up.

In spite of the British effort to blockade Palestine during World War II, a group of courageous and dedicated young Jews were able to rescue 800 children and smuggle them safely into the country. Eliav's retelling of this true story is thrilling from beginning to end.

Firer, Benzion. *The Twins.* New York: Feldheim Publishers, 1981. Grade level: 5 and up.

When the parents of Polish Orthodox twins choose to die for the sake of God, the boy becomes a partisan and his sister converts to Christianity. Through intense faith in Judaism and remarkable courage, the twins survive the Holocaust and are reunited in Israel.

Firer, Benzion. *The Long Journey Home.* Trans. by Bracha Slae. New York: Feldheim Publishers, 1984. Grade level: 6 and up.

Firer has skillfully combined the themes of the Holocaust and Zionism in this novel about Shlomo and Zissel, who flee Poland to help establish a Jewish homeland in Palestine. The two eventually return to Europe where they must come to grips with the secular and religious ideologies which tug at their senses of Jewish identity.

Forman, James. *My Enemy My Brother.* New York: Scholastic Inc., 1972. Grade level: 6 and up.

A young survivor of the battle of the Warsaw Ghetto is able to make his way to Israel after a dangerous journey through Nazi occupied Europe. The sense of movement from destruction to rebirth is very evident in this bold novel.

Forman, James. *The Survivor*. New York: Farrar, Straus & Giroux, Inc., 1976. Grade level: 6 and up.

> The children of a Dutch Jewish physician must call upon all of their resources in order to survive the terror of life in a Nazi concentration camp. The children's courage and will to survive are dramatically revealed.

Forman, James. *The White Crow*. New York: Farrar, Straus & Giroux, Inc., 1976. Grade level: 6 and up.

> The evil roots of the Holocaust become apparent in this fictionalized novel about the development of the Hitler Youth Movement between 1907 and 1923. Forman has provided a unique glimpse at the character of the people who allowed Hitler's eventual rise to power.

Frank, Anne. *The Diary of a Young Girl*. New York: Doubleday & Co., Inc., 1967. Grade level: 5 and up.

> Anne Frank's humor, courage, warmth and belief in humanity characterize the entries in this diary which she kept while her family was in hiding in Amsterdam.

Frank, Anne. *Tales From the Secret Annex*. Trans. by Michael Mok and Ralph Manheim. New York: Washington Square Press, 1983. Grade level: 5 and up.

> A collection of fables, short stories, essays, and personal reminiscences by the young girl whose diary became a classic in the field of Holocaust literature.

Friedman, Ira R. *Escape or Die: True Stories of Young People Who Survived the Holocaust*. New York: Addison-Wesley, 1982. Grade level: 5 and up.

> A collection of true stories about young Jews and gentiles who managed to escape death during the Holocaust. Friedman eloquently captures the intense emotions experienced by each of the young survivors.

Gabor, Georgia. *My Destiny: Survivor of the Holocaust*. Arcadia, CA: Amen Publishing Co., 1981, Grade level: 6 and up.

> The author has used personal photographs to illustrate this graphic autobiographical account of her experiences in a Hungarian ghetto during World War II. Gabor's postwar narrative is particularly effective in describing the problems with which Holocaust survivors must cope for the rest of their lives.

Green, Bette. *Summer of My German Soldier*. New York: Dial Press, 1973. Grade level: 6 and up.

> A provocative novel for more mature young readers about a twelve-year-old girl in an Arkansas town who becomes friends with a German prisoner of war.

Goldstein, Lisa. *The Red Magician*. New York: Timescape/Pocket Books, 1982. Grade level: 6 and up.

> This is a unique Holocaust legend in which an Elijah-like character appears to warn a village of impending danger. However, when the village Rabbi places his need for power above the survival of his people, disaster becomes inevitable. Goldstein has written a powerful novel about the delicate balance between selflessness and selfishness in a communal setting.

Grohskopf, Bernice. *Children in the Wind*. New York: Atheneum Publishers, 1977. Grade level: 5 and up.

> Among the characters in this fascinating novel are the daughter of an ex-Nazi in hiding and the daughter of a Holocaust survivor. The author has done a superb job of portraying the intricacies of teen-age relationships, as well as the sensitive issues arising from two very different Holocaust related experiences.

Haugaard, Erik Christian. *Chase Me, Catch Nobody*. Boston: Houghton Mifflin Co., 1980. Grade level: 6 and up.

> Erik, a fourteen-year-old Danish boy, embarks upon a far different journey than expected. As he enjoys a holiday ride on the ferry, Erik must complete a dangerous mission to Germany to deliver fifty Danish passports.

Hautzig, Esther. *The Endless Steppe: A Girl in Exile*. New York: Harper & Row Publishers, Inc., 1968. Grade level: 5 and up.

> Hautzig has chosen the Russian front of World War II as the setting for her story about a young Jewish girl from Vilna who is deported to Sibera with her family. The tragedy of being exiled from one's home is painfully evident in this novel.

Isaacman, Clara, as told to Joan Adess Grossman. *Clara's Story*. Philadelphia: The Jewish Publication Society of America, 1984. Grade level: 6 and up.

> After hearing Elie Wiesel speak at an interfaith conference on the Holocaust, Clara Isaacman was convinced that she

could no longer remain silent about her own Holocaust experience. This resulting account of the two and a half years Clara spend in hiding in Antwerp, Belgium with her family is among the most poignant Holocaust memoirs for young readers. Along with describing the devastating effects of the war, Clara reflects issues and concerns to which all young people can relate. One has the feeling that writing this book was, for Clara, like the "deep, full . . . free . . . breath of air" she first took after coming out of hiding.

Jackson, Livia Britton. *Ellie: Coming of Age in the Holocaust.* New York: Times Books, 1980. Grade level: 6 and up.

Family members often made extreme sacrifices during the Holocaust in order to help their loved ones survive. This is the heroic story of a thirteen-year-old girl who tries to keep her mother and older brother alive.

Jacot, Michael. *The Last Butterfly.* New York: Ballantine Books, Inc., 1974. Grade level: 6 and up.

This is an exquisite novel in which a group of children in Terezin are befriended by a professional clown after their parents have been murdered. The clown, in his own way, helps to bring a little sunshine into the otherwise melancholy atmosphere of Terezin concentration camp.

Jaffo, Joseph. *A Bag of Marbles.* Boston: Houghton Mifflin Co., 1974. Grade level: 6 and up.

The treacherous journey through Nazi-occupied France by two boys, ages ten and twelve, comes alive through Jaffo's fast paced narrative.

Kerr, Judith. *When Hitler Stole Pink Rabbit.* Illus. by the author. New York: Coward, McCann & Geoghegan, Inc., 1971. Grade level: 6 and up.

When a young girl's family is forced to flee Nazi Germany, she learns to adjust to being a refugee.

Kerr, Judith. *The Other Way Round.* New York: Coward, McCann and Geoghegan, 1975. Grade level: 6 and up.

In this fictionalized autobiographical sequel to *When Hitler Stole Pink Rabbit*, the author tells of a teen-age girl's growing up in wartime London after her family flees Nazi Germany.

Kerr, M.E. *Gentlehands.* New York: Harper & Row Publishers, Inc., 1978. Grade level: 6 and up.

Life is enjoyable for Buddy until he finds out through an investigative reporter that the grandfather he loves so much used to be known as "Gentlehands," the infamous Auschwitz murderer. Kerr's novel is a powerful reminder of the penetrating and chronic effects of anti-Semitism and the Holocaust.

Kluger, Ruth, and Mann, Peggy. *The Secret Ship.* New York: Doubleday & Co., 1978. Grade level: 5 and up.

This is a children's adaptation of Kluger's book, *The Last Escape*, in which Jewish refugees must free their icebound ship in a Rumanian port before making an illegal voyage to Palestine.

Koehn, Ilse. *Mischling, Second Degree: My Childhood in Nazi Germany.* New York: Greenwillow Books, 1977. Grade level: 5 and up.

Ilse Koehn's memoir describes how she survived the war by keeping secret the fact that her family was partly Jewish and anti-Nazi. This is a compelling novel in which the trauma of having to hide one's true identity is fully apparent.

Krueger, Horst. *A Crack in the Wall: Growing Up Under Hitler.* New York: Fromm International Publishing, 1982. Grade level: 6 and up.

Krueger offers scholarly insight into the quality of the German national character which allowed Hitler to rise to power and carry out his evil mission.

Levitan, Sonia. *Journey to America.* Illus. by Charles Robinson. New York: Atheneum Publishers, 1973. Grade level: 4-6.

When Lisa's father foresees the evil about to befall Nazi Germany in 1938, he leaves for America. Although his family intends to follow, their plans do not go smoothly and they must endure some very difficult hardships. Levitan realistically brings to life the emotional traumas experienced by the family.

Lingard, Joan. *The File on Fraulein Berg.* New York: Elsevier-Nelson, 1980. Grade level: 6 and up.

Unbeknownst to the Irish schoolgirls whom she teaches, Fraulein Berg is actually a Jewish Holocaust refugee. However, the girls believe their teacher is a Nazi and continue to persecute Fraulein Berg until they discover her true identity. Lingard has written a very powerful and fascinating novel that demonstrates the consequences of stereotyping and hiding one's true identity.

Lyttle, Richard. *Nazi Hunting*. New York: Franklin Watts, 1982. Grade level: 5 and up.

> The seven stories in this book dramatically reveal the capture of Nazi war criminals. Ongoing attempts to capture and bring other Nazis to trial are also described.

Mace, Elisabeth. *Brother Enemy*. New York: Beaufort Books, Inc., 1981. Grade level: 5 and up.

> A nine-year-old boy living in Germany in 1939 discovers that he is part Jewish when he, like his father before him, must leave Germany for England. Mace has written a dramatic story of the boy's war experiences and his eventual return to Germany where he discovers he no longer belongs.

Mazer, Harry. *The Last Mission*. New York: Delacorte Press, 1979. Grade level: 6 and up.

> This is the courageous story of Jack Raals, who wanted so much to join America's effort against Hitler's war machine, that he used false identification to enlist in the U.S. Air Force at age fifteen.

Meltzer, Milton. *Never to Forget: The Jews of the Holocaust*. New York: Harper & Row Publishers, Inc., 1976. Grade level: 6 and up.

> Meltzer received the National Jewish Book Award and Association of Jewish Libraries Award for this authoritative and superbly written account of the Holocaust. The narrative describes the historical background leading up to Hitler's rise to power, the concentration camps, and Jewish resistance.

Moskin, Marietta. *I Am Rosemarie*. New York: John Day Co., 1978. Grade level: 6 and up.

> The author has used autobiographical facts in this story about a young Jewish girl's courageous struggle to survive and grow up in Nazi occupied territory and, later, in a concentration camp.

Noble, Iris. *Nazi Hunter, Simon Wiesenthal*. New York: Julian Messner, 1979. Grade level: 6 and up.

> Noble has written a dynamic account of how Simon Wiesenthal's Holocaust experiences propelled him to dedicate the rest of his life to finding and bringing to trial Nazi war criminals. The book also includes a suggested bibliography for further reading.

Oberski, Jona. *Childhood*. New York: Doubleday & Co., Inc., 1983. Grade level: 5 and up.

> A small Jewish boy's experiences while imprisoned at Bergen-Belsen are retold in this poignant autobiographical novel. Oberski describes powerfully, yet compassionately, how Hitler's rise to power destroyed his previously peaceful childhood.

Orgel, Doris. *A Certain Magic*. New York: Dell Publishing Co., Inc., 1978. Grade level: 4 and up.

> As eleven-year-old Jenny reads her aunt's diary, she is deeply moved by the descriptions of her aunt's life as a young Jewish refugee in World War II England. Orgel received the Association of Jewish Libraries award for this poignant novel.

Orlev, Uri. *The Island on Bird Street*. Trans. by Hillel Halkin. New York: Houghton Mifflin Co., 1984. Grade level: 4 and up.

> When eleven-year-old Alex is separated from his father in the Warsaw Ghetto, he relies upon his inner faith, courage, and ingenuity to survive. Orlev has written an eloquent and heartwarming autobiographical account which demonstrates the powerful effects parental love can have for children, even in the parent's absence.

Patterson, Charles. *Anti-Semitism: The Road to the Holocaust and Beyond*. New York: Walker & Co., 1982. Grade level: 6 and up.

> Patterson provides an informative chronology of how anti-Semitism developed and erupted into the Holocaust. Consideration is also given to the continuing threat of anti-Semitism.

Rabinsky, Leatrice, and Mann, Gertrude. *Journey of Conscience*. Cleveland, OH: William Collins Publications, Inc., 1979. Grade level: 6 and up.

> The authors' powerful description of a trip to the concentration camps by two teachers, fifteen teen-age American students, and a Holocaust survivor is a most welcome addition to juvenile and adult Holocaust literature.

Reiss, Johanna. *The Journey Back*. New York: Harper & Row Publishers, Inc., 1976. Grade level: 5 and up.

> After spending the final two years of the war in hiding, two Dutch Jewish girls return home. This is a sequel to *The Upstairs Room*.

Reiss, Johanna. *The Upstairs Room*. New York: Harper & Row Publishers, Inc., 1972. Grade level: 5 and up.

> Reiss' autobiographical account of her experiences as a young girl in Holland during World War II won the National Jewish Book Award and was cited as a Newbery Honor Book. The emotions and experiences of the two Dutch Jewish girls in hiding are brought to life through lively narrative.

Rhue, Morton. *The Wave*. New York: Delacorte Press, 1981. Grade level: 6 and up.

> Teachers and students alike will enjoy this novel about how an energetic and creative teacher helps his class understand the reasons which propelled the spread of Nazism.

Romm, J. Leonard. *The Swastika on the Synagogue Door*. Chappaqua, NY: Rossel Books, 1984. Grade level: 4 and up.

> When a swastika and anti-Semitic slogan are painted on the entrance to a Long Island synagogue, two teen-agers join with their Rabbi and a Holocast survivor in an attempt to solve the crime. Romm has written an important novel which links the anti-Semitism of the Holocaust period to that which the young reader might, unfortunately, encounter today.

Rose, Anne. *Refugee*. New York: Dial Press, 1977. Grade level: 5 and up.

> When, at twelve, Elke is sent from Antwerp, Belgium to live in America, she wonders if she will ever see her parents and friends again. Her parents finally escape to America via Brazil. However, the family learns upon returning to Belgium after the war that their relatives and friends, including Elke's two best friends, have all been killed. Rose has captured the emotions of this family of survivors from the beginning of the war to the end.

Rossel, Seymour. *The Holocaust*. New York: Franklin Watts, 1981. Grade level: 6 and up.

> This is an easy to read historical account of the Holocaust. The author explains how the Nazis planned and executed the program for exterminating the Jews. In addition, Jewish resistance, concentration camp experiences, and the war crime trials are addressed.

Rubin, Arnold. *The Evil That Men Do: The Story of the Nazis*. New York: Julian Messner, 1977. Grade level: 6 and up.

> Rubin explores with great personal understanding the reasons why some individuals complied with Hitler's plans and why others resisted with all their might.

Rubinowicz, David. *The Diary of David Rubinowicz*. Trans. by Derek Bowman. Edmonds, WA: Creative Options, 1982. Grade level: 6 and up.

> David Rubinowicz was a young boy in rural Poland when Hitler rose to power. His daily diary entries chronicle how the Nazi occupation of Poland drastically changed the course of his life and millions of others.

Samuels, Gertrude. *Mottele*. New York: Harper & Row Publishers, Inc., 1976. Grade level: 6 and up.

> Actual experiences in the lives of Jewish partisans during World War II form the basis of Samuel's documentary novel.

Schwartz, Sheila. *Growing Up Guilty*. New York: Pantheon Books, 1978. Grade level: 5 and up.

> The late 1930s and beginning of World War II marked a time of intense political and social turmoil in Europe. This, in turn, triggered the intellectual and emotionally painful awakening of the young woman in this story.

Sommerfelt, Aimee. *Miriam*. New York: Criterion Books, 1963. Grade level: 6 and up.

> Miriam is a young Jewish girl living in Norway during World War II. When Nazi troops occupy the country, she and her family are forced to flee their home in Oslo. Fear of impending tragedy and loss of one's familiar surroundings are powerful elements in this engaging novel.

Spanjaard, Barry. *Don't Fence Me In*. Brookville, FL: B & B Publications, 1981. Grade level: 6 and up.

> Although Barry Spanjaard was born in America, his Dutch parents took him to Holland where his life was wonderful until the Nazi invasion. Spanjaard speaks from personal experience about what life was like for children in three concentration camps and reveals that one of his best friends turned out to be Anne Frank.

Suhl, Yuri. *On the Other Side of the Gate*. New York: Franklin Watts, 1975. Grade level: 6 and up.

> Suhl tells the story of a Polish-Jewish family living in the ghetto which attempts to send their son away in order to save his life. Suhl powerfully reveals the family's desire to have at least one of its members survive.

Szambelan-Stevinsky, Christine. *Dark Hour of Noon*. New York: J.B. Lippincott Co., 1982. Grade level: 4 and up.

> This is the fascinating story of five young Polish Christian partisans who join together to fight the Nazi occupation of Poland and avenge the murder of Jews.

Unsdorfer, Simcha Bunem. *The Yellow Star*. New York: Feldheim Publishers, 1983. Grade level: 6 and up.

> Maintaining one's identity and traditions under adverse circumstances is the major theme of this compelling novel. Unsdorfer, a Holocaust survivor, has courageously described how he was able to preserve his Jewish identity during the war.

von der Grun, Max. *Howl Like the Wolves: Growing Up in Nazi Germany*. New York: William Morrow & Co., Inc., 1980. Grade level: 6 and up.

> Von der Grun's novel is about a veteran of Hitler's army who attempts to warn people about the rise of neo-Nazi groups. The message of the book cries out painfully loud and clear: another Holocaust can happen if we choose to ignore the warning signals.

Werstein, Irving. *The Uprising of the Warsaw Ghetto*. New York: W.W. Norton & Co., Inc., 1968. Grade level: 6 and up.

> Personal accounts, together with authentic documents, vividly recapture the events of the Warsaw Ghetto uprising for young readers.

Wolf, Jacqueline. *Take Care of Josette: A Memoir in Defense of Occupied France*. New York: Franklin Watts, 1981. Grade level: 4 and up.

> Wolf has written a poignant story about two Jewish orphans who experience both the most kind and most evil of human actions during their struggle to survive World War II in Nazi occupied France.

Zar, Rose. *In the Mouth of the Wolf*. Philadelphia: The Jewish Publication Society of America, 1983. Grade level: 6 and up.

> Young Ruska Guterman is able to escape the Piotrkow Ghetto by using false papers. During the war she works as a housekeeper, nurse's aide, and laundress, always leery of suspicious people who might inform the Nazis of her Jewish identity. The narrative is fast paced and suspenseful.

Ziemian, Joseph. *The Cigarette Sellers of Three Crosses Square*. New York: Avon Books, 1977. Grade level: 5 and up.

> In 1942, a group of children managed to escape from the Warsaw Ghetto. They survived in the Aryan quarter of the Nazi occupied city by peddling cigarettes in the public square. Ziemian won the Literary Award of the World Jewish Congress for his marvelous retelling of this true story.

Zuker-Bujanowska, Liliana. *Liliana's Journal: Warsaw 1939-1945*. New York: Dial Press, 1980. Grade level: 6 and up.

> Liliana's journal describes how she escaped from the Warsaw Ghetto at age seventeen and managed to stay alive through the duration of the horrifying Holocaust.

HOLOCAUST: RESOURCES FOR ADULTS

Biographies and Personal Memoirs

Baker, Leonard. *Days of Sorrow and Pain: Leo Baeck and the Berlin Jews.* New York: Macmillan Publishing Co., Inc., 1978.

Bierman, John. *Righteous Gentile: The Story of Raoul Wallenberg, Missing Hero of the Holocaust.* New York: Viking Press, Inc., 1981.

Brin, Herb. *Ich Bin Ein Jude.* Preface by Elie Wiesel. New York: Jonathan David Publishers, Inc., 1983.

Carmel, Herman. *Black Days White Nights.* New York: Hippocrene Books, Inc., 1984.

Dorian, Emil. *The Quality of Witness: A Romanian Diary, 1937-1944.* Philadelphia: The Jewish Publication Society of America, 1983.

Eisenberg, Azriel (ed). *Witness to the Holocaust: Personal and Eyewitness Accounts of the Holocaust, Resistance and Rebirth.* Princeton, NJ: Pilgrim Press, 1981.

Fenelon, Fania. *Playing For Time.* New York: Atheneum Publishers, 1977.

Ferderber-Salz, Bertha. *And the Sun Kept Shining....* New York: Holocaust Library, 1980.

Goldstein, Charles. *The Bunker.* New York: Atheneum Publishers, 1973.

Gruber, Ruth. *Haven: The Unknown Story of FDR and 1000 World War II Refugees.* New York: Putnam Publishing Group, 1983.

Hanover, Nathan. *Abyss of Despair.* Trans. by Abraham J. Mesch. New Brunswick, NJ: Transaction Books, 1983.

Hans, Gerda. *These Do I Remember: Fragments from the Holocaust.* Freeport, ME: Cumberland Press, 1982.

Hausner, Gideon. *Justice in Jerusalem.* New York: Schocken Books, Inc., 1978.

Kaplan, Chaim, and Katsch, Abraham. *Scroll of Agony: The Warsaw Diary of Chaim Kaplan.* New York: Macmillan-Collier, 1981.

Klein, Gerda. *All But My Life.* New York: Hill & Wang, Inc., 1971.

Kohner, Hanna. *Hanna and Walter: A Love Story.* New York: Random House, Inc., 1984.

Korenblit, Michael, and Janger, Kathleen. *Until We Meet Again.* New York: G.P. Putnam's Sons, 1983.

Lester, Elenore. *Wallenberg: The Man in the Iron Web.* Englewood Cliffs, NJ: Prentice-Hall, Inc., 1972.

Lustig, Arnost. *Dita Saxiva.* New York: Harper & Row Publishers, Inc., 1979.

Meir, Lili, and Hellman, Peter. *The Auschwitz Album.* New York: Random House, Inc., 1981.

Noren, Catherine. *The Camera of My Family.* New York: Alfred A. Knopf, Inc., 1976.

Pomerans, Arno (trans). *An Interrupted Life: The Diaries of Etty Hillesum 1941-1943.* New York: Pantheon Books, 1983.

Reisman, Arnold, and Reisman, Ellen. *Welcome Tomorrow.* Shaker Heights, OH: North Coast Publishing, 1983.

Ringelblum, Emmanuel. *Notes from the Warsaw Ghetto.* New York: Schocken Books, Inc., 1974.

Rose, Leesha. *The Tulips Are Red.* Granbury, NJ: A.S. Barnes & Co., 1978.

Rubenstein, Erna F. *The Survivor in Us All: A Memoir of the Holocaust.* Hamden, CT: Archon Books/Shoestring Press, 1983.

Senesh, Hannah. *Letters, Diary, Poems.* New York: Herzl Press, 1972.

Shochet, Simon. *Feldafing.* Vancouver, BC: November House, 1983.

Starkopt, Adam. *There is Always Time To Die.* New York: Holocaust Library, 1981.

Stiffel, Frank. *The Tale of the Ring: A Kaddish.* Wainscott, NY: Pushcart Press, 1984.

Tec, Nechama. *Dry Tears: The Story of a Lost Childhood.* Westport CT: Wildcat Publishing, Inc., 1982.

Temchin, Michael. *Memoirs of a Partisan.* New York: Holocaust Library, 1983.

Ten-Boom, Carrie. *The Hiding Place.* New York: Bantam Books, Inc., 1971.

Wiesel, Elie. *Night.* New York: Avon Books, 1960.

_____. *One Generation After.* New York: Avon Books, 1972.

Children of the Holocaust

Bergmann, Martin, and Jucovy, Milton (eds). *Generations of the Holocaust.* New York: Basic Books, Inc., 1982.

Eisenberg, Azriel (ed). *The Last Generation: Children in the Holocaust.* Princeton, NJ: Pilgrim Press, 1982.

Epstein, Helen. *Children of the Holocaust.* New York: Bantam, Books, Inc., 1980.

Lustig, Arnold. *Children of the Holocaust Series.* Washington, DC: Inscape Corporation, 1976.

Moskovitz, Sarah. *Love Despite Hate: Child Survivors of the Holocaust and Their Adult Lives.* New York: Schocken Books, Inc., 1983.

Steinitz, Lucy (ed). *Living After the Holocaust: Reflections by the Post-War Generation in America.* New York: Bloch Publishing Co., 1976.

Comprehensive Holocaust Histories

Dawidowicz, Lucy. *Holocaust Reader.* New York: Behrman House, Inc., 1976.

_____. *The War Against the Jews 1933-1945.* New York: Holt, Rinehart & Winston, Inc., 1975.

Hilberg, Raul. *The Destruction of European Jews.* New York: Harper & Row Publishers, Inc., 1979.

Levin, Nora. *The Holocaust.* Harper & Row Publishers, Inc., 1968.

Essay Collections

Bauer, Yehuda, and Rotenstreich, Nathan (eds). *The Holocaust as Historical Experience: Essays and Discussions.* New York: Holmes and Meier Publishers Inc., 1980.

Friedman, Philip. *Roads to Extinction: Essays on the Holocaust.* Edited by Ada June Friedman. Philadelphia: The Jewish Publication Society of America, 1980.

Klausner, Carla L., and Schultz, Joseph P. *From Destruction to Rebirth: The Holocaust and the State of Israel.* Washington, DC: University Press of America Inc., 1978.

Historical Novels, Poetry, and Short Stories

Agel, Jerome, and Boe, Eugene. *Deliverance in Shanghai.* New York: Dembner Books, 1983.

Aichinger, Ilse. *Herod's Children.* New York: Atheneum Publishers, 1963.

Ajar, Momo. *Momo.* New York: Doubleday & Co., Inc., 1978.

Appelfeld, Aharon. *In the Wilderness.* Jerusalem: Ah'shav Press, 1965.

_____. *Badenheim 1939.* Boston: David R. Godine, Publisher, 1980.

_____. *The Age of Wonders.* Boston: David R. Godine, Publisher, 1981.

_____. *Tzili: The Story of a Life.* New York: E.P. Dutton & Co. Inc., 1983.

Barowski, Taedeusz. *This Way to the Gas, Ladies and Gentlemen.* New York: Penguin Books, Inc., 1967.

Feuchtwanger, Lion. *The Oppermans.* New York: Carroll & Graf Publishers, Inc., 1960.

Heifetz, Julie. *Oral History and the Holocaust.* Elmsford, NY: Pergamon Press, Inc., 1985.

Herzberger, Magda. *The Waltz of the Shadows.* New York: Philosophical Library, 1983.

Karmel, Ilma. *An Estate of Memory.* Boston: Houghton Mifflin Co., 1969.

Katzenelson, Yitzhak. *The Song of the Murdered People.* Kibbutz Hameuchad, Israel: Ghetto Fighters' House, 1980.

Kosinski, Jerzy. *The Painted Bird.* New York: Bantam Books, Inc., 1965.

Levin, Ira. *Boys From Brazil.* New York: Dell Publishing Co., Inc., 1976.

Lustig, Arnost. *A Prayer for Katerina Horovitzova.* New York: Harper & Row Publishers, Inc., 1973.

Roskies, David. *Nightwords: A Midrash on the Holocaust.* Washington, DC: B'nai B'rith Hillel, no publication date.

Sachs, Nelly. *O the Chimneys.* New York: Farrar, Straus & Giroux, Inc., 1967.

Schwarz-Bart, Andre. *Last of the Just.* New York: Bantam Books, Inc., 1960.

Singer, Isaac Bashevis. *Shosha.* New York: Farrar, Straus & Giroux, Inc., 1978.

Uris, Leon. *Mila 18.* New York: Doubleday & Co., Inc., 1961.

Wiesel, Elie. *Ani Maamin: A Song Lost and Found Again.* New York: Random House, Inc., 1973.

_____. *The Town Beyond the Wall.* New York: Holt, Rinehart & Winston, Inc., 1967.

Wolfe, Henia. *The Baders of Jacob Street.* New York: J.B. Lippincott Co., 1970.

Wouk, Herman. *War and Remembrance.* Boston: Little, Brown & Company, 1978.

_____. *Winds of War.* Boston: Little, Brown & Company, 1971.

Holocaust and Art

"Art of the Holocaust." *Keeping Posted.* Vol. XXIII, No. 4. New York: Union of American Hebrew Congregations, January 1978.

Blatter, Janet, and Milton, Sybil. *Art of the Holocaust.* New York: W.H. Smith Publishers, Inc. 1981.

Green, Gerald. *The Artists of Terezin.* Illus. by the Inmates of Terezin. New York: Hawthorne Books, Inc., 1969.

Holocaust and Literature

Eliach, Yaffa. *Hasidic Tales of the Holocaust.* New York: Oxford University Press, 1982.

Ezrahi, Sidra DeKoven. *By Words Alone: The Holocaust in Literature.* Chicago: University of Chicago Press, 1980.

Kaliszan, Jozet. *The Warsaw Ghetto: Drawings.* Compiled and edited by Czeslaw Z. Banbasiewicz. New York: Thomas Yoseloff, 1968.

Langer, Lawrence. *The Holocaust and the Literary Imagination.* New Haven, CT: Yale University Press, 1975.

Yuter, Alan J. *The Holocaust in Hebrew Literature: From Genocide to Rebirth.* Port Washington, NY: Associated Press, 1983.

Jewish Resistance and Self-Government

Epstein, Leslie. *King of the Jews.* New York: Avon Books, 1980.

Suhl, Yuri (ed). *They Fought Back: The Story of the Jewish Resistance in Nazi Europe.* New York: Schocken Books, Inc., 1975.

Syrkin, Maria. *Blessed Is the Match: The Story of Jewish Resistance.* New York: Alfred A. Knopf, Inc., 1948.

Trunk, Isaiah. *Judenrat: The Jewish Councils of Eastern Europe Under Nazi Occupation.* New York: Macmillan Publishing Co., Inc., 1972.

Wiesel, Elie. *The Gates of the Forest.* New York: Avon Books, 1967.

Library and Teaching Resources

Altshuler, David. *Hitler's War Against the Jews.* New York: Behrman House, Inc., 1978.

Gestapo: A Learning Experience About the Holocaust. Denver: Alternatives in Religious Education, Inc., 1976.

Mlotek, Eleanor, and Gottlieb, Malke (eds). *We Are Here: 40 Songs of the Holocaust.* Trans. by Roslyn Bresnick Perry. New York: Workmん's Circle Book Department, 1983.

The Holocaust Library Series. New York: Anti-Defamation League of B'nai B'rith.

Stadtler, Bea. *The Holocaust: A History of Courage and Resistance.* New York: Behrman House, Inc., 1973.

Szonyi, David. *Selected Readings on the Holocaust.* New York: Jewish Book Council.

Life in the Concentration Camps

Berkovits, Eliezer. *With God in Hell: Judaism in the Ghettos and Deathcamps.* New York: Sanhedrin Press, 1979.

Des Pres, Terrence. *The Survivor: An Anatomy of Life in the Death Camps.* London: Oxford University Press, 1976.

Kogon, Eugene. *The Theory and Practice of Hell.* New York: Octagon Books, 1972.

Rawcz, Piotr. *Blood from the Sky.* Trans. by Peter Wiles. New York: Harcourt Brace and World, 1964.

Rothchild, Sylvia. *Voices of the Holocaust.* New York: New American Library, 1981.

Teaching the Holocaust: Resources and Materials. Culver City, CA: Social Studies School Service.

Nazi Hunting

Conot, Robert. *Justice at Nurenberg.* New York: Harper & Row Publishers, Inc., 1983.

Ryan, Allan A. *Quiet Neighbors: Prosecuting Nazi War Criminals in America.* New York: Harcourt Brace Jovanovich, Inc. 1984.

Wiesenthal, Simon. *Max and Helen.* New York: William Morrow & Co., Inc., 1982.

_____. *The Sunflower.* New York: Schocken Books, Inc., 1976.

Philosophy and Theology

Berenbaum, Michael. *The Vision of the Void: Theological Reflections on the Works of Elie Wiesel.* Middletown, CT: Wesleyan University Press, 1979.

Berkovits, Eliezer. *Faith After the Holocaust.* New York: KTAV Publishing House, Inc., 1973.

Bettelheim, Bruno. *The Informed Heart.* Glencoe, IL: Free Press of Glencoe, 1960.

Braham, Randolph L. (ed). *Contemporary Views on the Holocaust.* Dordorecht, Netherlands: Kluuer Publications, 1983.

Cargas, Harry (ed). *When God and Men Failed: Non-Jewish Views of the Holocaust.* New York: Macmillan Publishing Co., Inc., 1981.

Charny, Israel. *How We Commit the Unthinkable?: Genocide, the Human Cancer.* Boulder, CO: Westview Press, 1982.

Eckhardt, A. Roy, and Eckhardt, Alice. *Long Night's Journey Into Day: Life and Faith After the Holocaust.* Detroit, MI: Wayne State University Press, 1982.

Fackenheim, Emil. *The Jewish Return Into History: Reflections in the Age of Auschwitz and a New Jerusalem.* New York: Schocken Books, Inc., 1980.

_____. *To Mend the World: Foundations of Future Jewish Thought.* New York: Schocken Books, Inc., 1982.

Fein, Helen. *Accounting for Genocide: National Responses and Jewish Victimization During the Holocaust.* Glencoe, IL: Free Press, 1979.

Frankl, Viktor. *Man's Search For Meaning.* New York: Pocket Books, 1963.

Levi, Primo. *The Periodic Table.* New York: Schocken Books, Inc., 1984.

Maccoby, Hyman. *The Sacred Executioner: Human Sacrifices and the Legacy of Guilt.* London: Thames and Hudson, 1982.

Morse, Arthur. *While Six Million Died: A Chronicle of American Apathy.* New York: Overlook Press, 1966.

Neher, Andre. *The Exile of the Word: From the Silence of the Bible to the Silence of Auschwitz.* Trans. by David Maisel. Philadelphia: The Jewish Publication Society of America, 1981.

Rosenbaum, Irving. *The Holocaust and Halakhah.* New York: KTAV Publishing House, Inc., 1976.

Rosenfeld, Alvin. *A Double Dying: Reflections on the Holocaust.* Bloomington, IN: Indiana University Press, 1980.

Roskies, David G. *Against the Apocalypse: Responses to Catastrophe in Modern Jewish Culture.* Cambridge, Mass: Harvard University Press, 1984.

Rubenstein, Richard L. *After Auschwitz: Essays on Contemporary Jewish Theology.* New York: Bobbs-Merrill Co., Inc., 1966.

Sklar, Dusty. *Gods & Beasts: The Nazis and the Occult.* New York: Thomas Y. Crowell Co., 1977.

Wiesel, Elie. *Legends of Our Time.* New York: Holt, Rinehart & Winston, Inc., 1968.

Significant Places and Events

Ainsztein, Reuben. *Warsaw Ghetto Revolt.* New York: Schocken Books, Inc., 1979.

Flender, Harold. *Rescue in Denmark.* New York: Holocaust Library, 1980.

Gilbert, Martin. *The Macmillan Atlas of the Holocaust.* New York: Macmillan Publishing Co., Inc., 1982.

Grossman, Mendel. *With a Camera In The Ghetto.* Kibbutz Hameuched, Israel: Ghetto Fighters' House, 1972.

Hallie, Philip. *Lest Innocent Blood Be Shed: The Story of the Village of Le Chambon and How Goodness Happened There.* New York: Harper & Row Publishers, Inc., 1980.

Kielar, Wieslaw. *Anus Mundi: An Eyewitness Account of Auschwitz.* New York: Times Books, 1980.

Kranitz-Sanders, Lillian. *Twelve Who Survived: An Oral History of the Jews of Lodz, Poland.* New York: Irvington Publishers, 1983.

Kuznetsov, Anatoli. *Babi Yar: A Documentary Novel.* New York: Farrar, Straus & Giroux, Inc., 1970.

Lengyel, Olga. *Five Chimneys: The Story of Auschwitz.* New York: Howard Fertig, 1983.

Marrus, Michael, and Paxton, Robert. *Vichy France and the Jews.* New York: Basic Books, Inc., 1981.

Michaelis, Meir. *Mussolini and the Jews: German-Italian Relations and the Jewish Questions in Italy, 1922-1945.* London: Oxford University Press, 1979.

Patkin, Benzion. *The Dunera Internees.* Berkeley, CA: Benmir Books, 1983.

Penkower, Monty. *The Jews Were Expendable.* Champaign, IL: University of Illinois Press, 1984.

Steiner, Jean-Francois. *Treblinka.* New York: New American Library, 1979.

Thomas, Gordon, and Watts, Max. *Voyage of the Damned.* Briarcliff Manor, NY: Stein & Day, 1974.

Wyman, David. *The Abandonment of the Jews.* New York: Pantheon Books, 1984.

Israel

VI

Nothing in life just happens. It isn't enough to believe in something; you have to have the stamina to meet obstacles and overcome them, to struggle.
Golda Meir

OVERVIEW

How appropriate it is that through the combined realization of alphabetical order and long awaited destiny, a chapter on Israel follows immediately after one on the Holocaust. Nowhere is the tragedy and the miracle of Jewish history more poignantly affirmed than in the connection between these two events.

Yet, to fully appreciate the emotional intensity and grandeur of the Proclamation of the State of Israel on May 14, 1948, we must consider the event not only in relation to the Holocaust, but in light of the two thousand year struggle to establish a Jewish homeland — a struggle which dates back to God's covenant with Abraham that God would make of Abraham a great nation and that one day his descendants would inherit the Land of Israel.

The study of Israel is both fascinating and extremely important if teachers are to help children become a part of the very intimate and vital connection between the Jews of the *Yishuv* (Israel) and those of the Diaspora. However, to accomplish this, teachers must begin by acquainting students with each dimension of Israel: her geography, her history, her struggles, and the everyday lifestyles and special customs of her varied inhabitants. The songs, dances, creative arts, and language of her people must all be brought together in the learning experience if the study of Israel is to be complete.

Finally, the students must also be allowed to "taste" of the well earned name of "sabra" which native Israelis have bestowed upon themselves. By comparing Israelis to the sabra fruit, students can better understand that the Israelis' outer toughness is not a stereotype. It is, rather, a very necessary protection against the extreme internal and external forces with which they must cope each day. Perhaps the best description of the dynamic relationship between the characteristic spirit of Israelis and the forces which have shaped it may be found in *Midrash Genesis Rabbah* (39:1). There Israel is compared to a dove because "... other birds, when tired, rest on a branch; but when the dove tires, she rests one wing and flies with the other."

Certainly one woman who has helped Israel to soar is Golda Meir. Her biography, *The Golda Meir Story*, is included to serve as an inspiration for Jewish youth and also to illustrate the impact that this great leader had on the establishment of the State of Israel.

When one is asked to name the great artists of this century, the name of Marc Chagall is certain to be mentioned. Marc Chagall's many artistic contributions to the State of Israel are looked upon with great pride by the Jewish people. *Marc Chagall: Art for Children* is an excellent introduction to the life and work of this famous artist.

Unfortunately, since the Proclamation of the State of Israel, the country has frequently been at war. The negative effects of war on children cannot be understated. Yet, throughout the turbulance, children have managed to maintain their humanity and hope for a more peaceful future. In *Smoke Over Golan: A Novel of the 1973 Yom Kippur War*, the friendship between an Israeli and Syrian youth thrives in spite of the war between their nations. *My Shalom, My Peace* is a collection of poetry and paintings which reflect the emotions of Jewish and Arab children while their countries are at war.

Regardless of the battles, many Jews still choose to make their home in Israel. *The House in the Tree: A Story of Israel* provides a view of a young American boy adjusting to and learning about life in Israel. *Alina: A Russian Girl Comes to Israel* documents a Russian girl's life after she and her family emigrate from Russia.

Two of the books selected give an excellent view of contemporary Israel. *This is Israel* may serve as an introduction to the country. Reading the book gives the feeling of actually traveling through the land of Israel. The photographs in *The Children of Israel* allow the reader to share in experiencing the daily lives of children.

To appreciate contemporary Israel, one must know something of the history of the country. *The Story of Masada* is an impressive book which carries students back in history to a crucial struggle for Jewish survival. *Path of the Orange Peels: Adventures in the Early Days of Tel Aviv* is, just as the title suggests, an exciting adventure story. The plot allows students to experience life in Palestine during World War I.

ISRAEL: BOOKS AND ACTIVITIES

Cone, Molly. *The House in the Tree: A Story of Israel.* **Illus. by Symeon Shimin. Springfield, IL: Thomas Y. Crowell Co., 1968. 41 pages. Grade level: 2-4.**

A young boy is determined to build a tree house in Israel just like the one he had in the United States. This leads him on a journey which reveals many interesting aspects of his new homeland. Wood is scarce, but Yaacov, through his persistence and belief in miracles, secures the materials he needs to construct the house in a gnarled old olive tree. Realistic pen and ink drawings highlight Yaacov's new environment, as well as his quest to retain a small piece of his old way of life.

Major Ideas

"If you will it, it is no dream" (Herzl).
Like the sabra fruit, a tough exterior often shelters a compassionate heart.

Activities

1. Grades 2-4: Yaacov wished to create a tree house in Israel so as to have a special place just like the one he had in his old home. Students can create a special place in the classroom to be used for quiet reading or small group activities. Secure an appliance box large enough to seat two or three children comfortably. Position it in a well lit corner of your room. Cut one side of the box away for an entrance. You may want to cut a skylight hole at the top of the box. The box should be decorated by the students using drawings depicting Israeli themes. Examples of possible themes include:

   Scenes of important places in Israel.
   Plant and animal life.
   Religious celebrations.
   Israel at work and play.

   Following the completion of the "house," hold a special dedication ceremony during which a *mezzuzah* is affixed to the entrance. The blessing is as follows:

   ברוך אתה יי אלהינו מלך העולם אשר
   קדשנו במצותיו וצונו לקבוע מזוזה.

   Baruch Atah, Adonai Eloheynu, Melech Ha'olam, Asher Kid'shanu B'mitzvotav, Vitzivanu Likbo'a Mezzuzah.

   Blessed is the Eternal our God, Ruler of the Universe, who sanctifies us by Your commandments and commands us to affix a *Mezzuzah*.

   Remind the children that Yaacov was going to use his tree house for pleasurable activity and that they now will have such a house.

2. Grades 3 and 4: When Yaacov moved to Israel, he had to learn Hebrew. Have the students imagine that they are Yaacov wanting to learn the vocabulary related to each part of his special house. Teach all of your "Yaacovs" the following vocabulary:

house	bayit	בית
window	chalon	חלון
roof	gag	גג
mezzuzah	mezzuzah	מזוזה
wood	eytz	עץ
chimney tree	arubah	ארבה
wall	kir	קיר
ladder	sulam	סלם
mailbox	tayvat doar	תבת דואר
flowers	p'rachim	פרחים
grass	desheh	דשה
bird	tzipor	צפור
door	delet	דלת
branches	anafim	ענפים

   After the words have been taught, play a vocabulary reinforcement game. Prepare the game as follows:

   a. Trace the tree house design in Diagram 7 onto a stencil.

   b. Make enough copies for twice the number of students in the class.

   c. Put aside one copy for each member of the class.

   d. Cut the remaining copies along the dotted lines as depicted in Diagram 8. Make sure to write the appropriate Hebrew name on each piece. Pieces may be decorated in color if desired.

   e. Place the pieces of each complete house in separate envelopes.

   f. Now you are ready to play the game with the students. Follow the steps in g., h., and i.

   g. Give each student an intact picture of the treehouse and a set of the pieces.

   h. Tell the students that when you call out an English word, they must hold up the piece on which the Hebrew translation is written without looking around at their classmates. Then, they may place it in the corresponding space on the picture. Once the students become proficient, you may wish to add novelty to the game by creating riddles about each piece.

Israel

Diagram 7

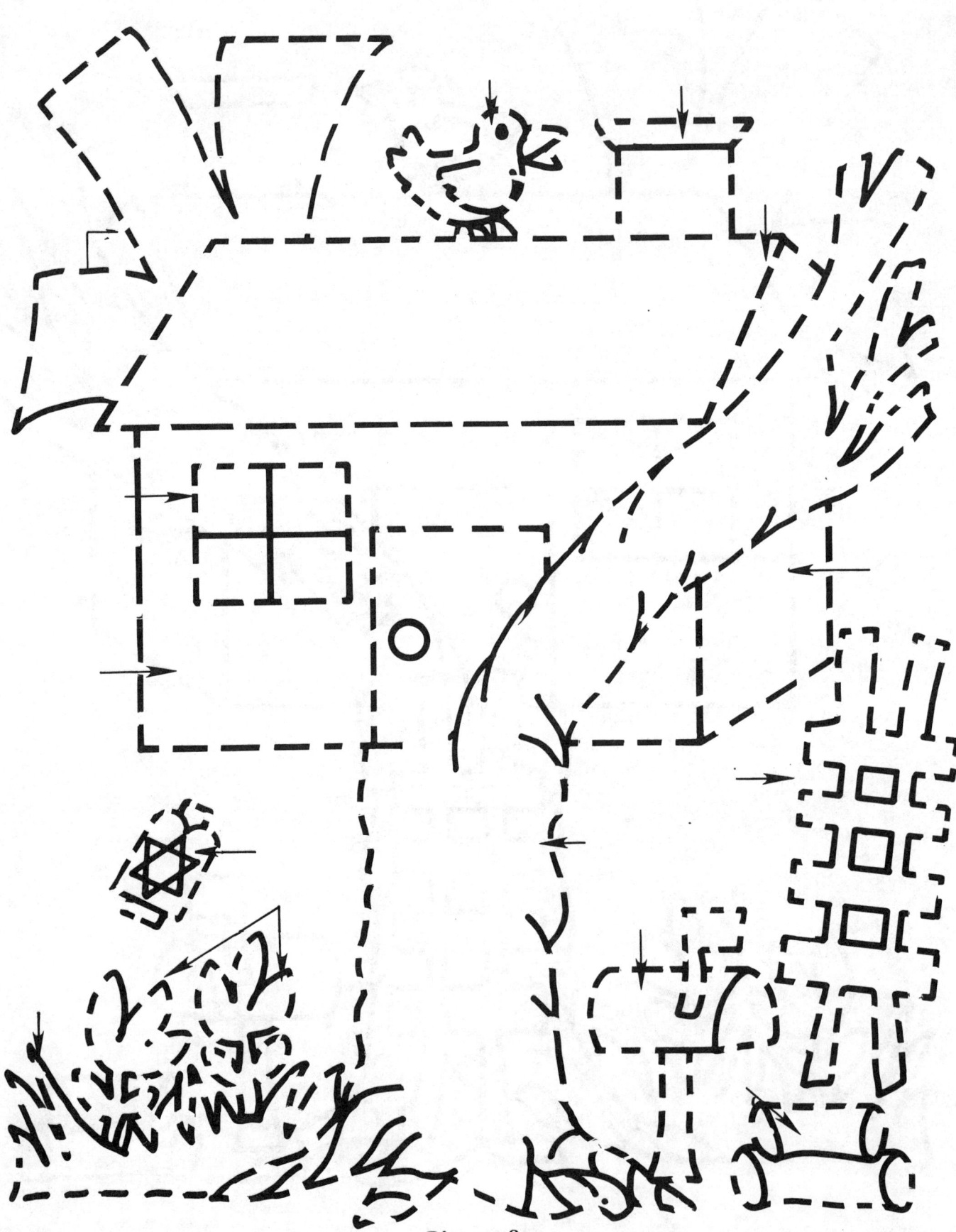

Diagram 8

i. The game ends when one or more of the students has completed the house.

3. Grades 2-4: Yaacov's effort to build a treehouse is an example of Theodor Herzl's maxim that "If you will it, it is no dream." Explain to the students that Herzl made this remark in reference to the long and difficult struggle involved in creating a Jewish homeland in Israel. In celebration of Yaacov's fulfillment of his dream in the Land of Israel, teach the song "*Im Tirtzu*" to the students. This song may be found on Debbie Friedman's Album, *Ani Ma-amin* (Sing Unto God). Words, music and lyrics.

Davidson, Margaret. *The Golda Meir Story*. Revised Edition. New York: Charles Scribner's Sons, 1981. 228 pages. Grade level: 4-7.

Golda Meir's life from Russia to Milwaukee and finally to Israel is dramatically retold in this book. The use of dialogue throughout the book and the special emphasis placed on Golda's early growing experiences create a story of particular interest for young readers. In addition, one can actually feel the struggles and joys of this remarkable woman's quest to establish a Jewish homeland. Davidson has written a biography which can serve as an inspiration for all who read it.

Major Ideas

Childhood experiences have a profound influence on the kind of person one becomes.

It is important not merely to establish goals, but to actually pursue them.

Golda Meir possessed qualities to which we should all aspire.

Activities

1. Grades 5-7: A page from Golda's high school yearbook is reproduced in *The Golda Meir Story*. In addition to listing some of her high school activities, the text beside her name reads "Those about her shall read the perfect ways of honor." Golda is one of the many important figures in the life and history of Israel. Have the students research the lives of other prominent Israelis. These may include political figures, poets, artists, writers, war heroes, religious leaders, and so on. After the research is completed, have the students create a separate page about their chosen figure for a "yearbook" entitled "Stars of Israel." One student should do a page for Golda. Students may draw pictures of stars, using source books as a basis. Each class member can create an original quote focusing on the virtues of his/her star. Compile the pages in a looseleaf binder for easy viewing. Place the yearbook in the Children's Biography or Israel section of the school library.

2. Grades 4-7: After discussing Golda's life and her accomplishments and contributions to the State of Israel, have each student design a coin to commemorate Golda Meir. Use an 8" piece of white circular cardboard. Allow the students the freedom of choosing their own medium. The coins may then be hung from the ceiling with string.

3. Grades 4-7: The highlight of Golda's life was her participation in the ceremony to proclaim the State of Israel. Signing her name to the Proclamation of Independence was her most memorable experience. As she listened to the speeches being made, memories of her life came to mind. In preparation for an upper grade school assembly program about Israel, or as part of a Yom HaAtzma'ut celebration, have each student in the class write one or two sentences about Golda's life beginning with "I remember when . . ." or "I remember the time . . ." The teacher should make sure that each student has selected a different event. If the class is large, students may need to work on one event in pairs. At the assembly program, the students can recite the events on stage, in chronological order. At the end of the presentations, one student, acting as Golda, can step forward and sign Golda's name to a large Proclamation of Independence which has been displayed prominently in the auditorium. At this point, the entire assembly should be asked to rise and sing "*Hatikvah*." Suggest to other teachers that they teach "*Hatikvah*" to their students before the assembly. Music may be found in *Israel in Song*, compiled, edited, and arranged by Velvel Pasternak.

Grand, Samuel, and Grand, Tamar. *The Children of Israel*. Illus. by Ilona Frankel. New York: Union of American Hebrew Congregations, 1972. 55 pages. Grade level: 2-4.

The Grands have created a sweeping panorama depicting the lives of Israeli children. Children are shown engaging in everyday activities, holiday celebrations, nature hikes, and explorations in the city of Jerusalem. Through photographs and the integration of Hebrew into the English narrative, the authors have captured the vibrant spirit of Israel.

Major Ideas

The lifestyles of Israeli children and American children are different, yet similar.

The lifestyles of Israeli children vary from place to place within the country itself.

Activities

1. Grades 2-4: One chapter of the book is entitled "The children of Israel at School." In this chapter we learn that after students' academic activities are finished,

many schools remain open as community centers for hobby groups. Some of the hobbies listed are folk dancing, reading, stamp collecting, and crafts. Plan a special day for your class in which the students will participate in activities similar to those engaged in by the children in this book. Activities can include:

- Israeli dancing
- Israeli singing
- Reading center with Hebrew books. (Many American favorites such as the Dr. Seuss books are now available in Hebrew.)
- Israeli games

The day should be organized so that each student has time to participate in all of the activities. A room larger than your classroom will most likely be required.

2. Grades 3 and 4: The chapter on Jerusalem shows a young boy praying at the Western Wall (*HaKotel*). It is customary for visitors to the Western Wall to write a prayer or a message on a piece of paper to be placed in a space between the stones. To allow your students to participate symbolically in this custom, arrange with a class of your students' age in Jerusalem to act as *shlichim* (messengers) for your students. To find a class willing to participate, contact the Jewish National Fund, 42 East 69th Street, New York, NY 10021. Once the class is selected, have a list of the names of the children in the class sent to you so that your students may have a pen pal. Along with the first letter your students write, enclose a message (on a very small piece of paper) to be placed in the Western Wall. Request of the pen pal that the message be "delivered."

3. Grades 2-4: Israelis, as it is noted in this book, take special pride in their natural environment. Hiking is a regular school activity. Arrange for the students to go on a nature hike for half a day. If you wish, take along a picnic lunch and, as depicted in the book, bring musical instruments for a sing-along. If this activity is used in a day school, you may wish to integrate the hiking activities with a science unit.

Gutman, Nahum. *Path of the Orange Peels: Adventures in the Early Days of Tel Aviv.* **Trans. from the Hebrew by Nelly Segal. Illus. by the author. New York: Dodd, Mead and Co., 1979. 140 pages. Grade level: 5 and up.**

Nahum Gutman has written a lively piece of fiction set during World War I in Palestine. The reader is introduced to the main character Nahum as he announces, "I always put my shoes on joyfully, happy to welcome a new day." Yet, this will be a difficult day, for Nahum must leave Petach-Tikvah because Turkish soldiers are forcing young men to join their army. Nahum's grandmother sends him off to Tel Aviv, telling him that along the way he will find oranges to eat. During his journey, a strange man tells him that he must look for orange peels instead and recruits Nahum in the search for a briefcase labeled "When All Hope Is Lost." So begins Nahum's mysterious adventures. Humorous cartoon illustrations and fast paced narrative add to the fun and suspense of this tale.

Major Ideas

Survival sometimes involves choosing to carry on with a mission even in the face of danger.

"What can be done... must be done" (Nahum Gutman).

Activities

1. Grades 5 and up: Nahum begins and ends his story with the motto "I always put my shoes on joyfully, happy to welcome a new day." This is illustrated with a cartoon style drawing depicting a bird perched on a boot, singing a happy tune. Keeping in mind that it was Nahum's type of dedication that helped the Jews to survive and Israel to be established, have the students discuss how Nahum's motto reflects their own personal Jewish beliefs and sense of commitment. Then ask the students to think up an original motto which characterizes their personality, and the way they live their lives. The mottos should be printed on individual banners with a cartoon illustration appropriate to the motto's theme. These can be used as desk decorations or hung in their bedrooms. In small groups, discuss how each student's motto reflects his/her Jewish beliefs and commitment.

2. Grades 5 and 6: The path of orange peels serves as a symbol to Nahum for "doing things that could be done and must be done." Have the students sit in a circle and eat oranges. As they eat, each student must formulate an idea for one thing he/she can do to make the world a better place in which to live. As an extra treat that can later serve as a reminder of the students' ideas, the peels from their oranges can be candied, dipped in chocolate, and eaten another day.

3. Grades 5 and up: The book is set in the early days of Tel Aviv. Before the story actually begins, the author presents the reader with four drawings illustrating how Tel Aviv looked in the early part of this century. As an update for the class, arrange to borrow slides from someone who has been to Israel and organize a slide presentation of Tel Aviv today. (This would be a perfect time to serve the candied orange peels!)

Meir, Mira. *Alina: A Russian Girl Comes to Israel.* Photo. by Yael Rozen. Trans. from the Hebrew by Zeba Shapiro. Philadelphia: The Jewish Publication Society of America, 1982. 48 pages. Grade level: 2-4.

This photo-documentary tells the story of a young Russian immigrant's adjustment to her new life in Israel. Language and cultural barriers contribute to Alina's sense of loneliness and frustration when she first arrives. Once Alina accepts the friendship extended to her by her classmates, she begins to enjoy exploring the curiosities of her new environment. Alina's strong identification with Israel as her homeland becomes apparent near the end of the story when she announces to her friends that she would like to be called Ilana which, in Hebrew, means a new tree. Finally, Ilana is shown befriending Sonia, who has just arrived from Russia.

Major Ideas

In order to find acceptance from others, one must also make an effort to reach out.

Israel is home to all Jews.

Adjusting to a new environment is challenging, yet rewarding.

Activities

1. Grades 2-4: Alina must become accustomed to Middle Eastern cuisine when she immigrates to Israel. To give the students the flavor of such delicacies, plan a luncheon at which the following foods are served:

   > falafel in pita bread (falafel mixes are available at grocery stores and delicatessens)
   > chopped cucumber and tomato salad
   > techina and humus
   > sabra fruit (sometimes available in the gourmet vegetable section of grocery stores)
   > halvah

   These should be served in small portions, as the flavors are quite different from those to which students are accustomed. The students may help in the preparation of the foods.

2. Grade 4: Before Alina learned Hebrew, the language differences created a barrier between her and the Israeli children. Have the students imagine that they are Israeli children who must create a picture dictionary to help Alina learn Hebrew. Each student will be responsible for one page in the dictionary. If the class is large, the students may work on one page in pairs. Each page will deal with a specific theme. Possible major themes to be included are:

   > members of the family
   > transportation
   > meal time
   > the grocery store
   > the classroom
   > parts of the body
   > clothing
   > colors
   > numbers
   > weather and seasons

   The number of items drawn on each page may vary according to the ages of the students, with older students able to include more vocabulary. Students should draw their pictures on dittos. Once the pictures are completed, each item should be labeled in Hebrew and Russian. The teacher should have Hebrew-English and Russian-English dictionaries on hand so that parent volunteers, together with the teacher, can help with the labeling. When each page is completed, run off enough copies for each student in the class. Bind each dictionary in a softcovered, loose leaf binder. Students may then keep the dictionaries for personal use.

3. Grades 2-4: Alina learns from a teacher that "Israelis are not always polite . . . they're known to be tough on the outside, but soft on the inside, like the sabra fruit." Ask the students to discuss how they, too, are like the sabra fruit. Then have them draw an X-ray picture of themselves with the sweet qualities written inside the figure and their less polite traits written around the outside. Display these on a bulletin entitled "Don't Forget to Look Inside!"

Ofek, Uriel. *Smoke Over Golan: A Novel of the 1973 Yom Kippur War in Israel.* Illus. by Lloyd Bloom. New York: Harper & Row Publishers, Inc. 1979. 184 pages. Grade level: 4-7.

When Eitan's family moves to a farm on the Golan Heights near the Syrian border, the young boy views the move as an inviting opportunity to become familiar with a strange, new environment. Israel is at peace and there is much time to be spent studying and tending to farm chores, both of which Eitan enjoys. What contributes even more to Eitan's pleasurable existence is two friendships he makes. The first is with Saleem, a young Syrian boy who often sneaks over the border to visit. The second is with Asher'ke, a soldier from a nearby Israeli army post. Eitan's simple life is shattered on a day when he is left alone on the farm, and the 1973 Yom Kippur War begins. Finally, following the violent war, Eitan is driven into an abandoned village in Syria to search for his young friend Saleem. When Saleem is found, Eitan realizes that the war has not come between them. Ofek has written an excellent adventure story with a message of peace and friendship.

Major Ideas

Sometimes the friendship between children can serve as a model for adults who are striving for peace.

Necessity can often lead to extraordinary resourcefulness and courage.

Activities

1. Grades 4-7: One of the themes of this book is hope for peace between Israel and the Arab nations. Many of the songs which have been written during and after Arab and Israeli wars speak of the strong desire for a peaceful future. One such song is "*Bashanah Haba'ah*." The song is a lively one which students enjoy singing. The music may be found in *Israel in Song*, edited and arranged by Velvel Pasternak. The song is on the album *El Al Songs of Israel* (Hed Arzi).

2. Grades 4-7: When Eitan and Saleem greet one another or say goodbye, they use the Hebrew and Arabic words for peace, *Shalom* and *Salaam*. It is evident from the story that Eitan and Saleem are crusaders for peace. Not even a war can come between their friendship. Tell half of the class that they are Eitan and the other half that they are Salaam. Give each student a 2" blank circular button with pins affixed to the back, such as those used during a political campaign. These may be obtained at a craft store or through companies that specialize in slogan buttons. The Eitans will design a peace button using the word "*Saleem*." The Saleems will design a peace button using the word "*Shalom*." First, have the students work out a design on scratch paper. The design should then be traced onto a paper disk the size of the button and decorated using permanent felt markers. After the disk is glued to the button, spray with fixative and wear proudly.

3. Grades 6 and 7: Both Eitan and Saleem are interviewed by reporters when they meet at Saleem's abandoned village. To have the students more fully explore the impact of war on people, videotape a mock television documentary in which the students, acting as various individuals affected by the 1973 Yom Kippur War, are interviewed. Suggestions for roles follow:

    news reporters
    Israeli soldiers
    Israeli children in an underground shelter
    a parent whose child has died
    a wife whose husband has been wounded
    Arabs forced to flee their village
    doctors and nurses at a field hospital
    Saleem, who has chosen to remain in his village even though his parents have fled
    Eitan, who travels to find Saleem

Assign roles to the students a week before the videotaping. Tell the news reporters who they will be interviewing so they may prepare questions and write a short introduction to the interview. Ask the other students to think about the impact that the war has had on their character. Send letters home to parents telling them about the project and asking their cooperation in discussing with their children the topic to be videotaped. The letter should also invite them to class to view the documentary together with their children. On the day of the taping, set up the equipment in another room so that the finished product will be a surprise for the children. An adult volunteer may operate the video camera. During class time, permit students to go to the taping room one at a time for their part to be taped. Urge them to take their roles seriously. Leave time for discussion after the tape is shown. Ask parents who have had actual war experiences to share them with the class. Note: If videotaping equipment is not available, this activity may be done as an on the spot class drama activity.

Raboff, Ernest. *Marc Chagall: Art for Children.* **Edited by Bradley Smith. Illus. by Marc Chagall and the author. New York: Doubleday & Co., Inc. 27 pages. Grade level: 3-6.**

Raboff has created an interesting introduction to the art of Marc Chagall whose Judaically informed works appear in Israel and throughout the world. The book is comprised of a brief biographical sketch followed by pictures and descriptions of the artist's work. The format of the book is colorful and inviting.

Major Idea

All of one's life experiences are a potential source of inspiration for creative expression.

Activities

1. Grades 4-6: After sharing the book with the students, tell them that Marc Chagall's stained glass windows of the Twelve Tribes of Israel beautifully adorn the chapel of Hadassah Hospital in Jerusalem. Show pictures of the windows, and have the students create their own stained glass windows. The windows should be designed on Jewish themes such as Bible stories, holidays, or Israel. Materials and procedure follow.

Materials:

black construction paper
scissors
felt marker (water repellent)
powdered tempera
liquid starch
1" paint brushes

Procedure:

a. Plan a design on scratch paper.

b. Using a marker, transfer the design onto a window in the classroom or another place in the school (to be decided on earlier by the teacher and principal).

c. Glue thin strips of black construction paper over the marker lines.

d. Mix tempera with equal amounts of liquid starch. Using a sponge, fingers, or brushes, fill in the spaces inside the black lines.

2. Grades 3-6: The last painting in the book is entitled "The Fiddler." The author of the book tells the reader that the fiddler is Chagall's favorite uncle. He also informs us that Chagall, to show the viewer that he enjoyed his uncle's music ("when he was small, when he was growing up and when he was a young man"), painted himself with three heads observing his uncle's playing. While showing this painting, be sure to point out the techniques Chagall used to focus attention on the fiddler. The techniques include:

   positioning the figure in a central location.
   exaggerating the size of the figure in relation to other parts of the composition.
   lighting the houses as if the people within have been listening to the music.

   Ask the students to think about a relative or older friend who has been special to them. Have each student articulate what particular trait or talent attracts them to this relative. Then, using Chagall's techniques, have them paint a picture of their relative engaged in utilizing the special trait or talent. The students should also include a three-headed visual representation of themselves in the painting, just as Chagall did in "The Fiddler."

3. Grades 3-6: One of the paintings included in this book is "Midsummer Night's Dream" based on the play by William Shakespeare. In the play, a man who is loved is turned into a donkey. The author calls the reader's attention to Chagall's depiction of a donkey's head atop a man's body. This image appears alongside a green clown playing a fiddle. Raboff suggests that Chagall may be saying that people, even though animals, have the ability within them to be clowns, lovers, and musicians. Ask the students to imagine that they are part human, part animal, part clown, and part musician. Have them do an oil pastel drawing of themselves as this four-part being. Display these on a bulletin board entitled "Clowning Around with Chagall."

Sasek, Miroslav. *This is Israel*. Illus. by Miroslav Sasek. New York: Macmillan Publishing Company, Inc. 1962. 60 pages. Grade level: K-4.

Vibrant illustrations and bold text carry the students on a journey through the land of Israel. The illustrations are a particularly inviting feature of this book. Their effect is to make readers feel as if they are actually wandering about the land. The author's humor and incorporation of biblical passages adds other pleasurable dimensions to the book. A poignant description of the Land of Israel concludes the book: "The wilderness and solitary place shall be glad for them; and the desert shall rejoice and blossom . . . " (Isaiah 35:1).

Major Ideas

Israel is the cradle of three civilizations: Judaism, Christianity, and Islam.

The creation of a state by Jews from diverse backgrounds was a difficult and miraculous task.

Israel is characterized by a rich combination of old and new.

A variety of different customs and people may be found as one travels through Israel.

Activities

1. Grades K-4: Teach some Israeli folkdances. The following are excellent records to use:

   Hora-Oranim Zabar Troop (Elektra Records).

   Israeli Folk Dance Medley. Dances for Children from Nine to Ninety (Tikvah Records T106).

   Rikuday-American Israeli Folk Dances (Tikvah Recording 138).

2. Grades 2-4: One of the most popular sights in old Jerusalem is the Arab *shuk* (market). Students can enjoy the atmosphere of the market in their own classroom. Have them create handicraft items (i.e., bookmarks, pot holders, paper flowers) to be bartered for. Students should decorate boxes to be used as store fronts and they can design costumes to be worn to the market. Nuts and raisins should be available as the means of exchange. You are now ready to open the market.

3. Grades K-4: The geography of Israel is varied and interesting. Use creative movement to develop a feeling of a journey through the land. Have the students push back their desks. Tell them to find a place of their own within the available space and to get ready for a marvelous trip through the Land of Israel. The narration should include walking through the hot desert, climbing Masada and Mt. Sinai, floating in the Dead Sea, walking through the Judean Hills up to Jerusalem, splashing in the Mediterranean, and so on.

Yadin, Yigael. *The Story of Masada.* Retold for children by Gerald Gottlieb. Photo. by the author. New York: Random House, Inc., 1969. 151 pages. Grade level: 5 and up.

The story of Masada unfolds as Gottlieb retells the fascinating details of an archaeological dig at the site. The narrative, which describes how the Zealots fought against the Romans and chose suicide rather than defeat, is exciting and inspiring. Photographs of the archaeological dig bring to life the historical reality of the event and help the reader to understand the process of archaeology.

Major Ideas

Masada is a symbol of strength and endurance for the country of Israel and the Jewish people.

Archaeology provides an important means of linking the past, present, and future.

Activities

1. Grades 5 and up: The Zealots chose suicide rather than defeat at the hands of the Romans. As suicide is a very serious topic, a discussion of the Zealots' decision should take place after the students have read the book. Possible discussion questions are:

    Why do you suppose the Zealots chose suicide over life under Roman rule?

    If you had been there, what would your choice have been, and why?

    What do you think the Romans were thinking when they finally reached the top of Masada and found the Zealots dead?

2. Grades 5 and up: Thanks to the efforts of Yigael Yadin and his archaeological team, we have been able to learn much about Masada and the saga of the Zealots. Suggest to the students that people many years from now may wonder about how they lived. Tell the students that one way of helping our descendants learn about us would be to bury a time capsule containing various items which we use or enjoy in our everyday lives. The capsule can be made of ceramic and buried on the school or synagogue grounds. Make sure that some of the items reflect the Jewish facets of their lives. Secure permission from the director of the facility to place a plaque on the wall reading:

    The Class of _____ (year) has buried a capsule containing relics of their lives. The capsule is located _____. Retrieve in year _____ (100 years from the date of burial).

3. Grades 6 and up: Before doing this next activity, check to make sure that permission will be granted. Masada has come to serve as a symbol of strength and survival for the Jewish people. This concept is expressed in the slogan "Masada will never fall again." In Israel this slogan is particularly meaningful. One way that Jews in the Diaspora help Israel to remain a strong Jewish homeland is through fund raising efforts. Write a class letter to the principal. Ask if the entire school can participate in a walk-a-thon entitled "The Masada-thon," with proceeds to be donated to charitable causes in Israel. If given the go ahead, the class should choose a date and route for the walk-a-thon and design an announcement to be reproduced. The flyers should be sent home with all students in the school. Announcements should also be printed in the school newspaper, synagogue bulletin, and Jewish newspaper. In addition to the flyer, give each student a pledge sheet on which supporters write their names and the amount they will donate for each mile the student walks.

Zim, Jacob (ed). *My Shalom My Peace. Paintings and Poems by Jewish and Arab Children.* Translated by Don Vardi. Selected by Uriel Ofek. New York: McGraw-Hill Book Co., 1975. 97 pages. Grade level: 3 and up.

This collection of poetry and paintings reflects the experiences of children growing up during the 1973 Yom Kippur War. Their anguish, as well as their hopes for a more peaceful future, are movingly expressed.

Major Ideas

War has varying effects on people.

The benefits of peaceful coexistence are worth striving for.

Activities

1. Grades 6 and up: This is an excellent book to share out loud with an entire class of upper elementary or junior high students. The oral reading will prepare them to participate in a multi-media slide presentation incorporating poetry and illustrations from the book, along with the students' original work. To facilitate this, the following steps are suggested.

    a. Assign each student either a poem or a picture from the book. The poems will be illustrated by individual students. The emotions and experiences depicted in the paintings will serve as springboards for the creation of original poetry.

    b. After the student assignments are completed, ask them to find a piece of music which conveys the mood of their work.

    c. Decide with the students the order in which the paintings and the poems should be presented in the program.

d. Have the students recite either their original poem or the poem from the book into a cassette tape recorder, while their selected piece of music is playing softly in the background.

   e. Using film that will produce slides, photograph the paintings that were assigned from the book, as well as the students' art work.

   f. Place the slides in the carousel in the order decided upon by the class in step c.

   g. Invite the students' parents to the slide presentation.

2. Grades 5 and up: Older students will find writing proposals for peace in the Middle East to be a challenging activity. Tell the students that they will be writing peace proposals in small groups. The proposals will be displayed in the hall on a bulletin board entitled "Our Shalom, Our Peace — The Choice is Yours." Next to the display, provide ballots and a collection box so that students in the upper grades may vote for the proposal of their choice. Tabulate the ballots. The winning proposal and a picture of its writers can be published in the school's paper or the local Jewish newspaper.

3. Grades 3 and up: To reinforce further the theme of peace, teach the song "*Oseh Shalom*." The traditional melody may be found in *Israel in Song*, compiled, edited, and arranged by Velvel Pasternak. A contemporary version of "*Oseh Shalom*" may be found on Debbie Friedman's album *And the Youth shall See Visions* (Sing Unto God). Words and music are in the accompanying songbook.

ISRAEL: BOOKS FOR CHILDREN

Adler, David. *Picture Book of Israel*. Illus. with Photo. New York: Holiday House, Inc., 1984. Grade level: K-3.

Through black and white photographs and brief narrative, Adler takes young children on a fascinating journey through the Land of Israel.

Adler, David. *Our Golda: The Story of Golda Meir*. Illus. by Donna Ruff. New York: Viking Press, Inc., 1984. Grade level: 3-4.

Adler's account of Golda Meir's life holds special appeal for children. It focuses on the early experiences which helped to shape the heroine's character and on her ultimate participation in the establishment of the State of Israel. Line drawings highlight the most memorable moments in Golda Meir's life.

Ameri, Heder. *1000 Milim Rishonot: A Hebrew-English Picture Dictionary*. Illus. by Steven Cartwright. Israel: Massada Press Ltd., 1980. Grade level: 3 and up.

Ameri and Cartwright's collaboration has resulted in a Hebrew-English dictionary that is easy to use and a visual treat. It is both practical and whimsical in its coverage of vocabulary.

Arnold, Paula. *Paula Arnold's Israel Nature Notes*. Illus. by Meir Ronnen and Brakha Avigad. Haifa, Israel: Shalit Publishers, Ltd., 1965. Grade level: 6 and up.

This volume contains entertaining and informative excerpts from Paula Arnold's column "Nature Notes," which appeared in *The Jerusalem Post* in the 1950s and 60s. The selections are arranged in chapters from January through December and are accompanied by humorous illustrations.

Aved, Joe. *Ami*. New York: Shengold Publications, Inc., 1981. Grade level: 6 and up.

Aved's novel is a gripping fictional account of the infant daughter of an Israeli army officer who is kidnapped and raised by a Palestinian terrorist.

Avner, Yehuda. *The Young Inheritors: A Portrait of Israel's children*. Photo. by Gemma Levine. New York: Dial Press, 1982. Grade level: K and up.

A magnificent photographic essay on Israel's children which portrays them in their everyday lives in locations throughout the country.

Banai, Margalit. *Yael and the Queen of Goats*. Illus. by Friedel. Tel Aviv: Sabra Books, 1968. Grade level: 1-3.

Israeli twins traveling south to Eilat take their readers on a wonderful tour of Israel.

Bergman, Denise, and Williams, Lorna. *Through the Year in Israel*. Illus. with photo. London: Batsford Academic and Educational Ltd., 1983. Grade level: 6 and up.

Holidays are the prime focus of this joyous celebration of Jewish life in Israel.

Berkman, Ted. *Cast a Giant Shadow: The Story of Mickey Marcus*. Philadelphia: The Jewish Publication Society of America, 1967. Grade level: 5 and up.

Mickey Marcus was a West Point graduate who died in the battle to save Jerusalem during Israel's War of Independence. This action packed biography is a take-off on the original adult version that was made into a movie.

Biber, Yehoash. *Adventures in the Galilee*. Philadelphia: The Jewish Publication Society of America, 1973. Grade level: 6 and up.

These short stories capture the adventurous quality of life in the Galilee settlements of Palestine during the time of the British Mandate. The courage and persistence of the *Yishuv* settlers in reclaiming the land is depicted with moving clarity.

Burstein, Chaya. *What's an Israel?* Illus. by the author. Rockville, MD: Kar-Ben Copies, Inc., 1983. Grade level: 1-4.

Burstein brings Israel alive for children in this fun filled book of activities, games, stories, pictures, and interesting facts about Israel. An excellent approach to the concept of learning through active participation.

Chaikin, Miriam. *Joshua and the Promised Land*. Illus. by David Frampton. New York: Clarion Books, 1982. Grade level: 3 and up.

> The many sides of Joshua's character as a leader, warrior, family man, and friend are evident in this dramatic account of how he led the ancient Israelites in conquering the Promised Land. Frampton's bold woodcuts beautifully enhance Chaikin's narrative.

Comay, Jean. *Ben-Gurion and the Birth of Israel*. New York: Random House, Inc., 1967. Grade level: 5-8.

> This novel is filled with the hopes, struggles, and successes of David Ben-Gurion's life from the time he came to Palestine from Russia in the early 1900s through the birth of the State of Israel.

Comay, Jean. *The Temple of Jerusalem*. Illus. with photo. New York: Holt, Rinehart & Winston, Inc., 1975. Grade level: 6 and up.

> Photographs and diagrams complement this very readable historical narrative about the First Temple in Jerusalem, built during the reign of King Solomon. The description of the Temple's structure, why and how it was built, and how it was used provides a fascinating look at ancient Jewish religious customs.

Dobin, Arnold. *A Life for Israel*. New York: Dial Press, 1974. Grade level: 3-4.

> Dobin provides children with a dynamic look at Israel as seen through the eyes of Golda Meir, late Prime Minister and influential founder of the country.

Edwardson, Cordelia. *Miriam Lives in a Kibbutz*. Photo. by Anna Riwkin-Brick. New York: Lothrop, Lee & Shepard Books, 1971. Grade level: 2-4.

> Miriam is a young immigrant living on a *kubbutz*. Life on the *kibbutz* and Miriam's adjustment process are described through narrative and photographs.

Eisenberg, Azriel, and Globe, Leah (eds). *Home at Last*. New York: Bloch Publishing Co., 1977. Grade level: 6 and up.

> This powerful collection contains sixteen stories about the efforts of Jews to return to Zion.

Eisenberg, Azriel, and Globe, Leah (eds). *Sabra Children*. New York: Jonathan David Publishers, Inc., 1979. Grade level: 3-5.

> The twenty-five short stories in this book provide a rare glimpse at the many facets of Israeli children's lives. By allowing young readers to compare and contrast their lives with their Israeli peers, this book helps to establish a vital link between Jews of the Diaspora and Israel.

Elkins, Dov. *Shepherd of Jerusalem: A Biography of Rabbi Abraham Isaac Kook*. New York: Shengold Publications, Inc., 1976. Grade 6 and up.

> Elkins retells the life story of the beloved Rabbi Abraham Isaac Kook. Kook, known for his great sensitivity and scholarly abilities, served as Chief Rabbi of Jerusalem during the first half of this century.

Ellis, Harry. *Israel: One Land, Two Peoples*. New York: Thomas Y. Crowell Co., 1972. Grade level: 6 and up.

> Ellis' exploration of the Israeli and Arab claims to the Land of Israel is both informative and interesting.

Elon, Amos. *Understanding Israel*. New York: Behrman House, Inc., 1976. Grade level: 6 and up.

> A very readable and intriguing social studies style book about life in Israel from the perspective of a prominent Israeli writer.

Feder Tal, Karah. *The Stone of Peace*. New York: Abelard Press, 1961. Grade level: 5 and up.

> This is an engaging and heartwarming story about the friendship between a Moroccan Jewish boy and an Arab boy in Israel. The ideal of a true and lasting peace between Israel and her Arab neighbors is eloquently symbolized through the boys' friendship.

Frankel, Max, and Hoffman, Judy. *I Live in Israel*. New York: Behrman House, Inc., 1979. Grade level: 3-5.

> With a child as guide, the reader is taken on a lively tour of Israel. Major sites and aspects of Israeli culture are highlighted in this combined activity textbook.

Gordon, Ayala. *Children of the World Paint Jerusalem*. New York: Bantam Books, Inc., 1978. Grade level: K and up.

Page after page of this brightly colored exhibit unite the artistic talent of young artists with the universal appeal of Jerusalem.

Gould, Jean and Maurice. *The Story of Israel in Coins*. Hollywood, CA: Wilshire Book, Co., 1971. Grade level: 4 and up.

Children will enjoy learning about the many aspects of Israeli life and history through the coins pictured and described in this book.

Gur, General Motta. *Azeet, Paratrooper Dog*. New York: Thomas Nelson, Inc., 1972. Grade level: 4-6.

An exciting collection of adventure stories about a dog that is part of an Israeli paratrooper unit patrolling the borders.

Hamori, Laszlo. *Flight to the Promised Land*. New York: Holt, Rinehart & Winston, Inc., 1963. Grade level: 6 and up.

This is the story of Shalom, a young Yemenite boy, and his family who emigrate to Israel on Operation Magic Carpet. Once in Israel, the family has much difficulty adjusting to Israeli life. Shalom chooses to leave his family in order to assimilate.

Hirschmann, Ira. *The Awakening: The Story of JNF*. Philadelphia: Porcupine Press, Inc. Reprint of 1946 edition. Grade level: 5 and up.

Hirschmann retells the amazing story of the Jewish National Fund, the organization which has been responsible for the successful reclamation of land in Israel since the early 1900s. The book provides vital insight into the extreme difficulty of the initial task of reclaiming the land and the continuing role of the Jewish National fund in maintaining the land.

Jordan, Ruth. *Daughter of the Waves: Memories of Growing Up in Pre-War Palestine*. New York: Taplinger Publishing Co., Inc., 1983. Grade level: 6 and up.

The true story of a young girl living in Haifa under the British mandate is revealed in this exciting novel. Jordan captures not only the struggles of the girl growing into adulthood, but also of Palestine growing into statehood.

Keller, Mollie. *Golda Meir*. New York: Franklin Watts/Impact Biography, 1983. Grade level: 5 and up.

Keller's well written biography illuminates Golda Meir's life accomplishments, as well as her personal, inner struggles.

Kovner, Abba (ed.) *Childhood Under Fire: Stories, Poems and Drawings, By Children, During the Six Day War*. Trans. by Don Vardi. Tel Aviv: United Artists Ltd., 1968. Grade level: 3 and up.

Kovner has compiled a stirring collection of drawings and creative writings by Israeli children who lived through the 1967 Six Day War. The honesty and sensitivity of these children provide the reader with remarkable insight into the traumas and dreams of a war torn nation.

Kubie, Nora. *Israel*. New York: Franklin Watts, 1979. Grade level: 3-5.

Kubie's third revised edition of this factual book on Israel includes an analysis of the Camp David peace initiatives. The text also includes a bibliography and topical index.

Lange, Suzanne. *The Year*. New York: S.G. Phillips, 1970. Grade level: 6 and up.

This glimpse at *kibbutz* life is offered through the eyes of eighteen-year-old Ann Sanger. Ann leaves America to live on a *kibbutz* where she subsequently meets her future husband.

Levine, Gemma. *We Live in Israel*. New York: Bookwright Press, 1984. Grade level: 5 and up.

Levine provides a fascinating picture of contemporary Israeli life through interviews with Israelis of various ages, backgrounds, and occupations.

Levin, Meyer. *The Story of Israel*. Photo. by Archie Lieberman. New York: G.P. Putnam's Sons, 1966. Grade level: 6 and up.

As always, Levin's approach to the topic at hand is heartfelt and scholarly. In this case, he retells the history of Israel from ancient to modern times, primarily through discussion of the country's most significant personalities and their contributions to Israel's development.

Litvinoff, Barnett. *Weizmann: Last of the Patriarchs.* New York: G.P. Putnam's Sons, 1976. Grade level: 6 and up.

A lively biography about Chaim Weizmann with special emphasis on his role as one of Israel's founding fathers.

Mann, Peggy, and Brodsky, Nina. *Israel in Pictures* (Visual Geography Series). New York: Sterling, 1980. Grade level: 4 and up.

This informative, updated source book on Israel includes sections on the Sadat-Begin peace negotiations, women in Israel, the Histadrut, the special challenges faced by inhabitants of Israel's occupied territories, and the problems of high inflation and taxes.

Miller, Shane. *Desert Fighter.* New York: Hawthorne Books, 1967. Grade level: 5 and up.

Miller describes the life of Moshe Dayan with emphasis on his major contributions to Israel as a settler, archaeologist, military and political leader. The life of the "Desert Fighter" is dramatically revealed.

Narell, Irene. *Joshua: Fighter For Bar Kochba.* Oakland, CA: Akiba Press, 1979. Grade level: 6 and up.

Joshua is a young participant in the revolt which Shimeon Bar Kochba led against the Romans beginning in 132 C.E. The intensity of the Jewish struggle to maintain self-rule is brought to life through a fast paced narrative.

Papas, William. *A Letter from Israel.* Illus. by the author. New York: Franklin Watts, 1968. Grade level: 3 and up.

A loving father blends colorful language and ink and watercolor drawings in a letter to his daughter about his experiences in Israel.

Omer, Devorah. *Path Beneath the Sea.* Tel Aviv: Sabra Books, 1969. Grade level: 4-6.

This is an exciting story about a young Moroccan man who becomes a member of the Israeli army's frogman team. Among the many challenges facing the young man in his new land is adjusting to the new way of life, while still maintaining his ethnic identity.

Omer, Devorah. *Rebirth: The Story of Eliezer Ben-Yehudah and the Modern Hebrew Language.* Philadelphia: The Jewish Publication Society of America, 1976. Grade level: 4 and up.

The daughter of Eliezer Ben-Yehudah retells the fascinating story of her father's successful struggle to revive the Hebrew language at the turn of this century.

Oz, Amos. *Soumchi.* Illus. by William Papas. New York: Harper & Row Publishers, Inc., 1980. Grade level: 4 and up.

After a series of trades ranging from a bike to a pencil sharpener, eleven-year-old Soumchi ends up meeting the girl who will become his first love. An intricate novel geared toward more mature young minds by one of Israel's most popular writers.

Reboul, Antoine. *Thou Shalt Not Kill.* Trans. by Stephanie Craig. New York: S.G. Phillips, 1969. Grade level: 4-6.

Reboul was awarded the grand prize of Salon de L'Enfrance for this moving novel about two young soldiers who become separated from their troops during the 1967 Arab-Israeli War. Slimane, the Egyptian soldier, initially wounds Simmi, a female Israeli soldier. However, their confrontation eventually leads to friendship as they struggle to survive together in the Sinai Desert.

Reit, Seymour. *A Week in Hagar's World: Israel.* New York: Crowell-Collier Press, 1969. Grade level: 1-3.

Reit introduces young readers to life on a *kibbutz* by taking them through a day in the life of Hagar, a young *kibbutznik.*

Rosenblum, Morris. *Heroes of Israel.* New York: Fleet Press Corporation, 1972. Grade level: 3 and up.

Rosenblum sheds a spotlight on the lives of twelve of Israel's most significant heroes, heroines, and leaders. The book is unique and useful in that it includes people who have made contributions to different aspects of Israeli life.

Rutland, Jonathon. *Take a Trip to Israel.* Illus. with photo. New York: Franklin Watts, 1981. Grade level: 1-3.

Actual photographs enhance this informational book about Israel for primary grade children. Topics include geography, historical sites, the economy, *kibbutz* life, and everyday home and school life. A glossary and maps are also provided.

Shamir, Maxim Gabriel. *The Story of Israel in Stamps*. Tel Aviv: Sabra Books, 1969. Grade level: 2-6.

A colorfully photographed display of over one hundred stamps relates the history of Israel in a most exquisite and interesting manner.

Speare, Elizabeth. *The Bronze Bow*. Boston: Houghton Mifflin, Co., 1961. Grade level: 4 and up.

Daniel Bar Jamin is the courageous main character in this novel about the ancient Israelites' struggle to free themselves from Roman rule.

Spector, Shoshannah. *Five Young Heroes of Israel*. Illus. by Aharon Shevo. New York: Shengold Publications, Inc., 1970.

A delightful story about five young *kibbutz* children who help to ensure Israel's safety in their own special way.

Spector, Shoshannah. *The Miraculous Rescue at Entebbe*. Illus. by Theo Phalieros. New York: Shengold Publications, Inc., 1978. Grade level: 3-6.

Yoram, an Israeli counselor, retells the miraculous story of Operation Thunderbolt to his campers at a Jewish camp in America. Spector has written an exciting novel which captures the intensity and drama of the event itself.

Stern, Ellen Norma. *Dreamer in the Desert: A Profile of Nelson Glueck*. New York: KTAV Publishing House, Inc., 1980. Grade level: 4 and up.

Nelson Glueck was an American archaeologist who led digs in Israel and Transjordan. This biography details his pioneering archaeological efforts which lent proof to the reality of biblical events.

Tribogoff, Joseph. *Abu*. New York: Lothrop, Lee & Shepard Books, 1975. Grade level: 6 and up.

A poignant novel about Itzhak, an Israeli soldier, and Abu, a nine-year-old refugee camp youngster, who struggle through their differences to become the best of friends.

Watson, Sally. *The Muktar's Children*. New York: Holt, Rinehart & Winston, Inc., 1968. Grade level: 5 and up.

The emotional conflicts between Arabs and Jews are explored in this novel about neighboring Arab and Jewish villages in Israel. A major theme in the book is that prejudices are learned through passage from one generation to the next.

Weinberg, Norbert. *Beyond the Wall*. New York: Bloch Publishing Co., 1978. Grade level: 6 and up.

The charactaers in Weinberg's alluring novel share the very special feelings evoked upon visiting the Western Wall in Jerusalem.

Worth, Richard. *Israel and the Arab States*. New York: Franklin Watts, 1983. Grade level: 6 and up.

Worth provides an interesting historical review of Israeli-Arab relations leading up the Sadat-Begin peace talks and the ensuing peace treaty between Egypt and Israel.

Zagoren, Ruby. *Chaim Weizmann: The First President of Israel*. New York: Garad, 1972. Grade level: 4 and up.

Zagoren skillfully uses the life story of Chaim Weizmann to recount the history of Zionism and Israel.

ISRAEL: RESOURCES FOR ADULTS

Ancient Israel

de Vaux, Roland. *Ancient Israel: Social and Religious Institutions.* New York: McGraw-Hill Book Co., 1965. (Two Volumes)

Josephus, Flavius. *The Jewish War.* New York: Penguin Books, Inc., 1959.

Kaufman, Yehezkel. *The Religion of Israel from its Beginnings to the Babylonian Exile.* Trans. by Moshe Greenberg. New York: Schocken Books, Inc., 1972.

Yadin, Yigael. *Bar-Kohba.* New York: Random House, Inc., 1971.

Celebrating Israel Through the Arts

Dayan, Ruth. *Crafts of Israel.* New York: Macmillan Publishing Co., Inc., 1974.

Elkins, Dov. *Rejoice With Jerusalem: Prayers, Readings and Songs for Israel Observances.* Bridgeport, CT: Prayer Book Press, Inc., 1972.

Joseph, Herbert S. (ed). *Modern Israeli Drama: An Anthology.* Rutherford, NJ: Farleigh Dickinson University Press, 1983.

Leymarie, Jean. *The Jerusalem Windows.* New York: George Braziller, Inc., 1967.

Levy, Emmanuel. *The Habima: Israel's National Theatre.* New York: Columbia University Press, 1979.

Ophir, Dan. *Israel in Painting.* Givatayim, Israel: Massada Press, 1982.

Famous Personalities

Dash, Joan. *Summoned to Jerusalem: The Life of Henrietta Szold.* New York: Harper & Row Publishers, Inc., 1979.

Dayan, Moshe. *Moshe Dayan: Story of My Life.* William Morrow & Co., Inc., 1976.

Dayan, Ruth. *And Perhaps... The Story of Ruth Dayan.* New York: Harcourt Brace Jovanovich, Inc., 1973.

Dudman, Helga. *Street People: Tel Aviv Streets Named After Famous People.* Jerusalem: Post-Carta, 1982.

Elon, Amos. *Herzl.* New York: Holt, Rinehart & Winston, Inc., 1975.

Handler, Andrew. *Dori: The Life and Times of Theodor Herzl in Budapest (1860-1878).* Birmingham: University of Alabama Press, 1983.

Kol, Moshe. *Mentors and Friends.* New York: Herzl Press, 1983.

Kurzman, Dan. *Ben Gurion: Prophet of Fire.* New York: Simon & Schuster, Inc., 1983.

Litvinoff, Barnet. *The Essential Chaim Weizmann: The Man, the Statesman, the Scientist.* New York: Holmes & Meier Publishers, Inc., 1982.

Maimon, Ada. *Women Build a Land.* New York: Herzl Press, 1962.

Meir, Golda. *My Life.* New York: G.P. Putman's Sons, 1975.

Meir, Menahem. *My Mother Golda Meir: A Son's Evocation of Life with Golda Meir.* New York: Arbor House, 1983.

Peres, Shimon. *From These Men: Seven Founders of the State of Israel.* New York: Wyndham Books, 1979.

Rabin, Yitzhak. *The Rabin Memoirs.* Boston: Little, Brown & Company, 1979.

Silver, Eric. *Begin: The Haunted Prophet.* New York: Random House, Inc., 1984.

Weizmann, Chaim. *Trial and Error: An Autobiography.* New York: Harper & Row Publishers, Inc., 1949.

Hebrew Language and Literature

Benari, Benjamin (ed). *The Student's Dictionary Including a Survey of Hebrew Grammar.* New York: Shulsinger Brothers, Inc., 1962.

Ben-Yehuda, Ehud, and Weinstein, David (eds). *Ben-Yehuda's English-Hebrew, Hebrew-English Dictionary.* New York: Pocket Books, 1961.

Birnbaum, Philip. *Ivrit Shotefet: Fluent Hebrew.* New York: Hebrew Publishing Company, 1966.

Carmi, T. *The Penguin Book of Hebrew Verse.* New York: Penguin Books Inc., 1981.

Glazer, Myra (ed). *Burning Air and a Clear Mind: Contemporary Israeli Women Poets.* Athens, OH: Ohio University Press, 1981.

Halkin, Abraham. *201 Hebrew Verbs: Fully Conjugated in All the Tenses.* Woodbury, NY: Barron's Educational Series Inc., 1970.

Horowitz, Edward. *How the Hebrew Language Grew.* New York: KTAV Publishing House, Inc., 1960.

Mintz, Ruth Finer (ed). *Modern Hebrew Poetry: A Bilingual Anthology.* Berkeley, CA: University of California Press, 1968.

Rolnik, Amos (ed). *Learn Hebrew: Tongue of the Prophets, Language of Today.* Illus. by Avner Katz. Tel Aviv: Rolnik Publishers, 1979.

History

Alexander, Yonahy and Miriam, and Chertoff, Mordecai. *A Bibliography of Israel.* New York: Herzl Press, 1981.

Alpert, Carl. *Technion: The Story of Israel's Institute of Technology.* New York: American Technion Society, 1983.

Avi-Yonah, Michael. *The Holy Land: A Historical Geography From the Persian to the Arab Conquest (536 B.C.-640 A.D.).* Grand Rapids, MI: Baker Book House, 1977.

Bahat, Dan (ed). *The Forgotten Generations: Twenty Centuries of Jewish Life in the Holy Land.* Jerusalem: Israel Economist Publishing House, 1975.

Bee, Noah. *In Spite of Everything: History of the State of Israel in Political Cartoons.* Ed. by Ernest Barbarash. New York: Bloch Publishing Co., 1973.

Ben-Gurion, David. *The Jews in Their Land.* Trans. by Mordechai Nurock and Misha Louvish. New York: Doubleday & Co., Inc., 1966.

Derogy, Jacques, and Carmel, Hasi. *The Untold History of Israel.* New York: Grove Press Inc., 1979.

Eban Abba. *My People: The Story of the Jews.* New York: Behrman House, Inc., 1968.

Efrati, Nathan. *Homecoming: The Saga of Immigration to the Holy Land From Biblical Times to the Present Day.* Illus. by Jossi Stern. Jerusalem: Israel Economist Publishing House, 1983.

Harris, Bill. *Israel: The Land of Promise.* New York: Smith Publications, Inc., 1980.

Kollek, Teddy, and Pearlman, Moshe. *Jerusalem: A History of Forty Centuries.* New York: Random House, Inc., 1968.

Lossin, Yigal. *Pillar of Fire.* New York: B'nai B'rith Anti-Defamation League, 1984.

Luttwak, Edward N., and Horowitz, Daniel. *The Israeli Army 1948-1973.* Lanham, MD: University Press of America, 1984.

Rath, Ari, and Frenkel, Erwin. *Front Page Israel: Major Events 1932-1978 as Reflected in the Front Pages of the Jerusalem Post.* Jerusalem: Palestine Post, Ltd., 1978.

Rosenblatt, Roger. *Children of War.* Garden City, NY: Doubleday & Co., Inc., 1983.

Rubashow-Katznelson, Rachel. *The Plough Woman.* New York: Herzl Press, 1975.

Sachar, Abram L. *The Redemption of the Unwanted: From the Liberation of the Death Camps to the Founding of Israel.* New York: St. Martin's Press, 1983.

Historical Landmarks

Avigad, Nahman. *Discovering Jerusalem.* Nashville, TN: Thomas Nelson, Inc., 1983.

Bartlett, John R. *Jericho.* Grand Rapids, MI: Eerdman's Publishing Co., 1983.

Ben-Dov, Meir; Naor, Mordechai; and Aner, Zeev. *The Western Wall.* Jerusalem: Ministry of Defense, 1983.

Bernstein, Burton. *Sinai the Great Terrible Wilderness.* New York: Viking Press Inc., 1979.

Gavron, Daniel. *Walking Through Israel.* Boston: Houghton Mifflin, Co., 1980.

Halevi, Ben Avraham. *A Modern Guide to Jewish Holy Places.* New York: Posner & Sons, 1982.

Hazelton, Lesley. *Where Mountains Roar: A Personal Report From the Sinai and Negev Deserts.* New York: Holt, Rinehart & Winston, Inc., 1980.

Model of the Second Temple. Tel Aviv: Jerusalem Catalogue House Ltd., 1978.

Pearlman, Moshe, and Yannai, Yaacov. *Historical Sites in Israel.* New York: Chartwell House, Inc., 1977.

Rosenberg, Stuart. *Great Religions of the Holy Land: A Historical Guide to Sacred Places and Sites.* Cranbury, NJ: A.S. Barnes & Co., 1971.

Uris, Jill and Leon. *Jerusalem: Song of Songs.* New York: Doubleday & Co., Inc., 1981.

Historical Novels

Bartov, Hanoch. *Whose Little Boy Are You?* Philadelphia: The Jewish Publication Society of America, 1978.

Collins, Larry, and LaPierre Dominique. *O Jerusalem.* New York: Pocket Books, 1980.

Golan, Aviezer, and Pibkas, Danny. *Shula: Code Name the Pearl.* New York: Delacorte Press, 1980.

Michener, James. *The Source.* New York: Fawcett Crest, 1965.

Uris, Leon. *Exodus.* New York: Doubleday & Co., Inc., 1958.

Israeli Dance and Song

Berk, Fred. *HaRikud: The Jewish Dance.* New York: American Zionist Youth Foundation, 1972.

Pasternak, Velvel (ed). *Great Songs of Israel.* New York: Tara Publications-Board of Jewish Education, 1976.

_____. *Israel in Song.* New York: Tara Publications-Board of Jewish Education, 1974.

_____. *Hassidic Style Songs of the 70's.* New York: Tara Publications, 1975.

Jewish-Arab Relations

Allen, Peter. *The Yom Kippur War.* New York: Charles Scribner's Sons, 1982.

Buber, Martin. *A Land of Two Peoples.* Ed. by Paul Mendes-Flohr. London: Oxford University Press, 1983.

Carroll, Raymond. *The Palestine Question.* New York: Franklin Watts, 1983.

Haber, Eitan; Schiff, Zeev; and Yaari, Ehud. *The Year of the Dove: The Israeli-Egyptian Peace Initiative.* New York: Bantam Books, Inc., 1979.

Herzog, Chaim. *The Arab-Israeli Wars: War and Peace in the Middle East, 1948-1982.* New York: Random House, Inc., 1982.

Memmi, Albert. *Jews and Arabs.* Merrick, NY: O'Hara Publishers, Inc., 1975.

Peters, Joan. *From Time Immemorial: The Origins of the Conflict Over Palestine.* New York: Harper & Row Publishers, Inc., 1984.

Sachar, Howard. *Egypt and Israel.* New York: Richard Marek Publishers, 1981.

Tawil, Raymonda. *My House, My Prison.* New York: Holt, Rinehart & Winston, Inc., 1979.

Kibbutz Life

Bettelheim, Bruno. *The Children of the Dream.* New York: Avon Books, 1969.

Gruber, Rifka (ed). *Village of the Brothers.* New York: Shengold Publishers, Inc., 1979.

Spiro, Melford. *Children of the Kibbutz.* New York: Schocken Books, Inc., 1965.

_____. *Gender and Culture: Kibbutz Women Revisited.* Durham, NC: Duke University Press, 1979.

Wilker, Shalom. *Kibbutz Judaism: A New Tradition in the Making.* New York: Herzl Press, 1982.

Learning Materials About Israel

The Arab-Israeli Wars. Baltimore, MD: Avalon-Hill Company. (Game)

Bamberger, David (adaptor). *My People: Abba Eban's History of the Jews.* New York: Behrman House, Inc., 1978. (Two Volumes)

The Battle for Jerusalem, 1967. New York: Simulations Publications, Inc. (Simulation Game)

Borovetz, Frances. *Israel Ditto Pak Grades K-3.* Denver: Alternatives in Religious Education, Inc., 1983.

_____. *Israel Ditto Pak Grades 4-6.* Denver: Alternatives in Religious Education, Inc., 1982.

Grishaver, Joel Lurie. *Bible Places Ditto Pak.* Denver: Alternatives in Religious Education, Inc., 1983.

_____. *Going Up: The Israel Game.* Denver: Alternatives in Religious Education, Inc., 1978. (Game)

Jaffe, Bernette. *Builders of Israel.* Cleveland: Jaffe Publications, 1977. Distributed by Alternatives in Religious Education, Inc., Denver, Colorado.

Kibbutz. Lebanon, OH: Saga Publications. (Game)

Kibbutz Town Meeting. Zionsville, IN: Goldman Union Camp Institute. (Simulation Game)

October War. New York: Simulations Publications, Inc. (Simulation Game)

Pioneers of Israel. Woodland Hills, CA: Educational Resources. (Game)

Legends of Israel

Vilnay, Zev. *Legends of Galilee, Jordon and Sinai.* Philadelphia: The Jewish Publication Society of America, 1978.

_____. *Legends of Judea and Samaria.* Philadelphia: The Jewish Publication Society of America, 1975.

Nature in the Holy Land

Asimov, Isaac. *Animals of the Bible.* Illus. by Howard Berelson. New York: Doubleday & Co., Inc., 1978.

Danin, Avinoam. *Desert Vegetation of Israel and Sinai.* Jerusalem: Cana Publishing, 1983.

Ferguson, Walter W. *Living Animals of the Bible.* Illus. by the author. New York: Charles Scribner's Sons, no publication date.

Hareuveni, Nogah. *Nature in Our Biblical Heritage.* Kiryat Ono, Israel: Neot Kedumim, Ltd., 1980.

Rabinowitz, Louis I. *Torah and Flora.* New York: Sanhedrin Press, 1977.

Rubin, Gail. *Psalmist With a Camera.* New York: Abbeville Press, Inc., 1979.

Political, Social, and Religious Issues

Grose, Peter. *Israel in the Mind of America.* New York: Alfred A. Knopf, Inc., 1983.

Liebman, Charles, and Don-Yehiya, Eliezer. *Civil Religion in Israel: Traditional Judaism and Political Culture in the Jewish State.* Berkeley, CA: University of California Press, 1983.

Rabinovich, Itamar, and Reinharz, Jehuda (eds). *Israel in the Middle East: Documents and Readings on Society, Politics and Foreign Relations, 1948-Present.* New York: Oxford University Press, 1984.

Avruch, Kevin. *American Immigrants in Israel: Social Identities and Changes.* Chicago: University of Chicago Press, 1981.

Banks, Lynne Reid. *Letters to My Israeli Sons: The Story of Jewish Survival.* New York: Franklin Watts, 1980.

Bellow, Saul. *To Jerusalem and Back.* New York: Viking Press Inc., 1976.

Elon, Amos. *Founders and Sons.* New York: Holt, Rinehart & Winston, Inc., 1971.

Friedlander, Saul. *When Memory Comes.* Trans. by Helen Lane. New York: Farrar, Straus & Giroux, Inc., 1979.

Fuchs, Esther. *Encounters With Israeli Authors.* Marblehead, MA: Micah Publications, 1982.

McNeish, James. *Belonging: Conversations with Men and Women Who Have Chosen to Make Israel Their Home.* New York: Holt, Rinehart & Winston, Inc., 1980.

Oz, Amos. *In the Land of Israel.* New York: Harcourt Brace Jovanovich, Inc., 1983.

Schoenbrun, David. *The New Israelis.* New York: Antheneum Publishers, 1973.

Smith, Rodney. *In the Land of Light: Israel, a Portrait of Its People.* Boston: Houghton Mifflin Co., 1983.

Stern, Geraldine. *Israeli Women Speak Out.* Philadelphia: J.B. Lippincott Co., 1979.

Zionism and the Birth of Israel

Avineri, Shlomo. *The Making of Modern Zionism: Intellectual Origins of the Jewish State.* New York: Basic Books, Inc., 1981.

Hertzberg, Arthur. *The Zionist Idea: A Historical Analysis and Reader.* Philadelphia: The Jewish Publication Society of America, 1960.

Postal, Bernard, and Levy, Henry. *And the Hills Shouted For Joy: The Day Israel Was Born.* New York: David McKay Co., Inc., 1973.

Rubinstein, Amnon. *The Zionist Dream Revisited: From Herzl to Gush Emunim and Back.* New York: Schocken Books, Inc., 1984.

Sachar, Howard. *A History of Israel from the Beginnings of Zionism to Our Day.* New York: Alfred A. Knopf, Inc., 1976.

Simon, Leon (ed). *Selected Essays of Ahad Ha-am.* New York: Atheneum Publishers, Inc., 1970.

Jewish Folklore
VII

Folklore is a vivid record of a people palpitating with life itself, and its greatest art is artlessness. It is a true and unguarded portrait, for where art may be selective, conceal, gloss over defects and even prettify, folk art is always revealing, always truthful in the sense that it is a spontaneous expression. It is therefore three-dimensional with the sense of "life" and "people." It proceeds in a straight line to the significant and ignores the trivial. By juxtaposing good with evil, light with shadow, grief with laughter, and honesty with sham, it achieves the harmonious unity of opposites that resides in objective truth.

A Treasury of Jewish Folklore, edited by Nathan Ausubel. New York: Crown Publishers, Inc., 1948, page xviii.

OVERVIEW

The folklore which has been passed orally from generation to generation is a colorful and dynamic chronicle of Jewish experience. Nowhere else in Jewish literature is the creative spirit of our people so much in evidence. Nowhere else is such a candid reflection encountered of the laughter and tears and the hope and despair which have followed us throughout our history. Folklore introduces in an entertaining and educational manner the ethical guidelines and psychological coping mechanisms which have enabled the Jewish people to overcome adversity and to thrive. Folklore acquaints Jewish children with the values, beliefs, and lifestyles of their culture.

In addition to the function of folk literature as culture medium, folktales can serve as pure entertainment; they are good stories. The plots are fast moving, the tales are often humorous, and, in most cases, the ending is happy. Children are comforted in knowing that good is rewarded, evil is punished, and that by fulfilling trials and tasks, wishes are granted. This gives them the sense that justice prevails in our world.

Jewish folklore is rooted in many sources. These include the Bible, *Midrashim*, Chasidic tales, Rabbinic legends, fables, parables, and the mystical writings in the Zohar and of the Kabbalists. Literally every aspect of Jewish history and culture has given birth to its own folklore. From the town of Chelm to our very own family rooms, the spinning of tribal yarns has been, and probably always will be, a favorite pastime.

The books reviewed in this chapter vary in theme and content. In *Honi and His Magic Circle*, a man is rewarded by God for doing good works, while in *King Solomon's Carpet* and *The Golem*, God is made angry when observing misuses of power.

Laughter is therapeutic for both children and adults; it serves to release tension. Fun and humor may be found in *Hershel of Ostropol*, *The Wise Men of Chelm*, and *Simon Boom Gets a letter*.

It is comforting to realize, when sad or depressed, that "tomorrow is another day." *The Magician*, *The Treasure*, and *It Could Always Be Worse* assure the reader that life can always take a turn for the better, even when one is least expecting this to happen.

Finally, for children who are frightened and sometimes hesitant to tackle the problems around them, *The Rabbi and the Twenty-nine Witches* will help instill in them the confidence that an individual's mind is certainly capable of formulating clever solutions to the most difficult of problems.

JEWISH FOLKLORE: BOOKS AND ACTIVITIES

Gershator, Phillis. *Honi and His Magic Circle* (A Talmudic legend from the Second Temple Period). Illus. by Shay Rieger. Philadelphia: The Jewish Publication Society of America, 1979. 28 pages. Grade level: 1-5.

Phillis Gershator has done a masterful job in retelling this Talmudic legend. Honi, with the aid of his magic circle, brings rain so that seedlings will blossom into carob bearing trees. He continues to do this even in his old age. God rewards Honi's efforts by throwing him into a deep sleep for seventy years and awakening him to behold with great pleasure the "fruits" of his efforts. Shay Rieger's washed line drawings work together with the narrative to bring out the richness and warmth of the legend.

Major Ideas

The dual symbolism of the circle may be viewed as

Jewish Folklore

(1) the continuing cycle of our lives, and (2) the joy of passing tradition from generation to generation.

The origin of the custom of eating carob on Tu B'Shevat is rooted in this legend from Talmudic times.

Activities

1. Grades 1-5: Planting a garden and/or a tree is a worthwhile follow-up activity for this book. To add significance, the planting could take place either at a local Jewish geriatric center or at the school, with older citizens of the community invited to participate. After the planting, have the students recite the blessing for dew and rain as taught in class. The blessing reads as follows:

   ותן טל ומתר לברכה על פני האדמה ושבעינו מטוביך וברך שנתינו כשנים הטובות. ברוך אתה יי נברך השנים.

   V'tain Tal U'matar Livrachah Al P'nei Ha'adamah V'sabeynu Mituvecha U'varech Sh'nateynu K'shanim Hatovot. Baruch Atah Adonai Nevarech Hashanim.

   Give dew and rain for a blessing upon the face of the Earth. O satisfy us with Your goodness and bless our year like other good years. Blessed are You, O Eternal, who blesses the years.

   End the event with refreshments, including carob.

2. Grades 1-5: Since this is an excellent book to use on Tu B'Shevat, have the class prepare carob and fruit delicacies. Two delicious and easy to prepare recipes follow:

   ### Ambrosia

   Peel two large oranges, removing all membranes.
   Cut three ripe bananas into thin slices.
   Add pineapple and other desired fruits.

   Combine and stir:
   ¼ cup confectioners sugar
   1½ cups shredded coconut

   Arrange alternate layers of oranges, bananas, and other fruits in a bowl. Sprinkle each layer with part of the coconut mixture, reserving some for the top. Chill well before serving.

   ### Carob Brownies

   2 eggs beaten
   1/2 cup honey plus 2 tbs.
   1/4 cup safflower oil
   1/2 tsp. vanilla extract
   1 cup whole wheat floor
   ¼ – ½ cup carob powder
   ½ tsp. salt
   ⅔ cup chopped walnuts

   Beat the eggs, honey, oil and vanilla together in a large mixing bowl. In a separate bowl sift together the flour, carob powder, and salt. Combine the wet and the dry ingredients. Mix well. Now add the nuts. Pour the batter into an oiled 8" square pan. Bake at 350 degrees for 35 minutes. Remove from the oven and cut into squares when cool. Makes 16 brownies.

3. Grades 1-5: Make thumbprint family trees. Needed are construction paper, tempera paint, small pieces of corrugated cardboard of varying thicknesses, a thumb of each student, and thin felt tipped markers. Dip the edge of the corrugated cardboard into tempera paint. Then use this paint dipped cardboard to print the trunk and branches of the tree. To make the members of the family tree, dip thumb into light colored paint and print along and around branches as desired. When the tree is dry, use felt markers to add facial details and to label each person.

Hirsh, Marilyn. *The Rabbi and the Twenty-nine Witches.* **Illus. by the author. New York: Holiday House, Inc. 1976. 29 pages. Grade level: K-6.**

This legend, from the Talmud, can provide a fun filled, enjoyable storytelling session for your class. Once a month, when the moon is full, twenty-nine frightening witches wreak their havoc on a small village. It is up to the village Rabbi to find a solution to this problem. Hirsh's writing style is reminiscent of the oral tradition of storytelling. Her black and white illustrations, sometimes accented with blue wash, convey both the joyous and the turbulent moments in the story.

Major Idea

The human mind has an extraordinary capacity to formulate clever solutions to difficult problems.

Activities

1. Grades K-3: After reading the story, give all the students in your class an opportunity to mimic the witches. Form a circle. Teach the following chant which can then be recited while students stir an imaginary brew.

   > Here we sit and stir our brew,
   > Stirring till the day is through.
   > At night we cast our magic spell,
   > Together we rise up (all children rise) and yell,
   > "Everyone become a _____.

   At this point the teacher will supply a word such as dog, cat, flower, egg, monster, etc., and the children will move around the given space as that character. Provide an opportunity to practice Hebrew vocabulary by using the Hebrew word when telling the children what to become (e.g., *kelev* for dog, *chatool* for cat, etc.). To halt each enactment, the teacher says "Witches, freeze." The children then return to their place in the circle and the chant begins again.

2. Grades K-6: At the feast which takes place at the end of the story, the illustration depicts the villagers as Chasidic Jews. Take time to share some of the beauty of Chasidic tradition, particularly the music and dance. Invite the Cantor or a musician to teach the children a simple *Nigun* (a melody without words). Once the children have learned it, have them sing it together while they do their own interpretive movements. Another possibility would be to teach an actual Chasidic dance, an example of which follows:

Zemer Atik (Ancient Song)

Formation:

Dancers form a circle facing counterclockwise. Right arm is extended forward so the right hand rests on the left palm of person in front. Left arm is extended back over left shoulder with palm facing upward.

Part One (4x through):

1. 4 steps forward, (counterclockwise), right-left-right-left.
2. Release hands. Small step to right.
3. Bend right knee and clap twice over right shoulder and once over the left shoulder while stepping slightly to the left.

Part Two:

Face center of circle (steps 1-4 repeated 4x)

1. Right step forward.
2. Bend right knee and snap fingers over right shoulder.
3. Left step forward.
4. Bend left knee and snap fingers over left shoulder.
5. 4 steps backward-right-left-right-left (gradually lowering arms).
6. Return to closed circle formation and Part One steps.

If desired, this dance may be done in a line moving like a snake throughout the room.

Yet another possibility is to listen to Klezmer music. If there are students who play instruments, form a Klezmer band using their talents. Klezmerim were Eastern European folk musicians known for their lively music played at weddings and holiday celebrations, such as Purim and Simchat Torah. Resources for music are *Hassidic Style Song of the 70's* (Tara Publications 1975); *The Klezmerim: Streets of Gold* (Arhoolie Records); Klezmer Conservatory Band, *Klez* (Vanguard Recording Society, Inc.); and The Klezmorim, *Metropolis* (Flying Fish Records, Inc.). Parents can be invited in for a presentation of song and dance.

3. Grades K-6: According to this legend, the witches always appeared at the time of the full moon to raise havoc on the town. As a way of celebrating their departure each month, the religious characters in this story may well have recited the traditional blessing over the new moon with extra fervor. This story provides excellent motivation for learning this blessing:

חדשינו הקדוש ברוך הוא עלינו ועל כל בית
ישראל לחיים ולשלום ולנחמה ונאמר אמן.

Y'chadsheynu Hakadosh Baruch Hu Aleynu V'al Kol Beit Yisrael L'chayim U'l'shalom, U'l'nechamah, V'nomar Amen.

May the new month bring to us all peace, joy, and comfort.

Ish-Kishor, Sulamith. *The Carpet of Solomon*. Illus. by Uri Shulevitz. New York: Pantheon Books, 1966. Grade level: 5 and up. 57 pages.

This adventurous legend of King Solomon, who dares to liken himself to God, captures the reader's interest from beginning to end. King Solomon uses a rug with evil qualities. The rug is curiously interwoven with threads spelling God's name. With the rug, he embarks on a magic carpet ride intending to survey the entire world so that he may rule it. Only after King Solomon is almost swept away like a speck of dust and, even worse, almost loses his son, does he realize that he is just a man. He comes to realize that wisdom is more important in guiding his people than vanity or selfish power. Uri Shulevitz's soft black and white illustrations capture the momentum of Solomon's journey.

Major Ideas

Attempting to be higher than God is arrogant.

Conceit can lead to destruction.

Wisdom can be gained from both failures and successes.

"All that glitters is not gold."

Activities

1. Grades 5 and up: Remind the students that Solomon's magic carpet was said to "glow with . . . mysterious rich colors." It was the glitter of the carpet which enticed King Solomon to purchase it even though he felt doubt in his heart. This is reminiscent of the old saying "All that glitters, is not gold." Ask the students the following questions:

What do you think this saying means? (If the children seem to have trouble with this concept, guide them to realize that it is not wise to judge the goodness of anyone or anything based on outer appearance.)

Can you give examples?

Why was this carpet not "gold" for Solomon?

What have you been attracted to which has glittered but which, in the end, turned out not to be so shiny?

How does the media persuade us to do things which may be harmful to ourselves or others?

After this discussion, have the students draw a scene depicting something which is alluring, but not necessarily beneficial. When the drawings are finished, have them apply glitter to the part of the scene which emphasizes that which is alluring. Public service announcements should then be written, focusing on the negative consequences of participating in the action depicted in their drawing. The announcements and drawings may be hung on a bulletin board entitled "Tikun Olam: Gold, Not Glitter." (*Tikun Olam* is the Hebrew phrase for repairing the world — making it a better place.)

2. Grades 5 and up: Have students write a folktale that is also entitled "The Carpet of Solomon." The twist is that in their stories Solomon will use the carpet wisely.

3. Grades 5 and up: Since the magic carpet is an important part of this legend, here is a golden opportunity to involve students in a weaving project. Two excellent source books for weaving are: *Yarn – The Things It Makes and How to Make Them* by Carolyn Meyer and *Fun With Weaving* by Alice Gilbrath. Suggestions for weavings with a Jewish theme are: a *kipah*, placemats to be used on Shabbat, a *matzah* cover for Passover.

Kimmel, Eric A. *Hershel of Ostropol*. Illus. by Arthur Friedman. Philadelphia: The Jewish Publication Society of America, 1981. 39 pages. Grade level: 2-4.

Four tales about the adventures of Hershel, a popular Jewish folk figure, are humorously retold by Kimmel. With his wisdom and wit, Hershel triumphs over the many trials and tribulations he encounters. Cartoon-like illustrations effectively punctuate the humor in the text.

Major Idea

A sense of humor and creative problem solving can get us through hard times.

Activities

1. Grades 3 and 4: Have students write a "sound story" with Hershel as the main character. Sound stories are stories in which much of the descriptive detail appeals to the sense of hearing. They are written to be read aloud so that the sounds may be supplied by the listeners. As the reading takes place, an arrow is used to inform the audience when they are to make the sound. When the arrow is pointed up, the sounds are supplied. When the arrow is pointed down the sounds cease. An example of the technique follows:

    Hershel jumped on his horse and rode proudly through the town square. (Arrow up - students supply clippity clop of horse. Arrow down - students listen.)

    Hershel walked into a large room where he heard the joyous singing of the townspeople. (Arrow up - students sing. Arrow down - students listen.)

2. Grades 2-4: Students often delight in writing to the author of a book which they have enjoyed reading. The author of *Hershel of Ostropol* is an Associate Professor of Education at Portland State University in Portland, Oregon. His mailing address is: Dr. Eric A. Kimmel, Department of Education, Portland State University, Box 751, Portland, Oregon 97207.

    Have the class compile a list of questions they wish to ask Kimmel. The students should also include a thank-you to the author for writing the book and perhaps a sentence or two about what they really enjoyed about the story. Possible interview questions are:

    When did you first hear about Hershel and why did you choose to write about him?

    Why do you enjoy writing books for children?

    Do you have any children? If so, what stories do you tell them?

3. Grades 2-4: In the story, Hershel is referred to as a "*luftmensch*." This is the Yiddish term for a person who seems to live without working — to live on air. Have each student think of a one or two word description of themselves to be translated by the teacher into Yiddish. A Yiddish/English dictionary is necessary for this activity. Someone from the community who speaks Yiddish could also be used as a resource. Once the name is chosen and translated, have the students write a cinquain. A cinquain is a poem that follows a specific structure. An example follows:

    First line – the chosen Yiddish description
    Second line – two words, describing themselves
    Third line – three words, expressing an action related to themselves
    Fourth line – four words, expressing a feeling
    Fifth line – their English name

Here is a cinquain written about Hershel

> *luftmensch*
> unique wisdom
> wandering, wondering fellow
> satisfied with his life
> Hershel

McDermott, Beverly Brodsky. *The Golem: A Jewish Legend*. Illus. by the author. New York: J.B. Lippincott Co., 1976. 41 pages. Grade level: 5 and up.

Dramatic, full page color illustrations convey both the good and evil which is inherent in the legend of the Golem. Rabbi Lev's dreams forewarn him of the harm which is about to befall the Jews of Prague. He shapes a lump of clay into a Golem which he hopes will protect his community. The Golem, however, is eventually commanded to return to dust as his powers turn from goodness to evil.

Major Ideas

One must use power wisely.

Gentle words can be more powerful than forceful actions.

Activities

1. Grades 5 and up: Have students sculpt golems from self-hardening clay. When dry, the statutes may be painted with acrylic paint if desired.

2. All ages: The Golem hears armed people in the secular community shouting "Kill the Jews." In response to the community's wrath, he employs *physical* means of revenge. The legend states that only God could have given the Golem the gift of speech. Have students imagine that they are the Golem confronted with a similar situation, but in our times. They, however, have been granted the gift of language. Tell them that they will be preparing a speech to persuade the aggressors that the world would lose much by taking up arms against the Jews. Give the students a week to prepare their speeches. To increase the persuasiveness of the speech, students may wish to include information about Jews who have made significant contributions to humanity. Examples are: Albert Einstein, Jonas Salk, Isaac Bashevis Singer, Sigmund Freud, Golda Meir, Marc Chagall, Itzak Perlman, Dr. Rosalyn S. Yalow (Nobel Price in Medicine, 1977), Leonard Bernstein, Beverly Sills, Dustin Hoffman, Joseph Pulitzer, Emma Lazarus, Henrietta Szold, Gloria Steinem, Bella Abzug, Barbara Streisand.

3. Grades 5 and up: Since this book deals with some very serious issues, a discussion period following its reading is especially important. Discussion questions can focus on the following:

> During some turbulent periods of history, Jews have been blamed for the hardships occurring at the time. In the book, the Jews are falsely accused of engaging in the practice of blood libel — killing Christian children so that their blood could be used in the baking of *matzah* or for some other ritual purpose. What might be the cause of these false accusations?

> When the Golem arises, he remembers another time in history when he was called upon to protect the Jewish community from harm. How can remembering the past better our lives today and help to shape the future?

> What are some times in history which are especially important to remember?

One of the major themes of the book is that power may be used toward constructive or destructive ends. Have students imagine times when they might have power in a given situation (i.e., being captain of a team, being an older brother or sister, being the president of the class). Then have them respond to the following questions:

> How could you use your power responsibly? How could you abuse your power?

> What would be the consequences of each action?

Shulevitz, Uri. *The Magician*. Illus. by the author. New York: Macmillan Publishing Co., Inc. 1973. 32 pages. Grade level: K-6.

Once again, Elijah reappears to bring good fortune into the world. This time the author masterfully recreates Elijah in the guise of a magician. Although this story takes place at Passover, it can be enjoyed year round as an uplifting reminder of Elijah's mission in our world. Fine line illustrations capture the gaiety of the text.

Major Ideas

When we are least expecting it, life can take a turn for the better.

The most important things in life cannot always be seen.

Activities

1. Grades 2 and up: Children are often enchanted by the mystery of magic. Have some simple magic books available in your classroom. Allow the students, individually or in pairs, to choose different magic acts to be learned and presented at a school program entitled "The Extraordinary Mr. Elijah." In between some of the acts the students may tell different tales of Elijah.

2. Grades K-6: Elijah uses his magic to bring about a

happy ending to the story. Have each student create an incantation such as "Bubble, bubble, toil and trouble," which will result in a happy ending for someone in need. After they have created their incantations, have them draw themselves dressed as magicians with the incantation floating out of their mouths. Finally, in the remaining space, have them draw the happy ending. If you are using this in Hebrew class, you might ask the students to write their incantations using Hebrew vocabulary. Have Hebrew/English dictionaries on hand to help them.

3. Grades 3 and up: One of the joyous qualities about the legends of Elijah is that each time he appears on the scene, he is in the guise of a different character. Have each student choose a character for their Elijah and develop it into a legend of their own. Possible character portrayals are:

    a politician
    a tailor
    a teacher
    a police officer
    a clown
    a forest ranger
    a computer programmer

Shulevitz, Uri. *The Treasure*. Illus. by the author. New York: Farrar, Straus & Giroux, Inc., 1978. 31 pages. Grade level: 3-6.

The literary and artistic qualities of this Caldecott Honor Book will delight children of all ages. The legend tells of a poor man, Isaac, who is told three times in his dreams to journey to the capital city to find a great treasure. Near the royal palace, Isaac hears the dream of a guard which causes him to return home and find the real treasure. His experience teaches him that "sometimes one must travel far to discover what is near."

Major Ideas

We should take the time to discover and explore the gifts and resources which are close at hand.

Sharing one's treasures with others is important.

Activities

1. Grades 3-6: Begin the storytelling session with a decorated trunk in front of the room. The book should be locked inside the trunk. Tell the students that inside the trunk is a treasure highly valued by the Jewish people. Play the game "Twenty Questions," in order to guess what is in the trunk. Instruct them to ask any questions which may be answered "yes" or "no" to help them solve the mystery. The student who guesses correctly gets the key to open the trunk. Introduce the book with the following discussion questions:

    Why would a book be considered a treasure by the Jewish people?

    What are some of your treasures?

    How could you use some of your treasures to help other people?

After the discussion say: "Here is a story about a poor man who finally discovers his treasure and uses it not only to help himself, but to help others as well."

2. Grades 3-6: On the cornerstone of the house of prayer which Isaac built as a treasure for the people of his town, he inscribed the following words of wisdom: "Sometimes one must travel far to discover what is near." Have the children analyze the meaning of this saying. Now the students are ready to explore the wisdom of sayings. After these discussions, tell them to imagine that they will be building a house of prayer. Their words of wisdom will be inscribed on the cornerstone. For the younger students, display poster board cut in various shapes. Have them choose the "plaque" which they like the best. The teacher, volunteer parents, or older students can act as scribes for students who cannot write. Plaques may be decorated with felt tipped markers after the inscription has been written. The older students should be allowed to cut their own design. The sophistication of the saying will depend on the age of the child. For example, a younger student may very well pass on such messages as: "Clean up your room," "Be nice to your mother and father," "Give *tzedakah*."

3. Grades 3-6: Send a letter to the parents of the students in your class telling them that you have shared with their children the Jewish legend, *The Treasure*. Ask them to send you a list of any Jewish treasures they might have at home that they would be willing to bring to school for one day. For example: a *tallit* passed on by a grandparent, a Siddur, a print done by an Israeli artist. To minimize duplication of items brought to school, tell them that you will return the list to them with one of the items circled. Give them a date on which they are to bring the requested item. Parent volunteers can set up a one day exhibit of the items. Each item should be labeled and historical information or an anecdote may be written on an index card to be placed beside the item. Your class and others have now constructed the "Museum of Jewish Treasures" which is open to visitors.

Simon, Solomon. *The Wise Men of Helm and Their Merry Tales*. Illus. by Lillian Fischel. New York: Behrman House, 1970. 135 pages. Grade level: 2-6. Also, *More Wise Men of Helm*. 119 pages. Grade level: 2-6.

This two volume set is a delightful collection of tales revolving around the follies of the people of Chelm.

Told during some of the harshest periods of Eastern European Jewish history, these tales continue to bring laughter and joy to listeners and readers even today. They contain a wealth of storytelling material for the teacher to share aloud. They may also be appreciated by older children for independent reading pleasure.

Major Ideas

Laughter is the best medicine.

Healthy survival is dependent upon the ability to laugh at oneself.

There are many different approaches to problem solving.

Activities

1. Grades 2-6: After reading several of the stories, have the class vote on three or four which will be presented as puppet shows using stick puppets. Instructions for simple stick puppets follow.

   Materials:

   heavy oak tag
   scraps of cloth material and paper
   felt tipped markers
   white glue
   dowel rods or ruler
   masking tape

   Procedure:

   a. Select a character from the story.

   b. Draw the character onto oak tag.

   c. Cut the character out of the oak tag.

   d. Embellish the character with markers, scraps of material and/or paper.

   e. Lay the character face down on a table. Place the dowel rod or ruler on the top and attach with masking tape.

   f. If your class wishes to use a different technique for puppet construction, a good source book is *Creative Puppetry for Jewish Kids* by Gale Solotar Warshawsky.

2. Grades 2-6: Have a Chelm Day in class. The teacher and each student must come dressed as a Chelm character. To add to the festivities, plan a crazy mixed up schedule in which all of the regular activities would be handled in a lighthearted manner. For example, you might tell a familiar Bible tale, injecting events or characters from other Bible tales. Or, the students could give absurd answers to any questions asked by the teacher. You could also institute a special set of Chelm rules to be followed during the day. For example, when the students move from place to place in the classroom, they must move in an out of the ordinary fashion.

3. Grades 2-6: In many of the Chelm stories, the focus is on the characters' foolish solutions to problems. In others, the characters offer foolish explanations for a variety of phenomena. Present the class with a list of problems or events to consider. Each student will select one problem to solve or one phenomenon to explain through a story modeled in style after the Chelm stories. Possibilities are:

Problems	Phenomena
how to make potato *latkes*	how Haman got his hat
how to cook chicken soup	where the sun goes during the night
how to get to Jerusalem	
how to keep your hair from growing long	how the angels got their wings
how to touch the sky	why strawberries are red
	why *matzah* balls don't bounce

Suhl, Yuri. *Simon Boom Gets A Letter*. Illus. by Fernando Krahn. New York: Scholastic Book Service, 1976. 34 pages. Grade level: K-6.

Simon Boom is a man who likes only the best. When he gets a letter from his brother, he insists on opening it with an intricately designed machine, rather than just ripping it open as suggested by his wife. In the end, he discovers that the "opener" is really the best paper shredder in town. The comic illustrations and humorous text keep the reader laughing.

Major Idea

What seems to be the best might really be the worst in disguise.

Activities

1. Grades 2-6: The letter written to Simon was shredded to pieces before he could read it. To console poor Simon, have each student write him a letter as his brother.

2. Grades K-6: Simon Boom's machine shredded paper. Tell the students that they are going to create a machine using themselves as the parts. Have one student come to the center of the room and start a motion which can be sustained. A sound should accompany the motion. One by one the members of the class will attach themselves to the machine, adding their unique motion and sound. If the class is large, you might need to have two machines. (To add a little Jewish humor to the activity, have students create music box machines and make their sounds to the tune of a popular Hebrew song, such as "*Hava Nagila*" or "*David Melech Yisrael*."

3. Grades K-6: What appeared to Simon Boom be a letter opener really turned out to be a paper shredder. When people who are not Jewish view our ritual objects, they may very well imagine that the objects are used for something other than their intended purposes. Have the students invite a non-Jewish friend to the class to learn the purpose of ritual objects used for Shabbat. This can be done through a reenactment of the following: Blessings at Shabbat dinner, reading the Torah during Shabbat services, the Havdalah service at the end of a Shabbat. Objects for this activity should include:

   Shabbat candlesticks
   Shabbat candles
   challah
   wine and cup
   a prayer book
   Havdalah candle
   spice box
   the Torah
   yad

   This activity is appropriate for any of the holidays.

Zemach, Margot. *It Could Always Be Worse (An old Yiddish folk tale)*. Illus. by the author. New York: Farrar, Straus & Giroux, Inc., 1976. 30 pages. Grade level: K-4.

Through folk art, Zemach tells a pointed, humorous story about a poor man living in cramped quarters who complains to the Rabbi about his plight. In this tale, the man follows the Rabbi's advice to take his farm animals into the already cramped quarters one by one. When he complains even more bitterly, the Rabbi suggests removing each animal. Finally, the man realizes "it could always be worse."

Major Ideas

No matter how bad we think things are, they could always be worse.

Painful adversity can help us to appreciate our blessings and view life from a more appropriate perspective.

Activities

1. Grades K-4: This is an excellent story for dramatization. For an exciting session, assign the following roles to class members:

   the Rabbi
   the discontented man
   the wife
   the children
   the mother-in-law
   goats
   cows
   chickens
   geese
   sheep
   other animals of your choice

   Rope off a section of the room to be the man's house. To help the students experience the frustration of the poor man, let them dramatize the story.

2. Grades 2-4: Have the students illustrate what the inside of their home would look like if they followed the Rabbi's advice.

3. Grades 2-4: Write a class poem listing students' complaints and have every other line read: "It could always be worse." Care must be taken here when students bring up personally or socially tragic situations.

JEWISH FOLKLORE: BOOKS FOR CHILDREN

Adler, David A. *The Children of Chelm*. New York: Bonim Books/Hebrew Publishing Co., 1979. Grade level: K-3.

A good book which serves as a fine introduction to the stories of Chelm. Humorous illustrations depict the silly antics of Chelm inhabitants.

Adler, David. *Children's Treasury of Chassidic Tales*. Illus. by Arie Haas. New York: Mesorah Publishers, Ltd., 1983. Grade level: 3-6.

Adler has adapted eight of the most poignant stories from Zevin's *Treasury of Chassidic Tales*. The blue, black, and beige drawings capture the spirit of the environment and times in which the characters lived.

Barash, Asher. *A Golden Treasury of Jewish Tales*. Illus. by Henry Hechtkopf. Ramat Gan, Israel: Massada Press Ltd., 1965. Grade level: 5 and up.

Forty stories from Rabbinic sources are included in this book of Jewish folklore. Each contains an illuminating lesson from the Torah. The text is well written and may be used as a source for oral storytelling.

Bialik, Hayyim. *Knight of Onions and Knight of Garlic*. Illus. by Emanuel Roman. New York: Hebrew Publishing Co., 1939. Grade level: 3-6.

In this exquisite allegory by a beloved Hebrew poet, a country which values onions offers a special reward to a visitor who comes bearing a gift of garlic.

Calisch, Edith Lindeman. *Fairy Tales from Grandfather's Big Book: Jewish Legends of Old Retold For Young People*. Illus. by Henriette Strauss. New York: Behrman House, Inc., 1938. Grade level: K-4.

Retold in a delightful manner, these stories will be enjoyed by younger children when read aloud and relished for individual reading by children in the intermediate grades.

Chapman, Carol. *The Tale of Meshka the Kvetch*. Illus. by Arnold Sobel. New York: E.P. Dutton, 1980. Grade level: PK-2.

Although not from the oral tradition, this tale has all the flavor of a Jewish folktale. The story revolves around the cure for "*kvetch's* itch." Lobel's illustrations are humorous and delightful.

Einhorn, David. *The Seventh Cradle and Other Folk Tales on Eastern Europe*. Trans. from the Yiddish by Gertrude Pashin. Illus. by Ezekiel Schloss. New York: KTAV Publishing House, Inc., 1968. Grade level: 4 and up.

Life in the *shtetl* is clearly depicted in this collection of stories based on Jewish folktales and legend. Einhorn, through his masterful storytelling, makes this book a memorable one.

Elkin, Benjamin. *The Wisest Man in the World*. Illus. by Anita Lobel. New York: Parents' Magazine Press, 1968. Grade level: 1-3.

When a tiny bee promises King Solomon to serve him, the King laughs, thinking that such a small creature would be incapable of helping a man. However, when Queen Sheba tries to humiliate the King in front of his people, it is the bee who saves the King from embarrassment. Vibrant illustrations and delightful text convey the moral that "the tiniest creatures are teachers of kings."

Ellenbuck, Shan. *Yankel the Fool*. Illus. by the author. New York: Doubleday and Co., Inc., 1973. Grade level: 4-6.

A fun, noodlehead story about the various mishaps in the life of Yankel the Fool. The eight chapters are humorous, fast moving, and good for a read aloud story time.

Fleischman, Paul. *Finzel the Farsighted*. Illus. by Marcia Sewall. New York: E.P. Dutton & Co., Inc., 1983. Grade level: 1-4.

Although Finzel's poor eyesight distorts his view of the present, his ability to see into the future earns him the honorable position of local fortune teller. Comical illustrations depict Finzel's mixed up dealings with the village simpleton and a crafty thief.

Freedlander, Gerald. *A Treasury of Jewish Fables*. Illus. by Beatrice Hirschfeld. New York: Blue Star Book Club, 1971. Grade level: 4 and up.

> The moralistic tales in this collection come from a variety of Jewish sources. The language is true to the oral tradition, thereby providing the teacher with good read aloud material.

Gross, Michael. *The Fable of the Fig Tree*. Illus. by Mila Lazarevich. New York: Henry Z. Walack, Inc., 1975. Grade level: K-4.

> A warm and charming fable about a good man who is rewarded for his noble deeds and love for future generations, and a selfish man who is punished for his greed. The lively illustrations convey both the joy and humor in the story.

Hirsh, Marilyn. *Captain Jiri and Rabbi Jacob*. Illus. by the author. New York: Holiday House, Inc., 1976. Grade level: 1-4.

> Captain Jiri's soldiers fight; Rabbi Jacob's students study. Each has a guardian angel, but when the angels get mixed up and deliver their messages to the wrong man, Captain Jiri and Rabbi Jacob learn lessons which benefit them and the people with whom they work. Colorful drawings highlight this lively tale.

Hirsh, Marilyn. *Could Anything Be Worse?* Illus. by the author. New York: Holiday House, Inc., 1974. Grade level: PK-4.

> A Rabbi gives some very sound advise to a man who is convinced that there could be nothing worse than the noise and commotion in his home. The Eastern European setting is handsomely depicted in Hirsh's lively and humorous illustrations.

Ish-Kishor, Sulamith. *The Master of the Miracle*. Illus. by Arnold Lobel. New York: Harper & Row Publishers, Inc., 1971. Grade level: 6 and up.

> Told in first person narrative, this exciting novel based on the legend of the Golem raises the same important questions about the misuse of power as the original tale. This is a suspenseful novel written by a distinguished writer.

Kimmel, Eric A. *Mishka, Pishka and Fishka and Other Galician Tales*. Illus. by Christopher J. Spollen. New York: Coward, McCann & Geoghegan, 1976. Grade level: 3-6.

> Warm, humorous folk tales for children of all ages to listen to and read. Lively etchings enhance the charming text.

Kimmel, Eric A. *Nicanor's Gate*. Illus. by Jerry Joymer. Philadelphia: The Jewish Publication Society of America, 1979.

> Nicanor is a wealthy Jew who wishes to give a beautiful doorway as a gift to the restored Temple in Jerusalem. He travels to Jerusalem to bestow his gift, but a storm at sea washes one of his doors away. A miracle occurs which allows the door and Nicanor to meet on shore. The Gate of Nicanor can now lead to the innermost court of the Temple. The joy that Nicanor's gift brings to him and to his people is poignantly felt by the reader.

Kranzler, Gershon. *The Golden Shoes and Other Stories*. New York: Feldman Publishers, 1960. Grade level: 6 and up.

> Realistic historical settings such as King Solomon's court, the Spanish Inquisition, and nineteenth century Poland lend special intrigue to Kranzler's stories.

Lisowski, Gabriel. *On the Little Hearth*. Illus. by the author. New York: Holt, Rinehart & Winston, Inc., 1978. Grade level: PK and up.

> Pen and ink drawings of *shtetl* life illustrate the verses to this popular Yiddish song. A beautiful book to own.

Muchnik, Michael. *The Cuckoo Clock Castle of Shir*. Illus. by the author. New York: Bloch Publishing Co., 1980. Grade level: PK-3.

> The beauty of the Sabbath and the holiness of the Sabbath day help to bring a wooden cuckoo clock bird to life. The illustrations are charming and add to the warmth of the tale.

Posy, Arnold. *Israeli Tales and Legends*. Middle Village, New York: Jonathan David Co., 1966. Grade level: 5 and up.

> Nineteen stories stressing the importance of love of God comprise this collection of tales based on the Jewish folklore of Israel. The style of writing will appeal to today's generation.

Rabinowicz, Harry M. *The Slave Who Saved the City and Other Hassidic Tales*. Illus. by Ahron Gelles. San Diego: A.S. Barnes and Co., Inc., 1960. Grade level: 5 and up.

> This fascinating book is made up of stories of the Baal Shem Tov and other Chasidic sages. Warm tales filled with wisdom are sure to delight the upper elementary student.

Rabinowitz, Shalom. *Tevye: Oh A Miracle!* Illus. by Kerman. New York: Fleet Press Corp., 1971. Grade level: K-3.

When poor Tevye gives two wealthy women a ride home in his wagon, they are so appreciative that they hold a party in his honor, pay him handsomely, and give him a cow which they believe can no longer produce milk. For Tevye and his family, the latter is the most precious reward, as Tevye is miraculously able to encourage the cow to give milk again. Rabinowitz and Kerman have colorfully retold this delightful Shalom Aleichem tale, supposedly shared with them by Tevye himself.

Rose, Ann. *The Trimphs of Fuzzy Fogtop.* Illus. by Tomie de Paola. New York: Dial Press, 1979. Grade level: K-3.

Fuzzy, a humorous character from Chelm, is a lovable man whose antics as he attempts to travel from Pinsk to Minsk will be enjoyed by all children. Both the text and the lively illustrations will leave children laughing.

Sever, Blanche. *Let's Steal the Moon: Jewish Tales Ancient and Recent.* Illus. by Trina S. Hyman. New York: Little, Brown & Co., 1970. Grade level: 3 and up.

Eleven tales, ranging from stories about witches and demons to nonsense tales about the citizens of Chelm, make up this collection of Jewish folklore. The illustrations of characters from the story are modeled after friends of the artist and they seem very real.

Schwartz, Howard. *Elijah's Violin and Other Jewish Fairy Tales.* Illus. by Linda Heller. New York: Harper & Row Publishers, Inc., 1983. Grade level: 6 and up.

The tales which are included in this collection come from sources which include the Middle East, the Far East, Eastern Europe, and Spain. The source for each tale is given. Children will enjoy making comparisons between the fairy tales commonly told in America and the Jewish versions. This is an excellent, comprehensive collection.

Silverman, Althea O. *The Harp of David: Legends of Mount Zion.* Illus. by Ezekiel Schloss. Hartford, CT: Hartman House, 1964. Grade level: 6 and up.

This is an exciting book about a young American boy, Moshe, who is told the tales and legends related to Mount Zion when he makes a summer visit to Jerusalem. The book will help students "grow" along with Moshe.

Simon, Solomon. *The Wandering Beggar . . . Or the Adventures of Simple Shmerel.* Illus. by Lillian Fischel. New York: Behrman House Inc., 1942. Grade level: 4 and up.

Simple Shmerel rises to stardom in the twelve miraculous and humorous adventure stories contained in this entertaining book.

Singer, Isaac Bashevis. *Elijah the Slave: A Hebrew Legend Retold.* Illus. by Antonio Frasconi. New York: Farrar, Straus & Giroux, Inc., 1973. Grade level: 3-6.

In this story, wandering Elijah comes to the aid of Tobias, a holy scribe who is ill and cannot find work. Elijah and Tobias meet and Elijah is sold as a slave so that Tobias may earn some money. A beautiful castle is constructed by Elijah which makes the angels and God happy. Thus, Elijah earns his freedom. Frasconi's woodcuts complement Singer's lively test.

Singer, Isaac Bashevis. *The Fearsome Inn.* Trans. by the author and Elizabeth Shub. Illus. by Nonny Hogrogian. New York: Charles Scribner's Son's, 1967. Grade level: 4 and up.

Three young men and women are held captive by a pair of devils who own a fearsome inn. The interest of young readers will be held as Leibel, a student of *Kabbalah*, outwits the devils and eventually rescues the young people. Watercolor illustrations create just the right mood for this excellent book.

Singer, Isaac Bashevis. *The Golem.* Illus. by Uri Shulevitz. New York: Farrar, Straus & Giroux, Inc., 1982. Grade level: 4 and up.

Singer retells the legend of the Golem, a clay giant, who helps the Jews in time of need. The story's theme relates to abuse of power. This version pointedly asks if love perhaps "has more power than a Holy Name." Shulevitz is a master artist and his dramatic illustrations are a fine addition to this exciting and meaningful story.

Singer, Isaac Bashevis. *Mazel and Shlimazel; or The Milk of the Lioness.* Trans. by the author and Elizabeth Shub. Illus. by Margot Zemach. New York: Farrar, Straus & Giroux, Inc., 1967. Grade level: K-4.

When the two spirits, Mazel and Shlimazel, decide to determine which of them is more powerful, they select the peasant Tam as their subject. This is fortunate for Tam because, through the spirits' fight, he becomes the king's son-in-law and advisor. Large, bright illustrations are amusing and well suited to the story.

Singer, Isaac Bashevis. *Nafatli the Storyteller and His Horse, Sus and Other Stories*. Illus. by Margot Zemach. New York: Farrar, Straus & Giroux, Inc., 1976. Grade level: 4 and up.

Eight stories, some funny, some tender, combine to make this book an excellent collection of tales. Pencil drawings enhance the beauty of the work.

Singer, Isaac Bashevis. *When Shlemiel Went to Warsaw and Other Stories*. Illus. by Margot Zemach. New York: Farrar, Straus & Giroux, Inc., 1968. Grade level: 4 and up.

These stories, often inspired by traditional Jewish folk tales, show Isaac Bashevis Singer at his best. Tales of treachery and nonsense, witches and demons, and tenderness in human relationships combine to make a book to be enjoyed by all children. Line drawings of the *shtetl* complement the fine text.

Singer, Isaac Bashevis. *Zlateh the Goat and Other Stories*. Illus. by Maurice Sendak. New York: Harper & Row Publishers, Inc., 1966. Grade level: 4 and up.

The illustrator Maurice Sendak once said that the drawings he composed for this book were the most satisfying of his career. When one reads the six stories, it is easy to see why Sendak was so inspired. A delightful book which leaves the reader with feelings of warmth and contentment.

Soyer, Abraham. *Adventures of Yemina and Other Stories*. Illus. by Raphael Soyer. New York: Viking Press, Inc., 1979. Grade level: 6 and up.

This father and son team of author and illustrator has utilized engaging text and soft pencil drawings to bring new life to six Hebrew legends from the first half of this century. The stories are based on themes of idealism and the meek rising above the mighty. Animals are skillfully used to portray human situations.

Strauss, Ludwig. *The Magic Kite Tail*. Trans. by Trude Parzin. Illus. by Arthur Wallower. New York: D. Van Nostrand Co., Inc., 1967. Grade level: 3 and up.

Jewish and German folk tales have been gathered to form this wonderful collection. Magical stories of love, travel, and longed for children will delight the young reader.

Suhl, Yuri. *Simon Boom Gives a Wedding*. Illus. by Margot Zemach. New York: Scholastic Book Service, 1972. Grade level: PK-3.

Simon is a show-off and wants "only the best" for his daughter's wedding. Through faulty, yet understandable reasoning, he ends up serving only sparkling spring water. Zemach's illustrations showing the faces of the disappointed wedding guests capture the humor of this tale. An excellent book to share aloud.

JEWISH FOLKLORE: RESOURCES FOR ADULTS

Collections of Legends and Stories

Barash, Asher. *A Treasury of Jewish Tales*. New York: Dodd, Mead & Co., 1966.

Certner, Simon (ed). *101 Jewish Stories*. New York: Board of Jewish Education, 1961.

Gaster, Moses (ed). *Ma'aseh Book: Book of Jewish Tales and Legends*. Philadelphia: The Jewish Publication Society of America, 1934.

Goldin, Hyman. *The Book of Legends: Tales From the Bible, Talmud and Midrash*. New York: Hebrew Publishing Co., 1929. (Three Volumes)

Harlow, Jules. *Lessons from Our Living Past*. New York: Behrman House, Inc., 1972.

Ish-Kishor, Judith. *Tales From the Wise Men of Israel*. Philadelphia: J.B. Lippincott, 1962.

Nadich, Judah. *Jewish Legends of the Second Commonwealth*. Philadelphia: The Jewish Publication Society of America, 1983.

Nahmad, H.M. *A Portion in Paradise and Other Jewish Folktales*. New York: Viking Press, Inc., 1973.

Patai, Raphael (ed). *Gates to the Old City: A Book of Jewish Legends*. Detroit, MI: Wayne State University Press, 1981.

Prose, Francine. *Stories for Our Living Past*. New York: Behrman House, Inc., 1981.

Rush, Barbara, and Marcus, Eliezer (eds). *Seventy and One Tales For the Jewish Year*. New York: American Zionist Youth Foundation, 1980.

Salamon, Nina (ed). *Apples and Honey*. New York: Doubleday & Co., Inc., 1922.

Schram, Penninah. *A Storyteller's Journey*. POM Records. (Record Album/Cassette)

Comprehensive Anthologies

Ausubel, Nathan (ed). *A Treasury of Jewish Folklore*. New York: Crown Publishers, Inc., 1948.

Bin Gorion, Micha Joseph. *Mimekor Yisrael: Classical Jewish Folktales*. Bloomington, IN: University of Indiana Press, 1976. (Three Volumes)

Eichhorn, David Max. *Joys of Jewish Folklore*. Middle Village, New York: Jonathan David Publishers, Inc., 1981.

Ginsberg, Louis. *Legends of the Jews*. Philadelphia: The Jewish Publication Society of America, 1968.

Schwartz, Howard (ed). *Gates to the New City: A Treasury of Modern Jewish Tales*. New York: Avon Books, 1983.

Fables and Fairy Tales

Hadas, Moses (trans). *Fables of a Jewish Aesop: Translated from the Fox Fables of Berechiah ha-Nakdan*. Woodcuts by Fritz Kredel. New York: Columbia University Press, 1967.

Podwal, Mark. *A Jewish Bestiary*. Philadelphia: The Jewish Publication Society of America, 1984.

Schwartz, Howard. *Elijah's Violin and Other Jewish Fairy Tales*. Illus. by Linda Heller. New York: Harper & Row Publishers, Inc., 1973.

Schwartz, Howard (ed). *Imperial Messages: One Hundred Modern Parables*. New York: Avon Books, 1976.

_____. *Midrashim: Collected Jewish Parables*. London: Menard, 1976.

Famous Characters

Braude, William, and Kapstein, Israel. *Tanna Debe Eliyahu: The Lore of the School of Elijah*. Philadelphia: The Jewish Publication Society of America, 1980.

Klapholtz, Yisroel. *Stories of Elijah the Prophet*. B'nai Brak, Israel: Pe'er Hasefer, 1971-73 (Four Volumes)

Pascheles, Wolff. *Jewish Legends of the Middle Ages*. London: Shapiro-Vallentine, no publication date.

Simon, Solomon. *More Wise Men of Helm*. New York: Behrman House, Inc., 1965.

_____. *The Wise Men of Helm*. New York: Behrman House, Inc., 1945.

Tenenbaum, Samuel. *The Wise Men of Chelm*. New York: Collier, 1965.

Wiesel, Elie. *The Golem: The Story of a Legend*. Illus. by Mark Podwal. New York: Summit Books, 1983.

Winkler, Gershom. *Dybbuk*. New York: Judaica Press, 1980.

Zabara, Joseph ben Meir. *The Book of Delight*. English trans. by M. Hadas, 1960. Philadelphia: The Jewish Publication Society of America, 1912.

Chasidic Tales

Band, J. Arnold. *Nachman of Bratslav: The Tales*. Ramsey, NJ: Paulist Press, 1978.

Ben-Amos, Dan (ed). *In Praise of the Baal Shem Tov*. Trans. by Dan Ben-Amos and Jerome Mintz. Bloomington, IN: University of Indiana Press, 1970.

Buber, Martin. *Tales of the Hasidim: Later Masters*. New York: Schocken Books, Inc., 1948.

_____. *Tales of the Hasidim: Early Masters*. New York: Schocken Books, Inc., 1949.

_____. *The Legend of the Baal Shem*. New York: Schocken Books, Inc., 1977.

Cordover, Moses. *The Palm Tree of Deborah*. New York: Sepher-Hermon Press, 1981.

Eliach, Yaffa. *Hasidic Tales of the Holocaust*. London: Oxford University Press, 1982.

Heinemann, Benno. *The Maggid of Dubno and His Parables*. New York: Feldheim Publishers, 1969.

Klein, Aaron, and Klein, Jenny Machlowitz. *Tales in Praise of the Ari*. Philadelphia: The Jewish Publication Society of America, 1970.

Levin, Meyer. *Classic Hassidic Tales*. Illus. by Marek Szwarc. New York: Penguin Books, Inc., 1975.

Schochet, Jacob Immanuel. *The Great Maggid: The Life and Teachings of Rabbi Dov Ber of Mezhirech*. New York: Kehot Publication Society, 1974.

Schwartz, Howard. *The Captive Soul of the Messiah: New Tales of Reb Nachman*. New York: Schocken Books, Inc., 1983.

_____. *Rooms of the Soul: A Novel Told in Hasidic Tales*. Illus. by Tsila Schwartz. Chappaqua, NY: Rossel Books, 1984.

Singer, Isaac Bashevis. *Reaches of Heaven: A Story of the Baal Shem Tov*. New York: Farrar, Straus & Giroux, Inc., 1980.

Steinsaltz, Adin (ed). *Beggars and Prayers: The Tales of Nachman of Bratzlav*. New York: Basic Books, Inc., 1979.

Weisel, Elie. *Souls on Fire: Portraits and Legends of Hasidic Masters*. St. Paul, MN: Vintage Book Co., 1972.

_____. *Four Hasidic Masters and Their Struggle Against Melancholy*. Notre Dame, IN: University of Notre Dame Press, 1978.

_____. *Somewhere A Master: Further Hasidic Portraits and Legends*. New York: Summit Books, 1982.

Jewish Folktales From Different Lands

Andrić, Ivo. *The Pasha's Concubine and Other Tales*. Trans. by Joseph Hitrec. London: George Allen and Unwin Ltd., 1968.

Einhorn, David. *The Seventh Candle and Other Folk Tales of Eastern Europe*. New York: KTAV Publishing House, Inc., 1978.

Goitein, S.D. (ed). *From the Land of Sheba: Tales of the Jews of Yemen*. New York: Schocken Books Inc., 1973.

Hanauer, J.E. *Folklore of the Holy Land*. London: Folcroft, 1977.

Kahana, S.Z. *Legends of Zion*. Ramat Hasharon, Israel: Royal Press, 1974.

Leslau, Wolf (ed). *Falasha Anthology: The Black Jews of Ethiopia.* New York: Schocken Books, Inc., 1969.

Noy, Dov. *Folktales of Israel.* Chicago: University of Chicago Press, 1969.

_____. *Moroccan Jewish Folktales.* New York: Herzl Press, 1966.

Saben, Yona. *The Folk Literature of the Kurdistani Jews: An Anthology.* New Haven CT: Yale University Press, 1982.

Magic, Mystery, and Mysticism

Ben Zion, Raphael (ed). *An Anthology of Jewish Mysticism.* New York: Judaica Press, 1981.

Dann, Jack (ed). *More Wandering Stars: An Anthology of Jewish Fantasy and Science Fiction.* New York: Doubleday & Co., 1981.

_____. *Wandering Stars: An Anthology of Jewish Fantasy and Science Fiction.* New York: Harper & Row Publishers, Inc., 1974.

Kaufman, William, *Journeys.* New York: Bloch Publishing Co., 1981.

Kushner, Lawrence. *The Book of Letters: A Mystical Alef-bait.* New York: Harper & Row Publishers, Inc., 1975.

_____. *Honey From the Rock.* New York: Harper & Row Publishers, Inc., 1977.

_____. *The River of Light.* New York: Harper & Row Publishers, Inc., 1981.

Meltzer, David (ed). *The Secret Garden: An Anthology in the Kabbalah.* New York: Seabury Press, 1976.

Neugroschel, Joachim. *Great Works of Jewish Fantasy.* London: Pan Books, Ltd., 1978.

Shahn, Ben. *The Alphabet of Creation.* New York: Schocken Books, Inc., 1954.

Wright, Wayne (ed). *The Chicken Prince and Other Older Tales of Cabala.* El Cerrito, CA: Rhinoceros Press, 1977.

Scholarly Studies on Folklore

Ben-Ami, Issachar, and Dan, Joseph. *Studies in Aggadah and Jewish Folklore.* Jerusalem: Magnes Press, 1983.

Lauterbach, Jacob. *Studies in Jewish Law, Custom and Folklore.* New York: KTAV Publishing House, Inc., 1968.

Patai, Raphael. *On Jewish Folklore.* Detroit, MI: Wayne State University Press, 1983.

Talmage, Frank (ed). *Studies in Jewish Folklore.* Cambridge, MA: Assocation for Jewish Studies, 1980.

Scholarly Studies on Mysticism

Berg, Philip. *Kabbalah for the Layman: A Guide to Cosmic Consciousness.* Jerusalem: Research Center of the Kabbalah, 1981.

Blumenthal, David. *Understanding Jewish Mysticism: The Merkavah Tradition and the Zoharic Tradition.* New York: KTAV Publishing House, Inc., 1978.

Levine, Etan. *The Burning Bush: Jewish Symbolism and Mysticism.* New York: Sepher-Hermon Press, 1981.

Reuchlin, Johann. *On the Art of Kabbalah.* Trans. by Martin and Sarah Goodman. New York: Abaris Books, 1983.

Schaya, Leo. *The Universal Meaning of Kabbalah.* Trans. by Nancy Pearson. Secaucus, NJ: University Books, Inc., 1971.

Scholem, Gershom. *Kabbalah and Its Symbolism.* Trans. by Ralph Manheim. New York: Schocken Books, Inc., 1965.

Scholem, Gershom (ed). *Zohar: The Book of Splendor.* New York: Schocken Books, Inc., 1949.

Schutz, Albert L. *Call Adonoi: Manual of Practical Cabala and Gestalt Mysticism.* Goleta, CA: Quantal Publishing, 1980.

Schutz, Albert L., and deSchaps, Hilda W. *Kosher Yoga: Cabalistic Roots of Western Mysticism.* Goleta, CA: Quantal Books, 1983.

Sperling, Harry, and Simon, Maurice. *The Zohar.* London: Soncino Press, 1933.

Steinsaltz, Adin. *The Thirteen Petaled Rose.* New York: Basic Books, Inc., 1980.

Trachtenberg, Joshua. *Jewish Magic and Superstition.* Philadelphia: The Jewish Publication Society of America, 1961.

Weiner, Herbert. *Nine and a Half Mystics: The Kabbalah Today*. New York: Collier, 1969.

Tales by Modern Hebrew and Yiddish Masters

Agnon, Shumel, Yosef. *In the Heart of the Seas*. New York: Schocken Books, Inc., 1947.

_____. *Two Tales: Betrothed, Edo and Adam*. Trans. by Walter Lever. New York: Schocken Books, Inc., 1966.

_____. *The Bridal Canopy*. Trans. by I.M. Lask. New York: Schocken Books, Inc., 1967.

_____. *A Guest For the Night*. Trans. by Misha Louvish. New York: Schocken Books, Inc., 1968.

_____. *Twenty-One Stories*. Ed. by Nahum Glatzer. New York: Schocken Books, Inc., 1970.

Aleichem, Sholom. *Inside Kasrilevke*. New York: Schocken Books, Inc., 1968.

_____. *Some Laughter, Some Tears: From the Old World and the New*. Ed. by Curt Leviant. New York: G.P. Putnam's Sons, 1968.

_____. *The Adventures of Menachem Mendl*. New York: Putnam Publishing Group, 1979.

_____. *The Adventures of Mottel the Cantor's Son*. New York: Henry Schuman, Inc., 1953.

Asch, Sholem. *Tales of My People*. Trans by Meyer Levin. New York: G.P. Putnam's Sons, 1948.

_____. *Children of Abraham*. New York: Irvington Publishers, 1982.

Hochman, Baruch. *The Fiction of S.Y. Agnon*. Ithaca, NY: Cornell University Press, 1970.

Howe, Irving, and Greenberg, Elizer (eds). *A Treasury of Yiddish Stories*. Illus. by Ben Shahn. New York: Schocken Books, Inc., 1973.

_____. *Selected Stories of Isaac L. Peretz*. New York: Schocken Books, Inc., 1975.

Howe, Irving, and Wisse Ruth (eds). *The Best of Sholom Aleichem*. Washington, DC: New Republic Books, 1973.

Mendele Mokher-Seforim. *The Parasite*. New York: Thomas Yoseloff, 1956.

_____. *Fishke the Lame*. London: Stanley Paul, 1928.

_____. *The Travels and Adventures of Benjamin the Third*. New York: Schocken Books, Inc., 1949.

Peretz, Isaac L. *The Sabbath Treasure and Other Stories*. Philadelphia: The Jewish Publication Society of America, 1976.

Jewish History VIII

Before the Jewish people a great book of human and Jewish destiny stands open; in it is mirrored its millenial experience in its progression through many civilizations. If only our present generation and its successors can become fully cognizant of their heritage, if only they will delve even deeper into the mysteries of their people's past and present, they will not only make certain of that people's creative survival, but also significantly help in charting mankind's path toward its ultimate, let us hope messianic, goals.

Salo Baron, Great Ages and Ideas of the Jewish People. *Leo W. Schwartz, editor. © Random House, Inc., 1956, page 484.*

OVERVIEW

Be it the Exodus or any other event, each moment of Jewish history is forever, an enduring moment, filled with invaluable lessons. As the four thousand years of Jewish history unfold before the mind, it is clear that although we must never live in the past, neither may we forget it. We are reminded also of the meaning and challenge of chosenness. Hence to be truly the Chosen People, children must be helped both individually and collectively to accept their historical inheritance, and to carry it on with dignity, sincerity, and the wisdom born of hindsight.

This goal is often difficult to achieve when students learn history by textbook. When a paragraph is being read aloud by one child, the interest of others in the class may wane. Rote memorization of dates and events is unproductive. Knowledge so learned is often short lived.

History can be exciting when the people who have created history, who have lived in history, are "brought to life." Supplementing the textbook with historical fiction can be a great help in this regard. Children's books can show students that history is created by people, that the events of times past affected the people who lived then, and that those events continue to have a direct bearing on the way we live our lives today.

The books included in this chapter capture important eras in Jewish history and reveal important truths. For example, persecution has plagued the Jewish people for centuries. *Butchers and Bakers, Rabbis and Kings* is the story of a group of Jews living in Spain in the 12th century who "force" their king to protect their rights. The Inquisition and the choices faced by Jews living in Spain in the fifteenth century are brought to light in *The Cardinal's Snuff Box*. *A Boy of Old Prague* recounts the prejudice against Jews that was so prevalent in Eastern Europe during the 16th century.

Perilous conditions in Eastern Europe at various times throughout history forced a great number of Jews to emigrate to the United States. Many books have been written illuminating the experiences of the uprooted. *Gooseberries to Oranges*, *The Leckachmacher Family*, and *Call Me Ruth* have been included here to illustrate the adjustment Jews had to make when forced to resettle.

Jewish people throughout history have made significant contributions worthy of recognition. Four books in this chapter reveal the lives of characters, fictional and real, who contributed to both Jewish and general history. Contemporary children will find special appeal in *Sarah Somebody*, the story of a young girl living in 19th century Poland who wants a formal education at a time when this is not the norm. Through *Haym Solomon: Liberty's Son*, youngsters will discover the contributions that Solomon made to the American Revolution. Stadtler's *The Adventures of Glueckel of Hameln* is a moving acount of one Jewish "woman of valor" who lived in Hamburg, Germany during the late seventeenth and early eighteenth centuries. Finally, the contributions Jews have made to the world of sports cannot be denied, nor should they be overlooked. Hence the book *Great Jews in Sports* is included as well.

By bringing Jewish history alive for our children, we allow them to take on the proud name of Yisrael, whose Hebrew root means "to wrestle." And wrestle they will, just as has each generation before us, with the multitude of ideas and events, both joyous and sad, which have punctuated Jewish history.

JEWISH HISTORY: BOOKS AND ACTIVITIES

Cohen, Barbara. *Gooseberries to Oranges.*

Illus. by Beverly Brodsky. New York: Lothrop, Lee & Shepard Co., 1982. 29 pages. Grade level: 2-4.

Striking illustrations colorfully depict young Fanny's early childhood in Russia, her journey to America, and the beginnings of her life in a new land. The narrator of the book recalls warm memories of the home left behind and the horror of the pogroms which forced her journey to America. At first frightened and disappointed in her new home, she slowly adjusts when she begins school and makes a new friend. The adjustment is symbolized as Fanny enjoys an American orange and states that she would not give this up for the gooseberries of her Russian birthplace.

Major Ideas

The immigrant experience is characterized by both struggle and reward.

For individuals fleeing oppression, the fruits of a new land are often sweeter than those of their native home.

Activities

1. Grades 3 and 4: Fanny knew that her long and treacherous journey across the ocean was coming to an end when she saw the Statue of Liberty. Explain to students that the Statue of Liberty has been a welcome sight for immigrants throughout the history of the United States. Also note that the poem inscribed on the Statue was written by Emma Lazarus, a Jewish poet. Read the poem. It may be found in *The World Book Encyclopedia*, 1981 edition, page 688b, and in *The American Poets 1800-1900*, edited by Edwin H. Cady (New York: Scott Foresman and Co.,1966). This poem may be difficult for younger students to understand. Therefore, you may wish also to paraphrase its meaning. After discussing the meaning of the Statue of Liberty and the poem, have the students create their own Statues of Liberty using the box sculpture technique. Materials and procedure follow.

   Materials:

   boxes of various sizes and shapes which students collect at home
   string
   white liquid glue or rubber cement
   straight pins
   X-acto knife (to be handled only by the teacher)
   scissors
   construction paper
   tempera paint
   glitter and collage materials

   Procedure:

   a. Sketch a rough design for the statue, if desired.

   b. Decorate individual boxes and/or pieces with paint, construction paper, and/or collage materials. Any holes cut in the boxes which cannot be cut by the children using scissors should be cut by the teacher with the X-acto knife.

   c. Fasten the separate boxes and/or pieces together with glue. Some pieces may need to be tacked on with a straight pin.

   d. Using string, tie the boxes together until the glue has dried, preferably overnight.

   e. On a piece of construction paper small enough to be glued to their statue, each student may write a poem welcoming new immigrants to this land. These can be displayed in your classroom or elsewhere in the school with a sign reading "ברוכים הבאים (*Baruchim HaBa'im* — Blessed is Your Coming")."

2. Grades 2-4: Just as Fanny and her family were immigrants to the United States, so, too, were our families at one time. To help students get in touch with their family's history, engage them in the following genealogical activity.

   a. Send the students home with the handout in Diagram 9.

   b. When the handouts are returned, collect them and compile four separate lists containing the information on birthplaces. The four separate lists are:

      a list of states in which the students were born.
      a list of states in which the parents were born.
      a list of countries in which the grandparents were born.
      a list of countries in which the great-grandparents were born.

   c. Also keep a list of all the cities in which the members of each generation were born and the number born in each city. These lists will be typed and later given to the students.

   d. Prepare the outline of four large graphs. Hang these in your room. There should be a graph for each generation. Each student should have a dittoed replica of each graph outline (see Diagram 10).

   e. Return the original family tree handouts and tell students to use them as a reference for the next activity. Starting with the students' generation, call out the name of a state and ask the students who were born in that state to raise their hands. Count the number and fill in the bar above that state to the appropriate number. The student should then fill in the same bar on their graphs.

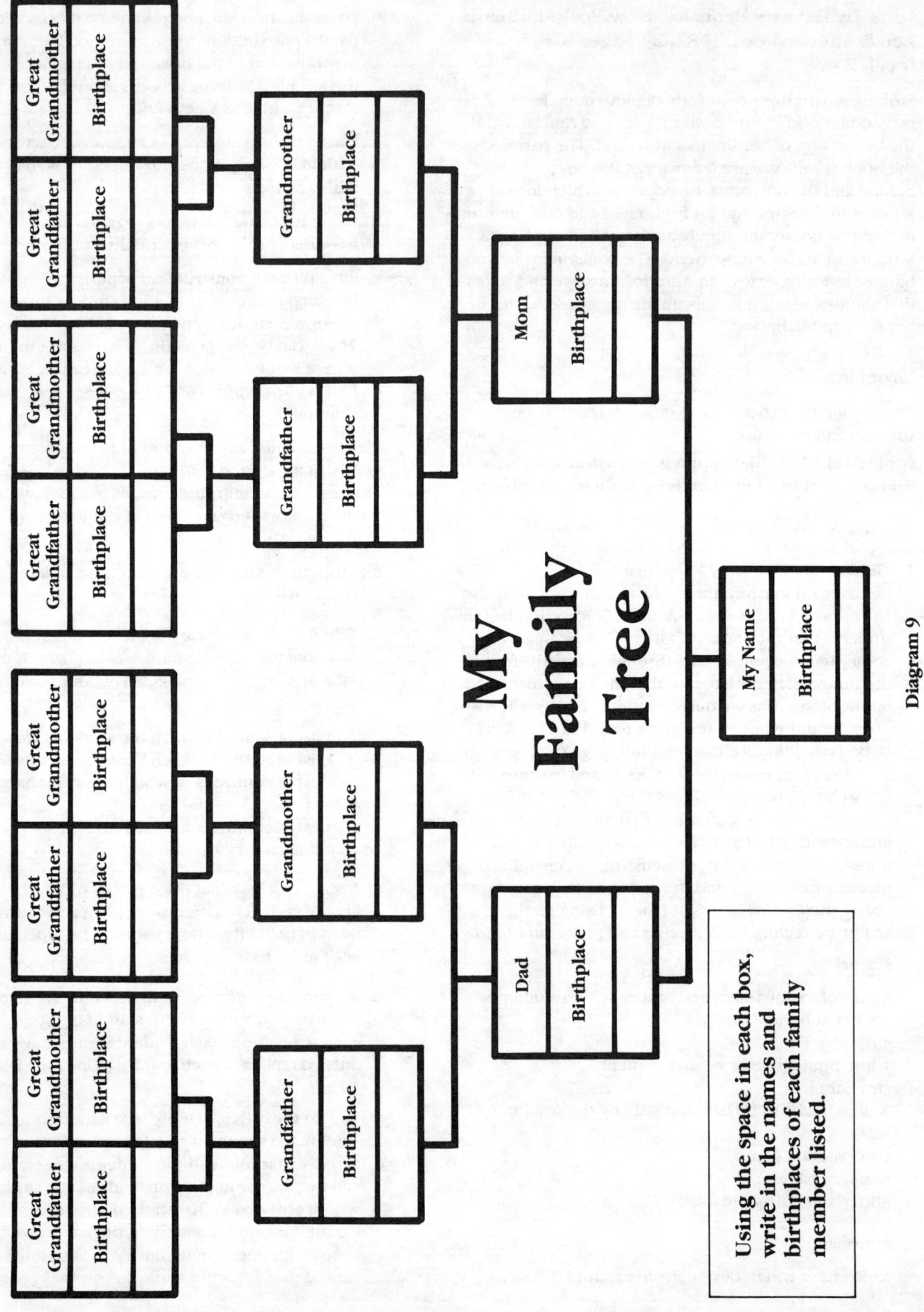

Diagram 9

Jewish History

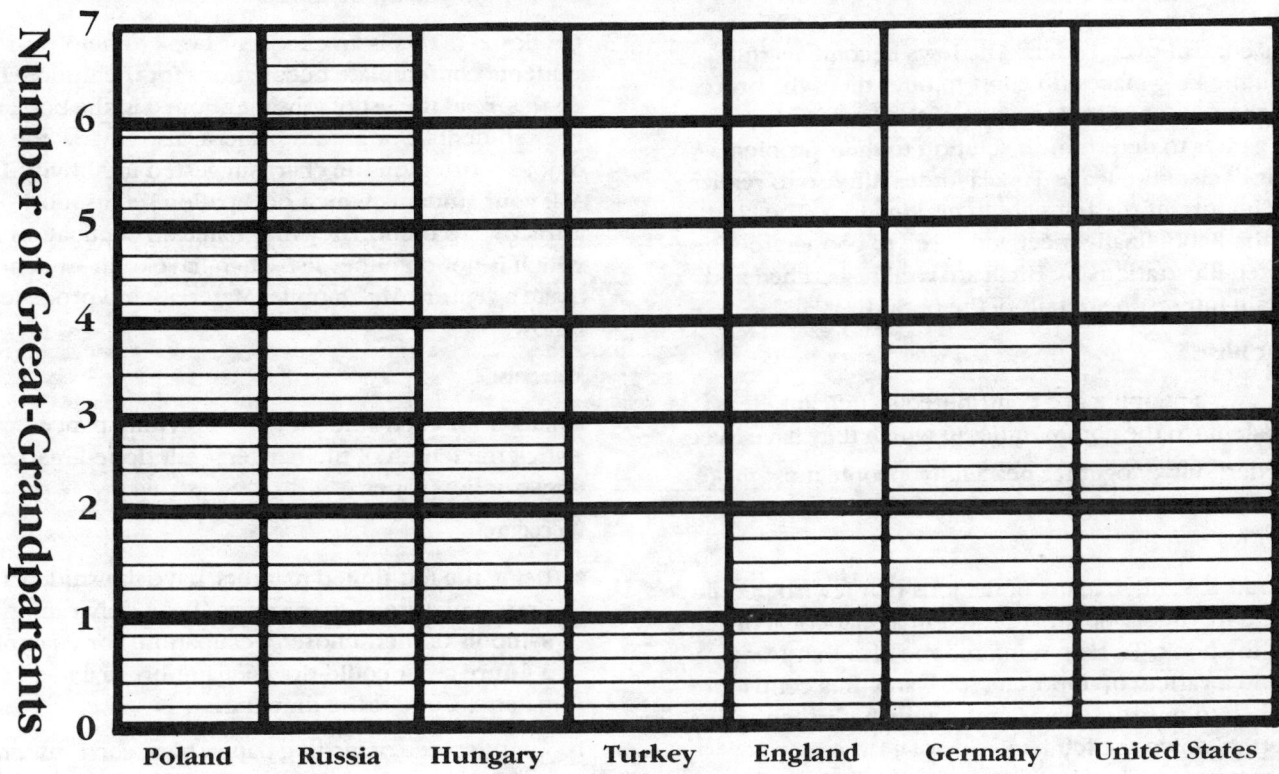

Diagram 10

This may be done with crayon, colored pencil, or marker. The same process should be used for filling in all four bar graphs. (In a day school, this activity can be integrated with secular math or social studies.)

f. Once the students have completed their graphs, attach the lists of the cities of birth and have the students take their work home to share with their families.

3. Grades 2-4: One of Fanny's memories is of her father reading from a Yiddish newspaper. Explain to the students that many of the Jewish immigrants who came here from European countries spoke Yiddish, which is a combination of many languages including German, Hebrew, English, Russian, and Polish. Take this opportunity to teach the students a few words of the language used by Fanny's father and many other Jewish immigrants. Some expressions and words you might want to teach the students are:

Terms of Endearment:

Shaineh madel – pretty girl
Shainkeit – beauty
tatele – little father
mamele – little mother
bubeleh – little grandmother

Members of the Family:

Mama – mother
Tate – father
bruder – brother
shvester – sister
tante – aunt
feter – uncle
bubby – grandma
zayde – grandpa

Greetings, Replies, and Other Common Phrases:

vus machs du? – How are you?
gut – good
gezuntheit – good health
mazel tov – good luck
zei gezunt – be well or goodbye
hab a gitten tog – have a good day.

For other ideas see *The Joys of Yiddish* by Leo Rosten; *Hooray for Yiddish: A Book About English* by Leo Rosten; *A Dictionary of Yiddish & Slang Idioms* by Fred Kogos.

Green, Jacqueline Dembar. *Butchers and Bakers, Rabbis and Kings.* Illus. by Marilyn Hirsh. Rockville, MD: Kar-Ben Copies, Inc., 1984. 30 pages. Grade level: K-4.

Based on an actual historical event, the author has told the story of a group of Jews living in Tudela, Spain in the 12th Century. A neighboring king, Alfonso the Warrior, gains control over Tudela. The Jews become fearful when the king makes no effort to offer them the protection they are used to. Members of the Jewish community gather to determine a solution to their problem. Their decision to leave Tudela forces Alfonso to realize how important the Jews are to his kingdom. The king and the Rabbi finally meet and agree to cooperate. The spirited illustrations by Hirsh are well researched and contain interesting details of the period.

Major Ideas

The Jewish people have contributed significant ideas and talents to the communities in which they have lived.

In order to live together peacefully, people must make the effort to communicate and cooperate.

Activities

1. Grades 3 and 4: Many of the jobs that Jewish people held in Tudela, Spain are listed in alphabetical order in the book. To help reinforce the idea that Jews hold a variety of important jobs, and thus contribute much to our society, print the alphabet in capital letters down the left hand side of a large piece of chart paper. Then have students brainstorm jobs which begin with each of the letters of the alphabet. Select only one job for each letter. Using capital letters, print the job title next to the appropriate letter of the alphabet. Depending on the size of class, assign each student or group of students to research the life of a Jewish person who is employed at the assigned jobs. The person need not be famous; he/she may be employed in the community. Print all persons' names in the appropriate space and display in the classroom. Have the students present oral reports based on the research. An example of jobs and names for the letters A-F follows:

A	RTIST	MARILYN	HIRSH
B	ARBER	VIDAL	SASSOON
C	OOK	JENNY	GROSSINGER
D	OCTOR	SIGMUND	FREUD
E	DUCATOR	(a teacher in the community)	
F	IDDLER	ISAAC	STERN

2. Grades K-4: It is stressed in the book that the talents of the Jewish people were sorely missed when they left Tudela. Take the opportunity to have the students reflect on the talents they have which would be missed if they left the community. Then have the class plan a talent show to be presented to their parents or at a school assembly. Begin the show with a retelling of *Butcher and Bakers, Rabbis and Kings*. When the story is completed, an announcer might say, "And now presenting some of the talented members of *our* Jewish community . . ."

3. Grades 2-4: This is an excellent book to help your students contemplate occupations for the future. To do this, read the list of jobs mentioned in the book to your students. For grades 3 and 4, also review the list of jobs written on the chart suggested in Activity 1. Ask your students which occupation seems most attractive to them. They may name an occupation which is not on either list. Then have each student make a "Future Me" mobile. Materials and procedure follow.

Materials:

a hanger for each student   writing paper
a stick the length of the hanger   felt tipped markers
construction paper   string

Procedure:

a. Using the felt tipped markers, have the students draw a picture of themselves (head only) and two symbols of their chosen occupation. For example, a future artist could draw a paint brush and a palette. Cut out the drawings.

b. On the piece of writing paper, have each student write a story about how they will use their chosen occupation to help both the Jewish and secular communities.

c. Punch holes at the top of the portrait, each symbol, and their story. Assemble the mobile as suggested in Diagram 11.

Diagram 11

Ish-Kishor, Sulamith. *A Boy of Old Prague.* **Illus. by Ben Shahn. New York: Pantheon Books, 1963. 90 pages. Grade level: 4 and up.**

Tomas, a young boy living in 16th century Czechoslovakia, works as a serf for a cruel and uncompassionate young lord. As many Christians of that time, Tomas believed that Jews could cast evil spells and were the property of the devil. When he is forced to become a servant for the father of Rachael, a young Jewess whom his lord finds attractive, Tomas's opinion of the Jewish people begins to change. He learns to respect, admire, and even love his new master. Thus, Tomas is devastated when he discovers that his lord is planning a pogrom against the people of the ghetto because Rachael has rebuked his advances. When the pogrom occurs, Tomas finds among the rubble and remains of a human bonfire a personal object which belonged to Rachael. Unable to believe that Rachael, her father, and little brother are dead, Tomas vows to continue to look for them and declares that "the God of mercy is the same God, no matter where we find Him." Ben Shahn's illustrations poignantly capture the scenes of old Prague.

Major Ideas

Stereotypes can cloud our ability to experience people as they really are.

More often than not, it is the stereotypes, rather than consideration of actual behavior, that cause us to discriminate against certain groups in our society.

God has compassion for all people no matter how they choose to worship. It is important for us to demonstrate that same compassion for one another.

Activities

1. Grade 6: Stereotypes often interfere with an individual's ability to perceive various groups accurately and also influence the way these groups are treated. This is a major theme in this book. To illustrate this concept to your students, list the names of several minority groups across the top of the blackboard. Some possibilities are Blacks, Native Americans, Mexican Americans, Puerto Ricans, Jews, and Orientals. Choose the groups which are most prevalent in the area in which you live. Ask the students to volunteer stereotypes that they hold, or know are held, about the groups which are listed. Write their responses under the appropriate columns, then transfer these to a chart labeled "Stereotypes." After this activity, assign groups of students to research the lifestyles and contributions of a specific minority group. Have the students creatively present their findings two weeks later. Presentations can include drama, art, music, song, films, dance, etc. After the presentations, take out the Stereotype Chart and discuss how the students' knowledge confirmed or dispelled the stereotypes.

2. Grades 4 and up: After living with the Jewish people, Tomas came to realize that Jews are not demons and that the actions of the Christian people against the Jews were inhumane and unjust. At the end of the book, he decides to help the Jewish people. Have the students imagine that they are Tomas and feel his compulsion to write a letter to their lord. Have them attempt to convince the lord that Jews should not be discriminated against and should not be terrorized through pogroms. Share the letters in small groups and discuss which aspects of each letter were convincing.

3. Grades 5 and up: The reader learns from the book that Christians in the sixteenth century attempted to convert the Jews by reason. Most Jews, however, were able to use their reasoning power to dispute the arguments for conversion presented by the Christians. The conversion activities employed by the various cults and missionary groups in this country are a contemporary parallel. After familiarizing adult volunteers with some typical conversion tactics, invite them to class to engage in role plays with the students. The adult will take the role of the one wishing to convert the student. The student must fight the pressure to convert through rational arguments. Those students not participating in the role playing at a given moment should observe. Conclude with a group discussion focusing on the following questions:

   How did you feel as the person tried to convert you?

   Which arguments proved most successful in combating the pressure to convert?

   How might you handle the situation now were it actually to arise?

   An excellent reference for the teacher is *You Take Jesus, I'll Take God* by Samuel Levine (Los Angeles, CA: Hamorah Press, 1980).

Milgrim, Shirley. *Haym Salomon: Liberty's Son.* **Illus. by Richard Fish. Philadelphia: The Jewish Publication Society of America, 1975. 119 pages. Grade level: 5 and up.**

Milgrim has given glorious tribute to a Jewish hero of the American Revolution. Haym Salomon, a Polish born Jew, was fiercely dedicated to the building of a free America. Imprisoned twice for his underground activities, Haym escaped and continued to work for the revolutionary cause. During the Revolution, America was faced with one financial crisis after another. Salomon not only raised the money necessary to fight the war, but often personally financed military units. This is an important book for children, as it relates how Jews contributed to the cause of freedom in the United States.

Major Ideas

Philanthropy is an important dimension of the Jewish way of life.

The preservation of human life takes precedence over all other commandments and obligations.

As American Jews, we must uphold our obligations not only to this country, but to the Jewish community as well.

The Jewish people played an important role in the establishment of the United States as a free country.

Activities

1. Grades 5 and up: Unfortunately, the role that Jews played in American history is not often included in the history curricula of public schools. After reading this book about Haym Salomon, help your children learn about some of the other important Jewish figures in American history. A good starting point for finding a list of important personalities is the *Pictorial History of the Jewish People: From Bible Times to Our Own Day Throughout the World* by Nathan Ausubel. Look specifically at the chapter entitled "The United States of America," pages 270-300. Once personalities have been chosen, direct the students to other sources, such as *Encyclopaedia Judaica*. After each student has researched an important Jewish figure, remind him/her that the United States Postal Service issued a series of stamps commemorating important figures in the American Revolution. Haym Salomon was commemorated in the stamp shown at the conclusion of Milgrim's book. A citation was also written summarizing Salomon's contributions. Now, ask each student to design a stamp and write a short citation commemorating the person he/she researched. Display the stamp on a bulletin board entitled "American Jewish History: Our Stamps of Pride."

2. Grades 5 and up: In the book, the author makes reference to the growth in population of the Philadelphia Jewish community during the Revolution and the decrease in New York's Jewish population. Help the students realize that although some large cities, such as New York and Los Angeles, have very large Jewish populations, there are actually Jews living in the cities and towns of all fifty states. To make this visually apparent, create a Jewish population map in your classroom. Assign each student the task of researching the Jewish population in one or more states. Have them also find out which cities in the state have the most sizable Jewish population. Good sources for obtaining this information are the Jewish Federations in each state. A list of federations may be found in *The Second Jewish Catalog* by Sharon Strassfeld and Michael Strassfeld. Look specifically at "The Jewish Yellow Pages" in the back of the book, pages 422-423. For best results, the students should write first to the Federations of the largest cities listed in each state. Federations for the following five states are not listed: Hawaii, Alaska, Wyoming, North Dakota, and Montana. The governor's office of these states or a synagogue in the state's largest city may be able to provide this information.

   Draw the map on a large piece of butcher paper that will fit on a bulletin board in your classroom. The teacher should supply each student with a cut-out drawing of a little person holding a sign. The student is responsible for writing the name of the state and its Jewish population on the sign. Each population marker should then be glued on the appropriate state on the map. Small circles can be made with a paper punch to be glued at the sites of the most sizable Jewish populations within each state.

3. Grades 5 and up: The importance of philanthropy is the major theme of this book. According to traditional Jewish law, we are to set aside ten to twenty percent of our earnings for philanthropic purposes (*tzedakah*). A fine way of teaching your students how to budget money for philanthropy is through a values clarification exercise done in small groups. Have each group imagine that they are one person and have $100.00 to budget for the coming week. Money must be budgeted for each of the following needs: food, transportation, household supplies, personal needs such as clothing, leisure activities, philanthropic purposes.

   Tell each group to share their budget with the rest of the class, giving a rationale for how they distributed their funds. After each group has shared its budget, explain that if they were budgeting according to Jewish law, they would have to allocate $10.00 to $20.00 for philanthropy. Those groups which did not do so must go over their budget again and discuss ways of redistributing their dollars. Remember that the emphasis of the exercise should be placed upon the values which determine how a decision is made.

Richman, Carol. *The Lekachmacher Family*. Illus. by the author. Seattle, WA: Madrona Publishers, Inc., 1976. 28 pages. Grade level: K-2.

The author's family history provided the inspiration for this story. Through the simple narrative and vivid ink and watercolor illustrations, children can better understand the immigrant experience. The book traces the progress of a family from Czarist Russia to their resettlement in the United States, capturing the wide range of emotions experienced in separation from the past and adjustment to life in a new environment.

Major Ideas

Adjusting to life in a new environment is difficult, yet rewarding.

We must cope with separation each time we say good-bye to significant people and places in our lives.

Persecution has different effects on people, including the necessity to leave the home one loves.

Freedom is a very important factor in our lives.

Activities

1. Grades K-2: Teach the song "Free To Be . . . You and Me." The words and music may be found in *Free To Be . . . You and Me* by Marlo Thomas (McGraw Hill, 1974). A recording of the song may be found on *Free To Be . . . You and Me* (Artista Records).

2. Grades K-2: Invite a guest to your classroom who has been through the process of immigration. Ask him/her to tell the students what life was like in the old country and how he/she adjusted to life in the United States. Using questions prepared in advance, students can ask questions during and after the presentation.

3. Grades K-2: The evening before the story is to be read, change the classroom arrangement as completely as possible. Dress in a style with which the students are unfamiliar. Speak in a foreign tongue, which may be imaginary. Allow the students to voice their reactions to the change. Use this as an introduction to the reading of the book.

Roseman, Kenneth. *The Cardinal's Snuff Box.* Illus. by Bill Negron. New York: Union of American Hebrew Congregations, 1982. 120 pages. Grade level: 3-6.

The stories in this book take place during the Spanish Inquisition. On the first page, the reader is asked to imagine that he/she is a wealthy Jewish child living in Spain in 1492. On the bottom of every other page, a choice is presented to the reader, such as converting to Christianity or leaving Spain to remain Jewish. Depending on the choice made, the reader is instructed to continue reading on a particular page. The eventual outcome of the story is determined by the choices the reader makes. Each story is an adventure, exposing children to the dilemmas which the Jews faced during the Inquisition and the consequences of their decisions. Key figures and important places from this period of history are also introduced.

Major Ideas

The choices made by individual Jews during the Inquisition had both personal and collective ramifications.

One of the greatest strengths of the Jewish people is the capacity to remain strong even through adverse times.

Activities

1. Grades 3-6: This book provides an excellent motivation for students to learn about Sephardic tradition. Share this book at the beginning of the semester, and then at class holiday celebrations throughout the school year, partake in Sephardic, as well as Ashkenazic, ways of celebrating. Some examples of Sephardic celebrations follow. These are taken from "Milk, Honey and Roses," an article by Gilda Angel in *Keeping Posted: The Sephardim*, Volume XXVIII, No. 3.

When studying Rosh Hashanah, serve pomegranate. Sephardim eat this fruit hoping that good deeds in the coming year will be as many as the fruit's seeds.

At Chanukah, along with potato *latkes*, serve *paneckuchen* (pancakes eaten by Dutch Sephardim), *birmuelos* (deep fried yeast doughnuts eaten by Turkish Jews), *lokoumades* (fried dough puffs eaten by Greek Jews), and funnel cakes (eaten by Persian Jews).

At Passover, serve Sephardic *charoset* which is made with dates.

On Shavuot, referred to by Persian Jews as the Festival of Roses, serve rice pudding made with milk and prepared in a ring mold with rose petals in the center as a decoration.

Four recipes follow, two of which include some interesting comments by the author. These and other Sephardic delicacies may be found in *Sephardic Holiday Cooking* by Gilda Angel, forthcoming from Decalogue Books, 7 North MacQuesten Parkway, Mount Vernon, NY 10550. This book is available for purchase from the publisher at $19.95 each.

Turkish Haroset (Cooked)

Makes 2 cups

Ingredients:
1 medium orange
1 pound pitted dates
½ cup sugar
½ tsp. cinnamon (or to taste)
2 tbs. sweet wine
½ cup chopped walnuts

Procedure:
a. Wash orange and cut into eighths. Remove pits but do not peel. Chop finely with knife, or coarsely grind in food mill. Coarsely chop dates.
b. In saucepan, combine orange, dates, sugar, cinnamon, and wine. Mix well. Cook over low heat, stirring often, until mixture is soft, about 20 minutes. Remove from heat and stir in walnuts.
c. Cover and refrigerate. Serve at room temperature.

Turkish Haroset (Uncooked)
Makes 3-3½ cups

Ingredients:
1 cup seedless raisins
1 pound pitted dates
1 orange, peeled, sliced crosswise and pitted
1 apple, peeled, cored and sliced
2 tbs. sweet wine

Procedure:
a. Soak raisins 30 minutes in hot water to cover. Drain.
b. Grind raisins, dates, orange, and apple together. Add sweet wine to make a thick paste.
c. Cover and refrigerate until 1 hour before serving.

Pepitas
(Toasted Pumpkin Seeds)
Makes 1 cup

Munching on *pepitas* is a favorite pastime throughout the Moslem world. *Sephardim* living in that region soon acquired the habit. To become a good *pepita* eater requires patience, but it is a skill worth developing. No reason other than their good taste is needed for eating *pepitas*, but this activity also offers relaxation and an opportunity for meditation.

Ingredients:
1 cup raw pumpkin or squash seeds
salt to taste

Procedure:
a. Wash seeds well and remove any remaining fibers. Dry 2 days at room temperature.
b. Preheat oven to 300° F.
c. Spread seeds in single layer on cookie sheet. Sprinkle with about 2 teaspoons water. Salt lightly. Bake 20-25 minutes, or until slightly golden and crisp. Cool completely. Store in covered container.

Foulares
(Turkish Hard Boiled Eggs Wrapped with Cheese Pastry)
Makes 8

Turkish and Greek Sephardic Jews make these foot-shaped pastries only once a year — just before *Purim*. The exact shape varies from community to community. In one typical version depicting Haman in jail, the villainous Haman is represented by an unshelled hard boiled egg. Strips of pastry surrounding the egg are meant to symbolize prison bars. Another interpretation of this foot-shaped pastry is that the secured egg represents Haman's ankle.

Traditionally, these unusual pastries are eaten on the Sabbath just before *Purim*, *Shabbat Zakhor*. In the *Torah* reading for that day, the treachery of Amalek is recalled. Jewish tradition has it that Haman descended from the evil Amalekites.

In my husband's family [Gilda Angel's husband's family], lunch after morning services on *Shabbat Zakhor* invariably includes *foulares*. Accompanied by salads and coffee, or milk for the children, *foulares* are considered a special treat. They are also used for *mishloach manot*, the sending of gifts, on *Purim*, since the two different blessings made on *Purim* can be recited before eating them (*mezonot* for the pastry and *shehakol* for the egg).

Ingredients:
1 cup vegetable oil
⅔ cup water
1 tsp. salt
⅛ tsp. pepper
4½ cups all-purpose flour
1¼ cups grated Cheddar cheese
8 hard-cooked eggs (leave shells on)

a. Preheat oven to 400° F. In a large bowl, combine oil, water, salt, pepper, flour, and cheese. Mix to form soft, pliable dough.
b. On lightly floured surface, roll dough to a thickness of ¼ inch. Cut foot-shaped pieces of dough measuring approximately 4½ x 2½ inches. Press an egg into heel end of foot and secure with strips of dough. Repeat with remaining dough and eggs. Left over dough can be shaped into small crackers and baked.
c. Bake on ungreased cookie sheets in preheated 400° F. oven 20 minutes, or until dough is golden brown. Serve hot, warm, or at room temperature.

2. Grades 3-6: In social studies texts commonly used in our American schools, Queen Isabella and King Ferdinand are described as good leaders who provided Columbus with the necessary ships to cross the Atlantic to the New World. Little, if anything is ever written about their role as leaders of the Inquisition. Have the students work in pairs, imagining that they are textbook writers assigned to write about Ferdinand and Isabella's role in the Inquisition. After the compositions are proofread, have each pair write a letter to a different social studies textbook publisher. The letter should request that in the next printing of the text, information about Queen Isabella and King Ferdinand's role in the Inquisition should be included. The students should conclude their letter by stating that they are enclosing facts on this event in history. Attach the students' compositions to the letters. Some names of their publishers, texts, and addresses of the publishers follows:

Follet Social Studies: *Our United States* (Grade 5)
Follet Publishing Co.
Division of Follet Corp.
1010 W. Washington Blvd.
Chicago, IL 60607

Ginn Social Science Series: *One Nation: The United States* (Grade 5)
Ginn & Co.
191 Spring St.
Lexington, MA 02173

Houghton Mifflin Social Studies: *America: Past & Present* (Grade 5)
Houghton Mifflin Co.
2 Park Street
Boston, MA 02107

McGraw Hill Social Studies Series: *Understanding the United States Our History* (Grade 5)
McGraw Hill Co.
1221 Avenue of the Americas
New York, NY 10020

Scott Foresman Social Studies: *America: Past & Present* (Grade 5)
Scott Foresman
1900 E. Lake Ave.
New York, NY 10017

3. Grades 3-6: As is indicated in the book, many of the Jews from Spain immigrated to other countries to seek religious freedom. Once there, they sought permission to build synagogues in their new home. Have the students imagine that they have just left Spain and have been granted permission to build a synagogue in their new homeland. Using drawing paper, have each student design a synagogue of their own showing an exterior and interior view. The synagogue's name should then be printed on the exterior view. These can be displayed on a bulletin board entitled: "Synagogues from Sephardic Souls." After the drawings are completed and put on display, invite in people in the community who have photographs or slides of Sephardic synagogues in Israel or elsewhere to share these with the students.

Sachs, Marilyn. *Call Me Ruth*. New York: Doubleday and Co., Inc., 1982. 134 pages. Grade level: 4 and up.

Rifka and her mother receive a letter from papa stating that he has finally saved enough money to pay for their transport to America. They are elated. For eight years Rifka's mother had waited for the opportunity to join her husband and to escape the oppression of Czarist Russia. In America the relationship between Rifka and her mother becomes strained. Rifka strives to become an ideal American and is uneasy with her mother's radical union activities. Sachs has written a moving story about the struggles of Jewish immigrants at the turn of the century in America. The somewhat typical distancing between an adolescent and her mother as depicted in this book adds to its universal appeal.

Major Idea

Oppression can lead to rebellion.

Children are often more flexible than adults in their ability to adjust to a new environment.

Childhood memories and family history play an important role in shaping the lives of children as they grow up.

Activities

1. Grades 4 and up: Rifka's mother finds her niche in the United States through involvement in the labor movement. Hold a discussion focusing on the conditions under which Rifka's mother worked. Ask the students to imagine how they would feel working under similar conditions. Then emphasize the fact that Samuel Gompers, along with many other Jews who were active in the early formation of labor unions, started the effort to protect the rights of workers in this county. Union songs were, and continue to be, a means of building cohesiveness among workers and inspiring them to fight for their rights. Teach students such songs as "We Shall Overcome" and "We Shall Not Be Moved." A source for these and other union songs is *Songs of Work and Freedom* by Edith Fowke and Joe Glazer.

2. Grades 4 and up: When Rifka and her mother were still living in Russia, Rifka's mother would often sing to her. One of the songs she sang expresses her mother's hopes for Rifka's future. Write a letter to the students' parents telling them a little about the book and how Rifka's mother communicates her hopes for Rifka through song. Ask the parents to write a poem or song for their child which expresses their personal hopes for the child's future. As an example, include the song of Rifka's mother found on page 4 of the book. Plan a special Shabbat family dinner or day in class when the poems or songs can be presented out loud.

3. Grades 4 and up: Rifka came to America when she was eight years old. Her father had never seen her because he had left Russia before she was born. Have students imagine that they are in the same situation as Rifka, eager to share with their father the years of their life which he has not known. Give each student a piece of 36" x 12" heavy weight white construction paper. Fold it accordian style, into nine equal sections. Label sections from birth to age eight. The students will then draw a self-portrait of how they looked during each year. They may also wish to draw other memories around the portraits. Actual photographs of the students taken during their first eight years may be brought to class to help them with this

project. When the portraits are completed, stand them up on display.

Slater, Robert. *Great Jews in Sports.* **New York: Jonathan David Publishers, Inc., 1983. 288 pages. Grade level: 4 and up.**

This book is a welcome treat for the young sports enthusiast. Included in the book are biographical sketches of famous Jewish sports figures. Photographs of the personalities in action add to the excitement of the text.

Major Ideas

Jews have made major contributions to the world of sports.

To achieve greatness in a sport or any other endeavor requires stamina, skill, and perservance.

Activities

1. Grades 4 and up: As described in the last chapter of the book, Israelis hold their own Olympic style events called the Maccabiah Games. Have your class plan a Maccabiah for the entire school. Depending on your scheduling needs, the event can last a full day or a half day. Begin your Maccabiah games by singing "*Hatikvah*" and your country's national anthem. A variety of sports events should be planned, and encourage all students to participate in at least one event. Have your class design a certificate to be given to each student. Leave space on the certificate to write in the student's name and event(s) participated in.

2. Grades 4 and up: Using the same format as Slater's book, have your students create their own book entitled *Great Jews in (teacher's name) Class, (date)*. Each student should write a short autobiographical sketch, including in the sketch a paragraph on what the student does well. A photograph of the student engaged in his/her special activity should accompany the autobiography. Photographs and compositions can be compiled with an introduction by the teacher and placed in the history section of the library. If possible, run off a copy of the book for each class member.

3. Grades 4 and up: Allow the students to share their knowledge of Jewish sports figures with other students in the school. Have them create a Jewish Sports Hall of Fame such as the one existing in Netanya, Israel. Assign each child to read one autobiographical sketch from *Great Jews in Sports*. After the research is completed, have students write a brief summary of what they have read. The summaries are then submitted for typing. Mount the typed summaries on colored cardboard. Now, give each student a three pound ball of self-hardening clay from which they will create a sculpture of their assigned figure in action. Secure a room in your facility and display the sculptures and biographical information. Send out invitations inviting other classes to the opening of your Jewish Sports Hall of Fame. Serve Gatorade, the drink of athletes.

Slobodkin, Florence. *Sarah Somebody.* **Illus. by Louis Slobodkin. New York: Vanguard Press, Inc., 1969. 72 pages. Grade level: 2-4.**

An inspiring book for children who no longer wish to accept gender role stereotypes. Sarah is a nine-year-old Jewish girl in a turn of the century Polish village. She wants to be educated at a time when it is not common for Jewish girls to receive a formal education. Sarah's parents find a teacher for her and she becomes an excellent student. Her handwriting is so beautiful that other girls in the school pay her to see their names in beautiful print. Sarah uses the money to help a poor friend. She also enables her grandmother to see her name in writing for the first time.

Major Ideas

Jewish tradition places emphasis on the importance of both Jewish and secular education.

Tzedakah is a hallmark of the Jewish way of life.

Maintaining Jewish tradition while adapting to the mainstream can be a great challenge.

"We walk alike . . . the very young and the very old." The generations are linked by shared dreams (*Sarah Somebody*, page 14).

Women have varied roles in traditional and contemporary Jewish life.

Activities

1. Grades 2-4: Sarah achieves an independent identity through various experiences. This provides an excellent introduction to the process of becoming a *mensch* (a good person). Have the students develop a *Me the Mensch Book*, perhaps over the period of an entire semester or two. Some of the thought provoking "chapters" could be:

    A self-portrait of the *Mensch*
    A "where the *Mensch* comes from" family tree
    Comic strip illustrations of moments that stand out in the *Mensch's* mind
    A recipe for becoming a *Mensch*
    The *Mensch's* meditation: A prayer about things for which I'm thankful

2. Grades 2-4: For a day, run the class like a *cheder*. This atmosphere can be achieved by dressing as a bearded teacher and accomplishing the day's tasks through rote learning.

3. Grades 2-4: Sarah shared her knowledge and expertise with the people around her. Give the students in your class an opportunity to do the same with "show and *kvell*." Set aside a time for each to share a hobby, special interest, or favorite Jewish activity with the class. Allow the students to ask questions of the "*kveller*."

Stadtler, Bea. *The Adventures of Glueckel of Hameln*. Illus. by Paul Sharon. New York: United Synagogue of America, 1967. 135 pages. Grade level: 5 and up.

Basing her book on the original memoirs of Glueckel of Hameln, Bea Stadtler has created a beautiful story about a fascinating, yet little known, figure in Jewish history. Glueckel lived in Hamburg, Germany during the late seventeenth and early eighteenth century. The warmth of Glueckel's family relationships is contrasted to the bitterness of the pogroms, the plague, and other tragic events of the time. The greatest joy of Glueckel's life was that she was able to share with her grandchildren the same treasured relationship that her grandmother shared with her. The Glueckel about whom Bea Stadtler writes is a strong and admirable woman.

Major Ideas

Women play a vital role in Jewish family life and history.

Strong family relationships are the heart of Jewish life.

Children learn through the example of their families.

It is important to avoid the temptations of false Messiahs.

Activities

1. Grades 5 and up: Glueckel of Hameln is but one example of the important role that women have played in Jewish family life and history. Other important women in Jewish history are:

    Women in the Bible
    Golda Meir (Prime Minister of Israel)
    Henrietta Szold (founder of Hadassah)
    Hannah Senesh (paratrooper during the Holocaust)
    Rebecca Gratz (founder of first Jewish religious school in America)

    As a tribute to these women, plan an *Ayshet Chayil* (Woman of Valor) Award ceremony. Separate your students into boy-girl pairs. Assign each couple the task of researching the life and contributions of one important woman in Jewish history. Tell the boy that he will be writing and delivering a one minute speech focusing on the qualities which have made her the woman deserving of the *Ayshet Chayil* Award. Tell the girl that she will be writing and delivering a one minute acceptance speech in the character of her assigned person. The ceremony will take place at an upper grade school assembly.

    The participating boys will wear suits and ties and each girl will come dressed as her character. The teacher or one of the students can serve as master/mistress of ceremonies. Each woman of valor will be presented with a tin foil covered Star of David. After the ceremony, hold a reception for the honored winners with punch and cookies.

2. Grades 5 and up: Bea Stadtler has dedicated this book to her mother, referring to her as "My *Ayshet Chayil*." On Friday night at the Shabbat table, it is traditional for husbands or other members of the family to read to the woman of the home "A Woman of Valor" — Proverbs 31:10-31. This reading reflects the traditional Jewish emphasis on the important role of women in the home. Share this reading with your class, pointing out and discussing that although today's women still play an important part in the home, they have taken on many other roles as well. Ask the students to choose a woman in their own family whom they consider to be a woman of valor. Have them write a Proverbs-style poem which focuses on the qualities which make the person they selected a woman of valor. It is written in the original Proverbs that "Her children shall rise up and call her blessed." Have students "rise up" and neatly print their poem on a piece of parchment paper, decorate the edges, and send or hand deliver the work to their woman of valor.

3. Grades 5 and up: As a child, Glueckel wanted very much to become an important person in the community. Have a discussion with students, focusing on their individual hopes and dreams for the future. After the discussion, have the students design a pair of sunglasses which reflect one or more of their dreams for the future. Make the frame for the glasses from construction paper or light weight cardboard. Embellish with a variety of materials. Use colored acetate for the lenses. An example follows in Diagram 12.

    After the children have fun wearing their glasses in class, display the glasses on a bulletin board entitled: "Looking Into Our Future."

Chapter VIII

Diagram 12

JEWISH HISTORY: BOOKS FOR CHILDREN

Barris, Sylvia. *Sir Moses Montefiore: The Champion in a Stage Coach.* New York: Bloch Publishing Co., 1964. Grade level: 3-6.

This fictional biography describes the great philanthropic works of Sir Moses Montefiore, whose generosity benefited Jews through the world.

Blaine, Marge. *Dvora's Journey.* Illus. by Gabriel Lisowski. New York: Holt, Rinehart & Winston, Inc., 1979. Grade level: 4-6.

This novel is based on the author's experience of trying to immigrate to America before the Russian Revolution. A suspenseful and sometimes somber story.

Blumenthal, Shirley. *Coming to America; Immigrants from Eastern Europe.* New York: Delacorte Press, 1981. Grade level: 6 and up.

One chapter in this well researched book deals with Jews who lived in Eastern Europe and made the decision to come to the United States.

Brodsky, Beverly. *Secret Place.* Illus. by the author. New York: J.B. Lippincott Co., 1979. Grade level: 4.

A sensory view into an old Jewish neighborhood, this book evokes memories of a time past. Children will travel to a neighborhood relatively unfamiliar in our contemporary life. Brodsky's watercolor illustrations are beautiful and reflect the setting well.

Burstein, Chaya M. *Joseph and Anna's Time Capsule: A Legacy From Old Prague.* Illus. by Nancy Edwards Calder. New York: Summit Books, 1984. Grade level: 5 and up.

This book was inspired by the museum exhibit, "A Precious Legacy: Judaic Treasures from the Czechoslovak State Collection." Burstein has skillfully used items from the exhibit to write the story of Joseph and Anna, two Jewish children living in nineteenth century Prague. Colorful illustrations and photographs complement the narrative which focuses on the Judaic and family dimensions of the children's lives. A warm and welcome addition to Jewish history books for children.

Burstein, Chaya M. *Rifka Grows Up.* Illus. by the author. New York: Hebrew Publishing Co., 1976. Grade level: 5 and up.

Life in a Russian village prior to the Russian Revolution is effectively recreated in this heartwarming and exciting book. The story focuses on Rifka, who is determined to go to high school and get an education. However, many obstacles stand in her way. The family, amidst the chaos of political upheaval, decides that in America "the world is open."

Colman, Hila, *Rachel's Legacy.* New York: William Morrow and Co., Inc. 1978. Grade level: 6 and up.

A clear picture of the Jewish immigrant experience in the early 1900s is conveyed in this well written book. The reader is exposed to the ways in which various individuals coped with life in the new land. The use of Yiddish terms adds realism to the story.

Ehrman, Herz Naftali. *The Kav.* New York: Feldheim Publishers, 1977. Grade level: 6 and up.

An interesting biography about the founder of the Lubavitcher movement, Rabbi Shneur Zalman.

Eiseman, Alberta. *Rebels and Reformers: Biographies of Four Jewish Americans.* Illus. by Herb Steinberg. New York: Doubleday and Co., Inc. 1976. Grade level: 5 and up.

This is a well researched book which offers profiles of the lives of Louis Brandeis, Uriah Phillips Levy, Ernestine Rose, and Lillian Waldman. The text is well written and makes for interesting reading.

Elkins, Dov Peretz. *God's Warriors: Dramatic Adventures of Rabbis in Uniform.* Illus. by Isobel Goldman. Middle Village, New York: Jonathan David Publishers, Inc., 1974. Grade level: 3-6.

In this exciting book, the adventures of Jewish chaplains from the Civil War to the War in Vietnam are recounted.

Faber, Doris. *Bella Abzug*. New York: Lothrop, Lee & Shepard Books, 1976. Illus. with photos. Grade level: 6 and up.

> A sprightly biography of Bella Abzug, the colorful and controversial New York Congressperson. Ms. Abzug's life is fascinating, as is this book.

Falstein, Louis. *The Man Who Loved Laughter: The Story of Sholom Aleichem*. Illus. by Adrienne O. Dudden. New York: The Jewish Publication Society of America, 1968. Grade level: 4 and up.

> Falstein has written an interesting biography which captures the highlights in the life of Sholom Aleichem, the beloved Yiddish writer and humorist.

Fast, Howard. *My Glorious Brothers*. New York: Bonim/Hebrew Publishing Co., 1977. Grade level: 6 and up.

> A skillful and moving novel about the Maccabean struggle against the Greek overlords of the Jews. The difficulty of life for the Jews during this period is stressed. A dramatic and well put together account.

Felton, Harold W. *Uriah Phillips Levy*. Illus. with photographs and prints. New York: Dodd, Mead and Co., 1972. Grade level: 5 and up.

> This interesting fictionalized biography recalls the attempts of Levy, the first Jewish commodore of the American navy, to apply Jewish values when in command.

Fisher, Leonard Everett. *A Russian Farewell*. Illus. by the author. New York: Four Winds Press, 1980. Grade level: 5 and up.

> The author has written a work of historical fiction about a Jewish family living in pre-revolutionary Russia. The powerful black and white illustrations are realistic and help to create the historical background.

Friedman, Russel. *Immigrant Kids*. Illus. with photos. New York: E.P. Dutton, 1980. Grade level: 4 and up.

> Fascinating photographs document the lives of immigrant children from a variety of backgrounds. The text is informative and interesting.

Geras, Adele. *Voyage*. New York: Atheneum Publishers, 1983. Grade level: 6 and up.

> Crossing the Atlantic to America was not easy for the immigrants whose stories are revealed in this book, but neither were their lives in Europe. This is an extremely well turned novel, depicting the dreams and fears of people of all ages who made the decision to come to America at the start of the century.

Gottesman, Meir. *Shpeter's Yesterday: Latecomer in Early History, From the Depths to the Heights*. New York: Judaica Press, Inc., 1981. Grade level: 3-5. (Two Volumes)

> The adventures of Shpeter are lovingly created by a grandfather whose grandchild is eager to learn about biblical times. In the first volume, Shpeter's experiences during the Exodus from Egypt are related. In the second volume, Shpeter is caught following the spies whom Moses sent ahead into Canaan.

Greenfeld, Howard. *Marc Chagall: An Introduction*. New York: Holt, Rinehart & Winston, Inc., 1981. Grade level: 6 and up.

> Reproductions of artist Marc Chagall's paintings add to the appeal of this concise biography.

Gray, Betty Anne. *Manya's Story*. Illus. with photographs. New York: Lerner Publications Co., 1978. Grade level: 6 and up.

> The life of the author's parents is depicted in this story of love and survival. Before arriving at Ellis Island in 1921, they experienced trauma and came close to death as the Red Army, White Army, and Ukranian Nationalists fought for control. The photographs beautifully enhance the book.

Gross, David C. *Pride of Our People: The Stories of One Hundred Outstanding Jewish Men and Women*. New York: Doubleday and Co., Inc., 1979. Grade level: 6 and up.

> Both modern day and historical Jewish personalities are highlighted in this book of short biographical sketches. Interesting anecdotal stories are told about the many figures included in the book.

Greenspan, Sophie. *Masada Will Not Fall Again*. Illus. by Unada. Philadelphia: The Jewish Publication Society of America, 1973.

> An interesting, although fictionalized, version of the Jews who chose suicide rather than defeat in their fight against the Romans.

Hartheimer, Eva. *Bustenai.* Brooklyn, New York: Merkos L'Inyonei Chinuch, 1982. Grade level: 4 and up.

> Hartheimer's novel is intriguing, in terms of its rapid style and of the little known figure in Jewish history about whom she writes. Bustenai, the last known descendant of the House of David, had, in fact, a tremendous impact on the Moslem world in which he lived.

Heller, Linda. *The Castle on Hester Street.* New York: The Jewish Publication Society of America, 1982. Grade level: K-2.

> Julie's grandfather has very fond memories of life on New York's Lower East Side. Julie listens to her grandfather's imaginative tales while her grandmother tells the stories as they actually occurred. A warm look at the past and love among the members of a close Jewish family.

Heyman, Anita. *Exit From Home.* New York: Crown Publishers, Inc., 1977. Grade level: 6 and up.

> Samuel is a young adolescent living in a Russian village just before the outbreak of the Revolution. He moves to a larger town to attend *Yeshiva.* There he meets people who influence his decision to break from the conventions of his religion and to participate instead in revolutionary activities. His decision to move to America is prompted by a pogrom. Heyman provides a realistic view of the Russian Jewish community's reaction to the Russian Revolution.

Hirsh, Marilyn. *Ben Goes Into Business.* Illus. by the author. New York: Holiday House, Inc., 1973. Grade level: 2-4.

> New York's Lower East Side is delightfully portrayed in this lively picture book. The story revolves around Ben, a ten-year-old, who starts his own business in a predominantly Jewish neighborhood.

Knight, Vick, Jr.. *Send For Haym Salomon.* Illus. by Joseph Hennger. Alhambra, CA: Borden Publishing Co., 1976. Grade level: 5 and up.

> The life of an important Jewish financier during the American Revolution is the subject of this fictionalized biography.

Kranzler, Gershon. *The Silver Matzoh and Other Stories.* Illus. by Betia Geffer. New York: Feldheim Publishers, 1981. Grade level: 5 and up.

> These ten stories, set in medieval times, are both exciting and historically accurate. The emphasis is on the importance of upholding Jewish tradition regardless of the hostile environment.

Lasky, Kathryn. *The Night Journey.* Illus. by Trina Schart Hyman. New York: Frederick Warne & Co., Inc., 1981. Grade level: 4 and up.

> Rachel, who lives in Czarist Russia, looks forward to hearing her great grandmother talk about her childhood. This book, winner of the National Jewish Book Award for Children's Literature in 1982, is vivid in the details of the period and locale. Hyman's drawings further enhance the story.

Lehman, Marcus. Jewish Youth Classics Series. New York: Feldheim Publishers, 1981. Grade level: 6 and up.
The Count of Coucy (12th Century France).
Banished (1849 Hungarian Revolution).
Faith and Courage (17th Century Chmielnicki Uprising in Poland-Lithuania).
Del Monte (18th Century Prague).
The Penknife (18th Century Berlin).
Ithamar (Second Temple Period of Palestine Under Herod's Rule).
The Agunah (19th Century German Struggle Between Reform and Traditional Judaism).
Just in Time (18th Century Frankfurt and Prague).
Portrait of Two Families (19th Century Europe).
The Royal Resident (Poland 1669, the Court of Augustus of Saxony).

> These historical romances originally appeared in German during the late 19th century. Each story focuses upon Jewish characters during a particular period of history. Lehman has done a masterful job of bringing these stories to life once again.

Lehman, Marcus. *Rabbi Joselman of Rosheim.* New York: Feldheim Publishers, 1981. Grade level: 6 and up. (Two Volumes)

> Lehman has a special knack for choosing the most interesting of Jewish historical personalities for his children's books. This time he writes about Rabbi Joselman and his work in the Holy Roman Empire to champion the rights of Jews.

Levitan, Tina. *Jews in American Life*. New York: Hebrew Publishing Co., 1969. Grade level: 5 and up.

Facts about ninety Jews who have made contributions to American and Jewish society are included in this informative and interesting work.

Levoy, Myron. *The Witch of Fourth Street and Other Stories*. Illus. by Gabriel Lisowski. New York: Harper & Row Publishers, Inc., 1972. Grade level: 3-6.

The eight stories in this book describe the experiences of families of different religions who journeyed to America in search of better lives. Lisowski's line drawings help to capture the unique atmosphere of New York's Lower East Side where each of the families live.

Lindenbaum, Ariel. *Great Jews in Stamps*. New York: Sabra Books, 1970. Grade level: 5 and up.

This book is a compilation of very short profiles of Jews whose accomplishments have won them the honor of being depicted on a stamp. Photographs of the stamps are included.

Marcus, Rebecca. *Moses Maimonides*. New York: Franklin Watts, Inc., 1969. Grade level: 6 and up.

Marcus has written an exciting account of the life and work of Moses Maimonides, the brilliant medieval philosopher, Rabbi, and physician. This is an inspiring book for children.

Meltzer, Milton. *Remember the Days: A Short History of the Jewish American*. Illus. by Harvey Dinnerstein. New York: Farrar, Straus & Giroux, Inc./Doubleday and Company, 1974. Grade level: 6 and up.

This is a thoroughly researched book focusing on the participation of Jews in American history. Included is a discussion of discrimination Jews have experienced, their cultural life, activism in public causes, and their support of Israel. An impressive work.

Meltzer, Milton. *The Jewish Americans: 1650-1950*. New York: Thomas Y. Crowell Co., 1982. Grade level: 5 and up.

Original documents and memoirs reveal the three hundred year history of American Jews. Meltzer's fine sense of history makes this a fascinating book to read.

Meltzer, Milton. *World of Our Fathers: The Jews of Eastern Europe*. New York: Farrar, Straus & Giroux, Inc., 1974. Grade level: 6 and up.

This serious and well written book examines Jewish life in Eastern Europe in the nineteenth century. The overwhelming problems of Jews living in these countries are discussed, as are the courage, strength, family unit, and religious conviction which helped them deal with poverty and persecution.

Moskin, Marietta D. *Waiting for Mama*. Illus. by Richard Lebenson. New York: Coward, McCann & Geoghegan Inc., 1975. Grade level: 3-5.

An engaging story about a Russian immigrant family at the turn of the century. When Papa takes the children to America to avoid their being subjected to Czarist persecution, Mama must stay behind. Finally, the children are able to contribute toward the purchase of Mama's ticket. A warm story depicting immigrant life on New York's Lower East Side.

Pearlman, Moshe. *The Maccabees*. Illus. with Photographs. New York: Macmillan Publishing Co., Inc., 1973. Grade level: 6 and up.

Excellent photographs and text combine to make this analysis of the political struggles which led to the celebration of Chanukah. An interesting historical book.

Postal, Bernard, and Koppman, Lionel. *Guess Who's Jewish in American History?* New York: New American Library/Signet. Grade level: 6 and up.

A very interesting read for the "Who's Who" buff. This book categorizes certain American Jews under a variety of headings such as medicine, religion, politics, science, etc. Information about each individual listed is provided.

Roseman, Kenneth. *The Melting Pot: An Adventure in New York*. New York: Union of American Hebrew Congregations, 1984. Grade level: 4-6.

The stories in this book are about Jews who immigrated to the United States at the turn of the century. The reader is asked to make a decision at the bottom of each page which will determine that person's future. The outcome of the story is affected by the choices made. A fun and informative book.

Rosenfeld, Max (ed). *Pushcarts and Dreamers: Stories of Jewish Life in America.* New York: Thomas Yoseloff, 1969. Grade level: 6 and up.

> The tales in this volume were originally written in Yiddish by ten different authors who immigrated to the United States between 1880 and 1920. Each story reflects the everyday struggles of immigrants at work and at home, as well as their quest to assert their Jewishness. A glossary of Yiddish terms is included.

Roskies, Diane K., and Roskies, David G. *The Shtetl Book.* Illus. with photos. New York: KTAV Publishing House, Inc., 1975. Grade level: 6 and up.

> Daily life in Tishevits is portrayed in first person accounts of the celebrations, games, and religious disputes which took place in the market town. Photographs add to the authenticity of the information related in the text.

Sevala, Ephraim. *Why There is No Heaven on Earth.* Trans. by Richard Lourie. New York: Harper & Row Publishers, Inc., 1982. Grade level: 6 and up.

> The experiences of a young boy during the Stalinist years are described in this compelling novel.

Singer, Isaac Bashevis. *A Day of Pleasure: Stories of a Boy Growing Up in Warsaw.* Photographs by Roman Vishniac. New York: Farrar, Straus & Giroux, Inc., 1969. Grade level: 5 and up.

> Each of the autobiographical stories in this book is accompanied by a documentary photo of the author's boyhood in Warsaw, Poland between 1908 and 1918. The characters who peopled Singer's childhood were without a doubt a major contributing factor to his rise to fame as a Nobel Prize winning author.

Skulsky, S. *Legends of Rabbi Akiva.* Trans. by I.M. Lask. Illus. by A. Luizada. New York: Shulsinger Brothers, 1968. Grade level: 3-5.

> Skulsky has retold the life story of the extraordinary Rabbi Akiva through narrative that is right in biographical facts and folklore. Detailed line drawings washed in green and gold highlight the emotional intensity of Rabbi Akiva's life from his modest beginnings as a shepherd through his rise to fame as a great scholar and, finally, his brutal execution by the Romans.

Sobol, Harriet Langsman. *Grandpa: A Young Man Grown Old.* Photographs by Patricia Agre. New York: Putnam Publishing Group, 1980. Grade level: PK and up.

> The nostalgia and value of personal family history are very much alive in this volume which preserves forever the life of one special grandfather. Photographs help to capture the most memorable moments as remembered by the grandfather and his granddaughter.

Steinberg, Fannie. *Birthday in Kishinev.* Illus. by Luba Hanushak. New York: The Jewish Publication Society of America, 1979. Grade level: 4 and up.

> Usually a twelfth birthday is a happy occasion. For Sarah, it becomes frightening, because it is the day of the Kishinev pogrom. The book revolves around Sarah's experiences. Despite the somber subject matter, this is a story of hope.

Vinberg, Ethel. *Grandmother Came From Dworitz: A Jewish Story.* Illus. by Rita Briansky. New York: Charles Scribner's Sons, 1978. Grade level: K-5.

> This lovely picture book features the life of the author's great-grandparents in Poland, her mother's journey to the United States, and her own childhood in Canada.

Waxman, Meyer; Ish-Kishor, Sulamith; and Sloan, Jacob. *Blessed is the Daughter.* New York: Shengold Publishers, Inc., 1980. Grade level: 6 and up.

> This is a fascinating reference book about important Jewish women from biblical times to the present. The book is lavishly decorated with photographs and paintings that, together with the narrative, reflect the courage and faith of the women included.

Wise, William, *Albert Einstein: Citizen of the World.* Illus. by Simon Jeruchim. New York: The Jewish Publication Society of America, 1960. Grade level: 4 and up.

> Einstein's scientific accomplishments and the expression of his Zionist beliefs and strong Jewish identity are the themes which make this an interesting and very worthwhile book.

Zemach, Margot. *Self- Portrait: Margot Zemach*. Illus. by the author. New York: Addison-Wesley Publishing Co., 1978. Self-Portrait Collections Series. Grade level: 4 and up.

> Margot Zemach is an illustrator of many books with Jewish content. This book reveals her family life and the influences on her artwork. The illustrations are typical of Zemach's colorful folk-like drawings.

JEWISH HISTORY: RESOURCES FOR ADULTS

American Jewish History

Angel, Marc. *LaAmerica: The Sephardic Experience in the United States*. Philadelphia: The Jewish Publication Society of America, 1982.

Baruch, Bernard. *Baruch: My Own Story*. New York: Henry Holt & Co., 1957.

Bernstein, Philip. *To Dwell in Unity: The Jewish Federation Movement in America, 1960-1980*. Philadelphia: The Jewish Publication Society of America, 1983.

Cohen, Naomi. *American Jews and the Zionist Idea*. New York: KTAV Publishing House, Inc., 1975.

Dawidowicz, Lucy. *On Equal Terms: Jews in America 1881-1981*. New York: Holt, Rinehart & Winston, Inc., 1982.

Feingold, Henry. *A Midrash on American Jewish History*. New York: University of New York Press, 1982.

_____. *Zion In America: The Jewish Experience from Colonial Times to the Present*. New York: Hippocrene Books, Inc., 1974.

Ford, Gertrude. *81 Sheriff Street*. New York: Frederick Fell, 1981.

Gittler, Joseph. *Jewish Life in the United States: Perspectives from the Social Sciences*. New York: New York University Press, 1981.

Glazer, Nathan. *American Judaism*. Chicago: University of Chicago Press, 1972.

Gurock, Jeffry. *American Jewish History: A Bibliographical Guide*. New York: B'nai B'rith Anti-Defamation League, 1983.

Handlin, Mimi, and Layton, Marilyn Smith. *Let Me Hear Your Voice: Portraits of Aging Immigrant Jews*. Photographs by Rochelle Casserd. Seattle, WA: University of Washington Press, 1983.

Handlin, Oscar. *Adventure in Freedom*. New York: McGraw-Hill Book Co., 1954.

Herscher, Uri. *Jewish Agricultural Utopias in America, 1880-1910*. Detroit, MI: Wayne State University Press, 1981.

Herscher, Uri D. (ed). *The East European Jewish Experience in America: 1882-1982*. Cincinnati, OH: American Jewish Archives, 1983.

Howe, Irving, and Libo, Kenneth. *How We Lived: A Documentary History of the Immigrant Jews in America, 1880-1930*. New York: Richard Marek Publishers, 1979.

_____. *We Lived There Too: In Their Own Words and Pictures - Pioneer Jews and the Westward Movement of America 1630-1930*. New York: St. Martin's/Marek, 1984.

Howe, Irving. *World of Our Fathers*. New York: Harcourt Brace Jovanovich, Inc., 1976.

Jacobs, Dan, and Paul, Ellen (eds). *Studies of the Third Wave: A Recent Migration of Soviet Jews to the United States*. Boulder, CO: Westview Press, 1981.

Karp, Abraham J. *Beginnings Early American Judaica: A Collection of Ten Publications, In Facsimile, Illustrative of the Religious, Communal, Cultural & Political Life of American Jewry, 1761-1845*. Philadelphia: The Jewish Publication Society of America, 1975.

Karp, Abraham. *To Give Life: The UJA in the Shaping of the American Jewish Community*. New York: Schocken Books, Inc., 1981.

Lebeson, Anita. *Recall to Life: The Jewish Woman in America*. New York: Thomas Yoseloff, 1970.

Marcus, Jacob. *The American Jewish Woman 1654-1980*. New York: KTAV Publishing House, Inc., 1981. (Two Volumes)

Paper, Lewis. *Brandeis: An Intimate Biography of One of America's Truly Great Supreme Court Justices*. Englewood Cliffs, NJ: Prentice-Hall, 1983.

Polne, Murray (ed). *American Jewish Biographies*. New York: Facts on File, Inc., 1982.

Raphael, Marc Lee (ed). *Jews and Judaism in the United States: A Documentary History*. New York: Behrman House, Inc., 1983.

Reisman, Bernard. *The Chavurah: A Contemporary Jewish Experience*. New York: Union of American Hebrew Congregations, 1977.

Ribalow, Harold. *Autobiographies of American Jews*. Philadelphia: The Jewish Publication Society of America, 1965.

Schappes, Morris U. (ed). *A Documentary History of Jews In the United States 1654-1875*. New York: Schocken Books, Inc., 1971.

Schumach, Murray. *The Diamond People*. New York: W.W. Norton, & Co., Inc., 1981.

Silverberg, Robert. *If I Forget Thee O Jerusalem: American Jews and the State of Israel*. New York: William Morrow & Co., Inc., 1970.

Schoener, Allon. *The American Jewish Album: 1654 To The Present*. New York: Rizzoli International Publications, 1983.

Sochen, June. *Consecrate Every Day: The Public Lives of Jewish American Women 1880-1980*. Albany, NY: State University of New York Press, 1981.

Biographies and Collections of Biographical Sketches

Altman, Alexander. *Moses Mendelssohn: A Biographical Study*. Philadelphia: The Jewish Publication Society of America, 1973.

Baker, Leonard. *Brandeis and Frankfurter: A Dual Biography*. New York: Harper & Row Publishers, Inc., 1984.

Bernstein, Leonard. *Findings*. New York: Simon & Schuster, Inc., 1982.

Black, David. *The King of Fifth Avenue: The Fortunes of August Belmont*. New York: Dial Press, 1981.

Bloch, Suzanne. *Ernest Bloch: Creative Spirit*. New York: Jewish Music Council, 1976.

Brown, Robert McAffe. *Elie Wiesel: Messenger to All Humanity*. Notre Dame, IN: University of Notre Dame Press, 1983.

Byrne, Frank, and Soman, Jean (ed). *Your True Marcus: The Civil War Letters of a Jewish Colonel*. Kent, OH: Kent State University Press, 1984.

Chagall, Bella. *First Encounter*. Trans. by Barbara Bray. New York: Schocken Books, Inc., 1983.

Clark, Ronald. *Freud: The Man and the Cause*. New York: Random House, Inc., 1980.

Comay, Joan. *Who's Who in Jewish History After the Period of the Old Testament*. New York: David McKay Co., Inc. 1974.

Drinnon, Richard. *Rebel in Paradise: A Biography of Emma Goldman*. Chicago: University of Chicago Press, 1961.

Feingold, Norman, and Silverman, William. *Kivie Kaplan: A Legend in His Own Time*. New York: Union of American Hebrew Congregations, 1976.

Feuer, Lewis Samuel. *Spinoza and the Rise of Liberalism*. Boston: Beacon Press, Inc., 1958.

Finkelstein, Louis. *Akiba: Scholar, Saint, and Martyr*. New York: Temple Books, 1970.

Friedlander, Albert H. *Leo Baeck: Teacher of Theresienstadt*. New York: Holt, Rinehart & Winston, Inc., 1968.

Freund, Else-Rahel. *Franz Rosenzweig's Philosophy of Existence: An Analysis of the Star of Redemption*. The Hague: Martinus Nijhoff, 1979.

Ginzberg, Louis. *Students, Scholars and Saints: Biographies of Jewish Scholars*. New York: Meridian Books, 1958.

Gross, David. *Pride of Our People: The Stories of One Hundred Outstanding Jewish Men and Woman*. Portraits by William D. Brahmall, Jr. New York: Doubleday & Co., Inc., 1979.

Grunfeld, Frederic. *Prophets Without Honour: A Background to Freud, Kafka, Einstein and Their World*. New York: Holt, Rinehart & Winston, Inc., 1979.

Halasz, Nicholas. *Captain Dreyfus: The Story of Mass Hysteria*. New York: Simon & Schuster, Inc., 1955.

Harris, Leon. *Merchant Princess: An Intimate History of Jewish Families Who Built Great Department Stores*. New York: Harper & Row Publishers, Inc., 1979.

Heschel, Abraham Joshua. *Maimonides: A Biography*. New York: Farrar, Straus & Giroux, Inc., 1982.

Howe, Irving. *A Margin of Hope: An Intellectual Autobiography*. New York: Harcourt Brace Jovanovich, Inc., 1982.

Kennington, Richard (ed). *The Philosophy of Baruch Spinoza*. Washington D.C.: Catholic University of America Press, 1980.

Klein, Gerda Weissman. *A Passion for Sharing: The Life of Edith Rosenwald Stern*. Chappaqua, NY: Rossel Books, 1984.

Kurzman, Dan. *Ben-Gurion: Prophet of Fire*. New York: Simon & Schuster, Inc., 1983.

Litvin, Martin. *The Journey: A Biography of August M. Bondi, The American Jewish Freedom Fighter Who Rode With John Brown in Kansas*. Galesburg, IL: Galesburg Historical Society, 1981.

Margolies, Morris. *Samuel David Luzzato: Traditionalist, Scholar*. New York: KTAV Publishing House, Inc., 1979.

Netanyahu, Benzion. *Don Isaac Abravanel: Statesman and Philosopher*. Philadelphia: The Jewish Publication Society of America, 1953.

Ovadyahu, Mordecai. *Bialik Speaks*. New York: Herzl Press, 1969.

Quasha, Solomon. *Albert Einstein: An Intimate Portrait*. Lake Forest, IL: Forest Publishing, 1980.

Peretz, Isaac Leib. *My Memoirs*. New York: Citadel Books, 1964.

Picon, Molly. *Molly!: An Autobiography*. New York: Simon & Schuster, Inc., 1980.

Rajak, Tessa. *Josephus: The Historian and His Society*. Philadelphia: Fortress, Press, 1983.

The Rishonim: Biographical Sketches of the Prominent Early Rabbinic Sages and Leaders From the 10th-15th Centuries. New York: Mesorah Publications, Ltd., 1982.

Rosenbloom, Noah. *Tradition in an Age of Reform: The Religious Philosophy of Samson Raphael Hirsch*. Philadelphia: The Jewish Publication Society of America, 1976.

Roth, Cecil. *Dona Gracia of the House of Nasi*. Philadelphia: The Jewish Publication Society of America, 1978.

Roth, Irene. *Cecil Roth Historian Without Tears: A Memoir*. New York: Sepher-Hermon Press, 1982.

Rothchild, Miriam. *Dear Lord Rothchild: Birds, Butterflies and History*. Glenside, PA: Balaban Books, 1983.

Sarna, Jonathan. *Jacksonian Jew: The Two Worlds of Mordecai Noah*. New York: Holmes & Meier, 1981.

Shershevsky, Ezra. *Rashi: The Man and His World*. New York: Sepher-Hermon Press, 1982.

Singer, Isaac Bashevis. *In My Father's Court*. New York: Signet Books/New American Library, 1967.

Sills, Beverly. *Bubbles: A Self-Portrait*. New York: Bobbs Merrill & Co., Inc., 1976.

Solomon, Flora, and Litvinoff, Barr. *A Woman's Way*. New York: Simon & Schuster, Inc., 1984.

Soloveitchik, Rabbi Joseph B. *Halakhic Man*. Trans. by Lawrence Kaplan. Philadelphia: The Jewish Publication Society of America, 984.

Suhl, Yuri. *Eloquent Crusader: Ernestine Rose*. New York: Julian Messner, 1970.

Umansky, Ellen M. *Lilly Montagu and the Advancement of Liberal Judaism: From Vision to Vocation*. New York: E.M. Mollen, 1983.

Wagenknecht, Edward. *Daughter of the Covenant: Portraits of Six Jewish Women*. Amherst, MA: University of Massachusetts Press, 1983.

Waife-Goldberg, Marie. *My Father Sholom Aleichem*. New York: Schocken Books, Inc., 1971.

Weisman, Seymour S. *Basher: Five Decades of Jewish Community Service*. Wilton, CT: Hadeira Press, 1984.

Werblowsky, R.J. Zwi. *Joseph Karo: Lawyer and Mystic*. Philadelphia: The Jewish Publication Society of America, 1977.

Wincelberg, Shimon and Anita (trans.) *The Samurai of Vishogrod: The Notebooks of Jacob Marateck.* Philadelphia: The Jewish Publication Society of America, 1976.

Young-Bruehl, Elizabeth. *Hannah Arendt: For Love of the World.* New Haven, CT: Yale University Press, 1982.

Comprehensive and Popular Histories

Ausubel, Nathan. *Pictorial History of the Jewish People.* New York: Crown Publishers, Inc., 1953.

Bloch, Abraham. *Day by Day in Jewish History: A Chronology and Calendar of Historic Events.* New York: KTAV Publishing House, Inc., 1983.

Dimont, Max. *Jews, God and History.* New York: Simon & Schuster, Inc., 1962.

Eban, Abba. *My People: The Story of the Jews.* New York: Behrman House, Inc. 1968.

Fast, Howard. *The Jews: Story of a People.* New York: Dial Press, 1968.

Grayzel, Solomon. *History of the Jews.* Philadelphia: The Jewish Publication Society of America, 1947.

Jospe, Raphael, and Wagner, Stanley (eds). *Great Schisms in Jewish History.* New York: KTAV Publishing House, Inc., 1981.

Margolis, Max, and Marx, Alexander. *History of the Jewish People.* New York: Harper & Row Publishers, Inc., 1965.

Potok, Chaim. *Wanderings.* New York: Fawcett Crest Books, 1978.

Rivkin, Ellis. *The Shaping of Jewish History: A Radical New Interpretation.* New York: Charles Scribner's Sons, 1971.

Roth, Cecil. *A History of the Jews from Earliest Times Through the Six-Day War.* New York: Schocken Books, Inc., 1970.

Sachar, Abram Leon. *A History of the Jews.* New York: Alfred A. Knopf, 1964.

Cultural, Religious, and Social Histories

Bamberger, Bernard. *The Story of Judaism.* New York: Schocken Books, Inc., 1957.

Baron, Salo. *A Social and Religious History of the Jews.* Philadelphia: The Jewish Publication Society of America, 1937-1983. (Eighteen Volumes)

Ben-Ami, Issachor (ed). *The Sephardi and Oriental Jewish Heritage.* Jerusalem: Magnes Press, 1982.

Eban, Abba. *Heritage: Civilization and the Jews.* New York: Summit Books, 1984.

Finkelstein, Louis (ed). *The Jews: Their History, Culture and Religion.* Westport, CT: Greenwood Press, 1979. (Two Volumes)

JPS Popular Judaic Library of Jewish Civilization. Philadelphia: The Jewish Publication Society of America, 1973-1974.
The Holocaust   *Germany*
Hasidism   *Age and the Aged*
Fasting and Fast Days   *Shavuot*
The Return to Zion   *Spain*
Marriage   *The Synagogue*
Sukkot   *The Sabbath*
England   *Messianic Movements*
Family   *The High Holy Days*
Passover   *Learning*

Gafni, Yeshayahu, et al. *Jerusalem to Jabneh: The Period of the Mishnah and Its Literature.* Tel Aviv: Everyman's University, 1980-81. Distributed by Alternatives in Religious Education, Inc., Denver, Colorado.

Kedouri, Elie. *The Jewish World: History and Culture of the Jewish People.* New York: Harry N. Abrams, Inc., 1979.

Peters, F.E. *Children of Abraham: Judaism, Christianity, and Islam.* Princeton, NJ: Princeton University Press, 1983.

Rotenstreich, Nathan. *Tradition and Reality: The Impact of History on Modern Jewish Thought.* New York: Random House, Inc., 1967.

Sandmel, Samuel. *Judaism and Christian Beginnings.* London: Oxford University Press, 1978.

Seltzer, Robert. *Jewish People, Jewish Thought: The Jewish Experience in History.* New York: Macmillan Publishing Co., Inc., 1980.

Silver, Daniel Jeremy. *History of Judaism.* New York: Basic Books, Inc., 1974. (Two Volumes)

Steinberg, Aaron. *History as Experience: Aspects of Historical Thought - Universal and Jewish.* New York: KTAV Publishing House, Inc., 1983.

Talmage, Frank Ephraim (ed). *Disputation and Dialogue: Readings in the Jewish-Christian Encounter.* New York: KTAV Publishing House, Inc./Anti-Defamation League, 1975.

Trepp, Leo. *A History of the Jewish Experience.* New York: Behrman House, Inc., 1973.

Famous Jewish Women

Fink, Greta. *Great Jewish Women: Profiles of Courageous Women from the Maccabean Period to the Present.* New York: Menorah Publishing Co., Inc., 1978.

Henry, Sondra, and Taitz, Emily. *Written Out of History: Our Jewish Foremothers.* Fresh Meadows, New York: Biblio Press, 1983.

Mazow, Julia Wolf (ed). *The Woman Who Lost Her Names: Selected Writings by American Jewish Women.* San Francisco: Harper & Row Publishers, 1980.

Sasso, Sandy Eisenberg, and Elwell, Sue Levi. *Jewish Women.* Denver: Alternatives in Religious Education, Inc., 1984.

Historical Perspectives on Jewish Family LIfe

Bermont, Chaim. *The Walled Garden: The Saga of Jewish Family Life and Tradition.* New York: Macmillan Publishing Co., Inc., 1974.

Gittleman, Sol. *From Shtetl to Suburbia: The Family in Jewish Literary Imagination.* Boston: Beacon Press, 1978.

Hubman, Franz, and Kochan, Miriam and Lionel. *The Jewish Family Album: The Life of a People In Photographs.* Boston: Little, Brown & Co., 1974.

Schneid, Hayyim (ed). *Family.* Jerusalem: Keter Publishing House, Ltd., 1973.

Jewish Communities Around the World

Awret, Irene. *Days of Honey: The Tunisian Boyhood of Raphael Uzan.* New York: Schocken Books, Inc., 1984.

Bach, Hans (ed). *The German Jew: A Synthesis of Judaism and Western Civilization, 1730-1930.* New York: Oxford University Press, 1983.

Bamberger, Nathan. *The Viking Jew: A History of the Jews of Denmark.* New York: Shengold Publishers, Inc., 1983.

Beinart, Haim. *Trujillo: A Jewish Community in Extramadura on the Eve of Expulsion from Spain.* Jerusalem: Magnes Press, 1980.

Calmann, Marianne. *The Carriere of Carpentras.* New York: Oxford University Press, 1984.

Chouraqui, Andre. *Between East and West: The Jewish Community of Northern Africa.* New York: Atheneum Publishers, 1973.

Comay, Joan. *The Diaspora Story.* New York: Random House, Inc., 1980.

Cowen, Ida. *Jews in Remote Corners of the World.* Englewood Cliffs, NJ: Prentice-Hall, 1971.

Dagen, Avigdor; Hirschler, Gertrude; and Weiner, Lewis. *The Jews of Czechoslovakia: Historical Studies and Surveys.* Philadelphia: The Jewish Publication Society of America/New York: Society for the History of Czechoslovak Jews, 1968-1984.

Dicker, Herman. *Piety and Perseverance: Jews from the Carpathian Mountains.* New York: Sepher-Hermon Press, 1981.

Dobroszycki, Lucjan, and Kirschenblatt-Gimblett, Barbara. *Image Before My Eyes: A Photographic History of Jewish Life in Poland 1864-1939.* New York: Schocken Books, Inc., 1977.

Elazar, Daniel J. *The Balkan Jewish Communities: Yugoslavia, Bulgaria, Greece and Turkey*. Lamhan, MD: University Press of America, 1984.

Elkin, Judith. *Jews of the Latin American Republics*. Chapel Hill, NC: University of North Carolina Press, 1980.

Endelman, Todd. *The Jews of Georgian England, 1714-1830: Tradition and Change in a Liberal Society*. Philadelphia: The Jewish Publication Society of America, 1980.

Freidenreich, Harriet Pass. *The Jews of Yugoslavia: A Quest for Community*. Philadelphia: The Jewish Publication Society of America, 1979.

Goitein, S.D. *A Mediterranean Society as Portrayed in the Documents of the Cairo Geniza*. Berkeley, CA: University of California Press, 1968-1983. (Four Volumes)

Gursan-Salzmann, Ayse. *The Last Jews of Radausta*. Photos by Lawrence Salzman. New York: Doubleday & Co., Inc., 1983.

Hacohen, Devora and Menahem. *One People: The Story of the Eastern Jews*. Tel Aviv: Sabra Books, 1969.

Haddad, Heskel M. *Jews of Arab and Islamic Countries: History, Problems, Solutions*. New York: Shengold Publishers, Inc., 1984.

Hughes, Stuart H. *Prisoners of Hope: The Silver Age of the Italian Jews, 1924-1974*. Cambridge, MA: Harvard University Press, 1983.

Kalechofsky, Robert and Roberta (eds). *South African Jewish Voices*. Marblehead, MA: Micah Publications, 1982.

Klepfisz, Heszel. *Culture and Compassion: The Spirit of Polish Jewry From Hasidism to the Holocaust*. Trans. by Curt Leviant. New York: KTAV Publishing House, Inc., 1983.

Kugelmass, Jack, and Boyarin, Jonathan (eds). *From a Ruined Garden: The Memorial Books of Polish Jewry*. New York: Schocken Books, Inc., 1984.

Mann, Vivian. *A Tale of Two Cities: Jewish Life in Frankfurt and Istanbul 1750-1870*. New York: The Jewish Museum, 1982.

Patai, Raphael. *The Vanished Worlds of Jewry*. New York: Macmillan Publishing Co., Inc., 1980.

Pollack, Michael. *Mandarins, Jews, and Missionaries: The Jewish Experience in the Chinese Empire*. Philadelphia: The Jewish Publication Society of America, 1979.

Rand, Baruch, and Rush, Barbara. *Jews of Kurdistan*. Toledo, OH: Board of Jewish Education/American Association of Jewish Education, 1978.

Rapoport, Louis. *The Lost Jews: Last of the Ethiopian Falashas*. Briarcliff Manor, NY: Stein and Day Publishers, 1980.

Ross, Dan. *Acts of Faith: A Journey to the Fringes of Jewish Identity*. New York: Schocken Books, Inc., 1984.

Shapiro, Sidney (ed). *Jews in Old China*. New York: Hippocrene Books, Inc., 1984.

Simonsohn, Shlomo (ed). *The Jews in the Duchy of Milan, 1378-1477*. Jerusalem: Israel Academy of Sciences and Humanities, 1982. (Two Volumes)

Stanislawski, Michael. *Tsar Nicholas I and the Jews: The Transformation of Jewish Society in Russia, 1825-1855*. Philadelphia: The Jewish Publication Society of America, 1983.

Sternberg, Ghitta. *Stefanesti: Portrait of a Romanian Shtetl*. Elmsford, NY: Pergamon Press, Inc., 1984.

Stillman, Norman. *The Jews of Arab Lands: A History and Source Book*. Philadelphia: The Jewish Publication Society of America, 1979.

Strizower, Schifra. *The Bene Israel of Bombay: A Study of a Jewish Community*. New York: Schocken Books, Inc., 1971.

Sutton, Joseph. *Magic Carpet: Aleppo-in-Flatbush: The Story of a Unique Ethnic Jewish Community*. New York: Thayer-Jacoby, 1979.

Tamir, Vicki. *Bulgaria and Her Jews: The History of a Dubious Symbiosis*. New York: Yeshiva University Press, 1979.

Vishniac, Roman. *A Vanished World*. New York: Farrar, Straus & Giroux, Inc., 1983.

Weisbrot, Robert. *The Jews of Argentina from the Inquisition to Peron.* Philadelphia: The Jewish Publication Society of America, 1979.

Williams, John A. *Last Flight from Ambo Ber.* Pelham, NY: American Association for Ethiopian Jews, 1983. (Play)

Jewish Contributions to Civilization

Caplan, Samuel, and Ribalow, Harold. *The Great Jewish Books and Their Influence on History.* New York: Horizon Press, 1952.

Ostow, Mortimer (ed). *Judaism and Psychoanalysis.* New York: KTAV Publishing House, Inc., 1982.

Raphael, Chaim. *Encounters with the Jewish People.* New York: Behrman House, Inc., 1979.

Roth, Cecil. *The Jewish Contribution to Civilization.* New York: Union of American Hebrew Congregations, 1940.

Schwarz, Leo (ed). *Great Ages and Ideas of the Jewish People.* New York: Random House, Inc., 1956.

Shapiro, Leon. *The History of ORT: A Jewish Movement for Social Change.* New York: Schocken Books, Inc., 1980.

Jewish Life Under Greek and Roman Influence

Steinberg, Milton. *As a Driven Leaf.* New York: Behrman House Inc., 1939.

Tcherikover, Victor. *Hellenistic Civilization and the Jews.* New York: Atheneum Publishers, 1970.

Jewish Life in the Middle Ages

Abrahams, Israel. *Jewish Life in the Middle Ages.* New York: Atheneum Publishers, 1969.

Ashtor, Eliyahu. *The Jews of Moslem Spain.* Philadelphia: The Jewish Publication Society of America, 1974. (Two Volumes)

Baer, Yitzhak. *A History of the Jews in Christian Spain.* Philadelphia: The Jewish Publication Society of America, 1966. (Two Volumes)

Bendiner, Elmer. *The Rise and Fall of Paradise: When Arabs and Jews Built a Kingdom in Spain.* New York: G.P. Putnam's Sons, 1983.

Lewis, Bernard. *The Jews of Islam.* Princeton, NJ: Princeton University Press, 1984.

Marcus, Jacob R. *Jews in the Medieval World: A Source Book.* Westport, CT: Greenwood Press, 1975.

Metzger, Theresa and Mendel. *Jewish Life in the Middle Ages.* New York: Alpine Fine Art Collections, 1983.

Millgram, Abraham. *An Anthology of Medieval Hebrew Literature.* New York: Burning Bush Press, 1935.

Roth, Cecil. *A History of the Marranos.* New York: Meridian Books, 1959.

_____. *The Jews in the Renaissance.* Philadelphia: The Jewish Publication Society of America, 1959.

Stern, Selma. *The Court Jew.* Philadelphia: The Jewish Publication Society of America, 1950.

Ruderman, David. *The World of a Renaissance Jew: The Life and Thought of Mordecai Farissal.* Cincinnati, OH: Hebrew Union College Press, 1981.

Jewish Literature

Babel, Isaac. *You Must Know Everything: Stories 1915-1935.* Trans. by Max Hayward. New York: Farrar, Straus & Giroux, Inc., 1969.

Goldreich, Gloria (ed). *A Treasury of Jewish Literature from Biblical Times to Today.* New York: Holt, Rinehart & Winston, Inc., 1982.

Gross, Theodore (ed). *The Literature of American Jews.* Glencoe, IL: Free Press, 1973.

Guttman, Allen. *The Jewish Writer in America: Assimilation and the Crisis of Identity.* New York: Oxford University Press, 1971.

Handler, Andrew. *Ararat: A Collection of Hungarian-Jewish Short Stories.* Rutherford, NJ: Farleigh Dickinson University Press, 1980.

Howe, Irving (ed). *Jewish American Stories*. New York: New American Library, 1977.

Howe, Irving. *Celebrations and Attacks: Thirty Years of Literary and Cultural Commentary*. New York: Horizon Books, 1979.

Kahn, Sholom J. (ed). *A Whole Loaf: Stories from Israel*. Tel Aviv: Karni Press, 1957.

Kalechofsky, Roberta (ed). *Echad I: An Anthology of Latin American Jewish Writings*. Marblehead, MA: Micah Publications, 1980.

_____. *Echad 2: South African Jewish Voices*. Marblehead, MA: Micah Publications, 1982.

_____. *Echad 3: Phoenix Rising: Contemporary Jewish Writers*. Marblehead, MA: Micah Publications, 1982.

_____. *Echad 4: Jewish Writing From Down Under: Australia and New Zealand*. Marblehead, MA: Micah Publications, 1982.

Lazar, Moshe (ed). *The Sephardic Tradition: Ladino and Spanish Jewish Literature*. New York: W.W. Norton & Company, 1972.

Michener, James (ed). *Firstfruits: A Harvest of 25 Years of Israeli Writing*. Philadelphia: The Jewish Publication Society of America, 1973.

Mozeson, Isaac (ed). *Ten Jewish American Poets*. New York: Downtown Poets, 1982.

Patterson, David (ed). *Studies in Modern Hebrew Literature Series*. New York: Cornell University Press, 1974.

Ribalow, Harold. *The Tie That Binds: Conversations With Jewish Writers*. Cranberry, NJ: A.S. Barnes & Co., 1980.

Rothenberg, Jerome. *A Big Jewish Book: Poems and Other Visions of the Jews from Tribal Times to the Present*. New York: Doubleday & Co., Inc., 1978.

Samuel, Maurice (ed). *Prince of the Ghetto: The Stories of Y.L. Peretz Retold*. New York: Schocken Books, Inc., 1973.

Schwartz, Howard, and Rudolf, Anthony (eds). *Voices Within the Ark: The Modern Jewish Poets*. Wainscott, NY: Pushcart Press, 1980.

Schwarz, Leo (ed). *The Menorah Treasury*. Philadelphia: The Jewish Publication Society of America, 1964.

_____. *The Jewish Caravan: Great Stories of Twenty-Five Centuries*. New York: Schocken Books, Inc., 1976.

Singer, Isaac B. *The Collected Stories of Isaac Bashevis Singer*. New York: Farrar, Straus & Giroux, Inc., 1982.

Siberschlag, Eisig. *From Renaissance to Renaissance*. New York: KTAV Publishing House, Inc., 1981. (Three Volumes)

Spicehandler, Ezra (ed). *Modern Hebrew Stories*. New York: Bantam Books, Inc., 1971.

Tammuz, Binyamin, and Yudkin, Leo (eds). *Meetings with the Angel: Seven Stories from Israel*. London: Deutsch, 1973.

Walden, Daniel (ed). *Studies in American Jewish Literature, #3: Jewish Female Writers and Women in Jewish Literature*. Albany, NY: State University of New York Press, 1983.

Zinberg, Israel. *A History of Jewish Literature*. New York: KTAV Publishing House, Inc., 1972. (Twelve Volumes)

Judaic Art and Historical Treasures

Altshuler, David (ed). *The Precious Legacy: Judaic Treasures From the Czechoslovak State Collections*. New York: Summit Books, 1983.

Davidovitch, David. *The Ketuba: Jewish Marriage Contracts Through the Ages*. Bat Yam, Israel: E. Lewin-Epstein Ltd., 1968.

Eisenberg, Azriel. *Jewish Historical Treasures*. New York: Bloch Publishing Co., 1968.

Kampf, Avram. *Contemporary Synagogue Art: Developments in the U.S., 1945-1965*. New York: Union of American Hebrew Congregations, 1966.

_____. *Jewish Experience in the Art of the Twentieth Century*. Philadelphia: The Jewish Publication Society of America/Bergin & Garvey, 1984.

Kanof, Abram. *Jewish Ceremonial Art and Religious Observance.* New York: Harry N. Abrams, no publication date.

Narkiss, Bezalel. *Hebrew Illuminated Manuscripts.* Jerusalem: Keter Publishing House, Ltd., 1969.

Shanks, Hershel. *Judaism in Stone: The Archaeology of Ancient Synagogues.* New York: Harper & Row Publishers, Inc., 1979.

Wigoder, Geoffrey (ed). *Jewish Art and Civilization.* New York: Walker Co., Inc., 1972. (Two Volumes)

Life in the Shtetl

Dawidowicz, Lucy (ed). *The Golden Tradition: Jewish Life and Thought in Eastern Europe.* Boston: Beacon Press, 1967.

Grupper, David, and Klein, David G. *The Paper Shtetl: A Complete Model of an Eastern European Jewish Town.* New York: Schocken Books, Inc., 1984.

Heschel, Abraham Joshua. *The Earth is the Lord's: The Inner World of the Jew in Eastern Europe.* New York: Henry Schuman, Inc., 1950.

Neugroschel, Joachim. *The Shtetl: A Creative Anthology of Jewish Life in Eastern Europe.* New York: Richard Marek Publishers, 1979.

Roskies, David. *The Shtetl Book.* New York: KTAV Publishing House, Inc., 1975.

Zborowski, Mark, and Herzog, Elizabeth. *Life is With People: The Culture of the Shtetl.* New York: Schocken Books, Inc., 1962.

Major Jewish Religious Movements

Borowitz, Eugene B. *Liberal Judaism.* New York: Union of American Hebrew Congregations, 1984.

Borowitz, Eugene. *Reform Judaism Today: How We Live, What We Believe, Reform in the Process of Change.* New York: Behrman House, Inc., 1978. (Three Volumes)

Bulka, Reuven P. (ed). *Dimensions of Orthodox Judaism.* New York: KTAV Publishing House, Inc., 1983.

Davis, Moshe. *The Emergence of Conservative Judaism.* Philadelphia: The Jewish Publication Society of America, 1963.

Dorff, Elliot. *Conservative Judaism: Our Ancestors to Our Descendants.* New York: United Synagogue of America, 1977.

Gordis, Robert. *Understanding Conservative Judaism.* New York: Rabbinical Assembly, 1978.

Kaplan, Mordecai. *Judaism as a Civilization.* New York: Reconstructionist Press, 1934.

Martin, Bernard, and Silver, Daniel Jeremy. *A History of Judaism.* New York: Basic Books, Inc., 1974. (Two Volumes)

Neusner, Jacob (ed). *Take Judaism, For Example: Studies Toward the Comparison of Religions.* Chicago: University of Chicago Press, 1983.

Rosenbloom, Herbert. *Conservative Judaism: A Contemporary History.* New York: United Synagogue of America, 1983.

Rosenthal, Gilbert. *Four Paths to One God: Today's Jew and His Religion.* New York: Bloch Publishing Co., 1973.

Segal, Abraham. *One People: A Study in Comparative Judaism.* New York: Union of American Hebrew Congregations, 1982.

Sklare, Marshall. *Conservative Judaism: An American Religious Movement.* Glencoe, IL: Free Press, 1965.

Waxman, Mordecai. *Tradition and Change: The Development of Conservative Judaism.* New York: Burning Bush Press, 1958.

Modern Jewish History

Chazen, Robert, and Raphael, Marc Lee (eds). *Modern Jewish History: A Source Reader.* New York: Schocken Books, Inc., 1974.

Ehrmann, Eliezer L. (ed). *Readings in Modern Jewish History from the American Revolution to the Present.* New York: KTAV Publishing House, Inc., 1977.

Eisenberg, Azriel, and Goodman, Hannah (eds). *Eyewitness to American Jewish History*. New York: Union of American Hebrew Congregations, 1976, 1978. (Two Volumes)

Grayzel, Solomon. *A History of the Contemporary Jews*. New York: Atheneum Publishers, 1975.

Howe, Irving. *World of Our Fathers*. New York: Harcourt Brace Jovanovich, 1976.

Mendes-Flohr, Paul, and Reinharz, Jehuda (eds). *The Jew in the Modern World: A Documentary History*. London: Oxford University Press, 1980.

Sachar, Howard. *The Course of Modern Jewish History*. New York: World Publishing Co., 1958.

Mystical and Messianic Trends

Jacobs, Louis. *Jewish Mystical Testimonies*. New York: Schocken Books, Inc., 1976.

Landman, Leo (ed). *Messianism in the Talmudic Era*. New York: KTAV Publishing House, Inc., 1979.

Scholem, Gershom. *Major Trends in Jewish Mysticism*. New York: Schocken Books, Inc., 1963.

_____. *Sabbatai Sevi: The Mystical Messiah*. Princeton NJ: Princeton University Press, 1973.

_____. *The Messianic Idea in Judaism and Other Essays on Jewish Spirituality*. New York: Schocken Books, Inc., 1971.

Sharot, Stephen. *Messianism, Mysticism, and Magic: A Sociological Analysis of Jewish Religious Movements*. Chapel Hill, NC: University of North Carolina Press, 1982.

Singer, Isaac B. *A Little Boy in Search of God: Mysticism in a Personal Light*. Illus. by Ira Moskowitz. New York: Doubleday & Co., Inc., 1976.

Sources for the Study of Jewish History

Ackerman, Walter (ed). *Out of Our People's Past: Sources for the Study of Jewish History*. New York: United Synagogue Commission on Jewish Education, 1977.

Bamberger, David. *My People: Abba Eban's History of the Jews*. New York: Behrman House, Inc., 1978, 1979. (Two Volumes)

Eisenberg, Azriel; Goodman, Hannah Grad; and Kass, Alvin (eds). *Eyewitness to Jewish History: From 586 B.C.E. to 1967*. New York: Union of American Hebrew Congregations, 1976, 1977, 1978, 1979. (Four Volumes)

Loeb, Sorel Goldberg, and Kadden, Barbara Binder. *Jewish History - Moments & Methods: An Activity Source Book for Teachers*. Illus. by Mae Shafter Rockland. Denver: Alternatives in Religious Education, Inc., 1982.

Simms, Laura, et al. *Exploring Our Living Past*. New York: Behrman House, Inc., 1979.

Unique Glimpses at Jewish History

Adler, Elkan Nathan (ed). *Jewish Travelers: A Treasury of Travelogues from Nine Centuries*. New York: Sepher-Hermon Press, 1966.

Davis, Eli and Elise. *Hats and Caps of the Jews*. Jerusalem: Massada Press, 1983.

Eldad, Israel, and Aumann, Moshe. *Chronicles News of the Past*. Jerusalem: Reubeni Foundation, 1967. (Three Volumes in Newspaper Form)

Goldberg, M. Hirsh. *The Jewish Connection: The incredible . . . ironic . . . bizarre . . . funny . . . and provocative in the story of the Jews*. Briarcliff Manor, NY: Stein and Day Publishers, 1976.

Kampf, Avram. *Jewish Experience in the Art of the Twentieth Century*. Philadelphia: The Jewish Publication Society of America, 1984.

Kobler, Franz. *Letters of Jews Through the Ages: A Self-Portrait of the Jewish People*. New York: East & West Library, 1952. (Two Volumes)

Roth, Cecil. *Gleanings: Essays in Jewish History, Letters and Art*. New York: Sepher-Hermon Press, 1967.

Rubens, Alfred. *A History of Jewish Costume*. New York: Crown Publishers, Inc., 1967.

Schwarz, Leo. W. (ed). *Memoirs of My People Through a Thousand Years*. Philadelphia: The Jewish Publication Society of America, 1943.

Yerushalmi, Yosef Hayim. *Zakhor: Jewish History and Jewish Memory*. Philadelphia: The Jewish Publication Society of America, 1982.

Yiddish Culture

Ayalti, Hanan. *Yiddish Proverbs*. Woodcuts by Bernard Reder. New York: Schocken Books, Inc., 1963.

Fishman, Joshua. *Never Say Die!: A Thousand Years of Yiddish Life and Letters*. Hawthorne, NY: Mouton Publishers, 1981.

Goldberg, Judith N. *Laughter Through Tears: The Yiddish Cinema*. Rutherford, NJ: Farleigh Dickenson University Press, 1983.

Howe, Irving, and Greenberg, Eliezer (eds). *A Treasury of Yiddish Poetry*. New York: Holt, Rinehart & Winston, Inc., 1969.

_____. *A Treasury of Yiddish Stories*. Illus. by Ben Shahn. New York: Schocken Books, Inc., 1973.

_____. *Voices From the Yiddish: Essays, Memoirs and Diaries*. Ann Arbor: University of Michigan Press, 1972.

Kogos, Fred. *A Dictionary of Yiddish Slang and Idioms*. Secaucus, NJ: Citadel Press, 1966.

Landis, J.C. (ed). *The Dybbuk and Other Great Yiddish Plays*. New York: Bantam Books, Inc. 1966.

Liptzin, Sol. *The Flowering of Yiddish Literature*. New York: Thomas Yoseloff, 1965.

Madison, Charles. *Yiddish Literature: Its Scope and Major Writers*. New York: Frederick Ungar Publishing Co., 1968.

Metzer, Isaac. *A Bintel Brief*. New York: Doubleday & Co., Inc., 1971.

Miron, Dan. *A Traveler Disguised: A Study in the Rise of Modern Yiddish Fiction in the Nineteenth Century*. New York: Schocken Books, Inc., 1973.

Rosten, Leo. *Hooray for Yiddish!: A Book About English*. New York: Simon & Schuster Inc., 1982.

_____. *The Joys of Yiddish*. New York: Pocket Books, 1970.

Rubin, Ruth. *Voices of a People: The Story of Yiddish Folksong with Musical Scores and Lyrics*. Philadelphia: The Jewish Publication Society of America, 1979.

Sandrow, Nahma. *Vagabond Stars: A World History of Yiddish Theater*. New York: Harper & Row Publishers, Inc., 1977.

Shepard, Richard F., and Levi, Vicki Gold. *Live & Be Well: A Celebration of Yiddish Culture in America from the First Immigrants to the Second World War*. New York: Ballantine Books, 1982.

Weiner, Leo. *The History of Yiddish Literature in the Nineteenth Century*. New York: Sepher-Hermon Press, 1972.

Jewish Identity IX

The table for the Jewish people, with its unique ceremonials, is an essential part of the Jewish religion. It is around the table that the ideals of Israel's home life find concrete expression. For the Jewish people the table is more than a piece of furniture upon which the daily meals are served. It is a symbolic altar of God.

Shulman, Albert M. Gateway to Judaism: Encyclopedia Home Reference. *New York: Thomas Yoseloff, 1971, page 441.*

OVERVIEW

Among the chapters in this book, this one on Jewish identity is unique. For Jewish identity is not a subject to be taught, but rather, the ultimate goal of Jewish education and upbringing. Rabbi Israel Goldstein has suggested that "true" Jewish identity may only be achieved through the following three actions subsequent to birth: ... the act of choice, choosing to remain Jewish despite its difficulties ... the act of cognition, learning to know the history and literature of [our] people so as to understand its soul and appreciate its place in the world ... and the act of transmission, transmitting to the next generation [our] heritage and the will to carry it on so that the Jewish people may not perish from the earth (*The Eternal Light.* Harper & Row Publishers, Inc., 1966, page 100).

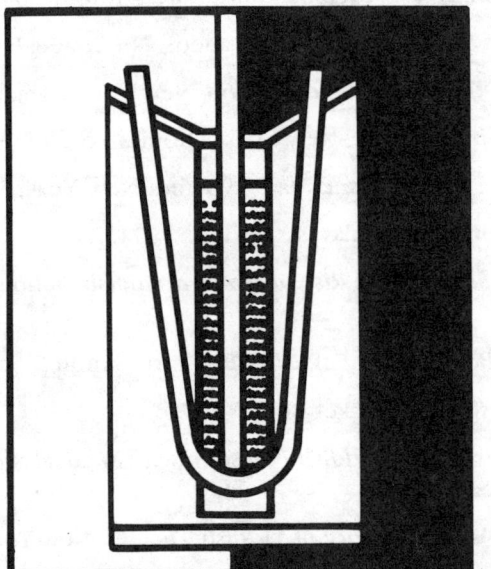

Jewish educators have little direct control over the acts of choice and transmission. These acts rest solely with each individual. The educator's efforts are therefore concentrated on the act of cognition. Providing students with creative learning opportunities, and exposing them to the tremendous wealth of Jewish knowledge and experience will encourage them to act desirably, to "choose" to remain Jewish," and to transmit their proud heritage to the next generation.

The books selected for this chapter fall under the heading of contemporary realistic fiction and informational literature. The stories are plausable and the events could actually happen to contemporary students. While reading the literature, students will be participating in the stories by trying out roles, making judgments about the characters' actions, and rehearsing experiences which they might someday confront. Because these books deal with Jewish issues, they are excellent ways to help the students develop a sense of their roots, family, and heritage, all of which combine to form one's Jewish identity.

Under this rubric are included books which mirror the concerns of many young Jewish people today. Several books were chosen because they address the issue of anti-Semitism, a plague in the past and a continuing threat today. *Chernowitz* seemed a particularly appropriate book for this chapter, since it discusses the insidious nature of prejudice in a suburban neighborhood and the effects of such hatred on its young Jewish protagonist. *Dmitry: A Young Soviet Immigrant* reflects the lack of religious freedom of Jews in the Soviet Union and one family's resettlement process. One cannot view today's anti-Semitism and make intelligent choices about action without looking back in history to the Holocaust. *The Children We Remember*, a touching informational book, establishes an immediate tie between children of today and those living under the Nazi regime.

Positive role models for students experiencing their Bar/Bat Mitzvah year may be found in *Season of Discovery* and *King of the Seventh Grade*. In reading these two stories, students will begin to discover the importance of living a meaningful Jewish life.

The conflict one faces to maintain Jewish tradition in a secular world is explored in two of the books included. The description of Orthodox customs in *I Am An Orthodox Jew* and *What Happened to Heather Hopkowitz?* contributes much to the understanding of a traditional Jewish lifestyle. Both present the often difficult choices that must be made in order to live by Orthodox traditions.

Family life in the Jewish home can do much to instill or defeat a sense of Jewish identity in the young child. In *Once I Was a Plum Tree*, Gerry Flam feels that she has been cut off from her Jewish heritage at home. She finds the meaning of being Jewish in a friendship she forms with a German Jewish refugee. However, eleven-year-old Carrie Levin in *The Rabbi's Girls*, learns what it means to be Jewish from her parents, who provide a traditional Jewish home.

Because Hebrew is the common language of our people, we have also included *A Book of Hebrew Letters*, an alphabet book which is sure to delight.

JEWISH IDENTITY: BOOKS AND ACTIVITIES

Abells, Chana Byers. *The Children We Remember*. Photographs from the Archives of Yad Vashem. Rockville, MD: Kar-Ben Copies, Inc., 1983. 42 pages. Grade level: 2-6.

This is a superb, heart-rending book about the children of the Holocaust. It immediately establishes a sense of identification on the part of Jewish children of today with those who actually experienced the horrors of pre-Holocaust Europe. One section depicts the hardships of Jewish families and the strength of children helping their people to survive. Photographs of children who died are followed by the hopeful faces of those who went on to rebuild their lives.

Major Ideas

We must not forget the Holocaust because it can happen again.

Even though one did not actually live during that time, the Holocaust experience will become a part of the heritage of all Jews down through the generations.

The courage of many of the children of the Holocaust is an example of behavior to which the children of today should aspire.

Activities

1. Grades 2-6: Interesting library displays are one way of capturing the attention of young readers. Share this book with your class. Then guide the students to realize that before the Holocaust began, the children of that time engaged in day-to-day activities that were basically the same as today. To establish a bond with the children portrayed in this book, invite the students to participate in the creation of a photographic essay on their lives. Photographs may be taken of the students by their families. The teacher may take additional photographs of the students engaged in Jewish activities. The photographs will be displayed on a bulletin board entitled "The Children We Are." Place a table directly under that bulletin board displaying the book *The Children We Remember*.

2. Grades 5 and 6: Show one of the following films/filmstrip about the Holocaust:

   Films:

   The Life That Disappeared (Scholastic Magazine, Inc.)

   The Legacy of Anne Frank (Eternal Light Kinescopes)

   I Never Saw Another Butterfly (National Academy for Adult Jewish Studies of the United Synagogue of America)

   Filmstrip:

   The Warsaw Ghetto: Holocaust and Resistance (Jewish Labor Committee)

   Be sure to leave ample time for discussion following the showing.

3. Grades 3 and up. The individual stories of the children whose photographs appear in this book are not told. Have each student in the class choose a picture of one child in the book. If the child who has been selected has not already been named in the book, the student should choose a name for the child. Have the student write a story about that child's life. These can be typed, reproduced, and compiled in individual books entitled "About the Children We Remember." The books may be kept in the student's personal library. Copies may also be given to the school library.

Arrick, Fran. *Chernowitz*. Scarsdale, NY: Bradbury Press, 1981. 165 pages. Grade level: 6 and up.

This book deals with the power of prejudice. Bobby Cherno's years in ninth and tenth grade are seen through his own eyes. Because he is Jewish, Bobby is chosen by the class bully, Emmett Sundback, to be a scapegoat. Recruiting others in his campaign, Sundback succeeds in torturing Bobby and alienating him from other boys his age. Bobby is hurt and seeks revenge. What he does to retaliate against Emmett is dishonest and the consequences of his actions are poignantly revealed. Arrick has written a book which is compelling, frightening, and, at the same time, hopeful.

Major Ideas

Bigotry is mindless.

We must fight openly against prejudice.

Bigotry inflicts hurt and is often contagious.

There are people who will always be prejudiced, but there are more people who are fair and just in their appraisal of others.

Activities

1. Grades 6 and up: The actions of Emmett Sundback illustrate the hurt that prejudice can inflict. At the end of the book, the principal of Bobby's school plans an assembly to reveal the history of the Holocaust. She hopes that the films and lectures will serve as a graphic lesson to the children that if history is not remembered, it will "soon become a present agony." An assembly planned in your school can

serve a similar purpose. Recruit several upper grade classes to plan a program focusing on incidents of discrimination throughout history. Each class may choose an historical event to present. Avoid duplication. Slavery, the Holocaust, apartheid, and the treatment of Native Americans are just a few suggested occurrences which may be included in the creative program. The message of the evils of prejudice may be conveyed through drama, music, creative interpretations of literature, slide presentations, etc. The program may be presented to other schools, as well as middle and upper grade non-participating classes in your school.

2. Grades 6 and up: At the end of the book, Bobby realizes that there will always be prejudice, but that many people are accepting of other people, regardless of race or religion. To help the students consider the contrast between prejudice and acceptance, have them write a poem in the form of a diamante comparing the meaning of prejudice and acceptance. The following form was created by Iris M. Tiedt, and may be found in *Language Arts Activities for the Classroom* by Sidney W. Tiedt and Iris M. Tiedt.

> Line one: subject – one word
> Line two: adjectives – two words
> Line three: participles – three words
> Line four: nouns – four words
> Line five: participles – three words
> Line six: adjectives – two words
> Line seven: noun, the opposite of the subject – one word.

The second, third, and fourth lines should relate to line one, and the next two lines to line seven.

An example follows:

> prejudice
> growing dangerous
> hating, breeding, stifling
> men, women, teens, infants
> loving, breathing, learning
> softer better
> acceptance

3. Grades 6 and up: This is a book that mandates discussion following its reading. Many important issues are raised which students can explore fully. Ideas for discussion questions follow:

> Bobby's best friend Brian followed Emmett in his persecution of Bobby. Why do you suppose he chose to do so?
>
> Imagine that you are Bobby. What actions would you have taken had a group of neighborhood boys or girls burned a cross on your lawn?
>
> Bobby celebrates both Jewish and Christian holidays. Until he was discriminated against, Bobby says he felt "like a Jewish boy, but not any different from any other boy." Now he does feel different. What, if anything, makes you feel different from other children who are not Jewish? When or in what circumstances do you feel the same?
>
> Bobby says that he always thought people judged him for who he was, not as a part of a race or religion. How do you judge people?
>
> Bobby decides to get back at Emmett by planning a scheme which makes Emmett look guilty of stealing Bobby's new radio. What is your opinion of what Bobby did? How might he have handled it differently?
>
> Could the persecution that Bobby endured happen to you? Explain.
>
> Bobby feels hope at the end of the book. What signs of hope for a less bigoted world do you see today?

Bernstein, Joanne. *Dmitry: A Young Soviet Immigrant*. Photographs by Michael Bernstein. New York: Clarion Books, 1981. 80 pages. Grade level: 3-5.

Through factual narrative and photographs, the Bernsteins document the experiences of Dmitry and his family as they leave Moscow and resettle in New York. Although everyday life in Russia was good for the Gindin family, they decided to give up their jobs and attachments in the land of their birth in order to pursue religious freedom in the United States. Once in the United States, the family struggles to adjust to the American way of life. They must be patient in their search for jobs commensurate with their skills. They must work hard at making new friends. Among the pleasurable opportunities that Dmitry's new life offers is the freedom to learn about Jewish holidays, customs, and history which he was not allowed to study in Russia. This story of Dmitry and his family illustrates the challenges and victories which are so much a part of the immigrant experience.

Major Ideas

The search for one's Jewish identity can be a rewarding challenge.

The sense of community responsibility and caring among both the Russian immigrants and the Jewish community at large is crucial to the resettlement process.

We must appreciate our freedom to live as Jews, as we remember that there are still governments which discriminate against our people.

Leaving a familiar way of life is difficult for young and old alike.

Jewish Identity

Activities

1. Grades 4 and 5: Dmitry's father, Edward, is a conductor and a musician. Students should be aware that there are many Jews who have made significant contributions to the field of music. Have each student research the life of one famous Jewish musician, singer, conductor, or composer. Some possibilities are: Leonard Bernstein, Beverly Sills, Isaac Stern, Itzak Perlman, Aaron Copeland, Vladimir Horwitz, Barbara Streisand, George Gershwin, Irving Berlin, Ernest Bloch, Oscar Hammerstein, Benny Goodman, Barry Manilow, Arthur Rubinstein, Richard Rogers, Jan Peerce, Richard Tucker, Roberta Peters, Bette Midler, Neil Diamond, Bob Dylan, Paul Simon, Neil Sedaka. After the research is completed, have the students write a brief summary of that person's life and select a short recorded piece of music presented by that person. Biographical information and records may be found at the public library. As a way of adding a bit of culture to your classroom, assign each student a day on which to present their report and musical selection.

2. Grades 3-5: One of the challenges which Dmitry and other immigrants face is learning a new language. Idioms pose a special problem for the immigrant who does not speak English. Have the students imagine that they are Dmitry trying to make sense of one of the following idioms:

   > Jonathan always needed to have a finger in the pie.
   > That's the last straw.
   > I could eat a horse.
   > Shoshana always barks up the wrong tree.
   > Rachel is a real bear if she doesn't get her way.
   > David flew into a rage.
   > Sometimes I think Stanley has bats in the belfry.
   > Mr. Stein kept his wife completely in the dark about her present.
   > Please weigh your words.
   > Let's hit the road.
   > I can't understand why she flew off the handle.
   > I jumped out of my skin when I heard the explosion.
   > After Robert spoke to Adam, he was fit to be tied.
   > Ann likes to pull Shira's leg.
   > Joshua is an old stick in the mud.
   > Let's get down to brass tacks.
   > I think Mrs. Klein has something up her sleeve.
   > They turned the tables on him.
   > Sarah didn't know which way the wind was blowing.
   > Joanne's parents have a difficult time keeping the wolf from the door.
   > It's on the tip of my tongue.
   > Out of sight, out of mind.

   Have the students illustrate on paper their understanding of the idiom, keeping in mind that English is not their native language. Display these on a bulletin board entitled: "It's All Greek to Me."

3. Grades 3-5: Invite a panel of Jewish people to your classroom who have emigrated from Russia or other countries. Select people of different ages. Beforehand, have the children prepare a list of questions to ask the panel members. Questions should focus on what Jewish and secular life was like in Russia, as well as soliciting information about the panel member's experiences as immigrants to this country. As a culminating activity, hold a freedom feast in honor of being Jewish in North America. The students may recite the following prayer which praises freedom and their country:

   > "May God bless the President [Prime Minister] and all other officials of our country. May they succeed in promoting a spirit of brotherhood [and sisterhood] among all the inhabitants of this land. May our country always be a champion of freedom and justice throughout the world. Amen."

This adapted English translation and the original Hebrew prayer by Louis Ginzberg may be found in *Siddureinu: Our Prayer Book*, edited by Rabbis Sydney Greenberg and Morris Silverman, (Bridgeport, CT: Prayer Book Press, 1969). Also, check your congregation's prayer book for prayers about freedom and country.

At the feast, serve traditional North American foods such as hot dogs, hamburgers, baked beans, french fries, and apple pie. If you wish to have a sing-along after the meal, include both Hebrew and English folk songs.

Cohen, Barbara. *King of the Seventh Grade.* New York: Lothrop, Lee & Shepard Books, 1982. 190 pages. Grade level: 5 and up.

Thirteen-year-old Vic hates Hebrew school. He is convinced that not even a big Bar Mitzvah party is compensation for attending classes. Vic devises a plan to be disruptive in school so that he will be dismissed permanently. When the teacher can no longer handle Vic, the Rabbi decides to give Vic private lessons. At a conference with Vic's parents, the Rabbi discovers that Vic's mother is not Jewish and, therefore, according to Jewish law, neither is Vic. Vic is informed by the Rabbi that he can no longer become a Bar Mitzvah. After much soul searching, a run-in with the law, and a positive Jewish experience at a friend's house on Shabbat, Vic decides to convert and proudly has his Bar Mitzvah ceremony. This is an excellent book which raises the important question of what it means to be a Jew.

Major Ideas

Becoming a Bar or Bat Mitzvah is a process which helps a person establish his/her Jewish identity and sense of "menschlikeit."

According to traditional Jewish law, a person is not a Jew unless born of a Jewish mother.

According to Reform and Reconstructionist thought, a person is a Jew if brought up as a Jew and committed to Jewish values and practices.

To become a Jew by Choice is difficult, but rewarding.

It is never too late to change one's ways and seek the righteous path.

Activities

1. Grades 6 and 7: Vic believes that his father is planning a big Bar Mitzvah party for him in order to show off to his family. Often, a big Bar Mitzvah party seems to outweigh the significance of the religious ceremony. It is important for children in their Bar or Bat Mitzvah year to be actively involved in planning the occasion. In this way, the ceremony and celebration can be in keeping with the meaning of becoming a Bar or Bat Mitzvah. With parental cooperation, have each student decide on at least one way to give personal and Jewish meaning to the *seudah* (meal) which follows the Bar or Bat Mitzvah. Some examples follow:

   For centerpieces, use children's books with a Jewish theme which will later be donated to the synagogue library.

   Buy cards from a charity organization and send these as invitations.

   Plan your celebration as a Shabbat retreat with time for leisure and study.

2. Grades 5 and up: Vic decides to go through conversion to become a Jew. Invite the Rabbi and some individuals who are Jews by Choice to class to discuss the conversion process. After the panelists have shared their expertise, have the students ask them questions which have been prepared beforehand. Appropriate questions include:

   Why did you choose to become a Jew?

   What were the most difficult changes you had to make once you became a Jew?

   What are some of the most rewarding aspects of being Jewish?

   What helps you to feel most Jewish?

   How did your family feel about your conversion?

   How do you (the Rabbi) feel about helping people convert to Judaism?

   After the panel leaves, conclude the discussion by asking the students whether, if they had been in Vic's position, they would have converted.

3. Grades 6 and 7: On the day that Vic is converted, he must sign a certificate declaring his desire to "accept the principles of the Jewish religion . . . " This certificate, which spells out his firm commitment to Judaism, is a rather lengthy document. This part of the book provides perfect motivation for the students to contemplate their own commitment to Judaism. Using the conversion document in the book as a model, have the students write a personal statement in which they pledge their determination to maintain their Jewish identity through the practice of a Jewish lifestyle. The individual statements may be included as part of the child's Bar or Bat Mitzvah ceremony.

Goldreich, Gloria. *Season of Discovery.* Nashville, TN: Thomas Nelson, Inc., 1976. 156 pages. Grade level: 4-6.

This book explores the meaning of becoming a Bat Mitzvah. All too often, Bar or Bat Mitzvah is seen as a time for parties and extravagant gift giving. However, Lisa, the main character in the book, finds the year of her Bat Mitzvah to be a time for self-discovery. It is then that she begins to deal with the fact that her twin brother is retarded. She is also faced with the cold reality of anti-Semitism. Through her friendship with an old woman who is a survivor of the Holocaust, Lisa learns to accept the challenges of adulthood and being a Bat Mitzvah. A pertinent story for upper elementary children. It portrays a sense of learning and growing through one's pain that is both challenging, comforting, and interesting.

Major Ideas

The Holocaust continues to influence both Jewish and secular life today.

It is crucial to cope constructively with anti-Semitism.

Bat Mitzvah involves a process of *becoming*, and of commitment to further learning and involvement in Jewish life.

One can mature through adversity and emotional change.

Intergenerational relationships can be of great value to young people in search of their identity.

Activities

1. Grades 4-6: Lisa matured through experience. The students can relive their growing experiences

Jewish Identity

through the creation of an autobiographical scroll outlining memorable times in their lives. See Diagram 13 for an example.

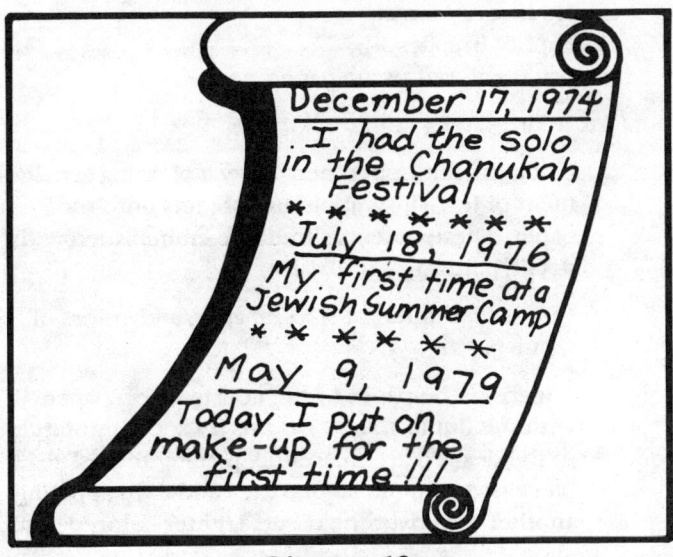

Diagram 13

2. Grades 5 and 6: Introduce acrostic poetry to children. Have each student write the word Bar or Bat Mitzvah horizontally down the left-hand margin of a sheet of paper. Tell the children to use each letter as the first letter of a phrase expressing some idea of what it means to become a Bar/Bat Mitzvah. An example follows:

   Blossoming into my adult life
   Agonizing over my Haftarah
   Teaching me lessons
   Most important
   Indeed.
   Triumph!
   Zigzag journey
   Victorious am I
   A Bat Mitzvah finally
   Haftarah, happiness, health, just beginning.

3. Grade 6: Bar/Bat Mitzvah is a time of both giving and receiving. So that the students can enjoy the pleasure of giving during their Bar/Bat Mitzvah year, allow them to decide on a project which will benefit the synagogue and/or its religious school. Some ideas are:

   Becoming teacher assistants in the religious school.
   Making a *parochet* (curtain for the Ark).
   Initiating a fund raising project to buy books for the library.

Greene, Laura. *I Am an Orthodox Jew*. Illus. by Lisa C. Wesson. New York: Holt, Rinehart & Winston, Inc., 1979. 37 pages. Grade level: K-3.

The narrator and central character in this story is Aaron Katz, an American Jew who attends an Orthodox Hebrew Day School. Through text and line drawings, the young reader is brought clearly in touch with Orthodox customs and, perhaps even more importantly, with the conflicts Aaron faces as an Orthodox Jew in a secular world. A welcome and necessary addition to Jewish literature for children.

Major Ideas

Traditional Jewish customs have specific purposes and meanings.

Being an Orthodox Jew in a secular society is both challenging and rewarding.

Exploring and understanding traditional beliefs and customs is a good way of becoming comfortable with them.

Activities

1. Grades 2 and 3: Arrange for the students to celebrate a traditional Shabbat. A weekend retreat is an excellent way to achieve this, inviting children from various synagogues in the community to join your class. Another way might be to ask observant families in your community to invite students to spend an entire Shabbat with them.

2. Grades K-3: Play "Guess This Tradition." Whisper Jewish traditions to one or more students. Allow them to pantomime the traditions. The audience will attempt to guess which tradition is being pantomimed. The student who guesses correctly pantomimes next. The following might be included:

   lighting Shabbat candles
   reading the Torah
   wearing a *kipah*
   putting on *tefillin*
   planting trees in Israel
   baking *challah*
   sitting separately in synagogue (*mechitzah*)
   Havdalah service

3. Grades K-3: Aaron Katz, the main character in the story, is obviously quite proud of his Jewish identity. Students will enjoy designing and wearing T-shirts with Jewish motifs to show their pride in being Jewish. Send a note home to the parents asking them to have the students bring a plain white T-shirt to class. After the students have created a design on scratch paper (with Jewish motifs), the designs can be drawn directly on the T-shirts with permanent fabric paint or ironed on after they have been drawn on paper with fabric crayons. If desired, the teacher can write each student's Hebrew name on his/her T-shirt with fabric paint. Arrange for the class to model their T-shirts.

Herman, Charlotte. *What Happened to Heather Hopkowitz?* New York: E.P. Dutton & Co., Inc., 1981. 176 pages. Grade level: 3-6.

When Heather's parents leave for a month-long vacation, Heather is left with family friends. She realizes that the adjustment will not be an easy one. After all, Heather's parents are not practicing Jews and the Greenwalds are Orthodox. During the month, something happens to change Heather. She begins to enjoy and find meaning in the Jewish traditions practiced by her surrogate family. After much thought, Heather decides to become a practicing Jew. When Heather's parents return from their trip, she practices her Judaism secretly. With guidance from a friend, Heather realizes that she is not living through the Spanish Inquisition and makes a decision to tell her parents. After a period of rejection, Heather's parents come to accept the change in Heather. The Passover *Seder* planned by the whole family symbolizes a new beginning. Herman has written a book showing a young girl's struggle to find meaning in her Judaism.

Major Ideas

Practicing one's Judaism adds meaning and fulfillment to one's life.

We should fight to uphold those values which are important to us.

Activities

1. Grades 3 and 4: Heather comes in contact with many Jewish symbols and religious objects during her stay at the Greenwald's. A tissue paper collage is a beautiful way to depict these symbols and objects. Tissue paper is adhered to a preliminary drawing, allowing the drawing to shine through. First, have your students brainstorm a list of symbols, objects, and their uses. A typical list might include:

    Magen David (Jewish Star)
    mezzuzah
    kipah
    candlesticks
    Shabbat candles
    Torah
    prayerbook
    Seder plate
    wineglass
    dreidle
    tallit
    menorah
    Torah mantle
    challah

    Then, using the objects named, have the children create a collage. Materials and procedure follow.

    Materials:
    12" x 18" white construction paper
    waterproof felt tipped black pens
    liquid laundry starch
    12" utility brushes
    assorted colored tissue paper

    Procedure:

    a. Using the felt tipped pen, draw a pleasing arrangement of Jewish symbols and objects onto the paper. These objects should be embellished with detail, pattern, and texture.

    b. Cut or tear different sizes, shapes, and colors of tissue paper.

    c. Adhere tissue paper to the construction paper with the liquid starch. Do this by applying starch to the desired area, carefully placing the tissue piece over the moistened area and then applying another coat over the tissue. Lighter colored tissue should be applied first and then darker colors. The various shapes of tissue paper should be overlapped. It is possible that very dark tissue will make the line drawing disappear. However, when the collage dries, the lines may be redrawn over the dried tissue.

    d. Display the collages on a bulletin board entitled: "Looking Into Our Jewish Identities."

2. Grades 5 and 6: When Heather informs her mother that she has decided to become religious, her mother replies, "That's ridiculous . . . " The only tradition which is followed in Heather's home is attending Yom Kippur services. That tradition is followed by a restaurant outing. As a way of having the students reflect on and become educated about the meaning of the traditions Heather learns to respect, assign small groups of students to research a tradition. Traditions might include:

    keeping kosher
    celebrating Shabbat
    separate seating in synagogue
    wearing a *kipah*
    naming a baby after a deceased relative
    lighting the *chanukiah* on Chanukah
    playing *dreidle*
    sitting *shiva*
    the Passover *Seder*

    Once the research is completed, have the students imagine that they are writing letters to Mrs. Hopkowitz explaining to her the significance of their assigned tradition. The letters should then be typed, duplicated, and compiled into a class book entitled "Dear Mrs. Hopkowitz: A Guide to Jewish Tradition." Give each child a copy of the book, and forward one copy to the author of *What Happened to Heather Hopkowitz?* with an explanatory letter. The author's name and address follows: Charlotte Herman, c/o E.P. Dutton Publishers, 2 Park Avenue, New York, NY 10016.

3. Grades 3-6: Heather crochets a *kipah* for a boy she met in youth group. Have the students choose someone for whom they would like to make a *kipah*. Provide each child with a plain white *kipah* and colored Vogart pens. (These are tubes of paint with a ballpoint pen tip which are made specifically for fabric.) Have the students decorate the *kipah* using a Jewish theme. The *kipah* should be nicely wrapped and presented to the chosen person, along with a letter of appreciation. Older students will enjoy learning how to crochet a *kipah* as Heather did in the book.

Hurwitz, Johanna. *Once I Was a Plum Tree*. Illus. by Ingrid Fetz. New York: William Morrow & Co., Inc., 1980. 160 pages. Grade level: 4-6.

Lacking an understanding of her Jewish identity means double trouble for ten-year-old Gerry Flam. Gerry is shunned by the non-Jewish children in her neighborhood for being Jewish. She is ostracized as well by the Jewish children because her family is non-observant. Gerry's father tries to explain that the family has assimilated in order to fit the American lifestyle. However, Gerry still feels that she has been cut off from her Jewish heritage and family roots. It is only through her friendship with Edgar, whose family members were refugees from Nazi Germany, that Gerry begins to learn the meaning of being Jewish. Hurwitz has integrated the common threads of the ancient Passover story, the lessons of the Holocaust, and the experiences of American Jewry in gaining acceptance. Her novel is a most powerful one for young readers.

Major Ideas

Jewish identify is not necessarily determined by one's level of observance.

It is possible to be both a good Jew and a good American without giving precedence to one identity over the other.

Jewish identity is dependent upon our connectedness to the past, present, and future as individuals, families, and also as a people.

Families can give their children important gifts — knowledge of their past heritage and the freedom to carry it on as desired.

Activities

1. Grades 4-6: Gerry begins to learn about her Jewish heritage through discussions with her friend Edgar and during a Passover *Seder* with his family. Explain to the students that there are many ways of learning about Judaism, including reading books. Then ask them to imagine that they are Gerry and that they have the opportunity to learn more about their Jewish identity through participating in a class read-a-thon. Your Jewish Identity Read-a-Thon can be scheduled to last an entire school year or one semester. Using the suggestions in *Jewish Literature for Children: A Teaching Guide* and your school librarian as resources, encourage the students to read at least one book in each of the following categories:

   Bible
   Death and Dying
   Ethics
   Jewish Folklore
   Jewish History
   Holidays
   Holocaust
   Israel
   Jewish Identity
   Prayer

   The teacher, together with the students, can decide how read-a-thon participants will share their knowledge of at least three of the books read. This can be accomplished through a variety of means, including formal written reports, small group book review sessions, or a creative presentation. At the end of the semester or school year, those students who have read the minimum of one book in each category should receive special recognition. The type of honor is a matter of personal choice and availability of funding. Possibilities include a certificate, the presentation of a Jewish book to the school library in the student's honor, or the giving of a Jewish book of their choice to eligible students.

2. Grades 5 and 6: After Edgar and Gerry become friends, he shares with her an essay he wrote for school about Jewish identity. Gerry is particularly touched by the following paragraph of the essay:

   "Now that I am in a new land with new traditions and customs, it would be simple enough to adopt all the new ways and forget the past of my ancestors. But I feel I have a responsibility to history and to all those relatives before me who held so firmly to their belief. Jews have a history of morality, compassion and courage. I am proud and not afraid to assume the responsibility that my heritage brings. I am proud to be a Jew" (page 81).

   As a means of teaching the students about the important role historical events have played in the shaping and strengthening of Jewish identity, have them plan and create a mural of important events in Jewish history. Begin the process with a discussion during which the students are asked to recall important events and explain why they believe them to be significant. List each event on the chalkboard in chronological order. It may be necessary to add events which your students have not mentioned. Depending on the number of students and the amount of space available, you may have to vote on the events to include in the mural. Following is a sample list of events:

> Abraham leaving Haran
> Slavery in Egypt
> Moses receiving the Law at Mt. Sinai
> Joshua conquering Jericho
> Destruction of the Temple
> Masada
> Hillel explaining the essence of Torah as the stranger stood on one foot
> The Spanish Inquisition
> *Shtetl* life in Eastern Europe
> Immigration of Jews to America at the turn of this century
> The Holocaust
> The establishment of the State of Israel
> Immigration of Soviet Jewry

Make sure in choosing events for your mural that you include ancient and contemporary happenings with which the students have some familiarity. Once the events have been chosen, work on the mural may begin. Materials and procedure follow.

Materials:
a long sheet of brown or white butcher paper (length will depend on amount of display space available and number of historical events to be illustrated)
oil pastels
pencils
scratch paper

Procedure:

a. Lay the paper out on a long table or on the floor.

b. The teacher should mark the paper off into even sections using black oil pastel or felt tipped marker.

c. Depending on the size of the class, assign individual or pairs of students one or two historical events to illustrate.

d. Have the students sketch designs on scratch paper and then lightly transfer them in pencil onto the mural in the appropriate choronological order.

e. Develop the illustrations using oil pastels.

f. Label each event with its name and, if desired, a quotation about the event (i.e., a line from the Haggadah under the illustration of slavery in Egypt).

g. After the students have signed their work, hang the mural in your classroom or along a prominent hall in your facility. In this way, the mural will serve not only as a work of art, but as a visual learning experience as well.

3. Grades 4-6: When Mrs. Wallace takes her dog Willie for an evening walk, she often stops to talk for a moment with Gerry. Inevitably, she leaves Gerry with the statement, "Be glad that you are you." By the end of the story, Gerry is able to appreciate fully Mrs. Walker's words, as she has finally begun to learn about the Jewish aspect of her identity.

To explore further the concept of identity, engage the students in a discussion. Focus on the following questions:

> What does the word identity mean?
> What elements go into making a person's identity?

Guide the students to realize that many elements or experiences comprise our identities including: ethnicity, race, religion, geographic location, special interests, occupation, and so on.

Next, ask each student to think about all the elements that make up their individual identities and to plan a collage reflecting who they are. Materials and procedure follow.

Materials:
a piece of heavy 12" x 18" cardboard for each student
old magazines, string, glitter, colored construction paper, scrap materials and any collage material's students wish to bring from home

Procedure:

a. Each student should design a collage reflecting the important elements of his or her identity, making sure to include aspects of his/her Jewishness.

b. Cut and glue collage material onto the heavy cardboard as desired.

c. Cut lettering to be included in the designs from magazines or write the letters in felt tipped or metallic markers.

d. Before the collages are displayed on a bulletin board entitled "Be Glad That You Are You," have the students share their work in small groups or in a circle of the entire class. Have each of them highlight the important aspects of his/her identity. Gerry's parents attempted to ignore one element of their identity. Ask the students to consider the consequences that might occur if they chose to "give up" Jewish practices and education in order to assimilate into the society around them.

Hurwitz, Johanna. *The Rabbi's Girls*. Illus. by Pamela Johnson. New York: Morrow Junior Books, 1982. 158 pages. Grade level: 4 and up.

This book is the account of one year in the life of eleven-year-old Carrie Levin and her family. The year is 1923 and Carrie's father, who is a Rabbi, has just moved the family to Lorrain, Ohio. Carrie's year is filled with both bitter and sweet experiences. Carrie is overjoyed at the birth of her new sister, yet saddened by the anti-Semitism she encounters in Ohio. When Papa dies, her family is forced to move once again. Hurwitz's characters are likable and real.

Major Ideas

Sometimes we do not appreciate the goodness in life until we experience the bitterness.

Family closeness is something to be treasured and preserved.

When living in a secular society, there may be temptations to break with Jewish tradition.

Anti-Semitism can sometimes be countered by setting a more compassionate example.

Activities

1. Grades 4 and up: After Papa's death, Carrie is comforted by a Chasidic story he once told her. The moral of the story is that the bitterness we experience in life helps us to appreciate life's goodness. Expand this concept to include the topic of Jewish history and identity. Have small groups dramatize both bitter and sweet moments in Jewish history. To generate a list of possible ideas for dramatizations, brainstorm historical events with the children. Each group should dramatize one bitter and then one sweet event. Some possible topics are:

Bitter	Sweet
The Holocaust	Proclamation of the birth of Israel
Slavery in Egypt	
1973 Yom Kippur War	Rescue at Entebbe
The Munich Olympic Tragedy	Exodus from Egypt
Quotas imposed on Jewish students during this century	Jewish immigration from Russia
	Chanukah or Purim Story

2. Grades 4 and up: The following activity would be appropriate to use after the class has studied the various dimensions of the traditional Jewish way of life. Carrie's oldest sister Betty breaks Jewish tradition when she chooses to attend the movies on Shabbat. Many Jews have chosen to modify the traditional way of life. Hold a discussion with the students focusing on the issue of maintaining Jewish traditions. Ask the following questions:

    What Jewish traditions have been maintained by your family?

    Of the traditions maintained, what modifications in the tradition, if any, has your family made?

    How might maintaining Jewish tradition help the Jewish people to survive?

3. Grades 4 and up: Carrie's father shares many words of wisdom with his children. These words help Carrie and her sisters cope with life. Have the students tell their parent(s) about how Carrie's father shared wisdom with her. Then, tell the students to ask their parents to share some of their own words of wisdom with them. The quotations from parents should be written down and brought to class. In class, have each student select one quotation from each parent. On separate pieces of paper, the children will then paint a portrait of the parent with his/her words of wisdom written on the page. Display these on a bulletin board entitled "Ethics of Our Parents." Plan a social hour. Invite parents so that they may view their portraits.

Podwal, Mark. *A Book of Hebrew Letters*. Illus. by the author. Philadelphia: The Jewish Publication Society of America, 1978. 57 pages. Grade level: K and up.

Artist Mark Podwal has set out to create pictographs which "seek to express in one form or another, the force and vitality of the twenty-two Hebrew letters in the enduring Jewish experience." He has accomplished this through Hebrew calligraphy and pen and ink drawings. Beginning with *aleph* for *aleph bet* and ending with *tav* for Torah, this exquisitely rendered book holds a spark of interest for readers of all ages.

Major Ideas

The letters of the Hebrew alphabet form the basis for all of the terms and concepts native to Jewish culture and language.

The letters of the Hebrew alphabet follow a specific order.

Although the letters look different, Hebrew and English have many similar sounds.

Activities

1. Grades K-3: Children will enjoy learning and reinforcing their knowledge of the Hebrew alphabet through Debbie Friedman's song "*Aleph Bet*." The song is on the record of *Hebrew and Heritage, Volume I* (Behrman House, Inc.). Music and words appear on duplicating masters, also available from Behrman House, Inc.

2. Grades 5 and up: In the introduction, the author notes that he relates to the letters of the Hebrew

alphabet not only for their artistic beauty, but also for the important role they have played in the development of Jewish experience and identity. Following the same format used by Mark Podwal, have the students create an art gallery style display entitled "The Aleph Bet of Jewish Experience." Materials and procedure follow.

Materials:

12" x 18" white drawing paper
black India ink
a variety of other colors of ink
calligraphy pens with nibs of different thickness (if desired, felt tipped markers of different thicknesses may be used instead of pen and ink)
Colored poster board

Procedure:

a. Depending on the size of the class, assign each student one or two letters of the Hebrew alphabet.

b. With the teacher's help, have each student choose an element of Jewish life which begins with his/her letter and which he/she finds particularly meaningful.

d. Give each student a piece of drawing paper to fold in half.

e. On the right half of the paper, have students use pen and ink or marker to create a black and white illustration of the chosen element.

f. On the upper left quarter of the paper and using a color of ink other than black, have students draw the Hebrew letter in bold print. Students may copy the calligraphic style employed by Mark Podwal or create a style of their own. The name of the letter should be printed neatly in Hebrew and/or English transliteration to the right of the letter.

g. To complete the drawings, the name of the object should be printed in Hebrew, English transliteration, and English in the lower right quarter of the page on which the letter appears.

h. Mount the drawings on colored poster board.

i. Display the exhibit in your classroom or along a prominent wall in the school.

3. Grades 2-4: Knowing and understanding the meaning of their Hebrew names can help the students achieve a greater sense of Jewish identity. Following are the materials and procedure for a Hebrew name game that will allow students to use their written, oral, and artistic communication skills.

Materials:

12" x 18" white drawing paper
crayons
felt tipped markers
a thick gold or silver metallic marker
pencils or pens
rulers

Procedure:

a. Inform students that on a given day, you will be talking to them individually about their Hebrew names. Students who do not know their Hebrew names should ask their parents so that they will be prepared for the activity. Some students may also need help in choosing a Hebrew name if they were not given one at birth. This should be done in consultation with each student's parents.

b. During a special time you have set aside, call the students to your desk one by one. Write the student's Hebrew name on a piece of paper (in Hebrew manuscript), as well as the meaning of the name. Name meanings may be found in *The Name Dictionary: Modern English and Hebrew Names* by Alfred Kolatch (New York: Jonathan David Publishers, Inc., 1967). If this or another source of Hebrew names is unavailable, ask your Rabbi for help in translating the names. Ask each student to keep the meaning of his/her name a secret. The slip of paper with the Hebrew name and its meaning should be taken home to help complete the following assignment:

Give each student a sheet of drawing paper with his/her Hebrew name written in metallic gold or silver letters at the top in bold Hebrew manuscript letters. The bottom should be marked off with a solid line as shown in Diagram 14.

Diagram 14

Jewish Identity

c. Ask students to do the following assignment at home in preparation for a game to be played in class on a specified date. In the box at the bottom of the page, they are to write a riddle about the meaning of their name and then draw an illustration of it in the middle section of the paper. The answer to the riddle will later be revealed in class. Some students may need help in planning their illustration, especially if their name represents an abstract concept such as "strength," as opposed to a concrete object such as "rose."

d. On the day of the game, have the students sit in a circle and one by one share their riddles. The student asking the riddle should begin by saying, "*Sh'me* (fill in the Hebrew name)," and then ask the riddle. The other students will try to answer the riddle in order to learn the meaning of their classmate's Hebrew name. Students should not view the illustration until the riddle has been solved.

e. After all the riddles have been shared, display the illustrations on a bulletin board entitled "What's in a Name?"

JEWISH IDENTITY: BOOKS FOR CHILDREN

Asher, Sandy. *Daughters of the Law.* New York: Beaufort Books, Inc., 1980. Grade level: 5 and up.

Ruthie cannot decide whether or not to become a Bat Mitzvah. Her Aunt Sarah has been encouraging her, but Ruthie does not want to go against her dead father, who was not religious at all. The trauma of an anti-Semitic incident helps Ruthie make her decision. Asher has written an exceptional book. He deals not only with a contemporary adolescent girl's dilemma, but also with her mother's fight to cope with the memories of the Holocaust.

Beatty, Patricia. *Melinda Takes a Hand.* New York: William Morrow & Co., Inc., 1983. Grade level: 4-6.

A young girl living in the Old West of 1893 involves herself in the life of the people living in her small frontier town. One of the families she decides to help is the Mittleman family who hope that other Jewish families will move nearby so that synagogue services may be held. A humorous depiction of some of the problems Jews faced in maintaining their identity in America's Old West.

Belth, Norton (ed). *The First World Over Story Book* (1952); *The Second World Over Story Book* (1963). Schloss, Ezekiel, and Epstein, Morris (eds). *The New World Over Story Book* (1968); *More World Over Stories* (1968). New York: Jewish Education Committee of New York, Inc.

These four volumes contain a rich assortment of stories that originally appeared in the children's magazine, *World Over*. Story topics relate to virtually every aspect of Jewish identity including holidays, history, prayer, ethics, folklore, and Bible.

Blue, Rose. *Cold Rain on the Water.* New York: McGraw-Hill Book Co., 1979. Grade level: 6 and up.

This is a contemporary story about the struggles of a Russian Jewish immigrant family. Although the young boy's father is robbed and murdered, the story ends on a note of hope as the boy learns that "each generation makes the next one." A powerful novel which rings true.

Bogot, Howard, and Syme, Daniel. *Books Are Treasures.* Illus. by Cara Goldenberg Marks. New York: Union of American Hebrew Congregations, 1982. Grade level: PK-2.

This book enables young children to appreciate the strong emphasis Judaism places on the importance of books. The line drawings are both entertaining and instructive, as is the text.

Bogot, Howard, and Syme, Daniel B. *My Body Is Something Special.* Photographs by Gay Block. New York: Union of American Hebrew Congregations, 1981. Grade level: PK-1.

Photographs of children involved in Jewish life highlight the way the senses and body can help us to enjoy the many traditions of Judaism. A beautiful book for the very young child.

Brand, Sandra. *Between Two Worlds.* New York: Shengold Publishers, Inc., 1982. Grade level: 6 and up.

The main character in this novel is a girl of eighteen in World War II Poland, the daughter of Chasidic parents. Brand explores the issue of being female in a man's world and wanting to achieve more than Orthodox tradition allowed.

Brooks, Jerome. *Make Me a Hero.* New York: E.P. Dutton & Co., Inc., 1980. Grade level: 6-9.

Jake Akerman is twelve years old. He is upset that his parents are more concerned about his older brothers, who are all in the military, than about him. Although he has not had a strong religious background, he decides to study for his Bar Mitzvah. With the help of Mr. Gold, his elderly employer, Jake finds his Jewish identity and matures. A well developed story with strong characters.

Chaikin, Miriam. *I Should Worry I Should Care.* Illus. by Richard Egielshi. New York: Harper & Row Publishers, Inc., 1979. Grade level: 4-6.

Warm and gentle family relationships punctuated by strong Jewish tradition are emphasized in this book about a young girl's adjustment in moving to a new neighborhood. Egielshi's realistic pencil illustrations capture the setting perfectly.

Cohen, Barbara. *Benny.* New York: Lothrop, Lee & Shepard Books. Grade level: 4-6.

This is a moving story about a twelve-year-old boy who, in 1939, gives up his self-centered life style. He shows compassion for a young German Jewish refugee whose mother is dead and who lives with his non-accepting father and stepmother, neither of whom is Jewish.

Jewish Identity

Cohen, Barbara. *Bitter Herbs and Honey.* New York: Lothrop, Lee & Shepard Books, 1976. Grade level: 6 and up.

Becky Levitzky grew up in a traditional Jewish family. She is torn between accepting her parents' values and plans for her and going on to college and marrying the non-Jewish man she loves. Becky's struggle is poignantly revealed in this touching, warm, and uplifting novel.

Coleman, Hila. *Ellie's Inheritance.* New York: William Morrow and Company, 1979. Grade level: 6 and up.

In this sequel to *Rachel's Legacy*, Ellie becomes friends with a Communist youth and falls in love with a refugee from Nazi Germany. Coleman's characters will appeal very strongly to children in search of their own identities as they grapple with the isues of adolescence.

Cone, Molly. *A Promise is a Promise.* Illus. by John Gretzer. Boston: Houghton Mifflin Co., 1964. Grade level: 4-6.

Ruthy Morgan is twelve years old and preparing for her Bat Mitzvah. As she studies, she begins to discover her Jewish identity and becomes a "*mensch*." A meaningful book with touches of humor.

Dolinger, Leah. *A Very Special Yarmulke.* Illus. by H. Hechtkopf. New York: Feldheim Publishers, 1979. Grade level: PK-1.

The merits of study and prayer are brought to life in a delightfully symbolic way when an ordinary *yarmulke* becomes encrusted with colorful jewels after it learns to love the Torah.

Drucker, Malka. *Celebrating Life: Jewish Rites of Passage.* New York: Holiday House, Inc., 1984. Grade level: 4-6.

Drucker has written a scholarly and fascinating book about the rites of passage which punctuate the Jewish life cycle from birth through death. The historical development of each rite is discussed, as well as the nature of the modern celebrations. An emphasis is placed on how these celebrations help strengthen Jewish identity and the sense of continuity from one generation to the next. Photographs of ritual objects used during the various ceremonies and of people observing the rites add to the appeal of the book.

Fredler, Jean. *The Year the World Was Out of Step with Jancy Fried.* New York: Harcourt Brace Jovanovich, Inc., 1981. Grade level: 5 and up.

A family brings to the United States their Austrian relatives who are under Hitler's threat. This causes a twelve-year-old girl to learn that her father's ties to Judaism are strong, despite his seemingly ambivalent attitude. A powerful story with convincing plot and characterization.

Fruchter, Yaakov (ed). *The Best of Olomeinu.* Illus. by Yosef Dershovitz. New York: Torah Umesorah, 1981-83. Grade level: 3 and up. (Four Volumes)

The stories in these volumes have been compiled from the children's magazine, *Olomeinu: Our World*. They are set in different periods of Jewish history and take place in various countries around the world. The common theme in the stories is that faith and courage have allowed the Jewish people to survive.

Ganz, Yaffa. *The Adventures of Jeremy Levi.* Illus. by Harvey Klineman. New York: Feldheim Publishers, 1981. Grade level: 3-6.

A young boy grows up and eventually becomes a person who respectfully observes the Torah. Fun adventures keep the reader's interest.

Ganz, Yaffa. *Who Knows One: A Book of Jewish Numbers.* Illus. by Harvey Klineman. New York: Feldheim Publishers, 1981. Grade level: 3-6.

The Jewish significance of consecutive numbers from one to thirteen, as well as various additional numbers, is illustrated through text and cartoon drawings. A glossary of Hebrew words used is included at the back of the book. A fun and informative number book.

Genet, Barbara. *Ta-poo-ach Means Apple.* Denver: Alternatives in Religious Education, Inc., 1985. Grade level: PK-3.

Genet has brought the Hebrew alphabet to life through wild and wonderfully colored graphics guaranteed to delight readers of all ages. The illustrations of intriguing everyday objects are labeled in Hebrew, English, and transliteration.

Girion, Barbara. *Like Everybody Else.* New York: Charles Scribner's Sons, 1980. Grade level: 5 and up.

It is Samantha's Bat Mitzvah year. She is excited and nervous and wonders whether her mother, who is a writer of some acclaim, will ever find time to plan the Bat Mitzvah celebration. Through her study of the proverb "A Woman of Valor," Samantha finds wisdom that helps her to cope with her own life. This book is funny and meaningful, especially for the young adolescent who is preparing to become a Bat Mitzvah.

Goffstein, M.B. *Family Scrapbook*. New York: Farrar, Straus & Giroux, Inc., 1978. Grade level: K-2.

Short simple stories of special memories in a young Jewish girl's life comprise this delightful book. Many of the soft line drawings have a greatly humorous quality.

Goldstein, Andrew. *My Very Own Jewish Home*. Photographs by Madeline Winkler. Rockville, MD: Kar-Ben Copies, Inc., 1979. Grade level: PK-2.

A little girl explains to the reader what makes her home Jewish. The pleasure the child draws from her Jewish lifestyle is evident in the narrative and photographs.

Greenfeld, Howard. *Bar Mitzvah*. Illus. by Elaine Grove. New York: Holt, Rinehart & Winston, Inc., 1981. Grade level: 4 and up.

Greenfeld discusses the historical origins and meaning of becoming a Bar Mitzvah, as well as how the three major branches of Judaism celebrate this important milestone.

Hautzig, Deborah. *Second Star to the Right*. New York: Greenwillow Books, 1981. Grade level: 5 and up.

Hautzig has written a very powerful novel about a teen-age girl with anorexia nervosa and her relationship with her mother, who is a survivor of the Holocaust.

Herman, Charlotte. *The Difference of Ari Stein*. Illus. by Ben Shecter. New York: Dial Press, 1976. Grade level: 5 and up.

Ari Stein is an eleven-year-old boy from an Orthodox family who realizes that he is quite different from the neighborhood boys who are trying to assimilate. Shecter's illustrations effectively capture the 1940s on the Lower East Side of New York.

Herman, Charlotte. *Our Snowman Had Olive Eyes*. New York: E.P. Dutton & Co., Inc., 1977. Grade level: 4 and up.

A heartwarming story about the very special relationship which is shared by Sheila and her Bubby. Herman has done a marvelous job of portraying the Jewish ideal of family and intergenerational reciprocity.

Hoban, Lillian. *I Met A Traveller*. New York: Harper & Row Publishers, Inc., 1977. Grade level: 4 and up.

A noted author of children's books has written a story about a girl who, when she is taken to Israel by her mother, learns to appreciate both the beauty and hardships of being Jewish. A rich novel which should appeal to both the pre-adolescent and adolescent reader.

Holman, Felice. *The Murder*. New York: Charles Scribner's Sons, 1978. Grade level: 5 and up.

Hershy Marks is a good-natured Jewish boy growing up in a small mining town in the 1930s. He is concerned about the anti-Semitism which appears to be rampant in his neighborborhood. Holman gives the reader a view of Hershy's childhood and his struggle to maintain an individual identity, yet gain acceptance by his neighbors.

Hull, Eleanor. *The Summer People*. New York: Atheneum Publishers, 1984. Grade level: 6 and up.

A young girl who spends her adolescent years in a small Colorado town realizes that her Jewishness will always set her slightly apart from her close friend. Interreligious understanding is the focus of the book.

Karp, Naomi J. *The Turning Point*. New York: Harcourt Brace Jovanovich, Inc., 1976. Grade level: 5 and up.

When twelve-year-old Hannah and her family move to the suburbs from the Bronx, she experiences her first taste of anti-Semitism. Hannah learns that despite tauntings and being excluded from a classmate's birthday party, she is a worthwhile person. Well drawn characters add to the reality of the plot.

Kitman, Carol, and Hurwitz, Ann. *One Mezuzah: A Jewish Counting Book*. Chappaqua, NY: Rossel Books, 1984. Grade level: PK-2.

Beautiful scenes of Jewish life are used to illustrate this special Jewish counting book. The text and photographs highlight the warm and happy moments experienced at home and in the synagogue.

Jewish Identity

Klass, Sheila Solomon. *Nobody Knows Me in Miami*. New York: Charles Scribner's Sons, 1981. Grade level: 4-6.

Miriam has a choice. She may stay with her poor, observant family which is struggling to make ends meet, or she can choose to be adopted by an aunt and uncle who are wealthy though unobservant Jews. Klass's style is engaging and children will appreciate Miriam's dilemma and decision.

Konigsberg, E.L. *About the B'nai Bagels*. Illus. by the author. New York: Atheneum Publishers, 1969. Grade level: 4-6.

A delightful story about Narj Setzer, a young Jewish boy who is studying for his Bar Mitzvah and also playing baseball for the team his mother coaches. This is a warm, humorous book about a boy who learns that becoming a man doesn't happen overnight, but rather happens when you "become more yourself."

Lebovics, Aydel. *The Teeny Tiny Yarmulke*. Illus. by Rochelle Cohen. New York: Merkos L'Inyonei Chinuch, 1982. Grade level: PK-1.

When a shopkeeper is given a tiny *yarmulke* in return for helping a stranger, he never imagined that such a *yarmulke* is just what the next customer needed. Poster style illustrations add extra appeal to this simple rhyming story.

Lehmann, Marcus. *Between Two Worlds*. New York: Feldheim Publishers, 1982. Grade level: 4 and up.

A search for his roots leads Paul, the main character in this powerful story, to rediscover Judaism. Lehmann's novel is particularly important and meaningful for young Jews in search of their Jewish identity and for those who question the merits of being Jewish.

Levin, Neil (ed). *Songs of the American Jewish Experience*. Illus. with photographs. Chicago: Board of Jewish Education, 1976. Grade level: 5 and up.

Historical background and musical arrangements are included in this collection of songs about the American Jewish experience. An excellent resource for both teacher and student.

Little, Jean. *Kate*. New York: Harper & Row Publishers, Inc., 1971. Grade level: 5 and up.

A poignant story about a young girl who considers herself Jewish, although she is the daughter of a mixed marriage and her mother is not Jewish. Kate revels in the stories her father tells her about his Jewish childhood and is surprised to discover that her father was disowned after marrying a non-Jew. This is an excellent book about self-discovery and acceptance.

Little, Jean. *Look Through My Window*. New York: Harper & Row Publishers, Inc., 1970. Grade level: 4 and up.

When Emily Blair moves to a different neighborhood, she becomes friends with Kate Bloomfield, who is half-Jewish. Through their friendship, Emily and Kate learn much about one another's religion and feelings, and how to survive in different types of family situations.

Metter, Bert. *Bar Mitzvah: How Jewish Boys and Girls Come of Age*. Illus. by Marvin Friedman. New York: Clarion Books, 1984. Grade level: 5 and up.

A clear and informative book which gives the historical background for the celebration of Bar/Bat Mitzvah. Preparation by the child, celebration in different countries, and the meaning of the Bar/Bat Mitzvah are included in the text.

Moskin, Marietta. *In the Name of God: Religion in Everyday Life*. New York: Atheneum Publishers, 1980. Grade level: 6 and up.

In this fascinating study on comparative religion, Judaism figures prominently. Religions are compared in terms of the factors that influenced their development, the role of women, and the relationship between religion and war. The differences between cults and traditional religions is also discussed. Maps, charts, and a bibliography add to the value of the book.

Naylor, Phyllis Reynolds. *The Solomon System*. New York: Atheneum Publishers, 1983. Grade level: 4 and up.

A grandmothers' support enables two brothers to cope with their parents' divorce and hold tight to their Jewish heritage. A warm story of Jewish family relationships.

Neville, Emily Cheney. *Berrie's Goodman*. New York: Harper & Row Publishers, Inc., 1975. Grade level: 5 and up.

This winner of the coveted Newbery Medal makes a strong statement against anti-Semitism. The influence that parents have on their children's beliefs and values is emphasized.

Pessin, Deborah. *The Aleph-Bet Story Book.* Illus. by Howard Simon. The Jewish Publication Society of America, 1946. Grade level: K-3.

    Learning the *aleph bet* becomes all the more enticing with this collection of stories about each of the twenty-two Hebrew letters. The author has drawn much of her source material from Jewish folklore and history.

Postman, Frederica. *The Yiddish Alphabet Book.* Illus. by Bonnie Stone. Palo Alto, CA: P'Nye, 1979. All grade levels.

    This informative book introduces the Yiddish alphabet. A transliteration into English is provided for each letter, accompanied by a word or words in Yiddish and the English translation. The illustrations in black, white, and brown add charm to this inviting book about an important part of Jewish culture.

Ruby, Lois. *Two Truths in My Pocket.* New York: Viking Press, Inc., 1982. Grade level: 6 and up.

    With sensitivity to the problems of youth, Ruby has written six short stories of young Jewish adolescents attempting to discover meaning in their Judaism. Adolescent boys and girls will be drawn to this excellent collection.

Showers, Paul. *Me and My Family Tree.* Illus. by Don Madden. New York: Thomas Y. Crowell Co., 1978. Grade level: K-3.

    A lively illustration of a child's family tree is used to explain the process of heredity. A good book to introduce the concept that family history and heredity have an influence on who we are.

Simon, Norma. *Why Am I Different?* Illus. by Dora Leder. Niles, IL: Albert Whitman & Co., 1976. Grade level: PK-K.

A variety of children give reasons for why they are different. Acceptance of differences is stressed. The lively illustrations emphasize different and similar aspects of each child.

Skolsky, Mindy Warshaw. *The Whistling Teakettle; and Other Stories about Hannah.* Illus. by Karen Ann Weinhaus. New York: Harper & Row Publishers, Inc., 1977. Grade level: 3-4. (Other books by the author: *Carnival and Kopeck and More About Hannah*, 1979; *Hannah is a Palindrome*, 1980. *Hannah and the Best Father on Route 9W*, 1982. New York: Harper & Row Publishers, Inc.)

    A series of delightful books about a young Jewish girl growing up in the surburbs of New York during the 1930s. Warm Jewish family relationships and concern for tradition are evident.

Spier, Peter. *People.* Illus. by the author. New York: Doubleday & Co., Inc. 1980.

    Spier emphasizes the point that although there are over four billion people in the world, all of us are special and should take pride in what makes us unique. Illustrations depict religious and cultural aspects of different societies.

Sussman, Susan. *There's No Such Thing As a Chanukah Bush, Sandy Goldstein.* Illus. by Charles Robinson. Niles, IL: Albert Whitman & Co., 1983. Grade level: 2-4.

    Robin knows that her friend Sandy Goldstein's "Chanukah bush" is really just a Christmas tree and that Jews don't celebrate Christmas. But Robin is jealous and wants a tree, too. With her grandfather's help, Robin realizes the beauty in celebrating Chanukah at home and the joy in sharing holidays with friends. Black and white illustrations realistically convey Robin's dilemma and solution.

Syme, Deborah Shayne. *The Jewish Home Detectives.* Illus. by Marlene Lobell Ruthen. New York: Union of American Hebrew Congregations, 1982. Grade level: PK-2.

    A fun book which gives children ideas for entertaining themselves at home in a Jewish way.

Taylor, Sidney. *Ella of All-of- A- Kind-Family.* Illus. by Gail Owens. New York: E.P. Dutton & Co., Inc., 1978. Grade level: 4-6. (Other books by the author in this series: *All-of-a-Kind Family*, 1951; *More All-of-a-Kind Family*, 1954; *All-of-a-Kind Family Uptown*, 1958; and *All-of-a-Kind Family Downtown*, 1972. Chicago: Follett Publishing Co.)

    Close Jewish family relationships abound in this "all-of-a-kind-family" book focusing on Ella, the oldest daughter.

Tene, Benjamin. *In the Shade of the Chestnut Tree.* Trans. by Reuben Ben-Joseph. Illus. by Richard Sigberman. Philadelphia: The Jewish Publication Society of America, 1981. Grade level: 4 and up.

    When Benjamin Tene returns to Poland after World War II, he finds that his childhood has been destroyed. The only remaining remnant is the old chestnut tree by which he used to meet with friends. Sitting beneath the tree, Tene takes the reader on twelve reminiscent journeys back into his childhood.

Terris, Susan. *Whirling Rainbows*. New York: Doubleday & Co., Inc., 1974. Grade level: 5-7.

Leah was adopted by the Friedmans when she was an infant. She led a very happy Jewish life until she decided to find out more about her Indian heritage. In the end, she learns that although she is part Chippewa, this is only a part of herself; she is also satisfied with her Jewish identity. Realistic dialogue, plot, and characterization make the book a pleasant addition to the literature on Jewish identity.

Weinberg, Yona. *Dov-Dov in Seattle*. Baltimore, MD: Dov-Dov Publishers, 1979. Grade level: 1-3.

The Orthodox children in this story use their problem solving skills to solve the dilemma of how to comply with various religious injunctions. Dov-Dov provides an excellent way of teaching children about the traditional commandments, stressing that one can assert his/her Jewishness comfortably in a secular society.

JEWISH IDENTITY: RESOURCES FOR ADULTS

Anti-Semitism

Abel, Ernest. *The Roots of Anti-Semitism*. Cranbury, NJ: Associated University Presses, Inc., 1975.

Belth, Nathan. *A Promise to Keep: A Narrative of the American Encounter With Anti-Semitism*. New York: Times Books, 1979.

Forster, Arnold, and Epstein, Benjamin. *The New Anti-Semitism*. New York: McGraw-Hill Book Co., 1974.

Freedman, Theodore (ed). *Anti-Semitism in the Soviet Union*. New York: Anti-Defamation League of B'nai B'rith, 1984.

Gager, John S. *The Origins of Anti-Semitism*. New York: Oxford University Press, 1983.

Kaplan, Kalman J., et al. *The Family: Biblical and Psychological Foundations*. New York: Human Sciences Press, 1984.

Maneli, Mieczyslaw. *Freedom and Tolerance*. New York: Hippocrene Books, Inc., 1984.

Poliakov, Leon. *The History of Anti-Semitism*. New York: Vanguard Press Inc., 1964. (Three Volumes)

Prager, Dennis, and Telushkin, Joseph. *Why the Jews? The Reason for Anti-Semitism*. New York: Simon & Schuster, Inc., 1983.

Sartre, Jean-Paul. *Anti-Semite and Jew*. New York: Schocken Books, Inc., 1948.

Slavin, Stephen L., and Prodt, Mary A. *The Einstein Syndrome: Corporate Anti-Semitism in America Today*. Lanham, MD: University Press of America, 1982.

Timmerman, Jacobo. *Prisoner Without a Name, Cell Without a Number*. New York: Alfred A. Knopf, Inc., 1981.

Trachtenberg, Joshua. *The Devil and the Jews: The Medieval Conception of the Jew and Its Relation to Modern Anti-Semitism*. Philadelphia: The Jewish Publication Society of America, 1983.

Cults and Missionaries

Colton, Lawrence (ed). *Cults and Missionaries: A "How To" Kit*. New York: Central Conference of American Rabbis, no publication date.

Fisch, Dov Aharoni. *Jew For Nothing*. New York: Feldheim Publishers, 1984.

Levine, Samuel. *You Take Jesus, I'll Take God: How to Refute Christian Missionaries*. Los Angeles: Hamorah Press, 1980.

Rudin, A. James, and Rudin, Marcia. *Prison or Paradise?: The New Religious Cults*. Philadelphia: Fortress Press, 1980.

Developing and Enhancing Jewish Self-Esteem

Aliyah. Ames, IA: Contemporary Jewish Learning Materials, Inc. (Game)

Barish, Shirley. *Six Kallot: Retreats for Jewish Settings*. Denver: Alternatives in Religious Education, Inc., 1978.

Benami, Aviva. *Hebrew Roots and Fruits*. New York: Bureau of Jewish Education, 1983.

Borowitz, Eugene. *The Masks Jews Wear: The Self-Deceptions of American Jewry*. New York: Simon & Schuster, Inc., 1973.

Canfield, Jack, and Wells, Harold. *100 Ways to Enhance Self-Concept in the Classroom: A Handbook for Teachers and Parents*. Englewood Cliffs, NJ: Prentice-Hall, 1976.

Cohen, Martin A., and Zevin, Jack. *Identity and Survival*. New York: Union of American Hebrew Congregations, 1976. (Two Volumes and Teacher's Manual)

Elkins, Dov. *Clarifying Jewish Values: Values Activities for Jewish Groups*. Rochester, NY: Growth Associates. (Other books by same author: *Glad To Be Me: Building Self-Esteem in Yourself & Others*, 1976; *Jewish Consciousness Raising: 50 Experiential Activities*, 1977; *Loving My Jewishness: Thoughts On Jewish Self-Pride*, 1977; *Meeting Your Jewish Self: Personal Growth for Jews*, 1978; *The Ideal Jew: A Values Clarification Program*, 1977. Rochester, NY: Growth Associates.)

Fein, L.; Chin, R,; Dauber, J.; Reisman, R.; and Spiro, R. *Reform is a Verb: Manual of Exercises*. New York: Union of American Hebrew Congregations, 1972.

Israel, Richard J. *Jewish Identity Games*. Washington, DC: B'nai B'rith Hillel Foundation, 1978.

Klein, Judith Weinstein. *Jewish Identity and Self-Esteem: Healing Wounds Through Ethnotherapy*. New York: American Jewish Committee, 1980.

Reisman, Bernard. *The Jewish Experiential Book: The Quest for Jewish Identity*. New York: KTAV Publishing House, Inc., 1979.

Rosenthal, Suzanne, and Schreiner, Nikki. *My Ancestors are Jewish*. Palos Verdes Estates, CA: Touch & See, 1975. Distributed by Educational Supply Co., Inc.

Sulkes, Zena. *Proud and Jewish: A Student Experience Book*. Denver: Alternatives in Religious Education, Inc., 1980.

Jewish Life Cycle Events

Donin, Hayim Halevy. *To Be a Jew: A Guide to Jewish Observance in Contemporary Life*. New York: Basic Books, Inc., 1972.

Efron, Benjamin, and Rubin, Alvan D. *Coming of Age: Your Bar/Bat Mitzvah*. New York: Union of American Hebrew Congregations, 1977.

Eisenberg, Azriel. *The Bar Mitzvah Treasury*. New York: Behrman House, Inc., 1952.

Eisenberg, Azriel, and Globe, Leah (ed). *The Bat Mitzvah Treasury*. Boston, MA: Twayne Publishers, 1965.

Fine, Irene, and Feinman, Bonnie. *Midlife and Its Rites of Passage Ceremony*. San Diego, CA: Women's Institute for Continuing Jewish Education, 1983.

Goodman, Philip and Hannah. *The Jewish Marriage Anthology*. Philadelphia: The Jewish Publication Society of America, 1965.

Grishaver, Joel Lurie. *The Life Cycle: A Workbook for Grades 4 to 6*. Denver: Alternatives in Religious Education, Inc., 1983.

Kaplan, Aryeh. *Made in Heaven: A Jewish Wedding Guide*. New York: Maznaim Publishing Corporation, 1983.

Katsh, Abraham. *Bar Mitzvah*. New York: Shengold Publishers, Inc., 1976.

Kolatch, Alfred. *The Name Dictionary: Modern English and Hebrew Names*. New York: Jonathan David Publishers, Inc., 1967.

Marcus, Audrey Friedman, et al. *Bar and Bat Mitzvah: A Family Education Unit*. Denver: Alternatives in Religious Education, Inc., 1983.

Marcus, Audrey Friedman; Bissell, Sherry; and Lipschutz, Karen. *Death, Burial & Mourning in the Jewish Tradition*. Denver: Alternatives in Religious Education, Inc., 1976.

Moskowitz, Nachama Skolnik. *The Jewish Life Cycle Game*. Denver: Alternatives in Religious Education, Inc., 1984. (Game)

Rittner, Stephen. *All That You Want To Know About the Bar-Bat Mitzvah: A Text That Isn't*. Boston, MA: Rittner's, 1976.

Romberg, Henry. *Bris Milah*. New York: Feldheim Publishers, 1982.

Schauss, Hayyim. *The Lifetime of a Jew: Throughout the Ages of Jewish History*. New York: Union of American Hebrew Congregations, 1950.

Strassfeld, Sharon, and Kurzweil, Arthur (eds). *Behold a Great Image: The Contemporary Jewish Experience in Photographs*. Philadelphia: The Jewish Publication Society of America, 1978.

Trepp, Leo. *The Complete Book of Jewish Observance*. New York: Behrman House, Inc., 1979.

Zwerin, Raymond A.; Marcus, Audrey Friedman; and Kramish, Leonard. *Circumcision*. Denver: Alternatives in Religious Education, Inc., 1983.

Jewish Symbols and Their Meaning

Klepper, Jeff; Freelander, David; and Nanus, Susan. *Especially Jewish Symbols: Sing-Along Songs for the Primary Grades*. Denver: Alternatives in Religious Education Inc., 1977. (Cassette and Song Book)

Raskin, Saul. *Aron Hakodesh: Jewish Life and Lore*. Drawings by the author. New York: Academy Photo Offset, Inc., 1955.

Novels and Autobiographies on the Theme of Jewish Identity

Cowan, Paul. *An Orphan in History: Retrieving a Jewish Legacy*. New York: Doubleday & Co., Inc., 1982.

Helmreich, William B. *Wake Up, Wake Up, To Do The Work of the Creator*. New York: Harper & Row Publishers, Inc., 1976.

Kukoff, Lydia. *Choosing Judaism*. New York: Union of American Hebrew Congregations, 1981.

Potok, Chaim. *The Chosen*. New York: Simon & Schuster, Inc., 1967.

Rappaport, Ness. *Preparing For Sabbath: A Young Woman in Search of God and Love*. New York: William Morrow & Co., Inc., 1981.

Roiphe, Anne. *Generation Without Memory: A Jewish Journey in Christian America*. New York: Linden Press, 1981.

Sherman, Schlomah. *Escape From Jesus: One Man's Search for Meaningful Judaism*. Mount Vernon, NY: Decalogue Books, 1983.

Wiesel, Elie. *A Jew Today*. New York: Random House, Inc., 1979.

The Family

Benson, Paulette, and Altschuler, Joanne. *The Jewish Family: Past, Present and Future*. Denver: Alternatives in Religious Education, Inc., 1979.

Bial, Morrison David. *Your Jewish Child*. New York: Union of American Hebrew Congregations, no publication date.

Donin, Hayim Halevy. *To Raise a Jewish Child*. New York: Basic Books, Inc., 1977.

Greenberg, Blu. *How to Run a Traditional Jewish Household*. New York: Simon & Schuster, Inc., 1983.

The Joy of Family. Norwalk, CT: Rutledge Books/C.R. Gibson Co., 1969.

Kaplan, Benjamin. *The Jew and His Family*. Baton Rouge, LA: Louisiana State University Press, 1967.

Kaplan, Kalman. *The Family: Biblical and Psychological Foundations*. New York: Human Sciences Press, 1984.

Latner, Helen. *The Book of Modern Jewish Etiquette: A Guide for All Occasions*. New York: Schocken Books, Inc., 1981.

Linzer, Norman. *The Jewish Family: Authority and Tradition in Modern Perspective*. New York: Human Sciences Press, 1984.

Matzner-Berkerman, Shoshana. *The Jewish Child: Halakhic Perspectives*. New York: KTAV Publishing House, Inc., 1984.

Morse, Charles and Ann. *Let This Be a Day for Grandparents*. Winona, MN: St. Mary's College Press, 1972.

Patz, Naomi, and Perlman, Jane. *In the Beginning: The Jewish Baby Book*. Illus. by Dianne Applebaum. New York: National Federation of Temple Sisterhoods/Union of American Hebrew Congregations, 1983.

Roseman, Kenneth. *All in My Jewish Family*. Photographs by Arthur Leipzig. New York: Union of American Hebrew Congregations, 1984.

Steichen, Edward. *The Family of Man*. New York: Museum of Modern Art, 1955.

Strassfeld, Sharon, and Green, Kathy. *The Jewish Family Book: A Creative Approach to Raising Kids*. Photographs by Bill Aron. New York: Bantam Books, Inc., 1981.

Thomas, Marlo. *Free To Be . . . You and Me*. New York: McGraw-Hill Book Co., 1974.

The Russian-Jewish Experience

Azbel, Mark. *Refusnik: Trapped in the Soviet Union.* Boston: Houghton Mifflin, 1981.

Bytensky, Bella. *From Russia With Luggage.* Toronto: Annic Press, 1980.

Gilbert, Martin. *The Jews of Hope: The Plight of Soviet Jews Today.* New York: Viking Press, Inc., 1984.

Gruzenberg, O. *Yesterday: Memoirs of a Russian Jewish Lawyer.* Berkeley, CA: University of California Press, 1981.

Howe, Irving, and Greenberg, Eliezer (eds). *Ashes Out of Hope: Fiction by Soviet-Yiddish Writers.* New York: Schocken Books, Inc., 1977.

On the Move: Soviet Jewry. Denver: Alternatives in Religious Education, Inc., 1974. (Game)

Rusinek, Alla. *Like a Song, Like a Dream: A Soviet Girl's Quest for Freedom.* New York: Charles Scribner's Sons, 1973.

The Russian Jewry Simulation Game. New York: Behrman House, Inc. (Game)

Shcharansky, Avital, and Ben-Joseph, Llana. *Next Year in Jerusalem.* Trans. by Stefani Hoffman. New York: William Morrow & Co., Inc., 1979.

Zaslavsky, Victor, and Brym, Robert J. *Soviet-Jewish Emigration and Soviet Nationality Policy.* New York: St. Martin's Press, 1983.

Tracing Jewish Roots

Kranzler, David. *My Jewish Roots: A Practical Guide to Tracing Your Geneology and Family History.* New York: Sepher-Hermon Press, 1979.

Kurzweil, Arthur. *From Generation to Generation: How to Trace Your Jewish Genealogy and Personal History.* New York: William Morrow & Co., Inc., 1980.

_____. *My Generations: A Course in Jewish Family History.* New York: Behrman House, Inc., 1983.

Rottenberg, Dan. *Finding Our Fathers: A Guidebook to Jewish Geneology.* New York: Random House, Inc., 1977.

Tarachow, Mike. *Toldoteinu — Finding Your Own Roots: An Activity Book.* Milwaukee, WI: Arbit Books, Inc., 1978.

Wagenvoord, James. *A Grandparent's Book: Thoughts, Memories, and Hopes For A Grandchild.* New York: Rawson Wade, Publishers, Inc., 1981.

_____. *A Parent's Book: Thoughts, Reflections, and Hopes For a Child.* Tuscon, AZ: H.P. Books, 1981.

Zimmerman, William. *How To Tape Instant Oral Biographies.* New York: Guarionex Press, Ltd., 1982.

Women and Judaism

Ben Maimon, Moses. *The Book of Women.* New Haven, CT: Yale University Press, 1972.

Greenberg, Blu. *On Women and Judaism: A View from Tradition.* Philadelphia: The Jewish Publication Society of America, 1981.

Henry, Sondra, and Taitz, Emily. *Written Out of History: Our Jewish Foremothers.* Fresh Meadows, NY: Biblio Press, 1983.

Heschel, Susannah (ed). *On Being a Jewish Feminist: A Reader.* New York: Schocken Books, Inc., 1983.

Koltun, Elizabeth (ed). *The Jewish Woman: New Perspectives.* New York: Schocken Books, Inc., 1976.

Marcus, Jacob R. (ed). *The American Jewish Woman: 1654-1980.* New York: KTAV Publishing House, Inc., 1981. (Two Volumes)

Patai, Raphael. *The Hebrew Goddess.* New York: KTAV Publishing House, Inc., 1968.

Sasso, Sandy Eisenberg, and Elwell, Sue Levi. *Jewish Women.* Denver: Alternatives in Religious Education, Inc., 1983.

Schneider, Susan Weidman. *Jewish and Female: Choices and Changes in Our Lives.* New York: Simon & Schuster, Inc., 1984.

Singer, Isaac B. *Yentl the Yeshiva Boy.* Woodcuts by Antonio Frasconi. New York: Farrar, Straus & Giroux, Inc., 1983.

Scholarly Studies on the Meaning of Judaism

Asheri, Michael. *Living Jewish: The Lore and Law of the Practicing Jew.* New York: Dodd, Mead & Co., 1983.

Baeck, Leo. *The Essence of Judaism.* New York: Schocken Books, Inc., 1974.

_____. *This People Israel: The Meaning of Jewish Existence.* New York: Holt, Rinehart & Winston, Inc., 1964.

Bleich, J. David (ed). *With Perfect Faith: The Foundations of Jewish Belief.* New York: KTAV Publishing House, Inc., 1983.

Buber, Martin. *For the Sake of Heaven: An Allegory of the Spiritual Struggle of the Jewish People.* Philadelphia: The Jewish Publication Society of America, 1958.

Cohen, Steven M. *American Modernity and Jewish Identity.* New York: Tavistok Books, 1983.

Feuerlicht, Roberta Strauss. *The Fate of the Jews: A People Torn Between Israel, Power and Jewish Ethics.* New York: Times Books, 1983.

Fleg, Edmond. *Why I Am a Jew.* New York: Bloch Publishing Co., 1975.

Gittelsohn, Roland. *The Modern Meaning of Judaism.* Cleveland: Collins Publishers, Inc., 1978.

Gordis, Robert. *Judaism in a Christian World.* New York: McGraw-Hill Book Co., 1966.

Haberman, Dr. Steven. *New Jews: The Dynamics of Religious Conversion.* New York: Union of American Hebrew Congregations, 1979.

Halevi, Judah. *The Kuzari: An Argument for the Faith of Israel.* New York: Schocken Books, Inc., 1964.

Heilman, Samuel C. *Synagogue Life: A Study in Symbolic Interaction.* Chicago: University of Chicago Press, 1973.

Herberg, Will. *Judaism and Modern Man.* New York: Atheneum Publishers, 1970.

Herman, Simon N. *Jewish Identity: A Social Psychological Perspective.* New York: Herzl Press, 1977.

Heschel, Abraham Joshua. *God in Search of Man: A Philosophy of Judaism.* New York: Octagon Books, 1972.

Hirsch, Samson Raphael. *Judaism Eternal.* Edited by I. Grunfeld. London: Soncino Press, 1976. (Two Volumes)

Holtz, Barry W. (ed). *Back to the Sources: Reading the Classic Jewish Texts.* New York: Summit Books, 1984.

Hyams, Ario. *Toward a One-World Jewry: An Essay in Jewish Identity.* Smithtown, NY: Exposition Press, Inc., 1979.

Karff, Samuel. *Agada: The Language of Jewish Faith.* Cincinnati, OH: Hebrew Union College Press, 1979.

Korn, Yitzhak. *Jews at the Crossroads.* Cranbury, NJ: Cornwall Books, 1983.

Levine, Etan (ed). *Diaspora: Exile and the Jewish Condition.* New York: Jason Aronson, 1983.

Miller, Alan W. *God of Daniel S.: In Search of the American Jew.* New York: Macmillan Publishing Co., Inc., 1969.

Neusner, Jacob. *The Jewish War Against the Jews: Reflections on Golah, Shoah, Torah.* New York: KTAV Publishing House, Inc., 1984.

Newsome, James. *By the Waters of Babylon: An Introduction to the History and Theology of the Exile.* Atlanta, GA: John Knox Press, 1979.

Prager, Dennis, and Telushkin Joseph. *Nine Questions People Ask About Judaism.* New York: Simon & Schuster, Inc., 1981.

Raphael, Chaim. *The Springs of Jewish Life.* New York: Basic Books, Inc., 1982.

Rosenberg, Stuart. *The New Jewish Identity in America.* New York: Hippocrene Books, Inc., 1984.

Schechter, Solomon. *Studies in Judaism.* Philadelphia: The Jewish Publication Society of America, 1924.

Silver, Abba Hillel. *Where Judaism Differed: An Inquiry into the Distinctiveness of Judaism.* Philadelphia: The Jewish Publication Society of America, 1957.

Steinberg, Milton. *Basic Judaism.* New York: Harcourt Brace Jovanovich, Inc., 1947.

_____. *The Making of the Modern Jew.* New York: Behrman House, Inc., 1967.

Wouk, Herman. *This is My God.* New York: Doubleday & Co., Inc., 1959.

Prayer

*Teach me, my God, a blessing, a prayer
On the mystery of a withered leaf,
On ripened fruit so fair,
On the freedom to see, to sense,
To breathe, to know, to hope, to despair.
Teach my lips a blessing, a hymn of praise,
As each morning and night
You renew Your days,
Lest my day be as the one before,
Lest routine set my ways.*

Leah Goldberg, translated from Hebrew by Pnina Peli, in The Second Jewish Catalog, edited by Michael Strassfeld and Sharon Strassfeld, page 304. Copyrighted by and used through the courtesy of The Jewish Publication Society of America.

OVERVIEW

The complexity of prayer is eloquently defined in the following conversation: The Tzanzer Rebbe was asked by a Chasid: "What does the Rebbe do before praying?" "I pray," was the reply, "that I may be able to pray properly" (*The Hasidic Anthology*, edited by Louis Newman. New York: Schocken Books, Inc., 1963), page 332.

Teaching children to participate in Jewish worship is a particularly challenging task. It requires introducing them to the basic format of the prayer book and the various services. Learning to understand and recite the traditional prayers in Hebrew and English is another key component to proper prayer. It is also important to familiarize them with those elements of worship unique to their congregation or school. Knowledge of the historical development of prayer, the prayer book, and the synagogue service can be very enlightening. Yet, is often neglected.

While all of the above represent fairly concrete knowledge which can be taught through equally concrete learning experiences, there are abstract elements to the vocabulary of prayer which also demand attention. These include most notably, an exploration of the Jewish concept of God and the idea of praying with "*kavanah*," or proper intent. The concept of *kavanah* goes hand-in-hand with encouraging children to add to the traditional prayers their own special thoughts and feelings. Creatively combining all of these dimensions of worship will hopefully lead to the same understanding Rabbi Bunam shared with the Chasid who complained that praying gave him headaches, namely that "worship is a service from the heart, not a labor of the head." Thus, books have been selected for this chapter which relate to both the concrete vocabulary of prayer, as well as to its abstract meaning.

Without freedom of worship, one may never cultivate the art of prayer. *Molly's Pilgrim* reinforces the idea that America is a country which values the basic human right to pray, regardless of religious orientation.

Prayers traditionally recited on the holidays may not hold much meaning for students unless they are presented within a framework that the young mind can understand. *A Children's Prayer Book for Rosh Hashanah and Yom Kippur* and *A First Haggadah* offer prayer within the context of storytelling and simple explananation. The meaning behind the Shabbat blessings introduced in *Shabbat Can Be* is highlighted by illuminating illustrations.

The idea of praying from the heart is clearly portrayed in two books. In *Prayer Is Reaching*, young students will be exposed to the concept that one much reach within and without to pray with purpose. *Lift Every Voice and Sing: Words and Music* shows people praying with conviction through both word and song.

One of the key objectives of teaching students to pray with *kavanah* is to provide them with the motivation to do so. A teacher cannot expect a student to memorize a prayer by rote and then recite that prayer with any real feeling. *Hear O Israel: First I Say the Shema* will furnish students with the inspiration for learning the *Shema*. *Hear, O Israel: About God* answers the young student's first questions about God, thereby giving students an understanding of God's role in prayer.

My Book of Prayer: Prayer For All Times and *Within Thy Hand: My Poem Book of Prayers* are two books which provide students with prayers appropriate to a wide variety of situations. The message evident in both of these books is that prayer can give one a feeling of peace and contentment and should be a part of one's everyday life.

PRAYER: BOOKS AND ACTIVITIES

Bogot, Howard, and Syme, Daniel B. *Prayer is Reaching.* Illus. by Marlene Lobell Ruthen. New York: Union of American Hebrew Congregations, 1981. 23 pages. Grade level: PK-1.

A simple, yet moving introduction to prayer for very young children. Prayer is defined as words, but — more importantly — as reaching out to attain a sense of completeness or peace in our lives. Sensitive illustrations of young children show that prayer is a natural part of the action of our everyday lives.

Major Ideas

Prayer can take many forms.

Reaching within and reaching out to others is necessary to lead a full and a good life.

Activities

1. Grades PK-1: In the book, it is written that "Prayer is reaching...." Have the students reach out and imagine they are grasping something for which they are thankful. The students will then pantomime what they have reached for — for example: their parent, a flower, an animal.

2. Grades K and 1: This book could be used as a choral speaking presentation for a kindergarten class consecration service. Because the students are so young, separate them into four groups. The text should be divided and memorized as follows:

    Group I: pages 1-6
    Group II: pages 7-13
    Group III: pages 14-17
    Group IV: pages 18-21
    All groups: pages 22-23

3. Grades PK-1: The book ends with the *Shehecheyanu* blessing. Teach the students the words to this blessing and explain to them that the *Shehecheyanu* is recited on many occasions to thank God for being alive. At this time, discuss why they are thankful to be alive. If desired, the *Shehecheyanu* may be sung using a traditional melody. Or, the contemporary melodies composed by Zvika Pik or Debbie Friedman could be taught. Zvika Pik's version may be found on the album *Israeli Chassidic Festival 1984* (Isra-Art Productions). Debbie Friedman's version is on the album *... and the Youth Shall See Visions* (distributed by Sing Unto God). Invite a Cantor or song leader to teach these melodies to the class.

Chanover, Hyman, and Zusman, Evelyn. *My Book of Prayer.* Illus. by Leonard Weisgard. New York: United Synagogue Commission on Jewish Education, 1959. 96 pages. Grade level: 2-4.

Included in this child's introduction to prayer are prayers for weekdays, Shabbat, country, and special times. English explanations in simple prose help the reader to understand the meaning of the Hebrew text. The many topics of prayer have been colorfully rendered by noted illustrator Leonard Weisgard.

Major Idea

There are many reasons for which to be thankful.

Activities

1. Grades 2 and 3: For a fun activity to help reinforce the learning of blessings recited over various foods, hold a "Blessing Banquet" in the classroom. Prepare a cup of grape juice for each student and a plate with small samples of bread, fruit, vegetables, cookies, or cake. Before each type of food is savored, the students should recite the appropriate blessing together. The blessings are found in *My Book of Prayer*. Conclude the banquet by having the students recite the short rendition of *Birkat HaMazon* (Grace after Meals) found on page 27 of *My Book of Prayer*.

2. Grades 2 and 3: The last chapter of the book includes "Prayers for Special Times." This chapter is most appropriate for younger students. Many of these prayers seem to be written as letters to God. After reading the prayers out loud, ask the students to talk about some times in their lives when they needed God or were thankful to God. Following the discussion, have them write short letters to God related to the topics they discussed. Invite the Rabbi or principal into the classroom so that the students may share their letters.

3. Grade 4: This book contains prayers for many occasions. Tell each student to choose one prayer in the book to be included in a creative story he or she will write. The story should have a beginning, middle, and end, with the prayer being recited at some point by one of the characters in the story. Some of these stories can be presented as skits for a school assembly.

Cohen, Barbara. *Molly's Pilgrim.* Illus. by Michael J. Deraney. New York: Lothrop Lee & Shepard Books. 32 pages. Grade level: K-3.

Molly is a Russian-Jewish immigrant living in a small American town at the turn of the century. She is taunted by the girls in school because she is different. Feeling hurt, she expresses a desire to go back to New York City where she was not the only Jewish girl in her class. When her mother informs her that it is financially impractical to return to New York, Molly asks to go home to Russia. She realizes that this is impossible when her mother tells her that synagogues in Russia were burned and Jews were not allowed to worship freely. Molly gains acceptance from her classmates when she explains to them during a school Thanksgiving lesson that, like the Pilgrims, her family also journeyed to America in search of religious freedom. Realistic black and white illustrations capture Molly's pain, humiliation, and eventual joy as she struggles to find acceptance from the other children.

Major Ideas

The freedom to worship as one pleases is a good reason for giving thanks.

America is a haven for people seeking religious freedom.

The freedom to worship as one pleases is a basic human right which should be respected by all.

Activities

1. Grade 3: A major theme of this book is the importance of having the freedom to worship as one pleases. Each religious group has unique ways of worshiping. To help the students see that America is a country which allows freedom of religion, plan for small groups of students to attend various religious services in the community. Parent volunteers should accompany each group. Ask the students to observe the service closely and note similarities and differences between Jewish worship and the worship of the group they are visiting. Arrange for the students to visit with the religious leader of each church, mosque, or synagogue. Ask that a teacher or leader spend some time with the students to explain their rituals and answer any questions the students may have. After the visit, give each group time during class to share their experiences.

2. Grades K-3: When Molly asks her mother if they can return to Russia, her mother informs her that the synagogues were burned. Obviously, this interferes with freedom of worship. Take the students into the sanctuary for a lesson on the physical aspects of the synagogue which help one to worship as a Jew. Point out the following items in the sanctuary:

    Siddur – Prayer Book
    Ner Tamid – Eternal Light
    Aron Hakodesh – Holy Ark
    Torah
    Seven branched *Menorah*
    Bimah – Pulpit
    Yahrzeit plaques – Memorial plaques

    Conclude this activity by discussing how these ritual objects are used and their symbolic meaning.

3. Grades K-3: This is a perfect book to share at Thanksgiving. Hold a special Thanksgiving feast in your class during which this book is read. Make special note of the section in the book in which it is mentioned that the idea for the American Thanksgiving was borrowed from the Jewish holiday of Sukkot.

Cone, Molly. *Hear, O Israel: About God.* Illus. by Clare and John Ross. New York: Union of American Congregations, 1973.

The first questions that children have about God are answered in this collection of engaging stories written in folktale style. Each story focuses on one question and ends with a line from a Hebrew prayer capturing the story's message. The illustrators have used a pleasing and colorful combination of folk and abstract art to complement the delightful text.

Major Idea

Although God cannot be seen, one can feel God's presence in a multitude of ways.

Activities

1. Grade K-2: In the story "The Fish That Looked for Water," a little fish consults with a wise old fish asking, "Where is water?" The old fish responds, "It's all under you and over you and in you and around you . . ." An analogy is then drawn between water and God through the use of a prayer which states that ". . . the whole earth is full of God's glory." Explain to the students that although God cannot be seen like other beings, God's presence is evident in a multitude of ways (i.e., a rainbow, roaring lions, flowers growing, the unique qualities humans possess). After the explanation, have students suggest ways in which God's presence is evident. Following the discussion, each student will draw two illustrations of God's presence in the world. One will be a self-portrait and the other may be of anything that reminds them of God's presence. The drawings can be displayed on a bulletin board entitled, "The Best of Creation."

2. Grades 3-4: The story "How Does God Talk to Us?" focuses on the importance of appreciating one's God-given ability to experience the world through physical senses and a compassionate heart. In the story, a little mouse learns to use all of his five senses, as well as his sense of compassion, through the gentle urging of his mother. The prayer quoted at the end of the story is the *Aleinu*. Present the major idea of this story in a choral reading before or after the singing of *Aleinu* during a Shabbat service. Separate your class into six groups. Assign the first five groups one of the five senses, and the sixth group, the sense of compassion. Tell each group to write a poem about the different ways in which they experience God's presence in the world through the sense they were assigned. An example follows:

    When I see the rising sun,
    I know that God is here.

An arching rainbow up above
Reminds me God is near.

When I see a baby smile,
I know that God smiles, too,
A happy, laughing, joyful smile.
At the sight of something new.

After the poems have been written and proofread, have each group rehearse reading their poem out loud together. The teacher and class can then decide in which order the poems will be read, leaving the poem about the sense of compassion for last.

3. Grades K-2: In the last story, "The Man Who Was Not Himself," the main character, Eli, wishes he were Mr. Jonathan, his next door neighbor, rather than himself. When Mr. Jonathan becomes sick, Eli becomes sick, too. The Rabbi who visits the sick patient takes pity on him, because Eli doesn't understand the value of his individuality. When Eli finally looks in the mirror, he realizes his foolishness and takes the Rabbi's words to heart that "... there is only one Eli." After sharing the story with the students, ask them to share one thing about themselves which makes them special. As a culminating activity, teach the song "Just One Me." The melody may be found on *My Sesame Street Record: All About Me!* (Record #CTW-22103, Distributed by Sesame Street Record Division of Distinguished Productions, Inc.).

Cone, Molly. *Hear, O Israel: First I Say the Shema*. Illus. by William L. Seinel. New York: Union of American Hebrew Congregations. 1971. 31 pages. Grade level: PK-2.

This is the first of a series of books which focus on the *Shema*. The importance of the prayer as a pledge of Jewish identity is underscored by the author's analogy between the American Pledge of Allegiance and the *Shema*. The text of the book has been carefully arranged to provide children with motivation for learning the *Shema* before the Hebrew words are taught. Narrative and realistic illustrations enumerate the occasions on which the prayer is recited and emphasize its role as the cornerstone of Jewish faith.

Major Ideas

Judaism is based on the belief in only one God.

The words of the *Shema* unite all Jewish people.

The many occasions on which the *Shema* is recited constantly remind us of the importance of its meaning.

Activities

1. Grades PK-2: To reinforce learning the *Shema*, take the students through a dramatic experience that encompasses the many occasions on which the *Shema* is recited. Following is a narrative the teacher may use. Make sure that you pause, giving students an opportunity to act out the narrative and to say the *Shema* each time it is mentioned.

    Let us imagine that it is nighttime and you are getting very sleepy. You crawl under the covers and before you close your eyes, you softly say the words of the *Shema*. Now the sun is shining. It is morning! You jump out of bed and run to your window to open it. You look around at the beautiful new day and happily say the *Shema* out loud. You get dressed, walk downstairs, and sit down at the kitchen table to enjoy your breakfast. Now breakfast is over. You get up and leave for synagogue because it is Shabbat. As you pass through the door of your home, you look up to see the *mezzuzah*. You remember the words of the *Shema* which are inside of it and say them as you close the door. You walk to the synagogue and, once inside, you sit down and open the prayer book. During the service, many Hebrew prayers are recited, but you are especially excited when you hear the Rabbi say "Let us say the *Shema*." You recite it proudly, just as you have learned in class. After services you begin walking home with your parents. As you're walking, they tell you how wonderful it is that you can recite the *Shema* in Hebrew. You think to yourself, "I can also say it in English." And then you do just that. You say it in English. When you come home, you are surprised to find that your teacher has been invited for a Shabbat visit. She/he sits down with you and together you sing some *zemirot* (Shabbat songs). (The teacher, keeping in role, should lead the children in these songs. The songs could include "Shabbat Shalom" or any other appropriate songs taught in class). After a peaceful Shabbat, you begin to feel sleepy. You walk back upstairs, brush your teeth, wash your face, put on your pajamas, and crawl under the covers. Just as your eyes begin to close, you softly say the last *Shema* of the day.

2. Grades PK-2: This activity is designed to help the students become aware that Jewish children have an English and Hebrew name as well. As indicated in the *Shema*, they also share the name *Yisrael* with all Jewish people. Have each student bring in a 3" x 5" photograph of themselves. Display these on a bulletin board across the top of which the words of the *Shema* are written. After the photographs have been arranged on the bulletin board, prepare three tags for each photograph. On one, print the student's English name. On another, print the student's Hebrew name. On the last, print the name *Yisrael*. Place the student's English name on one side of the

photograph. Place his/her Hebrew name on the other side. Place the name *Yisrael* at the bottom of the photograph.

3. Grades 1 and 2: On the last page of the book, the Hebrew and English words of the *Shema* appear together, surrounded by a colorful design. So that the students may see the words of the *Shema* every day in their homes and be reminded of the importance of prayer, have them create a *mizrach* out of heavy white drawing paper to display in their homes. A *mizrach* is a decorative plaque which is hung on the eastern wall of the room, indicating the direction of Jerusalem. Point out the illustration in the book of people praying at the Western Wall in Jerusalem. This is a holy place for Jewish people. For students who cannot yet write, the teacher can print the lines of the *Shema* on the paper as they appear on the last page of the book. Older students may need some help in printing the Hebrew. After finishing the lettering, have the students decorate their plaques. When these are completed, send a note home to parents asking for their cooperation in displaying the *mizrach* on an eastern wall in their home.

Johnson, James Weldon, and Johnson, J. Rosamond. *Lift Every Voice and Sing: Words and Music.* Illus. by Mozelle Thompson. New York: Hawthorn books, Inc., 1970. 28 pages. Grade Level: 2-6.

The song "Lift Every Voice and Sing" has been beautifully illustrated, stanza by stanza, on the pages of this book. In the words of Augusta Baker, who wrote the introduction to the book, this spiritual is a song of "faith and courage, hope and joy." Like the Psalms in Jewish liturgy, it speaks of the greatness of God and the gift of freedom.

Major Ideas

God can be extolled through word and song.

Music is a way of giving life to one's prayers.

Prayer and spirituals have the power to unite people.

Faith in God can ease past sorrows and provide hope for the future.

Activities

1. Grades 2-6: Although there have been differences in the backgrounds of Blacks and Jews, there have also been many similarities. The experience of having overcome a difficult past and the hope for a brighter future is reflected in the religious songs of both groups. After sharing this book with the class, point out some of the parallels in Jewish and Black history (e.g., Israelite enslavement in Egypt and Black slavery in the South; discrimination against Jews and Blacks in education, housing, job opportunities; victimization by the Ku Klux Klan). To help convey a sense of brotherhood/sisterhood between Blacks and Jews, invite a religious school class from a Black church to participate in a choral program at your school. Invite church and synagogue members as the audience. The program should consist of Black spirituals and Jewish liturgy and song. Arrange times when both classes can be together to rehearse. Secure the musical accompaniment, and create flyers to publicize the program. All songs should be learned by both groups. Sample songs are:

   "Swing Low, Sweet Chariot"
   "We Shall Overcome"
   "Somebody's Knocking At My Door"
   "Let My People Go"

   "*Tov L'Hodot*"
   "*Oseh Shalom*"
   "*Bashanah Haba'ah*"
   "*Hava Nagilah*"

   The program can conclude with "If I Had a Hammer" (a freedom song) and "Lift Every Voice and Sing." Program length may be adjusted according to the age of the students.

2. Grades 4-6: The lyrics of the spiritual "Lift Every Voice and Sing" not only praise God, but express a dream for a bright future in which freedom reigns. The lyrics have been illustrated stanza by stanza on individual pages of the Johnsons' book. Ask students to write a poem praising God that also expresses their dreams for a brighter future. Then, following the format of the book, have them neatly print each complete thought expressed in their poem on a separate page. Illustrate these pages in the medium and style of the student's choice. Create a cover out of poster board with the title of the poem printed on it. Punch holes along one edge of the cover and pages and fasten together with yarn or metal rings. Have the students share their books with one another and then take them home to enjoy.

3. Grades 3-6: In the book *Lift Every Voice and Sing*, there is a verse which proclaims:

   > Let our rejoicing rise
   > High as the list'ning skies
   > Let it resound loud as
   > the rolling sea.
   > Sing a song full of the faith that the dark past
   > has taught us
   > Sing a song full of the hope that the present
   > has brought us.

   Just as Blacks use spirituals as part of their religious worship, Jews use Psalms in religious services. The words of "Lift Every Voice and Sing" are reminiscent of Psalm 150 which speaks of praising God through music. When teaching Psalm 150 to the students, point out these similarities.

A beautiful melody to this Psalm was performed at the 1980 Oriental Song Festival in Israel. The melody may be found on a record called "*Lamenatseach Shir Mizmor*" Oriental Song Festival 1980 (#14826, Hed-Arzi Ltd.). Order the record from your local Jewish book store or gift shop. You might also want to check with a Cantor for other melodies to the Psalm.

Klausner, Abraham. *A Children's Prayer Book for Rosh Hashanah and Yom Kippur*. Illus. by Shraga Weil and Nachum Gutman. Yonkers, NY: Emanu-El Publications, 1974. 80 pages. Grade level: K-4.

This High Holy Day prayer book contains biblical tales, vivid illustrations, and concise English translations of Hebrew prayers. The skillful combination of these different modes of communication helps to bring Rosh Hashanah and Yom Kippur within the child's comprehension. Children exposed to this unique prayer book will gain an appreciation of High Holy Day worship services.

Major Ideas

The tasks for the High Holy Days are *teshuvah* (repentance), self-evaluation, and goal setting.

It is important to pray from one's heart.

Specific Torah portions are read on Rosh Hashanah and Yom Kippur because they illustrate the major themes of each holiday.

Activities

1. Grades K-4: One theme of this prayer book is repentance. Making peace with one's friends and family is an important aspect of repentance. To help students feel more comfortable in doing this, place them in paired role playing situations. One student asks for and the other grants forgiveness. Switch roles. Situations may be based on the students' actual experiences.

2. Grades 2-4: Have the students create a background design for a Rosh Hashanah card using the following "found object" printing technique.

   a. Have children bring in various objects with interesting relief surfaces.

   b. Each child should make a printing pad. To make the pad, use about twenty thicknesses of newspaper cut into " x 12" pieces. Saturate the pad with water, and sprinkle with dry powder paints or moist tempera paints.

   c. Press the object against the pad, picking up color.

   d. Firmly press the object against the paper on which the print is to appear. This process is repeated with each print.

3. Grades 3 and 4: In the story of "The Shepherd and His Flute," which is included in this prayer book, the shepherd boy is inspired to create a personal prayer through his music. Ask each student to write an original prayer, then find an appropriate piece of background music to be played as the prayer is shared with the class. The prayers may then be used at the synagogue's youth or adult service.

Kustanowitz, Shulamit, and Foont, Ronnie C. *A First Haggadah*. Illus. by Ronnie C. Foont. New York: Bonim Books, 1979. 63 pages. Grade Level: 2-5.

This is a beautiful and easy to understand Haggadah. Each step of the *Seder* is clearly explained in a manner which calls for the children's participation. Blessings and names of the symbols used in the celebration are provided in Hebrew and in English translation. The songs, prayers, and historical narrative as presented emphasize the importance of thanking God for our freedom. Bold, expressionistic illustrations embellish this retelling of the Passover story.

Major Ideas

Judaism emphasizes the importance of being thankful for one's freedom, both through prayer and action.

The origins of the *Haggadah* and other traditional Jewish liturgy are rooted in the biblical and historical narratives of the Jewish people.

Activities

1. Grades 3 and up: This activity focuses on the blessings and prayers which are a part of the Passover *Seder*. Create a Passover game according to the plan which follows.

   Materials:

   a piece of heavy oak tag
   felt tipped markers
   4" x 6" blank unlined index cards
   4 thimbles, each a different color
   1 die

   Procedure:

   a. Using felt tipped markers, draw a game board design on the piece of heavy oak tag (see Diagram 15 for an example). If desired, add original illustrations to your board or print the Hebrew names for the parts of the *Seder* and the Ten Plagues.

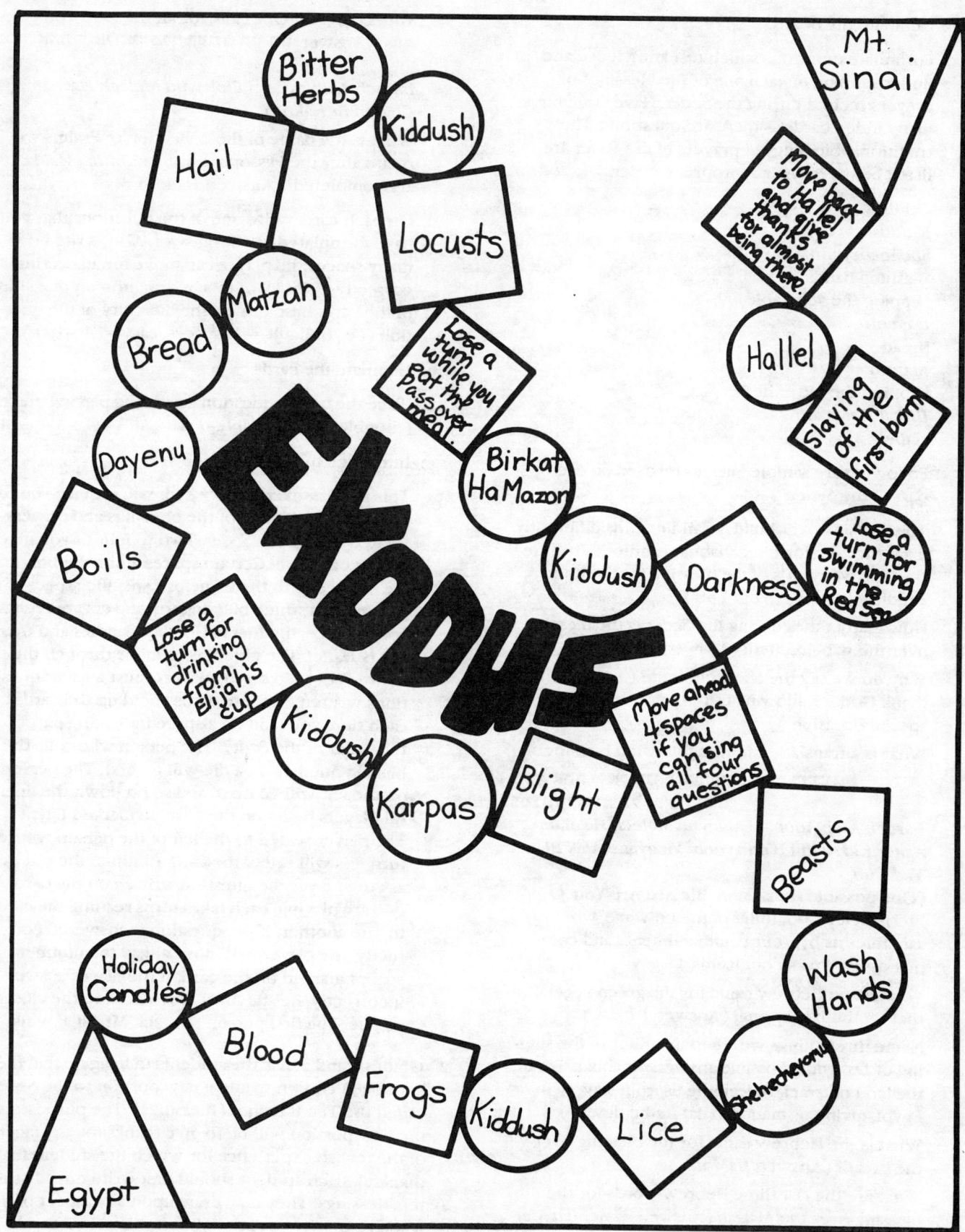

Diagram 15

b. Laminate the board.

c. Formulate questions which test knowledge and understanding of each one of the blessings or prayers recited during the *Seder*. Have available as many index cards as there are questions. The traditional blessings or prayers of the *Seder* are listed below in their appropriate order:

Candles
Kiddush
Shehecheyanu
Washing hands
Dipping the vegetable
Dayenu
Bread
Matzah
Dipping the bitter herbs
Birkat HaMazon
Hallel

Following are sample questions based on each part of the *Seder*:

The blessing over holiday candles ends differently from the blessing over Shabbat candles. What are the last two words of the blessing for the holiday candles? (Answer: *Yom Tov*.)

How many times during the *Seder* is the blessing over the wine recited? (Answer: 4.)

Why do we say the *Shehecheyanu*? (Answer: To thank God for allowing us to live to celebrate a special occasion.)

What is a translation for the following blessing?

ברוך אתה יי אלהינו מלך העולם אשר קדשנו במצותיו וצונו על נטילת ידים.

Baruch Atah Adonai Eloheynu Melech Ha'olam Asher Kid'shanu B'mitzvotav Vitzivanu Al N'tilat Yadayim.

(One possible translation: Blessed Are You, O Eternal Our God, Ruler of the universe, who sanctifies us by Your commandments and commands us to wash our hands.)

What is the Hebrew name for the green vegetable that symbolizes spring? (Answer: *karpas*.)

Name three things we are thankful for in the singing of *Dayenu*? (Possible answers: Shabbat, Torah, the land of Israel, redeeming us from slavery in Egypt, giving us manna to eat in the desert.)

What is the Hebrew name for the blessing over the bread? (Answer: *HaMotzi*.)

What are the last three Hebrew words for the blessing over the *Matzah* (Answer: *Al Achilat Matzah*.)

What is the Hebrew translation of "Blessed are You, O Eternal Our God, for all the food You give us? (Answer: ברוך אתה יי אלהינו מלך העולם חזן את הכל.

Baruch Atah Adonai Elohaynu Melech HaOlam Chazan Et Hakol.)

What is the name of the collection of Psalms we recite after the Passover meal and *Birkat HaMazon* are completed? (Answer: *Hallel*.)

d. On each card, write one of the questions that you have formulated and its answer. Also, write how many spaces the player can move for answering correctly. Print all of this information on one side of the card. Base this on the difficulty of the question (i.e., difficult = 3 spaces, easy = 1 space).

e. Laminate the cards.

f. Place the board, question cards, and playing pieces (thimbles) in a suitable box.

g. Introduce the game as follows:

This is a Passover game which will require you to use your knowledge of the blessings and prayers recited during the *Seder*. Two to four of you may play at one time. Certain spaces along the board are marked with the name of a specific aspect of the *Seder* in which blessings or prayers are recited. For instance, the first is Holiday Candles and the last is *Hallel*. The object is to move through the entire *Seder*. To do so, players must answer questions written on these cards (hold up the cards) each time you land on a space indicating part of the order of the *Seder*. The person who rolls the highest number on a die will go first. The person on the left will go next, and so on down the line. All players begin on the triangle marked Egypt. The player seated to the left of the person whose turn it is will select the card on top of the pile and ask the player the question written on the card. If two are playing, each takes turns reading the cards to one another. If the question is answered correctly, the player will move ahead the number of spaces marked on the card. If the player answers incorrectly, he/she must move back to the closest plague. The first person to reach Mt. Sinai wins.

2. Grades 4 and 5: Ask the students to imagine that they have been chosen to add a new portion to the *Seder* called the Ten B'rachot (Blessings). The purpose of the new portion will be to give thanks for any facet of the Jewish experience for which the student feels thankful. Each student should first write out a list of ten blessings. They may draw upon any aspect of the Jewish experience (i.e., holidays, historical events, biblical characters, ritual objects, Hebrew, etc.). After the lists are completed, give each student a piece of 12" x 18" white drawing paper on which has

Diagram 16

been printed a large outline of the Hebrew letters in the word *Baruch*. See Diagram 16 for an example.

Each student will then draw their Ten B'rachot inside the letters. The blessings should be spread throughout the letters (three blessings in two of the letters and two blessings in each of the other two letters). If desired, this project can also be done in collage form.

3. Grades 2-5: The *Hallel* is a collection of Psalms recited toward the end of the *Seder* thanking God for God's goodness. Have each student write a personal prayer of thanks to be recited along with the *Hallel* at their family *Seder*. The prayers may be written in poetry or prose.

Orleans, Ilo. *Within Thy Hand: My Poem Book of Prayers*. Illus. by Siegmund Forst. New York: Union of American Hebrew Congregations, 1961. 70 pages. Grade level: 4-6.

The editor states in the introduction to this book that "The worshiper must always fill out the poetry of the prayer with the artistry of his soul." In this innovative collection of prayers, the author has used lines from the original Hebrew liturgy, filling out the poetry of the liturgy with English poems or translations which capture the essence of the traditional prayers. Striking woodcuts illustrating the meaning of the prayers add to the appeal of the book.

Major Ideas

Each individual may add to the traditional prayers words which most meaningfully convey their innermost feelings and thoughts.

Jewish liturgy is composed of prayers which bring one closer to God, to others, and to oneself.

The activities of daily life are reflected in the themes of the traditional prayers.

Activities

1. Grades 4-6: The last prayer in the book is entitled "I Thank you, God." Have each student write a stanza thanking God, following the form of this prayer (four lines with the second and fourth rhyming). Compile the students' stanzas into a class prayer. Use the original first and last stanza to tie the prayer together. Submit the stanzas to the synagogue or school bulletin for publication. Or, arrange for the prayer to be included in a service which the students and their families attend.

2. Grades 4-6: In Orlean's book, hands are used as a theme for the title and for the artwork illustrating the prayers. One of the most striking illustrations appears on page 46 which shows hands providing support for God's creatures. Have the students trace their hands on the bottom of a piece of 12" x 18" drawing paper. Next, tell them to draw above the hands an element of life for which they are thankful or a situation when they need comfort or strength. Display these drawings on a bulletin board, repeating thereon the title of the book, "Within God's Hands."

3. Grade 6: Many of the prayers in this book are inspired by passages from the Tanach (Five Books of Moses, Prophets, and Writings). Help each student to choose a personally meaningful passage from one of the sections of the Tanach. After making the selection, have each student write and title a prayer based on the passage they have selected. As the author has done in his book, each student should write in bold letters (between the title and the beginning of the poem) a brief line of Hebrew taken directly from their chosen passage. Next, have the students paste the page on which their prayer is written onto a larger piece of colored construction paper. Felt markers or collage may be used to decorate the edges.

Display the prayers along the wall outside of the classroom or outside of the sanctuary.

Zwerin, Raymond A., and Marcus, Audrey Friedman. *Shabbat Can Be.* Illus. by Yuri Salzman. New York: Union of American Hebrew Congregations, 1979. 47 pages. Grade level: PK-2.

Zwerin and Marcus have written a book which carries the reader into the joyous dimensions of Shabbat. The text on each page begins with the enticing words "Shabbat can be." In each case, this is followed by a description of a special activity and feeling which may be experienced on Shabbat. The book provides an excellent introduction to Shabbat blessings and rituals, and invites young readers to explore what Shabbat means to them. Delightful illustrations of children enjoying Shabbat together with family and friends add to the text's beautiful depiction of this treasured day in Jewish life.

Major Ideas

Shabbat can be made even more special when we choose to spend it in traditional, as well as personally meaningful, ways.

Shabbat is the focal point for numerous blessings and prayers in Jewish life.

Shabbat is a day which evokes different feelings in each individual.

Activities

1. Grades 1 and 2: As illustrated in the book, it is customary for parents to bless their children on Shabbat. Send a note home to parents inviting them to a family Shabbat dinner. Ask the parents to prepare a two or three sentence personal blessing to recite to their child at the dinner. Guide the students in writing a short blessing to recite to their parent(s). At the dinner, traditional Hebrew blessings for children should also be recited by the entire group. The traditional blessings are as follows:

    For daughters:

    ישמך אלהים כשרה רבקה רחל ולאה.

    Y'simech Elohim K'Sarah, Rifka, Rachel V'Leah.
    May God bless you as He blessed Sarah, Rebekah, Rachel, and Leah.

    For sons:

    ישמך אלהים כאפרים וכמנשה.

    Y'simcha Elohim K'Ephraim V'chiMenasheh.
    May God bless you as He blessed Ephraim and Manasheh.

    Together:

    יברך יי וישמרך.

    Y'varecheha Adonai V'yishmerecha.
    May the Lord bless you and keep you.

    יאר יי פניו אליך ויחנך.

    Ya'eir Adonai Panav Eilecha Vichuneka
    May the Lord cause His spirit to shine upon you and be gracious unto you.

    ישא יי פניו אליך וישם לך שלום.

    Yisa Adonai Panav Eilecha V'yasem L'cha Shalom.
    May the spirit of the Lord turn unto you and grant you peace.

2. Grade 2: On one page in the book, children are shown being thankful to God for "making me me." One of the children is kicking his legs joyously in the air. Allow students to express thanks for being themselves and thanks for one another through creative movement. Clear a large space in the middle of the room or take the children outside on the lawn. Have the class form a large circle. Tell the students to practice reciting their first name silently to themselves in a rhythmic manner. The teacher might want to demonstrate using his/her own first name. After giving some time for reflection, tell the students that you will be calling them individually to the center of the circle to recite their name as practiced. They will also accompany the recitation with a rhythmic movement, expressing their thanks for being themselves. Again, a teacher demonstration would be helpful. The other students will imitate the movement and recitation of the child in the center of the circle. The teacher will signal for them to stop with a drum beat or other loud noise. After each student has had a turn in the center, have the entire group do their individual motions and names out loud together. For the finale, have the students shout out in Hebrew *Todah Rabbah* (thank you).

3. Grades K-2: Traditional Shabbat rituals will become all the more meaningful for students if they understand the origin and purpose of each ritual. First, teach the students the blessings for the following:

    Shabbat candles
    wine
    challah
    Havdalah spices
    Havdalah candle

    After the blessings are learned, invite the Rabbi to class to explain the origin and purpose of the ritual associated with each blessing. When the Rabbi arrives, a table should already be set up in the center or front of the classroom with Shabbat candles, grape juice, two *challot* covered with a decorative cloth, a spice box, and a Havdalah candle.

Ask the Rabbi to stimulate the students' curiosity by allowing them to suggest their own explanations for the various Shabbat blessings and rituals before offering the traditional explanations. Some possible discussion questions are:

- Why are two candles lit on Friday night?
- How does one know when it is time to light the Shabbat candles?
- What is the reason for the specific order of blessings on Friday night?
- Why is it customary to use two *challot*?
- Why are the *challot* kept covered until it is time to recite *HaMotzi*?
- Of what do the Havdalah spices remind one?
- Why is the Havdalah candle braided?
- Why are light (candles) and wine so much a part of the Shabbat celebration?

Invite the Rabbi to conclude the session with a Shabbat story, (perhaps related to the weekly Torah portion), then enjoy the grape juice and *challah* after reciting the appropriate blessings.

PRAYER: BOOKS FOR CHILDREN

Arian, Philip, and Eisenberg, Azriel. *The Story of the Prayer Book.* New York: Prayer Book Press, Inc., 1968. Grade level: 6 and up.

>A fascinating exploration of the development of prayer and the prayer book. Arian and Eisenberg's presentation is scholarly, readable, and covers an often neglected dimension of the study of prayer.

Blume, Judy. *Are You There God? It's me, Margaret.* Scarsdale, NY: Bradbury Press, 1970. Grade level: 4-6.

>Twelve-year-old Margaret Simon is the daughter of a mixed marriage. She often discusses with God her adolescent problems and the issue of choosing a religion. Great sensitivity and humor punctuate this children's favorite.

Bogot, Howard, and Syme, Daniel. *I Learn About God.* Illus. by Marlene Lobell Ruthen. New York: Union of American Hebrew Congregations, 1982. Grade level: PK-1.

>Bogot and Syme present the Jewish concepts of God and religion in a simple manner which relates to young children's everyday lives.

Brichto, Mira. *The God Around Us: A Child's Garden of Prayer.* Illus. by Clare and John Ross. New York: Union of American Hebrew Congregations, 1968. Grade level: K-2.

>Colorful illustrations and simple prayers in large Hebrew and English print provide a wonderful introduction to prayer for young children.

Cohen, Barbara. *Yussel's Prayer: A Yom Kippur Story.* Illus. by Joan Halpern. New York: Lothrop, Lee & Shepard Books, 1975. Grade level: 2-4.

>Warmly illustrated in shades of brown and white, this book tells the story of a poor young shepherd boy Yussel, who successfully opens the gates of heaven on Yom Kippur so that the prayers of the people in his village are received. Prior to Yussel's heartfelt prayer, the gates remained closed because the prayers of the villagers had not been offered with sincerity. This is an excellent book for teaching children the purpose and spirit of prayer.

Cone, Molly. *Hear, O Israel: About Learning.* Illus. by Iris Schweitzer. New York: Union of American Hebrew Congregations, 1971. Grade level: 1-3.

>This fourth book in the *Hear O Israel* series approaches learning as a key element of prayer. Each of the short stories is realistically illustrated and contributes to the ultimate understanding of the purpose of study and meaning of wisdom.

Curtis, Cecil. *He Looks This Way.* Illus. by the author. New York: Lothrop, Lee & Shepard Books, 1965. Grade level: 3-5.

>Nuru, an African boy, is like most children in that he often wonders what God looks like. After personifying God as a variety of animals, spirits, and a great light, Nuru concludes that God can be whatever Nuru desires God to be. Curtis has addressed a topic of great fascination through a bold combination of text and abstract illustrations.

Efron, Benjamin. *Pathways Through the Prayer Book.* Illus. by Uri Shulevitz. New York: KTAV Publishing House, Inc., 1962. Grade level: 6 and up.

>Efron combines history, major concepts, and the vocabulary of prayer in his discussion of the Reform prayer book. Shulevitz's illustrations help to explain further the topics covered by the text.

Ehrman, Yochaved. *My First Siddur.* New York: Bloch Publishing Co., 1979. Grade level: 1-3.

>This illustrated Siddur invites the young reader to explore and grasp the basic contents of the prayer book.

Freeman, Grace, and Sugarman, Joan. *Inside the Synagogue.* New York: Union of American Hebrew Congregations, 1984 (revised edition). Grade level: 2-4.

>Freeman and Sugarman take their reader's on an informative guided tour of the synagogue. A full page description of each aspect of the synagogue is accompanied by a photograph on the facing page in this large format book.

Friedman, Audrey, and Zwerin, Raymond A. *Our Synagogue Series*. New York: Behrman House, Inc., 1974. Grade level: 4 and up.

> A packet of 10 colorful mini-magazines is provided for each of three topics: The Synagogue, Holy Days and Shabbat, and Jewish Ideas. Each magazine focuses the student's attention on one element of the major topic through simple, bold text and photographs.

Greenberg, Sydney, and Silverman, Morris (eds). *Siddureinu: Our Prayer Book*. New York: Prayer Book Press, Inc., 1969. Grade level: 3 and up.

> This is an excellent Siddur in clear Hebrew print for children who can read Hebrew. The volume is comprehensive in its inclusion of all the daily, Shabbat, and holiday services, special blessings, and the *Birkat HaMazon*. Brief English explanations are provided for each prayer.

Miller, Deborah Uchill. *My Siddur: Prayer Readiness Book*. Illus. Jana Paiss. New York: Behrman House, Inc., 1984. Grade level: 2-3.

> An informative and enjoyable activity book that familiarizes children with the basic Hebrew and English vocabulary of prayer. Line drawings add to the appeal of the book.

Muchnik, Michael. *The Double Decker Purple Shul Bus*. Illus. by the author. New York: Merkos L'Inyonei Chinuch, 1977. Grade level: PK-2.

> Muchnik has created a mythical town where the bus serves as both a *shul* (synagogue) and a means of transportation. During the week, the passengers conduct their morning and evening services on board the bus as they travel to and from work. However, on Shabbat, the *shul*-bus is closed, as the townspeople go to pray at their regular *shuls*. The purple pictures of praying people add a delightful touch to the story.

Olivestone, Ceil and David. *Let's Go To Synagogue*. Illus. by Arien Seldich. Englewood, NJ: SBS Publishing, Inc., 1981. Grade level: PK-K.

> Through simple text and bright illustrations, the Olivestones have created an enticing invitation to the synagogue service for very young readers.

Rittner, Stephen. *The Why Do I Have to Pray Book*. Boston: Rittner's Publishing. Grade level: 5 and up.

> Rittner's approach to prayer is unique and refreshing, transforming the readers into participant theologians who must grapple with God-related issues.

Rossel, Seymour. *When a Jew Prays*. Illus. by Erika Weihs. New York: Behrman House, Inc., 1973. Grade level: 4-6.

> Rossel's explanation of what prayer is, the way we pray, and the order of prayers is superbly tailored to the needs and intellectual level of upper elementary students. The illustrations capture the emotional dimension of prayer and help to highlight major concepts.

PRAYER: BOOKS FOR ADULTS

Ceremonial Art and the Synagogue

Brooten, Bernadette, J. *Women Leaders in the Ancient Synagogue: Inscriptional Evidence and Background Issue.* Chico, CA: Scholars Press, 1982.

Debreffny, Brian. *The Synagogue.* New York: Macmillan Publishing Co., Inc., 1978.

Kanof, Abram. *Jewish Ceremonial Art and Religious Observance.* New York: Harry N. Abrams, Inc., no publication date.

Kaploun, Uri. *The Synagogue.* Philadelphia: The Jewish Publication Society of America, 1973.

Collections of Contemporary and Traditional Prayers and Meditations

Brin, Ruth. *A Rag of Love.* Minneapolis, MN: Emmet Publishing Co., 1969.

_____. *A Time to Search.* New York: Jonathan David Publishers, Inc., 1959.

Glatzer, Nahum (ed). *Language of Faith: A Selection From the Most Expressive Jewish Prayers.* New York: Schocken Books, Inc., 1974.

Hecht, Michael I. *The Fire Waits.* Bridgeport, CT: Hartmore House, 1972.

Quoist, Michel. *Prayers.* New York: Sheed & Ward, 1963.

Reznikoff, Charles. *By the Waters of Manhattan.* New York: New Directions Publishing Corporation, 1959.

Tagore, Rabindranath. *Contemporary Prayers and Readings.* Bridgeport, CT: Prayer Book Press, 1972.

Commentaries on the Prayers and Siddur

Arzt, Max. *Justice and Mercy: Commentary on the Liturgy of the New Year and the Day of Atonement.* New York: Holt, Rinehart & Winston, Inc., 1983.

_____. *Joy and Remembrance: Commentary on the Sabbath Eve Liturgy.* Bridgeport, CT: Hartmore House, 1979.

Baumgard, Herbert M. *Judaism and Prayer.* New York: Union of American Hebrew Congregations, 1974.

Cohen, Jeffrey M. *Understand the High Holyday Services: A Popular Commentary to the Mahzor.* London: Rutledge & Kegan Paul, 1983.

Colodner, Solomon. *Concepts and Values in Prayer.* New York: Cole Publications, 1972.

Donin, Hayim Halevy. *To Pray as a Jew: A Guide to the Prayer Book and the Synagogue Service.* New York: Basic Books, Inc., 1980.

Dresner, Samuel. *Prayer, Humility and Compassion.* Philadelphia: The Jewish Publication Society of America, 1957.

Finkel, Asher, and Frizzell, Lawrence (ed). *Standing Before God: Studies On Prayer in Scriptures and Tradition.* New York: KTAV Publishing House, Inc., 1981.

Garfiel, Evelyn. *Service of the Heart: A Guide to the Jewish Prayer Book.* North Hollywood, CA: Wilshire Book Co., 1958.

Goldstein, Rose. *A Time to Pray: A Personal Approach to the Jewish Prayer Book.* New York: National Women's League of the United Synagogue of America, 1972.

Greenberg, Moseh. *Biblical Prose Prayer.* Berkeley, CA: University of California Press, 1983.

Greenberg, Simon. *The Jewish Prayer Book: Its Ideals and Values.* New York: United Synagogue of America, 1957.

Gross, Sholom. *V'nomar Amen: The Amen Response.* New York: Mosad Brucha Tova, 1981.

Heiler, Friedrich. *Prayer: A Study in the History and Psychology of Religion.* London: Oxford University Press, 1958.

Hoffman, Lawrence. *Shaarei Bina: Gates of Understanding* (Volume I - For Weekdays, Sabbaths and Festivals). New York: Central Conference of American Rabbis, 1977.

_____. *Sharrei Bina: Gates of Understanding* (Volume II - For the High Holy Days). New York: Central Conference of American Rabbis, 1977.

Kadushin, Max. *Worship and Ethics*. Evanston, IL: Northwestern University, 1964.

Martin, Bernard. *Prayer in Judaism*. New York: Basic Books, Inc., 1968.

Mindel, Nissan. *As For Me - My Prayer*. New York: Merkos L'Inyonei Chinuch, Inc., 1972.

Petuchowski, Jacob J. *Understanding Jewish Prayer*. New York: KTAV Publishing House, Inc., 1972.

Posner, Raphael. *Jewish Liturgy*. Jerusalem: Keter Publishing House, Ltd., 1975.

The Artscroll Mesorah Prayer Series. New York: Mesorah Publications, Ltd.

Chasidic Prayer

Green, Arthur, and Holtz, Barry (eds). *Your Word is Fire: The Hasidic Masters on Contemplative Prayer*. Ramsey, NJ: Paulist Press, 1977.

Jacobs, Louis. *Hasidic Prayer*. New York: Schocken Books, Inc., 1978.

Kramer, Simon. *God and Man in the Sefer Hasidim*. New York: Bloch Publishing Co., 1966.

Historical Development of Jewish Liturgy

Goldstein, Rose. *A Time to Pray*. New York: Bloch Publishing Co., 1972.

Hoffman, Lawrence. *The Canonization of the Synagogue Service*. Notre Dame, IN: University of Notre Dame Press, 1979.

Idelsohn, A.Z. *Jewish Liturgy and Its Development*. New York: Schocken Books Inc., 1967.

Kon, Abraham. *Prayer*. London: Soncino Press, 1971.

Millgram, Abraham E. *Jewish Worship*. Philadelphia: The Jewish Publication Society of America, 1971.

Petuchowski, Jacob. *Prayer Reform in Europe: The Liturgy of European Liberal and Reform Judaism*. New York: World Union of Progressive Judaism, Ltd., 1968.

Posner, Raphael; Kaploun, Uri; and Cohen, Shalom (eds). *Jewish Liturgy: Prayer and the Synagogue Service Through the Ages*. New York: Leon Amiel Publishers, 1975.

Jewish Perspectives on God

Baeck, Leo. *God and Man in Judaism*. New York: Union of American Hebrew Congregations, 1958.

Baumgard, Herbert M. *Judaism and Prayer: Growing Towards God*. New York: Union of American Hebrew Congregations, 1964.

Bemporad, Jack (ed). *The Theological Foundations of Prayer: A Reform Jewish Perspective*. New York: Union of American Hebrew Congregations, 1967.

Berkovits, Eliezer. *God, Man and History: A Jewish Interpretation*. New York: Jonathan David Publishers, Inc., 1959.

Bissell, Sherry, with Audrey Friedman Marcus and Rabbi Raymond A. Zwerin. *God: The Eternal Challenge*. Denver: Alternatives in Religious Education, Inc., 1980.

Borowitz, Eugene. *A New Jewish Theology in the Making*. Philadelphia: Westminster Press, 1968.

Crenshaw, James L. *A Whirlpool of Torment: Israelite Traditions of God as an Oppresive Presence*. Philadelphia: Fortress Press, 1984.

Crenshaw, James L. (ed). *Theodicy in the Old Testament*. Philadelphia: Fortress Press, 1983.

Efron, Benjamin. *The Message of the Torah*. New York: KTAV Publishing House, Inc., 1963.

Fackenheim, Emil. *God's Presence in History: Jewish Affirmations and Philosophical Reflections*. New York: New York University Press, 1970.

_____. *Paths to Jewish Belief: A Systematic Introduction.* Illus. by Chet Kalm. New York: Behrman House, Inc., 1960.

Gertman, Stuart A. (ed). *What is the Answer.* New York: Union of American Hebrew Congregations, 1971.

Gittelsohn, Roland B. *Man's Best Hope.* New York: Random House, Inc., 1961.

Heschel, Abraham Joshua. *Quest for God: A Journey into Prayer and Symbolism.* New York: Crossroad Publishing Co., 1982.

_____. *Theology of Ancient Judaism.* London: Soncino Press, 1971. (Two Volumes)

Jacobs, Louis. *Jewish Thought Today.* New York: Behrman House, Inc., 1970. (Volume Three)

Joseloff, Samuel Hart (ed). *A Time to Seek: An Anthology of Contemporary Jewish American Poets.* Union of American Hebrew Congregations, 1975. (Chapter 5)

Kaplan, Aryeh. *The Infinite Light: A Book About God.* New York: National Conference of Synagogue Youth, 1981.

Kushner, Harold S. *When Children Ask About God.* New York: Schocken Books, Inc., 1976.

Levin, Meyer. *Beginnings in Jewish Philosophy.* New York: Behrman House, Inc., 1971.

Neusner, Jacob (ed). *Understanding Jewish Theology: Classic Issues and Modern Perspectives.* New York: KTAV Publishing House, Inc./B'nai B'rith Anti-Defamation League, 1973.

Silverman, William B. *The Still Small Voice.* New York: Behrman House, Inc., 1955. (Book One, Chapter 2)

Waskow, Arthur. *Godwrestling.* New York: Schocken Books, Inc., 1978.

Prayer Books for Weekdays, Sabbaths and Festivals

Birnbaum, Philip. *HaSiddur HaShalem: Daily Prayer Book.* New York: Hebrew Publishing Co., 1977.

Birnbaum, Philip (ed). *High Holiday Prayer Book.* New York: Hebrew Publishing Co., 1957.

De Sola Pool, David (ed). *The Traditional Prayer Book for Sabbath and Festivals.* New York: Rabbinical Council of America, Inc., 1960.

Green, Alan S. *Return to Prayer: Home and Student Devotions for Sabbath, Everyday and Special Occasions.* New York: Union of American Hebrew Congregations, 1971.

Greenberg, Rabbi Sidney. *Likrat Shabbat: Worship, Study and Song for Sabbath and Festival Services and for the Home.* New York: Prayer Book Press Inc., 1977.

_____. *The Junior Contemporary Prayer Book for the High Holy Days.* Bridgeport, CT: Prayer Book Press, 1972.

Greenberg, Rabbi Sidney, and Levine, Rabbi Jonathan. *The New Mahzor for Rosh HaShanah and Yom Kippur.* Bridgeport, CT: Prayer Book Press, 1977.

Harlow, Jules. *Mahzor for Rosh Hashanah and Yom Kippur.* New York: Rabbinical Assembly, 1972.

Harlow, Jules (ed). *Sim Shalom: A Prayerbook for Shabbat, Festivals and Weekdays.* New York: Rabbinical Assembly and United Synagogue of America, 1983. (Morning Service)

Hertz, Joseph H. *The Authorized Daily Prayer Book.* New York: Bloch Publishing Co., 1948.

Hirsch, Samson Raphael. *The Hirsch Siddur: The Order of Prayers for the Whole Year.* New York: Feldheim Publishers, 1972.

Jospe, Alfred, and Levy, Richard N. *Bridges to a Holy Time: New Worship for the Sabbath and Minor Festivals.* New York: KTAV Publishing House Inc., 1973.

Kaplan, Mordecai; Kohn, Eugene; and Eisenberg, Ira. *High Holiday Prayer Book: Prayers for Rosh HaShanah.* New York: Jewish Reconstructionist Foundation, Inc., 1948.

Malchuyot, Zichronot, Shofarot: Readings and Meditations for Rosh Hashanah Musaf. New York: Society for the Advancement of Judaism, 1980.

New Prayers For the High Holidays. Bridgeport, CT: Media Judaica Inc., 1973.

Scherman, Rabbi Nossen (ed). *The Complete Artscroll Siddur: Weekday, Sabbath, Festival.* New York: Mesorah Publications, Ltd., 1984.

Silverman, Morris. *Prayerbook for Weekdays, Sabbath and Festivals.* New York: United Synagogue of America, 1946.

Silverman, Morris. (ed). *High Holiday Prayer Book.* Bridgeport, CT: Prayer Book Press, 1951.

Stern, Chaim. *Gates of Joy.* New York: KTAV Publishing House, Inc., 1979.

_____. *Gates of Heaven.* New York: KTAV Publishing House, Inc., 1970.

Stern, Chaim (ed). *Shaarei HaBayit: Gates of the House (The New Union Home Prayer Book).* New York: Central Conference of American Rabbis, 1977.

_____. *Shaarei Teshuvah: Gates of Repentance (The New Union Prayer Book for the High Holy Days).* New York: Central Conference of American Rabbis, 1978.

_____. *Shaarei Tefilah: Gates of Prayer (The New Union Prayer Book for Weekdays, Sabbaths and Festivals).* New York: Central Conference of American Rabbis, 1975.

Vitaher Libenu. Sudbury, MA: Congregation Beth El of The Sudbury River Valley, 1980.

Teaching Prayer

Borovetz, Frances. *Hebrew Blessings Ditto Pak.* Denver: Alternatives in Religious Education Inc., 1980.

_____. *Hebrew Prayers Ditto Pak.* Denver: Alternatives in Religious Education Inc., 1980.

Brown, Steven. *Higher and Higher: Making Jewish Prayer Part of Us.* New York: United Synagogue of America, 1979.

Fields, Harvey J. *Bechol Levavcha: With All Your Heart.* New York: Union of American Hebrew Congregations, 1979.

Freehof, Solomon B. *In the House of the Lord.* New York: Union of American Hebrew Congregations, 1951.

Grishaver, Joel Lurie. *Shema is For Real: A Book on Prayer and Other Tangents.* Chicago: Olin-Sang Ruby Union Institute, no publication date.

Rittner, Stephen. *You Don't Have to Be Moses to Teach About God and Prayer.* Milwaukee, WI: B. Arbit Books, Inc., no publication date.

CROSS-REFERENCING SYSTEM

Note: The cross-referencing system includes only those books in each chapter for which activities are written.

Guide

    B = Bible Stories
    D = Death & Dying
    E = Ethics
    HOL = Holidays
    I = Israel
    JF = Jewish Folklore
    JH = Jewish History
    JI = Jewish Identity
    P = Prayer

I. Bible Stories

Alphabetized according to Author

Bulla, Clyde Robert. *Jonah and the Great Fish*. E, HOL (Yom Kippur), JH

Bulla, Clyde Robert. *Joseph, the Dreamer*. E, JH

Cohen, Barbara. *The Binding of Isaac*. E, JH

Ferguson, Walter W. *Living Animals of the Bible*. I

Fisher, Leonard Everett. *The Seven Days of Creation*. HOL (Simchat Torah), JH

L'Engle, Madeleine. *Ladder of Angels: Scenes from the Bible*. E, HOL (contains passages for each holiday), JH

Petersham, Maud and Mishka. *The Story of Ruth*. E, HOL (Shavuot), JH, JI

Singer, Isaac Bashevis. *The Wicked City*. E, JH

Spier, Peter, *Noah's Ark*. E, JH

Weisner, William. *The Tower of Babel*. E, JH

Alphabetized according to Title

The Binding of Isaac by Barbara Cohen. E, HOL (Rosh Hashanah), H, JH

Jonah and the Great Fish by Clyde Robert Bulla. E, HOL (Yom Kippur), JH

Joseph, the Dreamer by Clyde Robert Bulla. E, JH

Ladder of Angels: Scenes from the Bible by Madeleine L'Engle. E, HOL (contains passages for each holiday), JH

Living Animals of the Bible by Walter W. Ferguson. I

Noah's Ark by Peter Spier. E, JH

The Seven Days of Creation by Leonard Everett Fisher. HOL (Simchat Torah), JH

The Story of Ruth by Maud and Mishka Petersham. E, HOL (Shavuot), JH, JI

The Tower of Babel by William Weisner. E, JH

The Wicked City by Isaac Bashevis Singer. E, JH

II. Death and Dying

Alphabetized according to Author

Ancona, George. *Growing Older*. E

Cohen, Barbara. *Thank You, Jackie Robinson*. E

Krementz, Jill. *How It Feels When a Parent Dies*. E, P

Lowry, Lois. *A Summer To Die*. E

Mann, Peggy. *There Are Two Kinds of Terrible*. E

Miles, Miska. *Annie and the Old One*. E

Paterson, Katherine. *Bridge to Terabithea*. E

Pomerantz, Barbara. *Bubby, Me, and Memories.* E, JI

Townsend, Maryann, and Stern, Ronnie. *Pop's Secret.* E

Viorst, Judith. *The Tenth Good Thing about Barney.* P

Alphabetized according to Title

Annie and the Old One by Miska Miles. E

Bridge to Terabithea. by Katherine Paterson. E

Bubby, Me, and Memories by Barbara Pomerantz. E, JI

Growing Older by George Ancona. E

How It Feels When a Parent Dies by Jill Krementz. E, P

Pop's Secret by Ronnie Stern and Maryann Townsend. E

A Summer to Die by Lois Lowry. E

Thank You, Jackie Robinson by Barbara Cohen. E

There Are Two Kinds of Terrible by Peggy Mann. E

The Tenth Good Thing About Barney by Judith Viorst. P

III. **Ethics**

Alphabetized according to Author

Asher, Sande. *Summer Begins.* HOL (Chanukah), JI

Blau, Judith. *The Bagel Baker of Mulliner Lane.* HOL (Chanukah), JI

Chaiken, Miriam. *Finders Weepers.* HOL (Rosh Hashanah), JI

Eisenberg, Phyllis Rose. *A Mitzvah Is Something Special.* JI

Klein, Gerda. *The Blue Rose.*

Rittner, Stephen. *Rabbi Simon and His Friends: Values.* B, JI

Schotter, Roni. *Northern Fried Chicken.* JH, JI

Snyder, Carol. *The Great Condominium Rebellion.*

Snyder, Carol. *Ike and Mama and the Once-In-A-Lifetime Movie.* JH

Silverstein, Shel. *The Giving Tree.* D, HOL (Tu B'Shevat)

Alphabetized according to Title

The Bagel Baker of Mulliner Lane by Judith Blau. HOL (Chanukah), JI

The Blue Rose by Gerda Klein.

Finders Weepers by Miriam Chaiken. HOL (Rosh Hashanah), JI

The Giving Tree by Shel Silverstein. D, HOL (Tu B'Shevat)

The Great Condominium Rebellion by Carol Snyder.

Ike and Mama and the Once-In-A-Lifetime Movie by Carol Snyder. JH

A Mitzvah is Something Special by Phyllis Rose Eisenberg. JI

Northern Fried Chicken by Roni Schotter. JH, JI

Rabbi Simon and His Friends: Values by Stephen Rittner. B, JI

Summer Begins by Sandy Asher. HOL (Chanukah), JI

IV. **Jewish Folklore**

Alphabetized according to Author

Gershator, Phillis. *Honi and His Magic Circle.* E, HOL (Tu B'Shevat)

Hirsh, Marilyn. *The Rabbi and the Twenty-nine Witches.* HOL (Rosh Chodesh)

Ish-Kishor, Sulamith. *The Carpet of Solomon.* B, E

Kimmel, Eric A. *Hershel of Ostropol.*

Cross-Referencing System

McDermott, Beverly Brodsky. *The Golem: A Jewish Legend*. E, JH

Shulevitz, Uri. *The Magician*. B, HOL (Passover)

Shulevitz, Uri. *The Treasure*. E, JI

Simon, Solomon. *The Wise Men of Helm and Their Many Tales*. JH

Suhl, Yuri. *Simon Boom Gets a Letter*.

Zemach, Margot. *It Could Always Be Worse*. E

Alphabetized according to Title

The Carpet of Solomon by Sulamith Ish-Kishor. B, E

The Golem: A Jewish Legend by Beverly Brodsky McDermott. E, JH

Hershel of Ostropol by Eric A. Kimmel.

Honi and His Magic Circle by Phyllis Gershator. E, HOL (Tu B'Shevat)

It Could Always Be Worse by Margot Zemach. E

The Magician by Uri Shulevitz. B, HOL (Passover)

The Rabbi and the Twenty-nine Witches by Marilyn Hirsh. HOL (Rosh Chodesh)

Simon Boom Gets a Letter by Yuri Suhl.

The Treasure by Uri Shulevitz. E, JI

The Wise Men of Helm and Their Many Tales by Solomon Simon. JH

V. **Jewish History**

Alphabetized according to Author

Cohen, Barbara. *Gooseberries to Oranges*. JI

Ish-Kishor, Sulamith. *A Boy of Old Prague*. D, E, JI

Hirsch, Marilyn. *Butchers and Bakers, Rabbis and Kings*. E, JI

Milgrim, Shirley. *Haym Salomon: Liberty's Son*. E

Richman, Carol. *The Lekachmaker Family*. JI

Roseman, Kenneth. *The Cardinal's Snuff Box*. E, JI

Sachs, Ruth. *Call Me Ruth*. E, JI

Slater, Robert. *Great Jews in Sports*. JI

Slobodkin, Florence. *Sarah Somebody*. E, JI

Stadtler, Bea. *The Adventures of Glueckel of Hameln*. JI

Alphabetized according to Title

The Adventures of Glueckel of Hameln by Bea Stadtler. JI

A Boy of Old Prague by Sulamith Ish-Kishor. D, E, JI

Butchers and Bakers, Rabbis and Kings by Marilyn Hirsh. E, JI

Call Me Ruth by Ruth Sachs. E, JI

The Cardinal's Snuff Box by Kenneth Roseman. E, JI

Gooseberries to Oranges by Barbara Cohen. JI

Great Jews in Sports by Robert Slater. JI

Haym Salomon: Liberty's Son by Shirley Milgrim. E

The Lekachmaker Family by Carol Richman. JI

Sarah Somebody by Florence Slobodkin. E, JI

VI. **Holidays**

Alphabetized according to Author

Adler, David A. *The House on the Roof: A Sukkot Story*. E, JI

Aronim, Ben. *The Secret of the Sabbath Fish*. E, JH, JI

Cashman, Greer Fay. *Jewish Days and Holidays*. B, JH, JI

Cohen, Barbara. *Yussel's Prayer*. E, P

Cone, Molly. *Who Knows Ten?* B, E, JH

Hirsh, Marilyn. *Potato Pancakes All Around*. JI

Levitan, Sonia. *A Sound to Remember*. E, JI

Rosten, Norman. *The Wineglass*. E, JI

Udry, Janice. *A Tree Is Nice*. E

Weil, Lisl. *Esther*. B, JH, JI

Alphabetized according to Title

Esther by Lisl Weil. B, JH, JI

The House on the Roof: A Sukkot Story by David A. Adler. E, JI

Jewish Days and Holidays by Greer Fay Cashman. B, JH, JI

Potato Pancakes All Around by Marilyn Hirsh. JI

The Secret of the Sabbath Fish by Ben Aronim. E, JH, JI

A Sound to Remember by Sonia Levitan. E, JI

A Tree is Nice by Janice Udry. E

Who Knows Ten? by Molly Cone. B, E, JF

The Wineglass by Norman Rosten. E, JI

Yussel's Prayer by Barbara Cohen. E, P

VII. **Holocaust**

Alphabetized according to Author

Baldwin, Margaret. *The Boys Who Saved the Children*. D, E, JH

I Never Saw Another Butterfly: Children's Drawings and Poems from Terezin Concentration Camp. D, JH, JI

Kerr, Judith. *When Hitler Stole Pink Rabbit*. JH

Klein, Gerda Weissmann. *Promise of a New Spring: The Holocaust and Renewal*. D, JH, JI

Levoy, Myron. *Alan and Naomi*. D, E, JH

Orgel, Doris. *The Devil in Vienna*. E, JH

Richter, Hans Peter. *Friedrich*. D, E, JH, JI

Sachs, Marilyn. *A Pocket Full of Seeds*. D, E, JH, JI

Siegal, Aranka. *Upon the Head of the Goat: A Childhood in Hungary 1939-1944*. D, JH, JI

Suhl, Yuri. *Uncle Misha's Partisans*. JH, JI

Alphabetized according to Title

Alan and Naomi by Myron Levoy. D, E, JH

The Boys Who Saved the Children by Margaret Baldwin. D, E, JH

The Devil in Vienna by Doris Orgel. E, JH

Friedrich by Hans Peter Richter. D, E, JH, JI

I Never Saw Another Butterfly: Children's Drawings and Poems from Terezin Concentration Camp. D, JH, JI.

A Pocket Full of Seeds by Marilyn Sachs. D, E, JH, JI

Promise of a New Spring: The Holocaust and Renewal by Gerda Weissmann Klein. D, JH, JI

Uncle Misha's Partisans by Yuri Suhl. JH, JI

Upon the Head of the Goat: A Childhood in Hungary 1939-1944 by Aranka Siegl. D, JH, JI

When Hitler Stole Pink Rabbit by Judith Kerr. JH

VIII. **Israel**

Alphabetized according to Author

Cone, Molly. *The House in the Tree: A Story of Israel.* JI

Davidson, Margaret. *The Golda Meir Story.* JH, JI

Grand, Samuel, and Grand, Tamar. *The Children of Israel.* JI

Gutman, Nahum. *Path of the Orange Peels: Adventures in the Early Days of Tel Aviv.* E, JH

Meir, Mira. *Alina: A Russian Girl Comes to Israel.* JH, JI

Ofek, Uriel. *Smoke Over Golan: A Novel of the 1973 Yom Kippur War in Israel.* E, JH

Raboff, Ernest. *Marc Chagall: Art for Children.* JH

Yadin, Yigael. *The Story of Masada.* B, D, JH, JI

Sasek, Miroslav. *This is Israel.* B

Zim, Jacob. *My Shalom, My Peace.* E, JH, JI

Alphabetized according to Title

Alina: A Russian Girl Comes to Israel by Mira Meir. JH, JI

The Children of Israel by Samuel Grand and Tamar Grand. JI

The Golda Meir Story by Margaret Davidson. JH, JI

The House in the Tree: A Story of Israel by Molly Cone. JI

Marc Chagall: Art for Children by Ernest Raboff. JH

My Shalom, My Peace by Jacob Zim. E, JH, JI

Path of the Orange Peels: Adventures in the Early Days of Tel Aviv by Nahum Gutman. E, JH

Smoke Over Golan: A Novel of the 1973 Yom Kippur War in Israel by Uriel Ofek. E, JH

The Story of Masada by Yigael Yadin. B, D, JH, JI

This is Israel by Miroslav Sasek. E, JH, JI

IX. **Jewish Identity**

Alphabetized according to Author

Abells, Chana Byers. *The Children We Remember.* D, H, JH

Arrick, Fran. *Chernowitz.* E

Bernstein, Joanne. *Dmitry: A Young Soviet Immigrant.* JH

Cohen, Barbara. *King of the Seventh Grade.* E

Goldreich, Gloria. *Season of Discovery.* H

Greene, Laura. *I am an Orthodox Jew.* E

Herman, Charlotte. *What Happened to Heather Hopkowitz?* E

Hurwitz, Johanna. *Once I Was a Plum Tree.* E, HOL (Passover), H, JH.

Hurwitz, Johanna. *The Rabbi's Girls.* D, E

Podwal, Mark. *A Book of Hebrew Letters* B, E, HOL (contains symbols of Shabbat, Rosh Hashanah, and holidays in general), JF, JH

Alphabetized according to Title

A Book of Hebrew Letters by Mark Podwal. B, E, HOL (contains symbols of Shabbat, Rosh Hashanah, and holidays in general), JF, JH

Chernowitz by Fran Arrick. E

The Children We Remember by Chana Byers Abells. D, H, JH

Dmitry: A Young Soviet Immigrant by Joanne Bernstein. JH

I am an Orthodox Jew by Laura Greene. E

King of the Seventh Grade by Barbara Cohen. E

Once I Was a Plum Tree by Johanna Hurwitz. E, HOL (Passover), H, JH

The Rabbi's Girls by Johanna Hurwitz. D, E

Season of Discovery by Gloria Goldreich. H

What Happened to Heather Hopkowitz? by Charlotte Herman. E

X. **Prayer**

Alphabetized according to Author

Bogot, Howard, and Syme, Daniel B. *Prayer is Reaching*. E

Chanover, Hyman, and Zusman, Evelyn. *My Book of Prayer*. HOL (Shabbat)

Cohen, Barbara. *Molly's Pilgrim*. E, JH, JI

Cone, Molly. *Hear, O Israel: First I Say the Shema*. JI

Cone, Molly. *Hear, O Israel: About God*. E, JI

Johnson, James Weldon, and Johnson, J. Rosamond. *Lift Every Voice and Sing: Words and Music*. E

Klausner, Rabbi Abraham. *A Children's Prayer Book for Rosh Hashanah and Yom Kippur*. E, HOL (Rosh Hashanah and Yom Kippur)

Kustanowitz, Shulamit, and Foont, Ronnie C. *A First Haggadah*. B, HOL (Passover), JH

Orleans, Ilo. *Within Thy Hand: My Poem Book of Prayers*. HOL (Shabbat)

Zwerin, Raymond A., and Marcus, Audrey Friedman. *Shabbat Can Be*. HOL (Shabbat), JI

Alphabetized according to Title

A Children's Prayer Book for Rosh Hashanah and Yom Kippur by Rabbi Abraham Klausner. E, HOL (Rosh Hashanah and Yom Kippur)

A First Haggadah by Shulamit Kustanowitz and Ronnie C. Foont. B, HOL (Passover), JH

Hear, O Israel: About God by Molly Cone. E, JI

Hear, O Israel: First I Say the Shema by Molly Cone. JI

Lift Every Voice and Sing: Words and Music by Weldon James Johnson and J. Rosamond Johnson. E

Molly's Pilgrim by Barbara Cohen. E, JH, JI

My Book of Prayer by Hyman Chanover and Evelyn Zusman. HOL (Shabbat)

Prayer is Reaching by Howard Bogot and Daniel B. Syme. E

Shabbat Can Be by Raymond A. Zwerin and Audrey Friedman Marcus. HOL (Shabbat), JI

Within Thy Hand: My Poem Book of Prayers by Ilo Orleans. HOL (Shabbat)

GENERAL ADULT REFERENCES

BOOK LISTS AND CATALOGUES

Association of Jewish Book Publishers. *Combined Jewish Book Catalog.* Combined Book Service, P.O. Box 577, Conshohocken, PA 19428.

Davis, Enid. *Comprehensive Guide to Children's Literature with a Jewish Theme.* New York: Schocken Books, Inc., 1981.

Jewish Education Service of North America. *Materials Resource Guide for Jewish Educators.* Miami: Central Agency of Jewish Education, 1980. (Updates in 1982, 1984)

Kaplan, Jonathan (ed). *2000 Books and More.* Jerusalem: Magnes Press, 1983.

Lubetski, Edith and Meir. *Building a Jewish Library Collection.* Littleton, CO: Libraries Unlimited, Inc., 1983.

Posner, Marcia. *Selected Jewish Children's Books: An Annotated List.* New York: Jewish Welfare Board Jewish Book Council, 1982. (Updated 1984)

Schram, Peninnah. *Eeyore's Books of Jewish Interest for Children.* New York: Eeyore's Books for Children, 1983.

Studies in Bibliography and Booklore. 3101 Clifton Avenue, Cincinnati, OH 45220.

CATALOGUES AND REFERENCE BOOKS

Ausubel, Nathan. *The Book of Jewish Knowledge.* New York: Crown Publishers, Inc., 1964.

Ben-Asher, Naomi, and Leaf, Hayim. *Junior Jewish Encyclopedia.* New York: Shengold Publishers, Inc., 1978. (Eighth Edition)

Burstein, Abraham. *The Illustrated New Concise Jewish Encyclopedia.* Edited. by Robert Milch. New York: KTAV Publishing House, Inc., 1978. (Revised Edition)

Patai, Raphael. *Encyclopedia of Zionism and Israel.* New York: Herzl Press/McGraw-Hill Book Co., 1971. (Two Volumes)

Posner, Raphael (ed). *My Jewish World: The Encyclopedia Judaica for Youth.* Jerusalem: Keter Publishing House, Ltd., 1975.

Rockland, Mae Shafter. *The New Jewish Yellow Pages.* Englewood, NJ: SBS Publishing, Inc., 1980.

Roth, Cecil (ed). *Encyclopedia Judaica.* Jerusalem: Keter Publishing House, Ltd., 1972.

Siegel, Richard; Strassfeld, Michael; and Strassfeld, Sharon (eds). *The First Jewish Catalog: A Do-It-Yourself Kit.* Illus. by Stuart Copans. Philadelphia: The Jewish Publication Society of America, 1973.

Strassfeld, Michael, and Strassfeld, Sharon (eds). *The Second Jewish Catalog: Sources and Resources.* Illus. by Stuart Copans. Philadelphia: The Jewish Publication Society of America, 1976.

_____. *The Third Jewish Catalog: Creating Community.* Illus. by Stuart Copans. Philadelphia: The Jewish Publication Society of America, 1980.

Wigoder, Geoffrey. *Encyclopedia Dictionary of Judaica.* New York: Leon Amiel, Publishers/Jerusalem: Keter Publishing House, Ltd., 1974.

_____. *The New Standard Jewish Encyclopedia.* New York: Doubleday & Co., Inc., 1977. (Fifth Edition)

FINE ARTS

Arts and Crafts

Anderson, Mildred. *Paper Maché and How to Use It.* New York: Sterling Publishing Co., Inc., 1965.

Barford, George. *Clay in the Classroom.* Worcester, MA: Davis Publications Inc., 1963.

Becker, Joyce. *Bible Crafts.* New York: Holiday House, Inc., 1982.

_____. *Jewish Holiday Crafts.* Illus. by the author. New York: Hebrew Publishing Co., 1977.

Boylson, Elsie Reid. *Creative Expression with Crayons.* Worcester, MA: Davis Press Inc., 1954.

Brinn, Ruth Esrig. *Let's Celebrate! 57 Jewish Holiday Crafts for Young Children.* Rockville, MD: Kar-Ben Copies, Inc., 1977.

Elefant, Leah, and Gary, Esther. *Holiday Crafts Come Alive.* New York: Feldheim Publishers, 1981.

Galbraith, Alice. *Fun With Weaving.* Illus. by Judith Hoffman Corwin. New York: William Morrow and Co., 1976.

Gooch, Peter H. *Ideas for Art Teachers.* New York: Reinhold Publishing Corp., 1972.

Hoover, Francis Louis (ed). *Young Printmakers.* Normal, IL: Art Resources Publications, 1964.

Hooper, Grizella H. *Puppet Making Through the Grades.* Schenectady, NY: Davis Publications, Inc., 1966.

Lynch, John. *How to Make Mobiles.* New York: Studio-Crowell, 1953.

Meilach, Dona, and Ten Hoor, Elvie. *Collage and Found Art.* New York: Reinhold Publishing Corp., 1964.

Meyer, Carolyn. *Yarn — The Things It Makes and How to Make Them.* New York: Harcourt Brace Jovanovich, Inc., 1972.

Pattemore, Arnel W. *Printmaking Activities for the Classroom.* Worcester, MA: Davis Publications, Inc., 1966.

Sharon, Ruth. *Arts and Crafts the Year Round.* Illus. by the author. New York: United Synagogue of America, 1965. (Two Volumes)

Wachowiak, Frank, and Ramsey, Theodore. *Emphasis: Art.* New York: Thomas Y. Crowell Co., 1977. (Third Edition)

Warshawsky, Gale Solotar. *Creative Jewish Puppetry for Kids.* Denver: Alternatives in Religious Education, Inc., 1985.

Weiss, Harvey. *Clay, Wood, and Wire.* New York: William R. Scott, 1966.

Calligraphy

Greenspan, Jay. *Hebrew Calligraphy: A Step-by-Step Guide.* New York: Schocken Books, Inc., 1981.

Creative Writing

Arnstein, Flora J. *Poetry in the Elementary Classroom.* New York: Appleton-Century-Crofts. 1963.

Cheyney, Arnold B. *The Writing Corner.* Santa Monica, CA: Goodyear Publishing Co., Inc., 1979.

Burrows, Alvina Trent, et al. *They All Want to Write.* New York: Holt, Rinehart & Winston, Inc., 1964. (Third Edition)

Grimm, Gary, and Mitchell, Don. *The Good Apple Creative Writing Book.* Carthage, IL: Good Apple, Inc., 1976.

Hawley, Robert C.; Simon, Sidney B.; and Britton, D.D. *Composition for Personal Growth: Values Clarification Through Writing.* New York: Hart Publishing Co., Inc., 1973.

Jeep, Elizabeth. *Classroom Creativity: An Idea Book for Religion Teachers.* New York: Seabury Press, 1977.

Koch, Kenneth. *Wishes, Lies, and Dreams: Teaching Children to Write Poetry.* New York: Vintage Books, 1970.

Mearns, Hughes. *Creative Power.* New York: Doubleday, Doran & Co., 1952.

Petty, Walter, and Bowen, Mary. *Slithery Snakes and Other Aids to Children's Writing.* Englewood Cliffs, NJ: Prentice-Hall, 1967.

Tiedt, Sidney W., and Tiedt, Iris M. *Language Arts Activities for the Classroom.* New York: Allyn and Bacon, Inc., 1978.

Walter, Nina Willis. *Let Them Write Poetry.* New York: Holt, Rinehart & Winston, Inc., 1962.

Drama

Aldrich, Dorothy, and Schwartz, Dorothy Thames (eds). *Give Them Roots and Wings: A Guide to Drama in the Elementary Grades.* New York: American Theatre Association, 1972.

Barlin, Anne. *Teaching Your Wings to Fly: The Nonspecialists Guide to Movement Activities for Young Children.* Santa Monica, CA: Goodyear Publishing Co., 1979.

Beiner, Stan J. *Sedra Scenes: Skits for Every Torah Portion*. Denver: Alternatives in Religious Education Inc., 1982.

Cheifetz, Dan. *Theater in My Head*. Boston: Little Brown and Co., 1971.

Citron, Samuel. *Dramatics the Year Round*. New York: United Synagogue of America, 1956.

_____. *Israel: Dream and Fulfillment*. New York: Jewish Education Committee Press, 1968.

Cohen, Edward (ed). *Plays of Interest: A Preliminary Catalogue*. New York: Jewish Theatre Association, National Foundation for Jewish Culture, 1982.

Ferguson, Helen. *Bring on the Puppets*. Wilton, CT: Morehouse-Barlow Co., Inc., 1975.

Fredericks, M., and Segal, J. *Creative Puppetry in the Classroom*. Rowayton, CT: New Plays and Books, 1979.

Gabriel, Michell. *Jewish Plays for Jewish Days: Brief Holiday Plays for Ages 8-12*. Denver: Alternatives in Religious Education, Inc., 1978.

Goodman, Hannah Grad. *An Annotated and Selected Bibliography of Dramatic Scripts on American Jewish Themes*. New York: Jewish Book Council of the Jewish Welfare Board, 1975.

Goodridge, Janet. *Creative Drama and Improvised Movement for Children*. Boston: Plays, Inc., 1970.

Lepkin, Bela. *Creative Drama in the Hebrew School*. New York: Bloch Publishing Co., 1978.

McClaslin, Nellie. *Creative Dramatics in the Classroom*. David McKay Co., Inc., 1974.

Nanus, Susan. *Five In One: Holiday Plays for Jewish Children*. New York: Union of American Hebrew Congregations, 1981.

Rembrandt, Elaine. *Heroes, Heroines & Holidays: Plays for Jewish Youth*. Denver: Alternatives in Religious Education Inc., 1981.

Schram, Peninnah. *"Kernels of a Pomegranate": Storytelling Programs for Jewish Settings*. New York: National Jewish Welfare Board, 1975.

Siks, Geraldine Brian. *Creative Dramatics, An Art for Children*. New York: Harper Bros., 1958.

Sims, Judy. *Puppets for Dreaming and Scheming: A Puppet Source Book*. San Francisco, CA: Early Stages Press, Inc., 1978.

Sterling, Carol. *Puppetry in the Classroom*. Princeton, NJ: EIC Central, 1979.

Value Prompters. Denver: Alternatives in Religious Education, Inc., 1973.

Way, Brian. *Development Through Drama*. Atlantic Highlands, NJ: Humanities Press, Inc., 1967.

Winters, Shirley. *Creative Rhythmic Movement for Children of Elementary School Age*. Dubuque, Iowa: William C. Brown, 1975.

Wykell, Esther. *Creative Dramatics in the Jewish School*. Chicago: Board of Jewish Education, 1962.

Wyenn, Than R. *Parallel Dramatics*. Los Angeles: Bureau of Jewish Education, no publication date.

Music

Coopersmith, Harry (ed). *The New Jewish Song Book*. New York: Behrman House, Inc., 1965.

_____. *The Songs We Sing*. New York: United Synagogue Books, 1950.

Coopersmith, Harry, and Neumann, Richard. *Music For the Jewish School*. New York: Board of Jewish Education, 1975. (2nd Revised Edition)

Coopersmith, Harry (ed). *More of the Songs We Sing*. New York: United Synagogue Commission on Jewish Education, 1971.

Fouke, Edith, and Glazer, Joe. *Songs of Work and Freedom*. Chicago, IL: Labor Education Division Roosevelt University, 1960.

Friedman, Debbie. *Sing Unto God, Not By Might, Ani Ma-amin, If Not Now, When?, . . . and the Youth Shall See Visions*. Distributed by Sing Unto God. *Hebrew and Heritage Children's Album*. Distributed by Behrman House, Inc.

Idelsohn, A.Z. *Jewish Music in its Historical Development.* New York: Schocken Books, Inc., 1967.

Lersy, James (ed). *The Good Times Songbook: One Hundred and Sixty Songs for Informal Singing.* Nashville, TN: Abingdon Press, 1974.

Levin, Neil (ed). *Songs of the American Jewish Experience.* Chicago: Board of Jewish Education of Metropolitan Chicago, no publication date.

Levin, Neil, and Pasternak, Velvel (eds). *Z'mirot Anthology.* New York: Tara Publications, 1981.

Pasternak, Velvel (ed). *Great Songs of Israel.* New York: Tara Publications and Board of Jewish Education, 1976.

_____. *Israel in Song.* New York: Tara Publications & Board of Jewish Education, 1974.

_____. *The New Children's Songbook: 110 Hebrew Songs for the Young.* Cedarhurst, NY: Tara Publications, 1981.

_____. *The Sephardic Oriental Songbook.* Cedarhurst, NY: Tara Publications, 1984.

Rivkin, Nacha, and Shurin, Ella. *Come Sing With Me: Hebrew Songs for the Young.* Edited by Velvel Pasternak. Cedarhurst, NY: Tara Publications, 1984.

Rubin, Ruth (ed). *A Treasury of Jewish Folksong.* New York: Schocken Books, Inc., 1964.

Searles, Susan Claire, and Glicksberg, Dr. Avraham Abba. *Hebrew Songs For All Seasons.* Toledo, OH: Board of Jewish Education, 1978-1979. (Two Volumes)

Silverman, Jerry. *The Yiddish Song Book.* Briarcliff Manor, NY: Stein & Day, 1983.

Slobin, Mark (ed). *Old Jewish Folk Music: The Collections and Writings of Moshe Beregovski.* Philadelphia: University of Pennsylvania Press, 1982.

Vinkovetsky, Aharon; Kovner, Abba; and Leichter, Sinai. *Anthology of Yiddish Songs, Volume I.* Jerusalem: Magnes Press, 1983.

Warembud, Norman H. (ed). *Great Songs of the Yiddish Theater.* New York: New York Times Book Co., 1975.

CURRICULUM RESOURCES and TEACHING GUIDES

Bulletin Boards and Classroom Displays

Barnes, Donald L. *How To Make Bulletin Board Designs.* Minneapolis, MN: T.S. Denison & Co., Inc., 1977.

Dexter, Kerry. *The Display Book.* Wilton, CT: Morehouse-Barlow Co., Inc., 1977.

Fiarotta, Phyllis, and Fiarotta, Noel. *Pin It, Hang It, The Big Book of Kids' Bulletin Board Ideas.* New York: Workman Publishing Co., 1975.

Comprehensive Guides for Jewish Educators

Furfine, Sandy S., and Nowak, Nancy Cohen. *The Jewish Preschool Teachers Handbook.* Denver: Alternatives in Religious Education, Inc., 1981.

Goodman, Robert. *A Teachers Guide to Jewish Holidays.* Denver: Alternatives in Religious Education, Inc., 1983.

Loeb, Sorel Goldberg, and Kadden, Barbara Binder. *Teaching Torah: A Treasury of Insights and Activities.* Denver: Alternatives in Religious Education, Inc., 1984.

Marcus, Audrey Friedman, and Zwerin, Raymond A. (eds). *The Jewish Principals Handbook.* Denver: Alternatives in Religious Education, Inc., 1983.

Marcus, Audrey Friedman (ed). *The Jewish Teachers Handbook.* Denver: Alternatives in Religious Education, Inc., 1981-83. (Three Volumes)

Creating Instructional Materials

Bullough, Robert V. *Creating Instructional Materials.* Columbus, OH: Charles E. Merrill Publishing Co., 1974.

Morlan, John E. *Preparation of Inexpensive Teaching Materials.* New York: Chandler, 1973.

General Adult References

Pearson, Craig, and Marfuggi, Joseph. *Creating and Using Learning Games.* Palo Alto, CA: Learning Handbooks, no publication date.

Purdy, Susan. *Books For You To Make.* Philadelphia: J.B. Lippincott Co., 1973.

Simons, Robin. *Recyclopedia.* Boston: Houghton Mifflin Co., 1976. Distributed by The Children's Museum, Boston.

Developing Curriculum

Fox, Seymour, and Rosenfield, Geraldine (eds). *From the Scholar to the Classroom: Translating Jewish Tradition into Curriculum.* New York: Melton Research Center, 1977.

Gittelson, Abraham, and Freidenreich, Fradle. *Interdisciplinary Integration in the Jewish Day School.* Miami and New York: Central Agency for Jewish Education and American Association for Jewish Education, 1979.

Experiential and Group Activities

Ball, Geraldine. *The Magic Circle Human Development Program.* La Mesa, CA: Human Development Training Institute, Inc., 1974. (Seven Volumes)

Canfield, Jack, and Wells, Harold C. *100 Ways to Enhance Self Concept in the Classroom.* Englewood Cliffs, NJ: Prentice-Hall, Inc., 1976.

Reichert, Richard. *Self-Awareness Through Group Dynamics.* Dayton, OH: Pflaum/Standard, 1970.

Reisman, Bernard (ed). *Experiential Learning in Jewish Groups: Principles and Activities.* Waltham, MA: Philip W. Lown Graduate Center for Contemporary Jewish Studies, Brandeis University. (Two Volumes)

Stanford, Gene. *Developing Effective Classroom Groups.* New York: Hart Publishing Co., 1977.

There Is a Season: A Values Clarification Approach to Jewish Holidays. Denver: Alternatives in Religious Education, Inc., 1978.

FILM/FILMSTRIP DISTRIBUTORS

Anti-Defamation League
823 United Nations Plaza
New York, NY 10017

Alden Films
7820 20th Avenue
Brooklyn, NY 11214

Alternatives in Religious Education, Inc.
3945 South Oneida Street
Denver, Colorado 80237

American Federation of Jewish Fighters
Camp Inmates and Nazi Victims
823 United Nations Plaza
New York, NY 10017

Behrman House, Inc.
1261 Broadway
New York, NY 10001

American Zionist Youth Foundation
515 Park Avenue
New York, NY 10022

BFA Education Media
2211 Michigan Avenue
Santa Monica, CA 90404

B'nai B'rith Youth Organization
1640 Rhode Island Avenue, N.W.
Washington, DC 20036

Board of Jewish Education of Greater New York
426 W. 58th Street
New York, NY 10019

Bureau of Jewish Education
6505 Wilshire Boulevard
Los Angeles, CA 90048

Contemporary Films Inc.
267 West 25 Street
New York, NY 10001

Contemporary Films/McGraw Hill
Princeton Road
Hightstown, NJ 08520

Educational Resources
24010 Oxnard Street
Woodland Hills, CA 91367

Films, Inc.
1144 Wilmette Avenue
Wilmette, IL 60091

Gratz College
10th and Tabor Rd.
Philadelphia, PA 19141

Hadassah
50 West 58th Street
New York, NY 10019

Jewish Chatauqua Society
838 Fifth Avenue
New York, NY 10021

Jewish Media Service
Jewish Welfare Board
15 East 26th Street
New York, NY 10010

Jewish National Fund
42 E. 69th St.
New York, NY 10021

Kol R'ee Associates
1923 Springfield Avenue
Maplewood, NJ 07040

Learning Corporation of America
1350 Avenue of the Americas
New York, NY 10019

The Learning Plant
6950 Country Place Road
West Palm Beach, FL 33411

Macmillan Audio-Brandon Films
34 MacQuesten Parkway
Mt. Vernon, NY 10550

Mass Media Ministries
2116 North Charles Street
Baltimore, MD 21218

Michigan State University
Instructional Media Center
East Lansing, MI 48823

Miller-Brody Publications
342 Madison Avenue
New York, NY 10017

Multi-Media Productions
P.O. Box 5097
Stanford, CA 94305

National Film Board of Canada
680 Fifth Avenue
New York, NY 10019

Neot Kedumim
4080 Morrison Drive
Gurnee, IL 60031

New Day Films
P. O. Box 315
Franklin Lakes, NJ 07417

The New Media Bible
The Genesis Project Inc.
Box 327828T
Washington, DC 20013

Ohio Poster Co.
4077 Cedar Road
Cleveland, OH 44118

Pyramid Films
Box 1048
Santa Monica, CA 90406

Quad Films Inc.
Box 2086
University City, MO 63130

Religious Media Inc.
Box 8626
Rochester, NY 14619

Ru-Barb Productions
608 West Matson Run Parkway
Wilmington, DE 19802

Rutenberg and Everett Yiddish Film Library
Philip Lown Bld.
Brandeis University
Waltham, MA 02154

Phoenix Films
470 Park Avenue South
New York, NY 10016

Shimbal Studios
P.O. Box 313
Flushing, NY 11367

Skirball Museum Hebrew Union
College-Jewish Institute of Religion
3077 University Avenue
Los Angeles, CA 90007

Tape Tours (Israel) Ltd.
9 Pines Street
P.O. Box 2260
Jerusalem, Israel

Tarbuth Foundation Inc.
2 Penn Plaza
New York, NY 10001

Torah Umesorah Publications
229 Park Avenue South
New York, NY 10003

Union of American Hebrew Congregations
838 Fifth Avenue
New York, NY 10021

U.A.H.C. Commission on Synagogue Administration
838 Fifth Avenue
New York, NY 10021

United Jewish Appeal
1290 Avenue of the Americas
New York, NY 10019

United Synagogue-National Academy for
    Adult Jewish Studies
155 Fifth Avenue
New York, NY 10010

General Adult References

University of California
Extension Media Center
Berkeley, CA 94720

University of Colorado A/V Department
Folsom Stadium
Boulder, Co 80302

University of Minnesota
Dept of AV Extension
2037 University Ave., SE
Minneapolis, MN 55455

University of Southern California
Division of Cinema
Film Distribution Section
University Park
Los Angeles, CA 90007

Weston Woods Studio
Weston, CT 06833

World Zionist Organization
515 Park AVenue
New York, NY 10022

Yeshiva University Museum
2520 Amsterdam Ave.
New York, NY 10033

YIVO Slide Bank-Max Weinreich Center for
  Advanced Jewish Studies
1048 Fifth Ave.
New York, NY 10028

JEWISH COMPUTER PROGRAMS

Alef-Byte Computer Software
3515 South 50th Street
Omaha, NE 68106

Davka Jewish Computer Programs
Davka Corporation
845 North Michigan Avenue, Suite 843
Chicago, IL 60611

The Hebrew Scribe
Gamma Productions, Inc.
817 10th Street, Suite 102
Santa Monica, CA 90403

LEARNING CENTERS

Dolores Kohl Education Foundation. *Teacher Centering: Ideas Shared By the Kohl Jewish Teacher Center*. Wilmette, IL: Dolores Kohl Education Foundation, 1978.

Forte, Imogene; Prangle, Mary Ann; and Tupa, Robbie. *Center Stuff for Nooks, Crannies and Corners.* Nashville, TN: Incentive Publications, Inc., 1973.

Schrank, Jeffrey. *The Seed Catalogue*. Boston: Beacon Press, 1974.

MEETING SPECIAL EDUCATIONAL NEEDS

Curry, Robert C. *Training for Trainers: Serving the Elderly, the Technique*. Durham, NH: New England Gerontology Center, 1980.

Greene, Roberta, and Heavenrich, Elaine. *A Question in Search of an Answer: Understanding Learning Disability in Jewish Education*. New York: Union of American Hebrew Congregations, 1981.

Hammer, Reuven. *The Other Child in Jewish Education*. New York: United Synagogue Commission on Jewish Education, 1979.

Know, Allan B. *Educational Programs for Older Adults*. Los Angeles: University of Southern California, 1974.

Lipnick, Bernard. *An Experiment that Works in Teenage Religious Education*. New York: Bloch Publishing Co., 1976.

Rowen, Betty; Byrne, Joan; and Winter, Lois. *The Learning Match: Developmental Guide to Teaching Young Children*. Englewood Cliffs, NJ: Prentice-Hall, Inc., 1980.

Sanderlin, O. *Teaching Gifted Children*. Cranbury, NJ: A.S. Barnes & Co., 1973.

Seltzer, Sanford. *So Teach Us to Number Our Days: A Manual on Aging for Synagogue Use*. New York: Union of American Hebrew Congregations, no publication date.

That Thy Days May Be Long in the Good Land: A Guide to Aging Programs for Synagogues. Washington, DC: Synagogue Council of America, 1975.

Zola, Gary P., and Olitzky, Kerry M. *My People Jacob: Thy Tents Have Grown Old: A Manual for Planning Weekend Kallot for Older People*. New York: Union of American Hebrew Congregations, 1981.

PARENTAL AND PARAPROFESSIONAL INVOLVEMENT

Aft, Martha. "Parent Involvement" In *The Jewish Principals Handbook*. Denver: Alternatives in Religious Education, Inc., 1983.

DaSilva, Benjamin, and Lucas, Richard D. *Practical School Volunteer and Teacher Aide Programs*. New York: Citation Press, 1974.

Gattman, Eric. "Creatively Using Teacher's Aides in Our Classrooms." *Alternatives Magazine*, Spring, 1975.

Gordon, Ira, and Breivogel, William F. *Building Effective Home-School Relationships*. Boston: Allyn & Bacon Publishers, 1976.

Hakimian, Leah. "Parents Participate." *Pedagogic Reporter*, Spring 1979.

SELECTED LIST OF PUBLISHERS/DISTRIBUTORS OF MATERIALS OF JEWISH INTEREST

Abingdon Press
201 Eighth Avenue South
Nashville, TN 37202

Addison-Wesley Publishing Co., Inc.
One Jacob Way
Reading, MA 01867

Agudath Israel of America
5 Beekman Street
New York, NY 10038

Alfred A. Knopf
201 East 50th Street
New York, NY 10022

Alternatives in Religious Educaction, Inc.
3945 South Oneida Street
Denver, CO 80237

American Association for Jewish Education
(see Jewish Education Service of North America)

American Jewish Committee
165 East 56 Street
New York, NY 10022

American Jewish Congress
Commission on Jewish Life & Culture
15 East 84th Street
New York, NY 10028

American Jewish Historical Society
2 Thornton Road
Waltham, MA 02154

American Zionist Youth Foundation
Education and Programming Department
515 Park Avenue
New York, NY 10022

Ani Po
11805 Monticello Avenue
Silver Spring, MD 20902

Anti-Defamation League
823 United Nations Plaza
New York, NY 10017

Arbit Books, Inc.
8050 North Port Washington Road
Milwaukee, WI 53217

Arhoolie Records
10341 San Pablo Avenue
El Cerrito, CA 94530

Artista Records
1776 Broadway
New York, NY 10019

Avalon Hill Company
4517 Hartford Road
Baltimore, MD 21214

Behrman House, Inc.
1261 Broadway
New York, NY 10001

Bloch Publishing Co.
915 Broadway
New York, NY 10010

B'nai B'rith Adult Jewish Education Department
1640 Rhode Island Avenue, N.W.
Washington, DC 20036

B'nai B'rith Youth Organization
1640 Rhode Island Avenue, N.W.
Washington, DC 20036

Board of Jewish Education
Publications Department
5800 Park Heights Avenue
Baltimore, MD 21215

Board of Jewish Education
426 West 58th Street
New York, NY 10019

Board of Jewish Education
2727 Kenwood Blvd.
Toledo, OH 43606

Board of Jewish Education
62 East 11th Street
Chicago, IL 60605

General Adult References

Bradbury Press, Inc.
2 Overhill Road
Scarsdale, NY 10583

B'ruach HaTorah Publications
P.O. Box 391221
Miami Beach, FL 33139

Bureau of Jewish Education
6505 Wilshire Boulevard
Los Angeles, CA 90048

Central Agency for Jewish Education
4200 Biscayne Blvd.
Miami, FL 33137

Charles Scribner's Sons
597 Fifth Avenue
New York, NY 10017

The Children's Museum
Jamaicaway
Boston, MA 02139

Clarion Books
Two Park Street
Boston, MA 02108

Contemporary Jewish Learning Materials Inc.
1414 Glendale
Ames, IA 50010

Czigler
331 Beardsley
Dayton, OH 45426

Decalogue Books
7 North McQuesten Parkway
Mt. Vernon, NY 10550

Delacorte Press
One Dag Hammarskjold Plaza
New York, NY 10017

Dial Press
245 Park Avenue
New York, NY 10017

Dodd, Mead & Co.
79 Madison Avenue
New York, NY 10017

Educational Horizons
15445 Ventura Blvd., Suite 10
Sherman Oaks, CA 91413

Educational Resources
24010 Oxnard Street
Woodland Hills, CA 91367

Educational Supply Co., Inc.
2823-25 East Gage Avenue
Huntington Park, CA 90255

Eeyore's Books of Jewish Interest
2252 Broadway
New York, NY 10024

Elektra Records
15 Columbus Circle
New York, NY 10023

Emanu-El Publications
Temple Emanu-El
306 Rumsey Road
Yonkers, NY 10705

Elsevier/Nelson
Two Park Avenue
New York, NY 10016

Enjoy-a-Book Club
25 Lawrence Avenue
Lawrence, NY 11559

E.P. Dutton
Two Park Avenue
New York, NY 10016

Eternal Light Film Library
155 Fifth Avenue
New York, NY 10010

Eric Feldheim
86 Wooley Lane
Great Neck, NY 10023

Farrar, Straus & Giroux, Inc.
19 Union Square West
New York, NY 10003

Feldheim Publishers
96 East Broadway
New York, NY 10002

Flying Fish Records, Inc.
1034 West Schubert
Chicago, IL 60614

Four Winds Press
730 Broadway
New York, NY 10003

Growth Associates
PO Box 8429
Rochester, NY 14608

Hadassah Education Department
50 West 58th Street
New York, NY 10019

Harcourt Brace Jovanovich, Inc.
757 Third Avenue
New York, NY 10164

Harper & Row Publishers, Inc.
10 East 53rd Street
New York, NY 10022

Hawthorn Books
Two Park Avenue
New York, NY 10016

Hebrew Publishing Co.
100 Water Street, 3rd Floor
Brooklyn, NY 11201

Hed-Arzi Ltd.
The Israel Records Manufacturing Co.
Ramat Gan, Israel

Holt, Rinehart & Winston, Inc.
383 Madison Avenue
New York, NY 10017

Houghton-Mifflin
Two Park Street
Boston, MA 02108

Howard Wasserman
541 Sedgwick St.
Philadelphia, PA 19119

Isra-Art Productions
157 West 57th St.
New York, NY 10019

The Israel Records Manufacturing Co.
Ramat Gan, Israel

J.B. Lippincott Co.
East Washington Square
Philadelphia, PA 19105

Jerusalem Catalog House, Ltd.
P.O. Box 11303
Tel Aviv, Israel

Jewish Book Council
15 East 26 Street
New York, NY 10010

Jewish Educational Materials
Temple Emanu-El
99 Taft Avenue
Providence, RI 02906

Jewish Education Service of North America
730 Broadway, 2nd floor
New York, NY 10003

Jewish Labor Committee
25 East 78 Street
New York, NY 10021

Jewish National Fund Youth & Education Department
42 East 69th Street
New York, NY 10021

The Jewish Publication Society of America
117 South 17th Street
Philadelphia, PA 19103

Jewish Welfare Board
15 East 26th Street
New York, NY 10010

Jonathan David Publishers, Inc.
68-22 Eliot Avenue
Middle Village, NY 11379

Julian Messner
1230 Avenue of the Americas
New York, NY 10020

Kar-Ben Copies, Inc.
6800 Tilden Lane
Rockville, MD 20852

Kohl Jewish Teacher Center
161 Green Bay Road
Wilmette, Il 60091

KTAV Publishing House, Inc.
900 Jefferson Street
Box 6249
Hoboken, NJ 07030

Lawrence Hill & Co.
520 Riverside Avenue
Westport, CT 06880

The Learning Plant
6950 Country Place Road
West Palm Beach, FL 33411

Little Brown & Co.
34 Beacon Street
Boston, MA 02106

Lothrop, Lee & Shepard Books
105 Madison Avenue
New York, NY 10016

Luckey Educational Publications
89 Abbotsford Road
Brookline, MA 02146

Macmillan Publishing Co., Inc.
866 Third Avenue
New York, NY 10022

Madrona Publishers, Inc.
P.O. Box 22667
Seattle, WA 98122

McGraw Hill
1221 Avenue of the Americas
New York, NY 10020

Media Judaica
1363 Fairfield Avenue
Bridgeport, CT 06605

General Adult References

Melton Research Center
3080 Broadway
New York, NY 10027

Merkos L'Inyonei Chinuch, Inc.
770 Eastern Parkway
Brooklyn, NY 11213

Morrow Junior Books
105 Madison Avenue
New York, NY 10016

M.U.S.E.
Hebrew Union College
3077 University Avenue
Los Angeles, CA 90007

National Academy for Adult Jewish Studies
United Synagogue
155 Fifth Avenue
New York, NY 10010

National Conference on Soviet Jewry
10 East 40th Street
New York, NY 10016

National Council of Jewish Women
15 East 26th Street
New York, NY 10010

National Jewish Resource Center
250 West 57th Street, Suite 216
New York, NY 10019

National Foundation for Jewish Culture
122 East 42 Street, Suite 1512
New York, NY 10068

Ner Tamid Book Distributors
P.O. Box 10401
Riviera Beach, FL 33404

North American Jewish Students Network
15 East 26th Street
New York, NY 10010

Pantheon Books
201 East 50th Street
New York, NY 10022

Philip Lown Graduate Center For
Contemporary Jewish Affairs
Brandeis University
South Street
Waltham, MA 02154

POM Records
525 West End Avenue
New York, NY 10024

Random House, Inc.
201 East 50th Street
New York, NY 10022

Reconstructionist Foundation
432 Park Avenue, South
New York, NY 10016

Resler Publication Fund
5419 East Broad St.
Columbus, OH 43212

Rittner's
345 Marlborough Street
Boston, MA 02115

Rocket Press
5409 Rawlings Road NE
Albuquerque, NM 87111

Rossel Publishing
P.O. Box 87
Chappaqua, NY 10514

Saga Publications
4833 Greentree Road
Lebanon, OH 45036

SBS Publishing, Inc.
14 West Forest Avenue
Englewood, NJ 07631

Schocken Books, Inc.
200 Madison Ave.
New York, NY 10016

Scholastic Magazines, Inc.
730 Broadway
New York, NY 10003

The Seabury Press
815 Second Avenue
New York, NY 10017

Sesame Street Records
Division of Distinguished Productions, Inc.
1 Lincoln Plaza
New York, NY 10023

Shilo Publishing House
73 Canal Street
New York, NY 10002

Shulsinger Brothers, Inc.
121 West 17th Street
New York, NY 10001

Simulations Publications, Inc.
44 East 23 Street
New York, NY 10010

Sing Unto God
7700 San Felipe-Suite 240
Houston, TX 77607
Attn: Velva Levine

Social Studies School Service
10,000 Culver Boulevard
Culver City, CA 90232

Student Struggle for Soviet Jewry
200 West 72nd Street
New York, NY 10023

Synagogue Council of America
327 Lexington Avenue
New York, NY 10016

Tarbuth Foundation
515 Park Avenue
New York, NY 10022

Teacher's Press
P.O. Box 3105
Orange, CA 92665

Thomas Y. Crowell Co.
10 53rd Street
New York, NY 10022

Tikvah Records
1650 Broadway
New York, NY 10019

Torah Toys
c/o J. Levine
58 Eldrige Street
New York, NY 10002

Torah Umesorah Publications
229 Park Avenue South
New York, NY 10003

Union of American Hebrew Congregations
838 Fifth Avenue
New York, NY 10021

Union of Orthodox Congregations
116 East 27th Street
New York, NY 10016

United Synagogue of America
Department of Youth Activities
155 Fifth Avenue
New York, NY 10010

Vanguard Press, Inc.
424 Madison Avenue
New York, NY 10017

Vanguard Recording Society, Inc.
71 West 23 Street
New York, NY 10010

Walker & Co.
720 Fifth Avenue
New York, NY 10019

William Morrow & Co., Inc.
105 Madison Avenue
New York, NY 10016

Workmen's Circle Book Dept.
45 East 33rd Street
New York, NY 10016

THEORETICAL PERSPECTIVES AND PRACTICAL SOLUTIONS

Bubis, Gerald. *Serving the Jewish Family*. New York: KTAV Publishing House, Inc., 1977.

Collins, Myrtle, and Collins, Dwane R. *Survival Kit for Teachers (and Parents)*. Santa Monica, CA: Goodyear Publishing Co., Inc., 1975.

de Zafra, Carlos. *62 Suggestions to Improve Classroom Discipline*. Fairfield: Economics Press, 1968.

Ginott, Haim. *Teacher and Child*. New York: Macmillan Publishing Co., 1972.

Goldman, Ronald. *Religious Thinking from Childhood to Adolescence*. New York: Seabury Press, 1964.

Noar, Gertrude. *Individual Instruction: Every Child a Winner*. New York: John Wiley & Sons, Inc., 1972.

Osborn, D. Keith, and Osborn, Jamie Dyson. *Discipline and Classroom Management*. Athens, GA: Education Associates, 1981.

Silberman, Melvin. *How to Be Assertive With Children*. New York: Hawthorne Books, 1980.

Simon, Sidney B. *Meeting Yourself Halfway*. Niles: MA: Argus Communcations, 1974.

TREASURIES OF TEACHING IDEAS

Blackburn, Jack E., and Powell, W. Conrad. *One at a Time, All at Once: The Creative Teacher's Guide to Individualized Instruction Without Anarchy*. Pacific Palisades, CA: Goodyear Publishing Co., Inc., 1976.

Cardozo, Peter. *The Whole Kids Catalogue*. New York: Bantam Books, Inc., 1975.

Dolores Kohl Education Foundation. *A Jewish Tapestry: Learning Activities for Classrooms and Living Rooms.* Wilmette, IL: Dolores Kohl Educational Foundation, 1982.

Hawley, Robert, and Hawley, Isabel. *Developing Human Potential.* Amherst, MA: Education Research Associates, 1975, 1977. (Two Volumes)

Holman, Marilyn. *Using Our Sense: Hands-On Activities for the Jewish Classroom.* Denver: Alternatives in Religious Education, Inc., 1984.

Kopin, Rita. *The Lively Jewish Classroom: Games and Activities for Learning.* Illus. by Judye Kopin. Denver: Alternatives in Religious Education, Inc., 1980.

Moore, Nancy. *Everything Under the Sun for Teaching.* New York: Instructo/McGraw Hill Book Co., 1980.

Read, Don, and Simon, Sydney B. *Humanistic Education Sourcebook.* Englewood Cliffs, NJ: Prentice-Hall, 1975.

Schrank, Jeffrey. *Teaching Human Beings: 101 Subversive Activities for the Classroom.* Boston: Beacon Press, 1972.

Stanford, Gene, and Stanford, Barbara Dodds. *Learning Discussion Skills Through Games.* New York: Citation Press, 1969.

Jewish Humor and Wisdom

B'nai B'rith Adult Jewish Education. *Jewish Heritage Reader.* New York: Taplinger Publishing Co., Inc., 1965.

Golden, Harry. *The Golden Book of Jewish Humor.* New York: G.P. Putnam's Sons, 1972.

Greenspan, Ezra. *The Schlemiel Comes to America.* Metuchen, NJ: Scarecrow Press, 1983.

The Jewish Publication Society of America (eds). *The Eternal Light: A Heritage Album Mirroring Four Thousand Years of Jewish Inspiration and Wisdom.* New York: Bloch Publishing Co., 1966.

Novak, William, and Waldoks, Moshe (eds). *The Big Book of Jewish Humor.* Harper & Row Publishers, Inc., 1981.

Rosten, Leo. *Treasury of Jewish Quotations.* New York: Bantam Books, Inc., 1972.

Spalding, H.D. *Jewishlaffs.* New York: Jonathan David Publishers, Inc., 1982.

Van Buren, Abigail. *The Best of Dear Abby.* Fairway, KS: Andrews and McMeel, Inc., 1981.

PERIODICALS

Magazines and Newspapers for Students

Achshav, United Synagogue of America Department of Youth Activities, 155 Fifth Avenue, New York, NY 10010.

Chicken Soup, 15445 Ventura Blvd., Suite 10, Sherman Oaks, CA 91413.

Keeping Posted, Union of American Hebrew Congregations, 838 Fifth Avenue, New York, NY 10021.

Noah's Ark, 5514 Rutherglen, Houston, TX 77096.

Olomeinu: Our World, National Society for Hebrew Day Schools, 229 Park Avenue South, New York, NY 10003.

Shofar: The Magazine for Jewish Kids on the Move. Senior Publications Ltd., 43 Northcote Drive, Melville, NY 11747.

Young Judean, 50 West 58th Street, New York, NY 10019.

Creative Publications on a Variety of Jewish Topics

Lilith: The Jewish Women's Magazine, 250 West 57th Street, New York, NY 10019.

Moment Magazine, Jewish Educational Ventures, Inc., 462 Boylston Street, Suite 301, Boston, MA 02116.

Response: A Contemporary Review, 15 East 26th Street #1350, New York, NY 10010.

Sh'ma: A Journal of Jewish Responsibility, P.O. Box 567, Port Washington, NY 11050.

Historical and Literary Journals

American Jewish Archives, 3101 Clifton Avenue, Cincinnati, OH 45220.

American Jewish Historical Quarterly, 2 Thornton Road, Waltham, MA 02154.

Jewish Social Studies, 250 West 57th Street, New York, NY 10019.

Prooftexts: A Journal of Jewish Literary History, Johns Hopkins University Press, Journals Division, Baltimore, MD 21218.

Studies in Zionism: An International Journal of Social Political and Intellectual History, Johns Hopkins University Press, Journals Division, Baltimore, MD 21218.

Toledot: The Journal of Jewish Geneology, 808 West End Avenue, Suite 1006, New York, NY 10025.

Yiddish: A Quarterly Journal Devoted to Yiddish and Yiddish Literature, Queens College Press, Flushing, NY 11367.

Israel

Ariel: A Review of Arts and Letters in Israel, Jerusalem Post Publications, Ltd., POB 3349, Jerusalem, Israel 91002.

Israel Magazine, 110 East 54th Steet, New York, NY 10022.

Near East Report, 1341 G Street, Washington, DC 20005.

Newsview: The Israel Weekly, Israel Expo, 68-36 108 Street, Forest Hills, NY 11375.

Jerusalem Post, 120 East 56th Street, New York, NY 10022.

Jewish Current Events and Issues

Commentary, American Jewish Committee, 165 East 56th Street, New York, NY 10022.

Jewish Post and Opinion, P.O. Box 449097, Indianapolis, IN 46202.

Midstream: A Monthly Jewish Review, Theodor Herzl Foundation, Inc., 515 Park Avenue, New York, NY 10022.

Present Tense: The Magazine of World Jewish Affairs, American Jewish Committee, 165 East 56th Street, New York, NY 10022.

Journals for Jewish Communal Workers, Educators, and Librarians

Compass: New Directions in Jewish Education, Union of American Hebrew Congregation, 838 Fifth Avenue, New York, NY 10021.

Jewish Education, National Council for Jewish Education, 730 Broadway, 2nd Floor, New York, NY 10003.

The Melton Journal: Issues and Themes in Jewish Education, Melton Research Center, 3080 Broadway, New York, NY 10027.

Journal of Jewish Communal Service, 15 East 26th Street, New York, NY 10010.

Medium: A Jewish Media Review, National Jewish Welfare Board, 15 East 26th Street, New York, NY 10010.

Pedagogic Reporter, Jewish Education Service of North America, 730 Broadway, 2nd floor, New York, NY 10003.

Publications of Jewish Civic Organizations

Hadassah Magazine, Women's Zionist Organization of America, 50 West 58th Street, New York, NY 10019.

Jewish Monthly, B'nai B'rith International, 1640 Rhode Island Avenue, N.W., Washington, DC 20036.

Women's American ORT Reporter, 1250 Broadway, New York, NY 10001.

Women's League Outlook, 48 East 74th Street, New York, NY 10021.

Publications of Major Jewish Religious Movements

Conservative Judaism, 3080 Broadway, New York, NY 10027.

Jewish Action: The News Magazine of the Orthodox Union, Union of Orthodox Jewish Congregations of America, 45 West 36th Street, New York, NY 10018.

Reconstructionist, 2521 Broadway, New York, NY 10025.

Reform Judaism, Union of American Hebrew Congregations, 838 Fifth Avenue, New York, NY 10021.

Treasuries of Jewish Knowledge and Trivia

Birnbaum, Philip (ed). *Encyclopedia of Jewish Concepts.* New York: Sanhedrin Press, 1979.

Greenberg, Martin H. *The Jewish Lists: Physicists and Generals, Actors and Writers and Hundreds of Other Lists of Accomplished Jews.* New York: Schocken Books, Inc., 1979.

Gross, David (ed). *The Jewish People's Almanac.* Illus. by Robert Leydenfrost. New York: Doubleday & Co., Inc., 1981.

Isaacson, Ben. *Dictionary of the Jewish Religion.* Edited by David Gross. Englewood, NJ: SBS Publishing, Inc., 1979.

Kolatch, Alfred. *The Jewish Book of Why.* New York: Jonathan David Publishers, Inc., 1981.

_____. *Jewish Information Quiz Book.* New York: Jonathan David Publishers, Inc., 1967.

Siegel, Richard, and Rheins, Carl (eds). *The Jewish Almanac: Traditions, History, Religion, Wisdom, Achievements.* New York: Bantam Books, Inc., 1980.

The American Jewish Year Book. New York: American Jewish Committee/Philadelphia: The Jewish Publication Society of America. 1900 (Eighty-Five Volumes)

Tillem, Ivan L. (ed). *The Jewish Directory and Almanac.* New York: Pacific Press, 1984.